Monster Musume

Everyday Life with Monster Girls

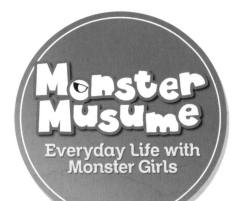

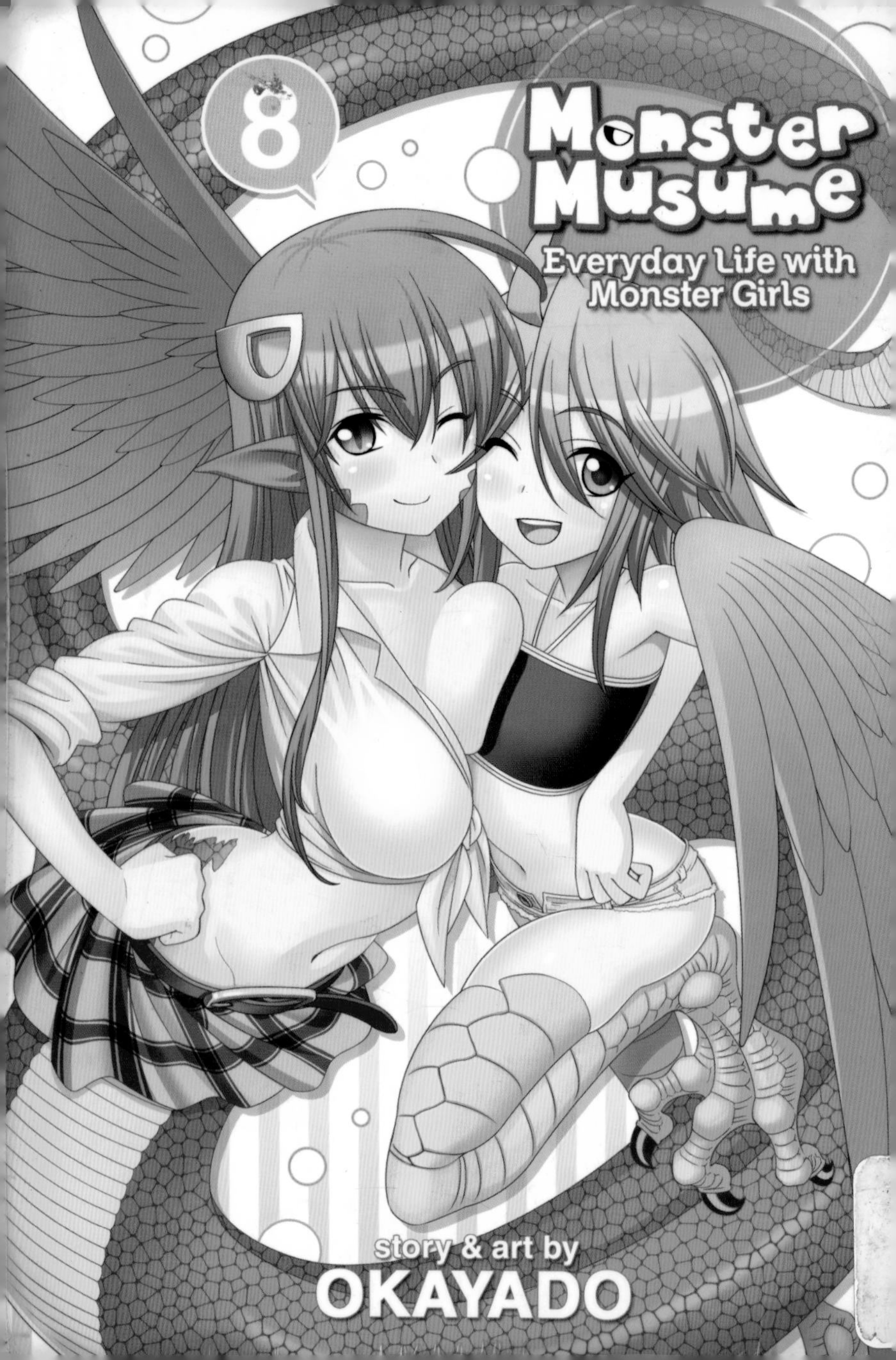
8
Monster Musume
Everyday Life with Monster Girls
story & art by
OKAYADO

SEVEN SEAS ENTERTAINMENT PRESENTS

Monster Musume

story and art by **OKAYADO**

VOLUME 8

TRANSLATION
Ryan Peterson

ADAPTATION
Shanti Whitesides

LETTERING AND LAYOUT
Ma. Victoria Robado

LOGO DESIGN
Courtney Williams

COVER DESIGN
Nicky Lim

PROOFREADER
Janet Houck

PRODUCTION MANAGER
Lissa Pattillo

EDITOR-IN-CHIEF
Adam Arnold

PUBLISHER
Jason DeAngelis

MONSTER MUSUME NO IRU NICHIJO VOLUME 8
© OKAYADO 2015
Originally published in Japan in 2015 by TOKUMA SHOTEN PUBLISHING
CO., LTD., Tokyo. English translation rights arranged with TOKUMA SHOTEN
PUBLISHING CO., LTD., Tokyo, through TOHAN CORPORATION, Tokyo.

No portion of this book may be reproduced or transmitted in any form without
written permission from the copyright holders. This is a work of fiction. Names,
characters, places, and incidents are the products of the author's imagination
or are used fictitiously. Any resemblance to actual events, locals, or persons,
living or dead, is entirely coincidental.

Seven Seas books may be purchased in bulk for educational, business, or
promotional use. For information on bulk purchases, please contact Macmillan
Corporate & Premium Sales Department at 1-800-221-7945 (ext 5442)
or write specialmarkets@macmillan.com.

Seven Seas and the Seven Seas logo are trademarks of
Seven Seas Entertainment, LLC. All rights reserved.

ISBN: 978-1-626922-13-6

Printed in Canada

First Printing: February 2016

10 9 8 7 6 5 4 3 2 1

FOLLOW US ONLINE: www.gomanga.com

READING DIRECTIONS

This book reads from *right to left*, Japanese style.
If this is your first time reading manga, you start
reading from the top right panel on each page and
take it from there. If you get lost, just follow the
numbered diagram here. It may seem backwards at
first, but you'll get the hang of it! Have fun!!

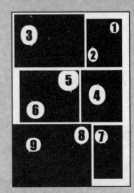

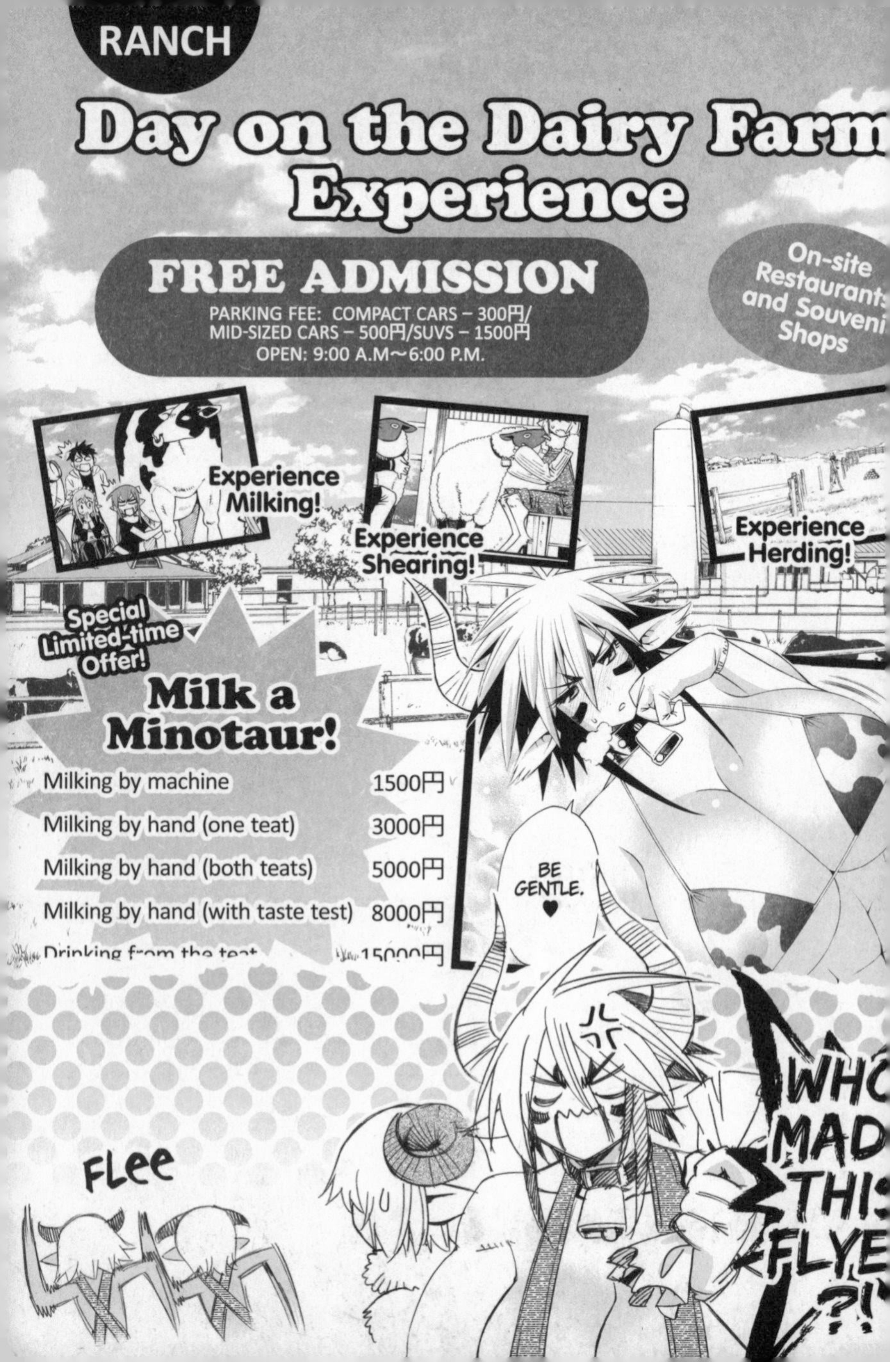
RANCH
Day on the Dairy Farm Experience
FREE ADMISSION
PARKING FEE: COMPACT CARS – 300円/ MID-SIZED CARS – 500円/SUVS – 1500円
OPEN: 9:00 A.M～6:00 P.M.
On-site Restaurant and Souveni Shops
Experience Milking!
Experience Shearing!
Experience Herding!
Special Limited-time Offer!
Milk a Minotaur!
Milking by machine 1500円
Milking by hand (one teat) 3000円
Milking by hand (both teats) 5000円
Milking by hand (with taste test) 8000円
Drinking from the teat 15000円
BE GENTLE. ♥
WHO MAD THIS FLYE ?!
FLEE

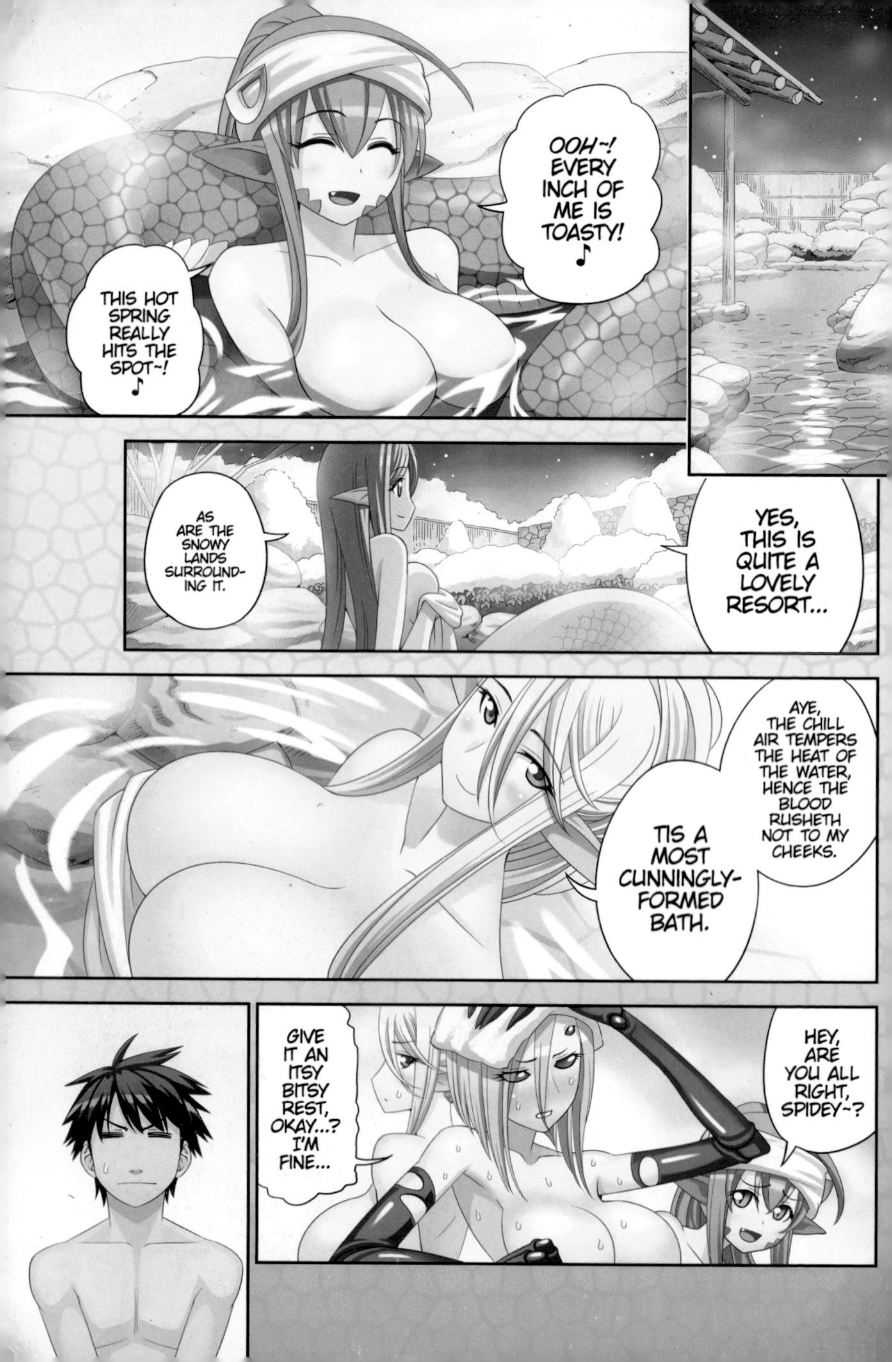
OOH~! EVERY INCH OF ME IS TOASTY! ♪
THIS HOT SPRING REALLY HITS THE SPOT~! ♪
YES, THIS IS QUITE A LOVELY RESORT...
AS ARE THE SNOWY LANDS SURROUNDING IT.
AYE, THE CHILL AIR TEMPERS THE HEAT OF THE WATER, HENCE THE BLOOD RUSHETH NOT TO MY CHEEKS.
TIS A MOST CUNNINGLY-FORMED BATH.
HEY, ARE YOU ALL RIGHT, SPIDEY~?
GIVE IT AN ITSY BITSY REST, OKAY...? I'M FINE...

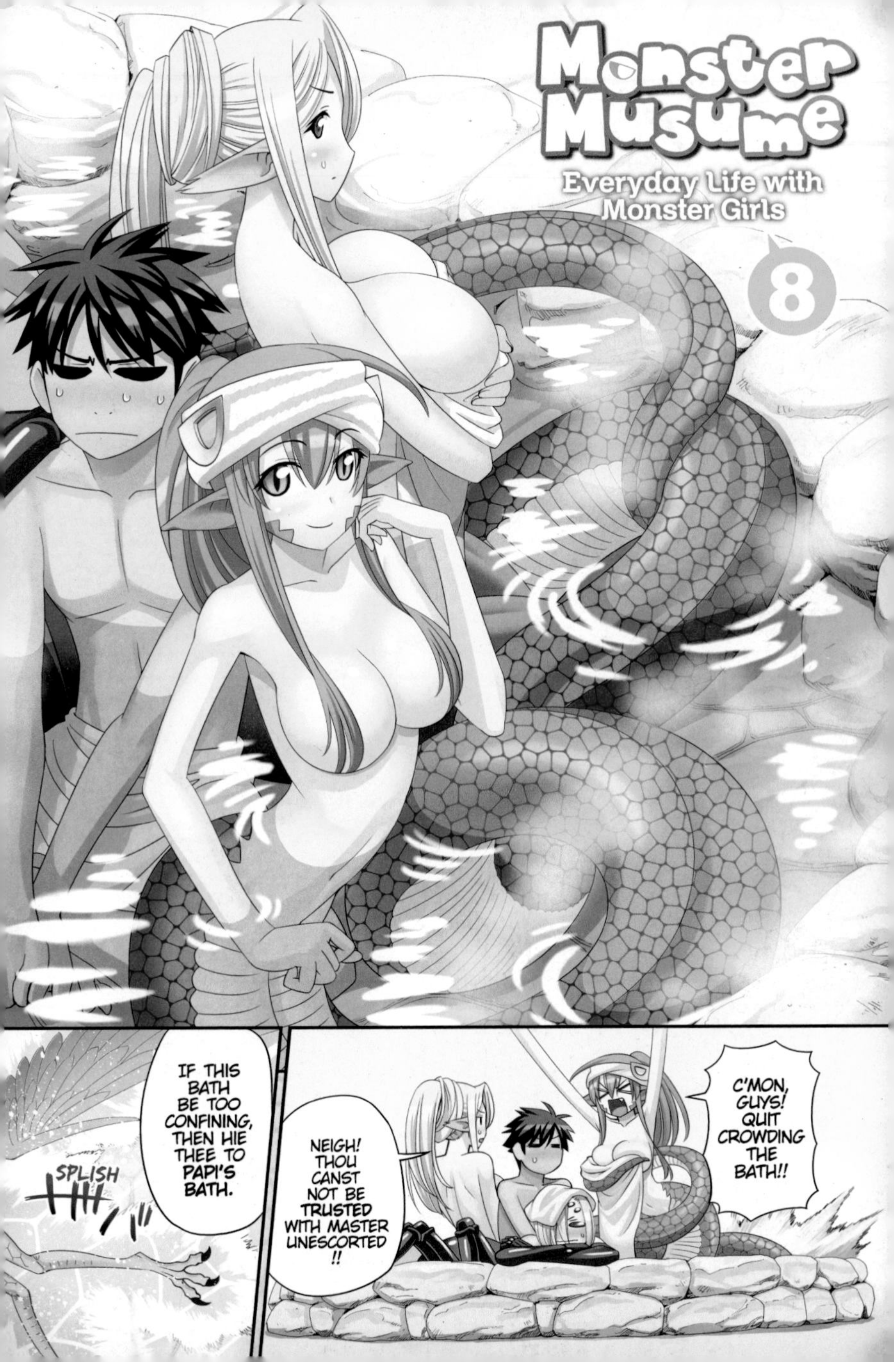
Monster Musume
Everyday Life with Monster Girls
8
C'MON, GUYS! QUIT CROWDING THE BATH!!
NEIGH! THOU CANST NOT BE TRUSTED WITH MASTER UNESCORTED!!
IF THIS BATH BE TOO CONFINING, THEN HIE THEE TO PAPI'S BATH.
SPLISH

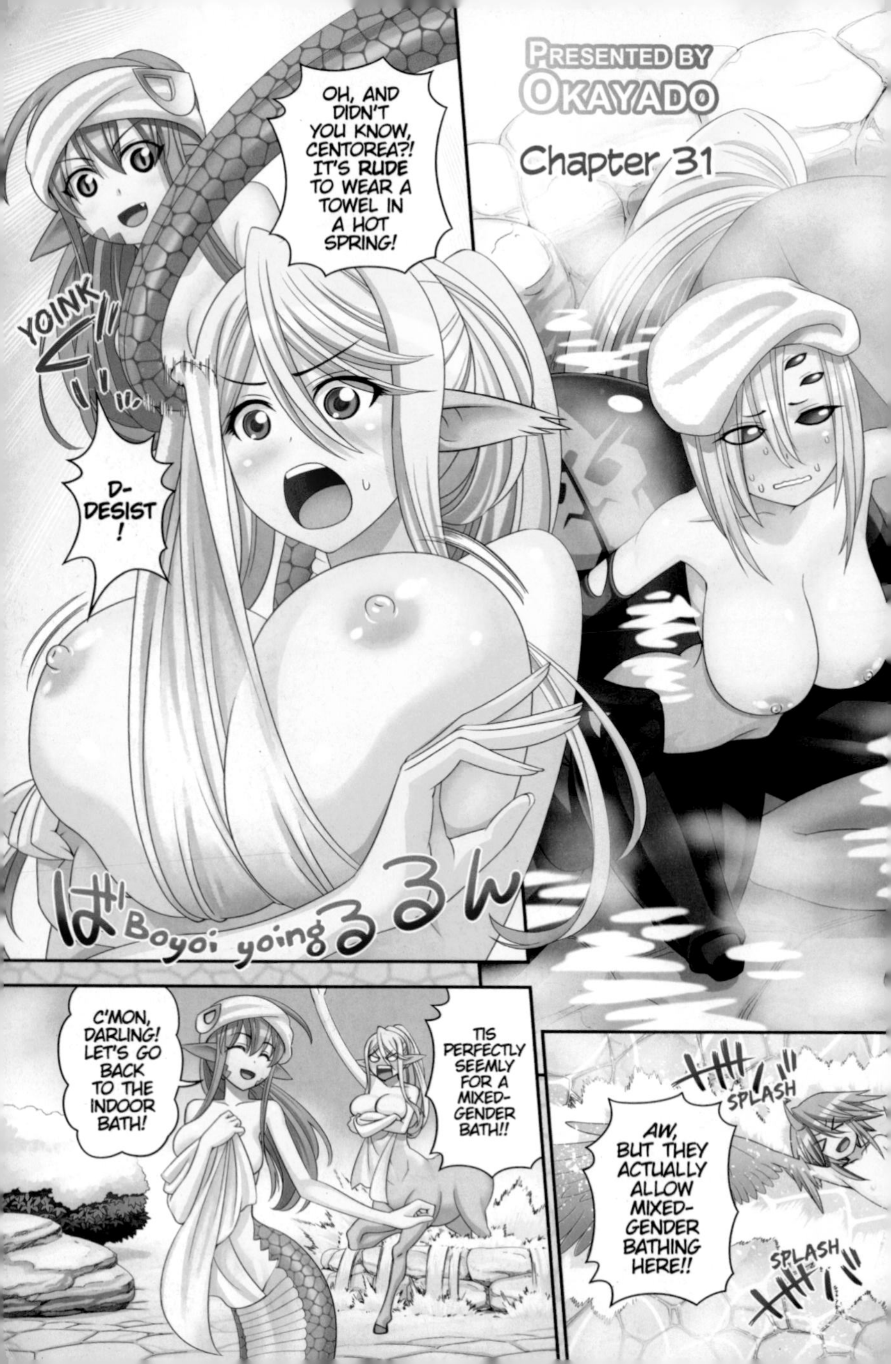
PRESENTED BY OKAYADO
Chapter 31
OH, AND DIDN'T YOU KNOW, CENTOREA?! IT'S RUDE TO WEAR A TOWEL IN A HOT SPRING!
YOINK
D-DESIST!
Boyoi yoing
SPLASH
AW, BUT THEY ACTUALLY ALLOW MIXED-GENDER BATHING HERE!!
SPLASH
TIS PERFECTLY SEEMLY FOR A MIXED-GENDER BATH!!
C'MON, DARLING! LET'S GO BACK TO THE INDOOR BATH!

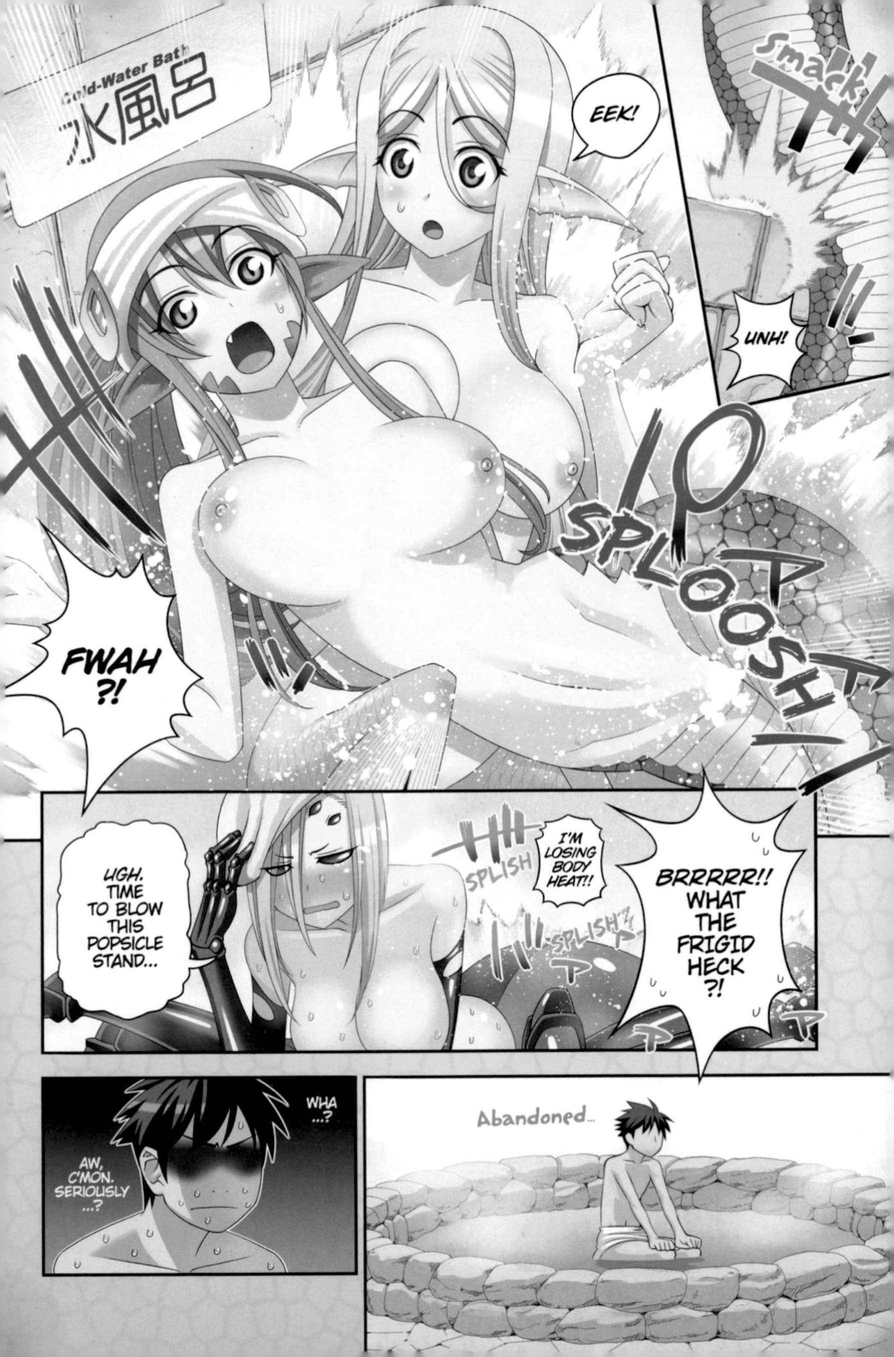
Smack!
UNH!
EEK!
Cold-Water Bath
水風呂
SPLOOSH
FWAH ?!
BRRRRR!! WHAT THE FRIGID HECK ?!
I'M LOSING BODY HEAT!!
SPLISH
SPLISH
UGH. TIME TO BLOW THIS POPSICLE STAND...
Abandoned...
WHA ...?
AW, C'MON. SERIOUSLY ...?

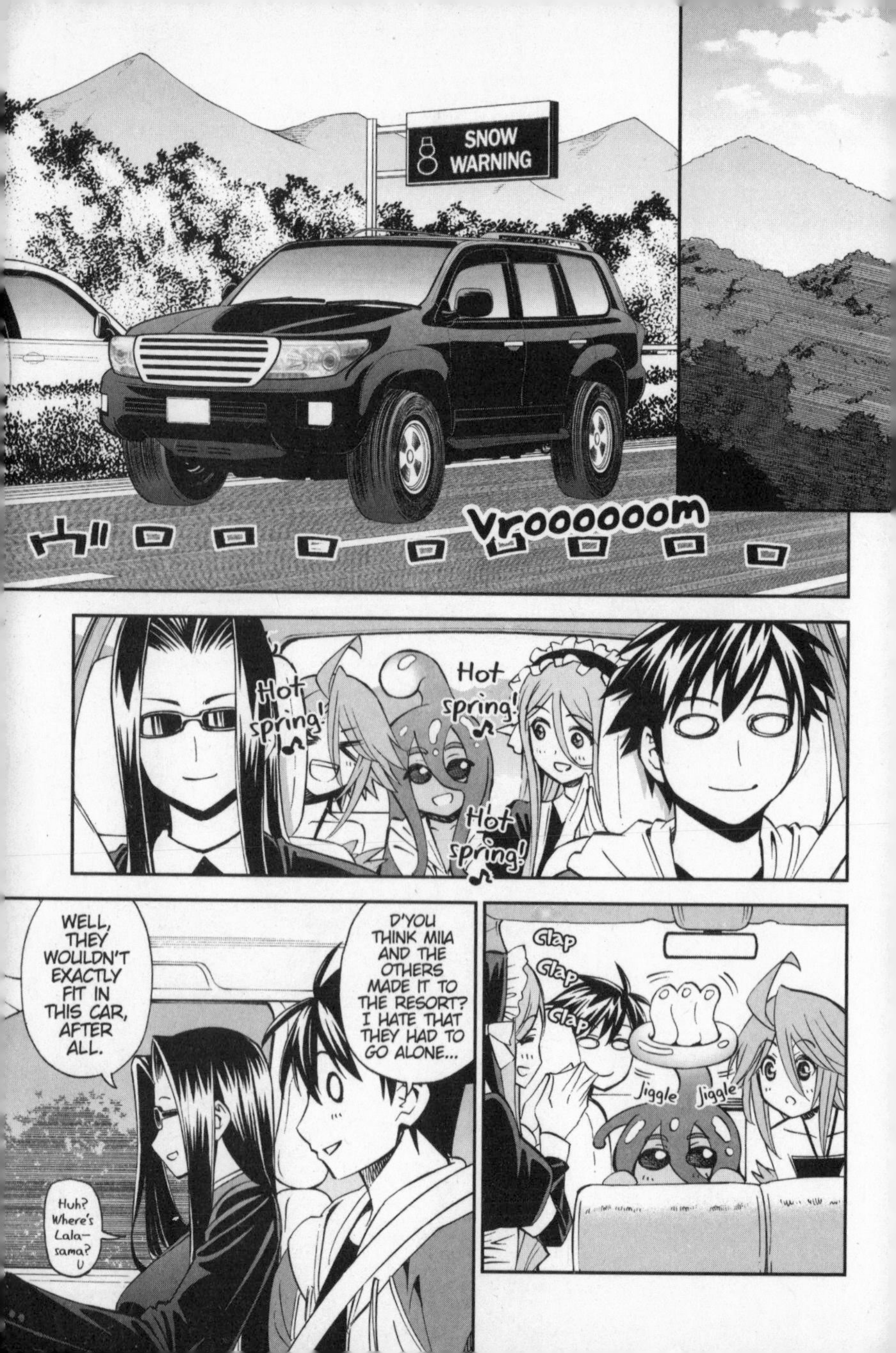
SNOW WARNING
Vroooooom
Hot spring!
Hot spring!
Hot spring!
Clap
Clap
Clap
Jiggle
Jiggle
D'YOU THINK MIIA AND THE OTHERS MADE IT TO THE RESORT? I HATE THAT THEY HAD TO GO ALONE...
WELL, THEY WOULDN'T EXACTLY FIT IN THIS CAR, AFTER ALL.
Huh? Where's Lala-sama?

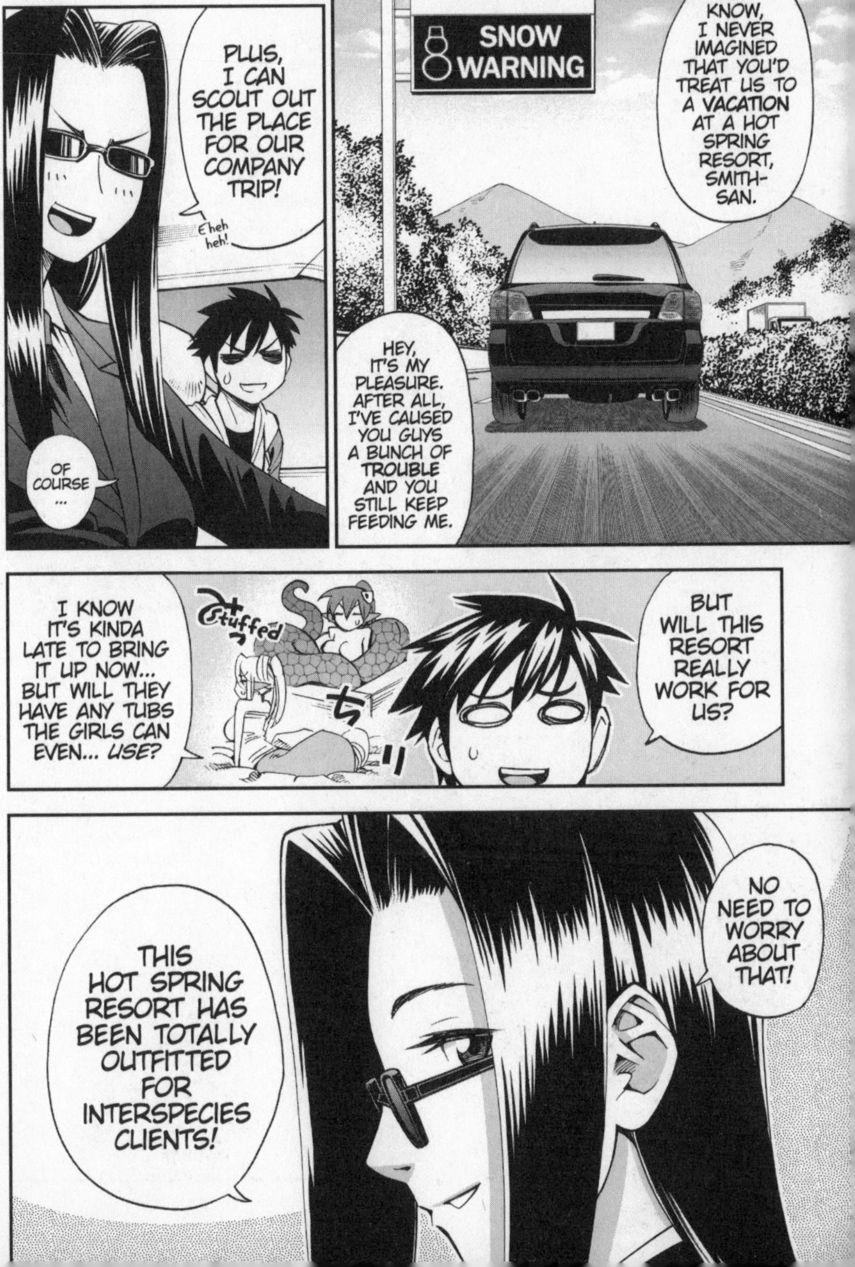
SNOW WARNING
YOU KNOW, I NEVER IMAGINED THAT YOU'D TREAT US TO A VACATION AT A HOT SPRING RESORT, SMITH-SAN.
HEY, IT'S MY PLEASURE. AFTER ALL, I'VE CAUSED YOU GUYS A BUNCH OF TROUBLE AND YOU STILL KEEP FEEDING ME.
PLUS, I CAN SCOUT OUT THE PLACE FOR OUR COMPANY TRIP!
Eheh heh!
OF COURSE...
BUT WILL THIS RESORT REALLY WORK FOR US?
Stuffed
I KNOW IT'S KINDA LATE TO BRING IT UP NOW... BUT WILL THEY HAVE ANY TUBS THE GIRLS CAN EVEN... *USE*?
NO NEED TO WORRY ABOUT THAT!
THIS HOT SPRING RESORT HAS BEEN TOTALLY OUTFITTED FOR INTERSPECIES CLIENTS!

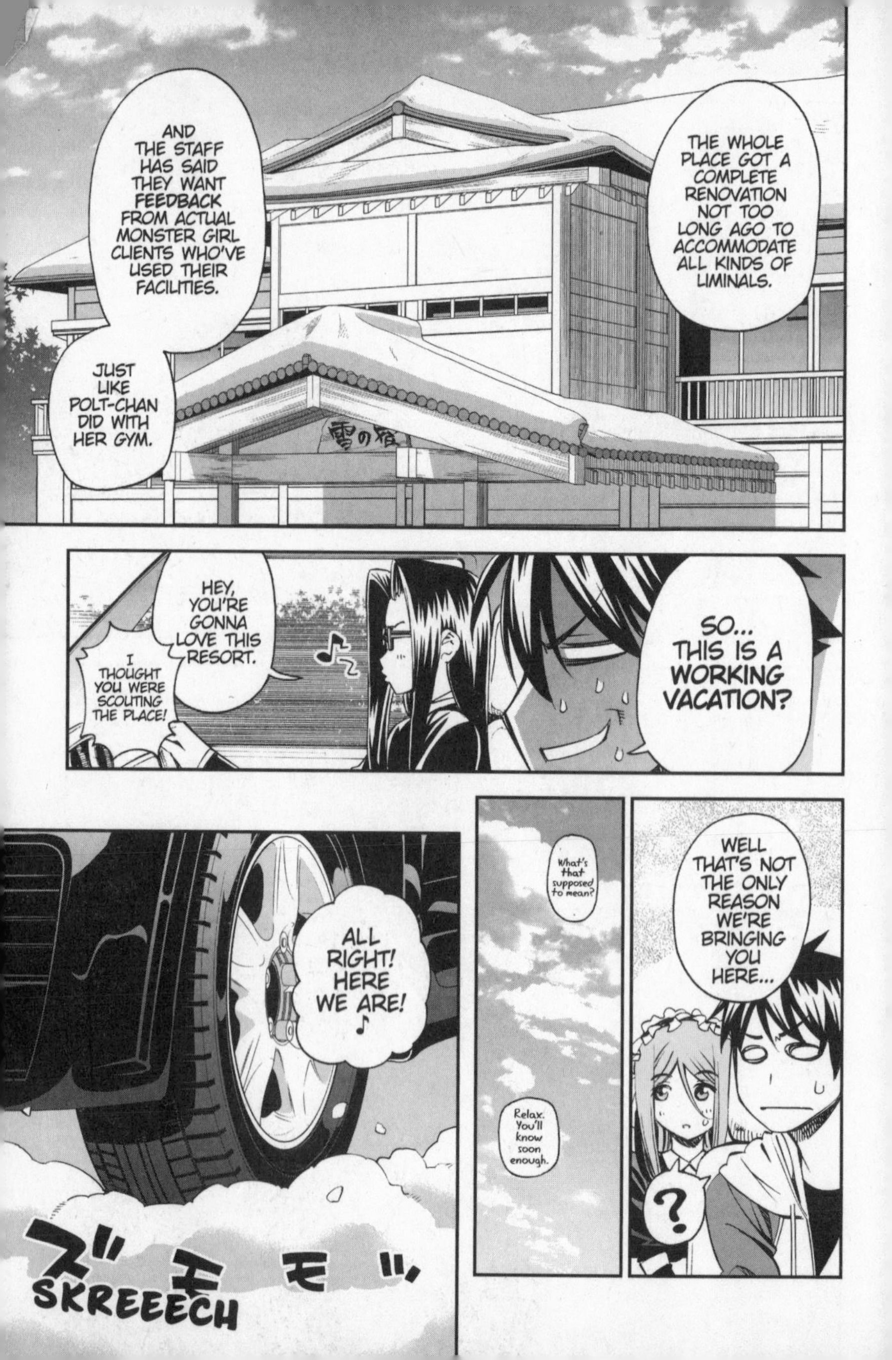
THE WHOLE PLACE GOT A COMPLETE RENOVATION NOT TOO LONG AGO TO ACCOMMODATE ALL KINDS OF LIMINALS.
AND THE STAFF HAS SAID THEY WANT FEEDBACK FROM ACTUAL MONSTER GIRL CLIENTS WHO'VE USED THEIR FACILITIES.
JUST LIKE POLT-CHAN DID WITH HER GYM.
SO... THIS IS A WORKING VACATION?
HEY, YOU'RE GONNA LOVE THIS RESORT.
I THOUGHT YOU WERE SCOUTING THE PLACE!
WELL THAT'S NOT THE ONLY REASON WE'RE BRINGING YOU HERE...
?
What's that supposed to mean?
Relax. You'll know soon enough.
ALL RIGHT! HERE WE ARE! ♪
ズモモッ
SKREEEECH

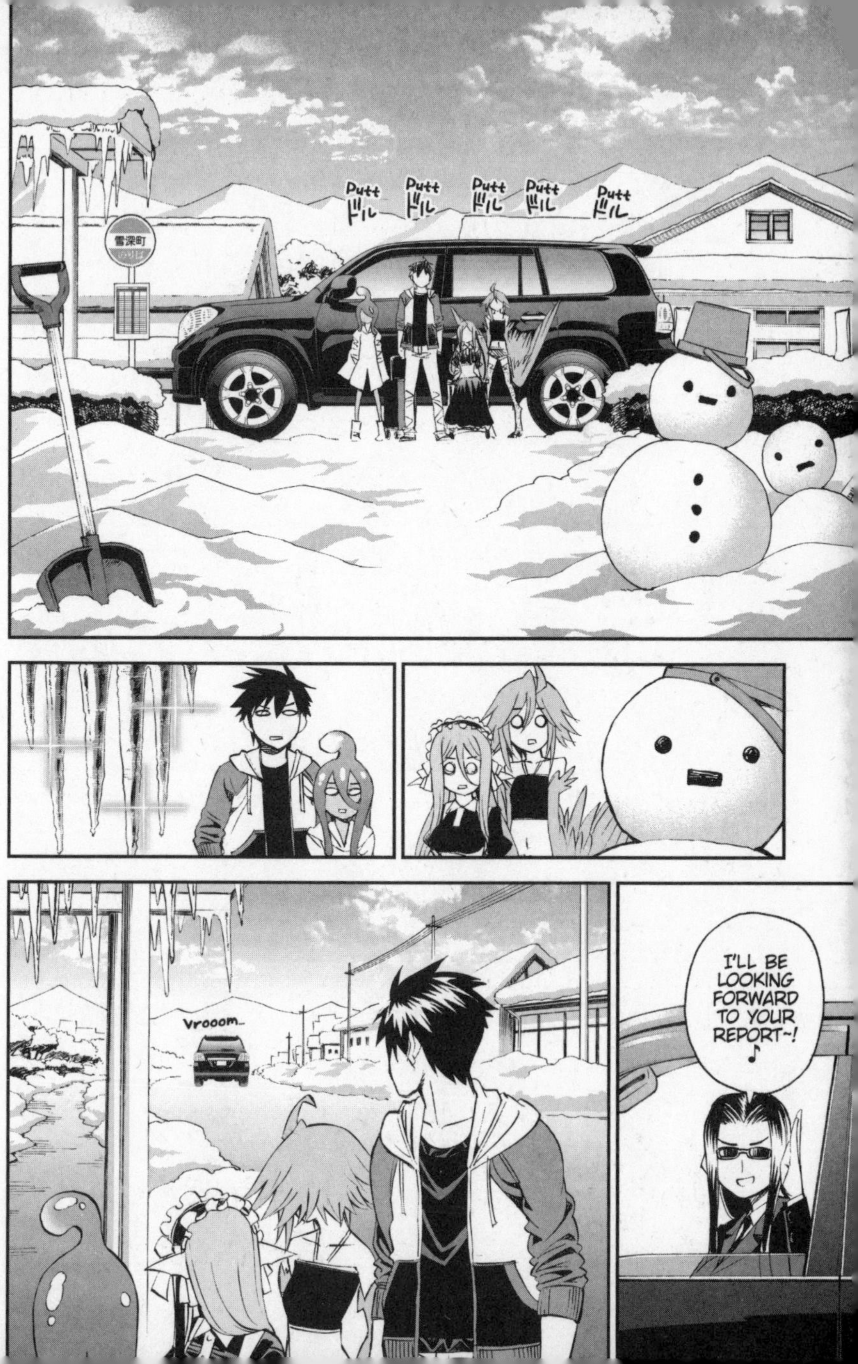
Putt ドル
Putt ドル
Putt ドル
Putt ドル
Putt ドル
雪深町
I'LL BE LOOKING FORWARD TO YOUR REPORT~! ♪
Vrooom...

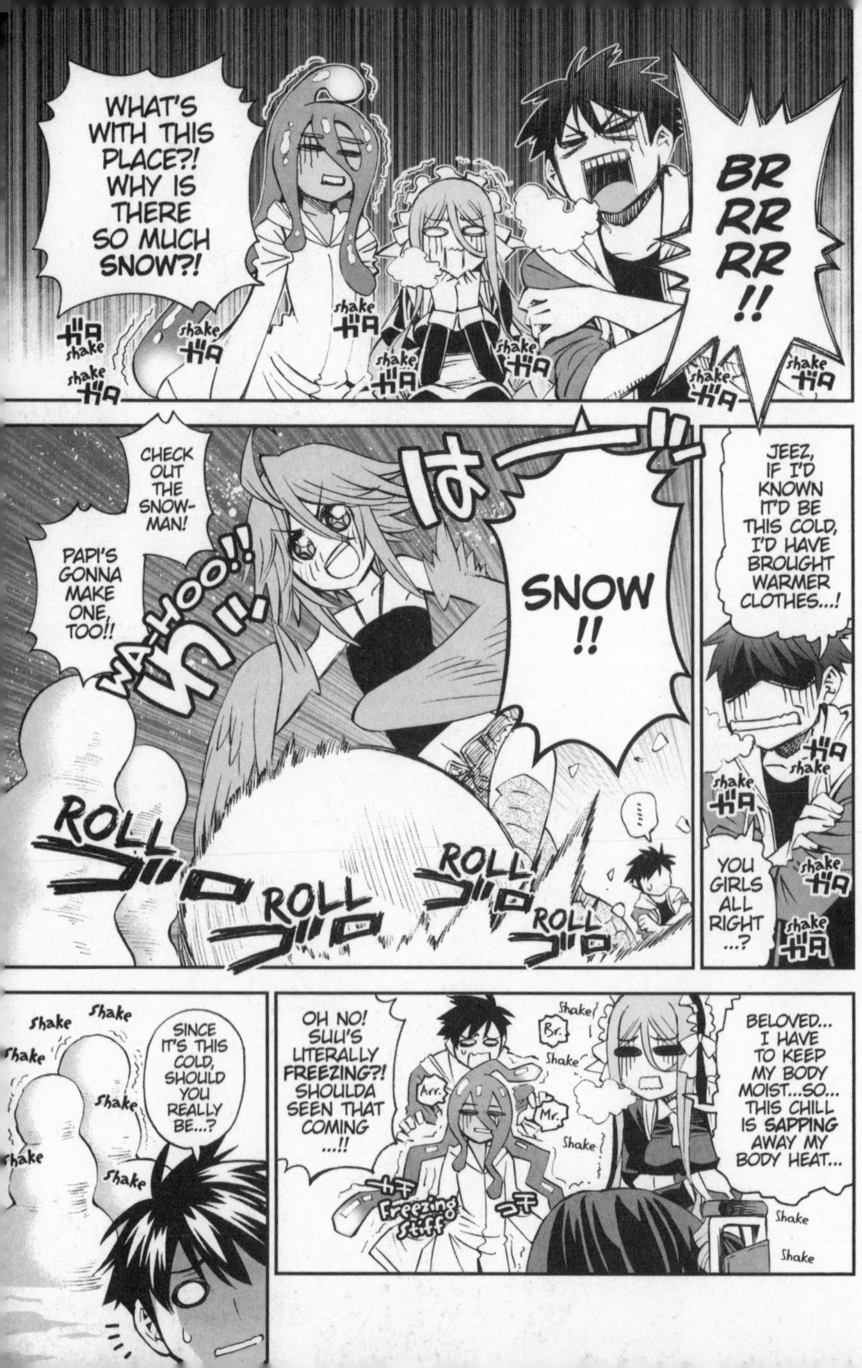

BRRRRRR!!
WHAT'S WITH THIS PLACE?! WHY IS THERE SO MUCH SNOW?!
shake ガタ
JEEZ, IF I'D KNOWN IT'D BE THIS COLD, I'D HAVE BROUGHT WARMER CLOTHES...!
YOU GIRLS ALL RIGHT ...?
shake ガタ
はーっ
SNOW !!
CHECK OUT THE SNOW-MAN!
PAPI'S GONNA MAKE ONE, TOO!!
WA-HOO!! わー!!
......
ROLL ゴロ
ROLL ゴロ
ROLL ゴロ
ROLL ゴロ
BELOVED... I HAVE TO KEEP MY BODY MOIST...SO... THIS CHILL IS SAPPING AWAY MY BODY HEAT...
Shake
Br.
Arr.
Mr.
OH NO! SUU'S LITERALLY FREEZING?! SHOULDA SEEN THAT COMING ...!!
カチコチ Freezing Stiff
Shake
SINCE IT'S THIS COLD, SHOULD YOU REALLY BE...?
Shake

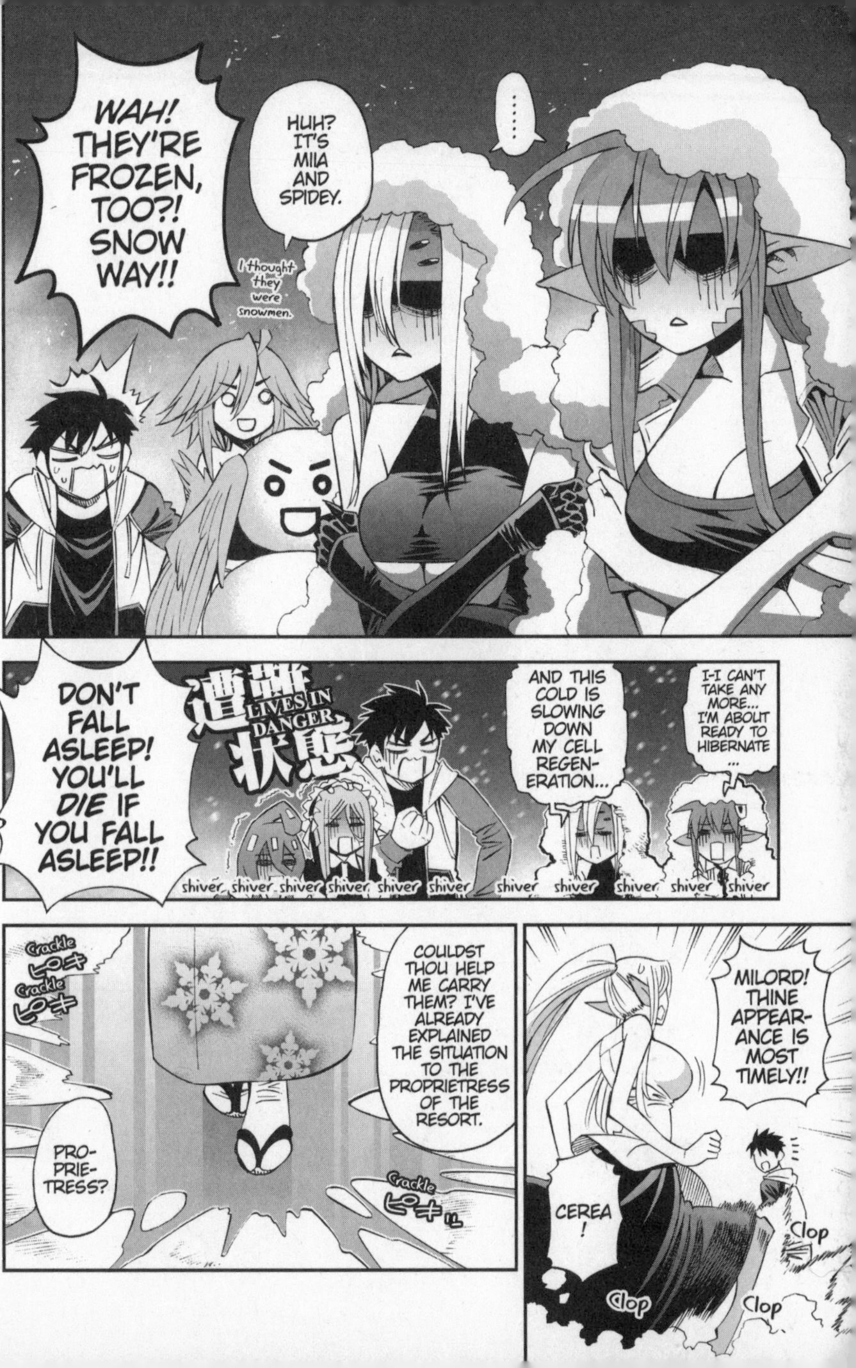

......
HUH? IT'S MIIA AND SPIDEY.
I thought they were snowmen.
WAH! THEY'RE FROZEN, TOO?! SNOW WAY!!
I-I CAN'T TAKE ANY MORE... I'M ABOUT READY TO HIBERNATE ...
AND THIS COLD IS SLOWING DOWN MY CELL REGENERATION...
遭難状態
LIVES IN DANGER
DON'T FALL ASLEEP! YOU'LL DIE IF YOU FALL ASLEEP!!
shiver shiver shiver shiver shiver shiver shiver shiver shiver shiver shiver
MILORD! THINE APPEARANCE IS MOST TIMELY!!
CEREA!
Clop
Clop
Clop
COULDST THOU HELP ME CARRY THEM? I'VE ALREADY EXPLAINED THE SITUATION TO THE PROPRIETRESS OF THE RESORT.
Crackle ピキ
Crackle ピキ
PRO-PRIE-TRESS?
Crackle ピキッ

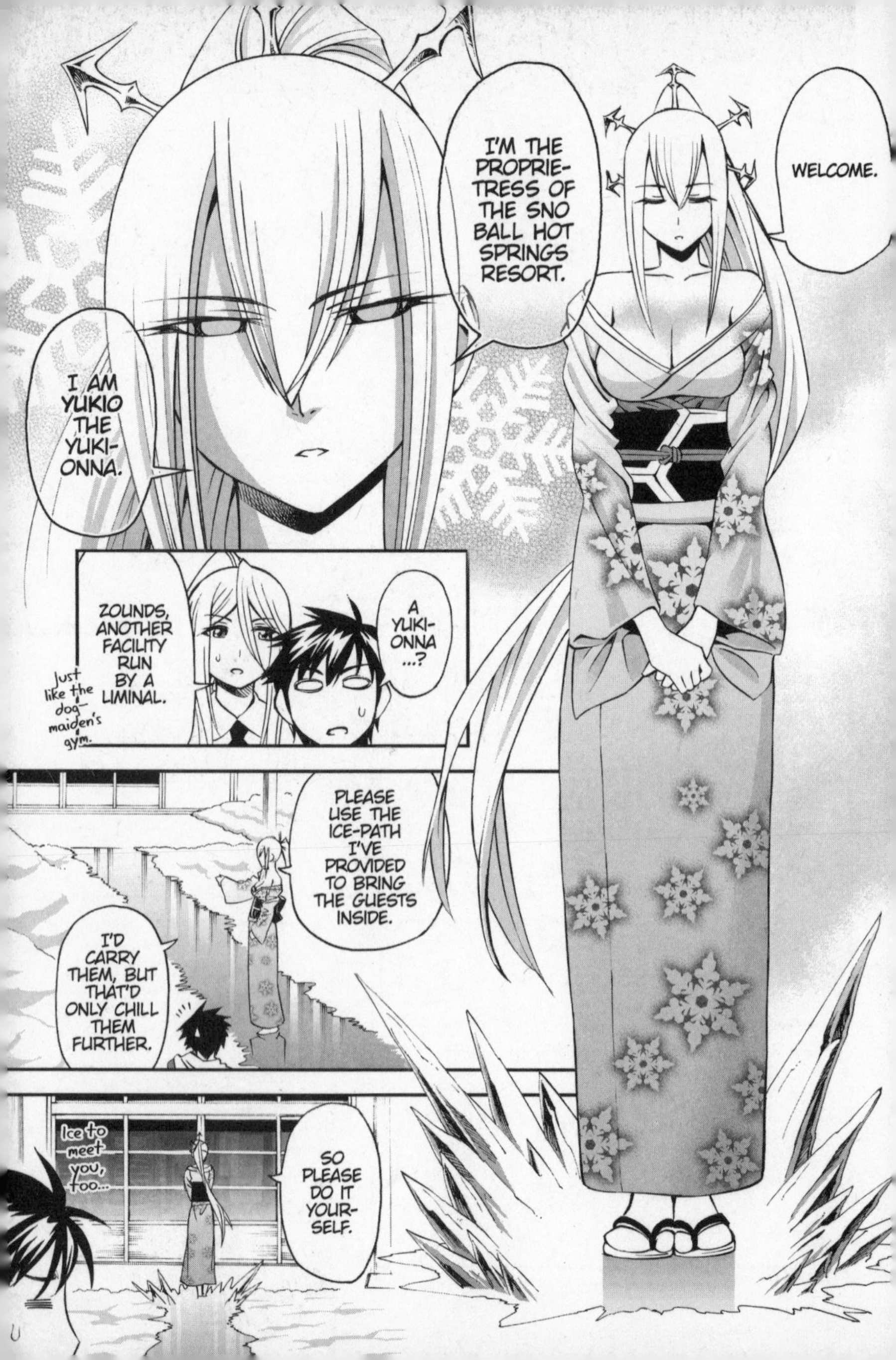
WELCOME.
I'M THE PROPRIETRESS OF THE SNO BALL HOT SPRINGS RESORT.
I AM YUKIO THE YUKI-ONNA.
A YUKI-ONNA...?
ZOUNDS, ANOTHER FACILITY RUN BY A LIMINAL.
Just like the dog-maiden's gym.
PLEASE USE THE ICE-PATH I'VE PROVIDED TO BRING THE GUESTS INSIDE.
I'D CARRY THEM, BUT THAT'D ONLY CHILL THEM FURTHER.
SO PLEASE DO IT YOURSELF.
Ice to meet you, too...

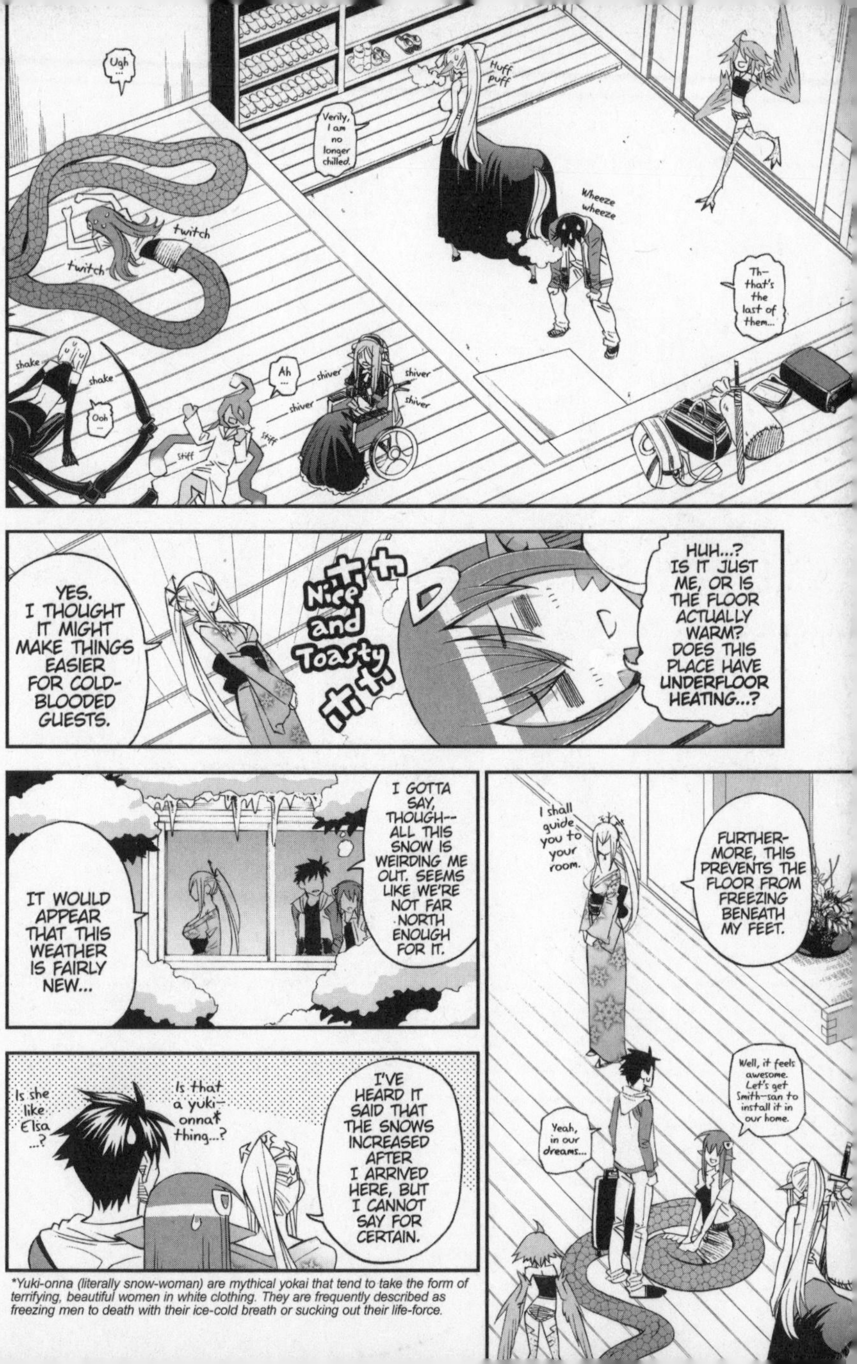
Huff puff
Verily, I am no longer chilled.
Ugh...
twitch
twitch
Wheeze wheeze
Th-that's the last of them...
shiver
shiver
Ah...
shiver
shiver
shake
shake
Ooh...
stiff
stiff
HUH...? IS IT JUST ME, OR IS THE FLOOR ACTUALLY WARM? DOES THIS PLACE HAVE UNDERFLOOR HEATING...?
Nice and Toasty
YES. I THOUGHT IT MIGHT MAKE THINGS EASIER FOR COLD-BLOODED GUESTS.
FURTHER-MORE, THIS PREVENTS THE FLOOR FROM FREEZING BENEATH MY FEET.
I shall guide you to your room.
Well, it feels awesome. Let's get Smith-san to install it in our home.
Yeah, in our dreams...
I GOTTA SAY, THOUGH--ALL THIS SNOW IS WEIRDING ME OUT. SEEMS LIKE WE'RE NOT FAR NORTH ENOUGH FOR IT.
IT WOULD APPEAR THAT THIS WEATHER IS FAIRLY NEW...
I'VE HEARD IT SAID THAT THE SNOWS INCREASED AFTER I ARRIVED HERE, BUT I CANNOT SAY FOR CERTAIN.
Is that a yuki-onna* thing...?
Is she like Elsa...?

*Yuki-onna (literally snow-woman) are mythical yokai that tend to take the form of terrifying, beautiful women in white clothing. They are frequently described as freezing men to death with their ice-cold breath or sucking out their life-force.

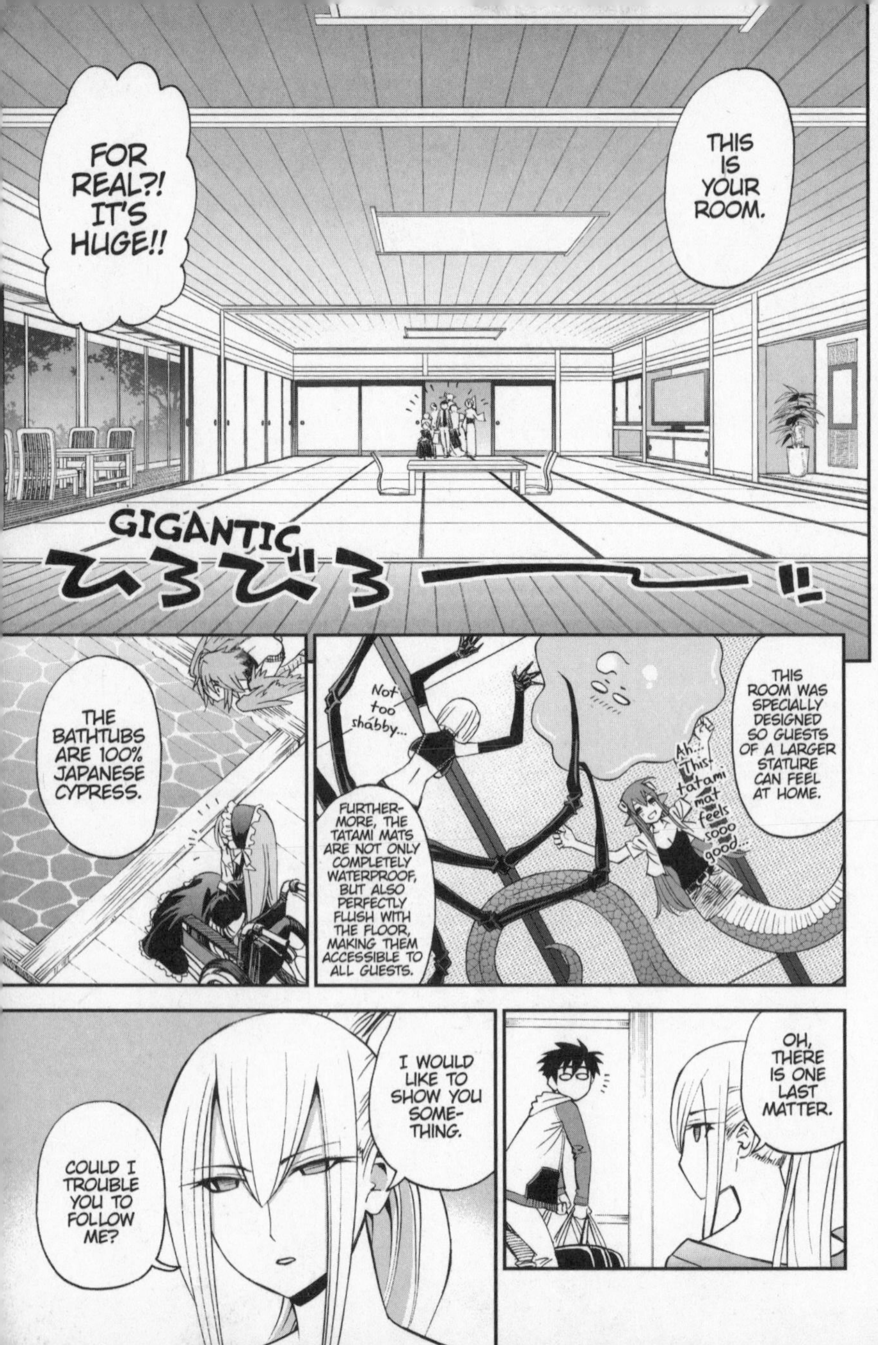
THIS IS YOUR ROOM.
FOR REAL?! IT'S HUGE!!
GIGANTIC
ひろびろーー!!
THIS ROOM WAS SPECIALLY DESIGNED SO GUESTS OF A LARGER STATURE CAN FEEL AT HOME.
Ah... This tatami mat feels sooo good...
Not too shabby...
FURTHERMORE, THE TATAMI MATS ARE NOT ONLY COMPLETELY WATERPROOF, BUT ALSO PERFECTLY FLUSH WITH THE FLOOR, MAKING THEM ACCESSIBLE TO ALL GUESTS.
THE BATHTUBS ARE 100% JAPANESE CYPRESS.
OH, THERE IS ONE LAST MATTER.
I WOULD LIKE TO SHOW YOU SOME-THING.
COULD I TROUBLE YOU TO FOLLOW ME?

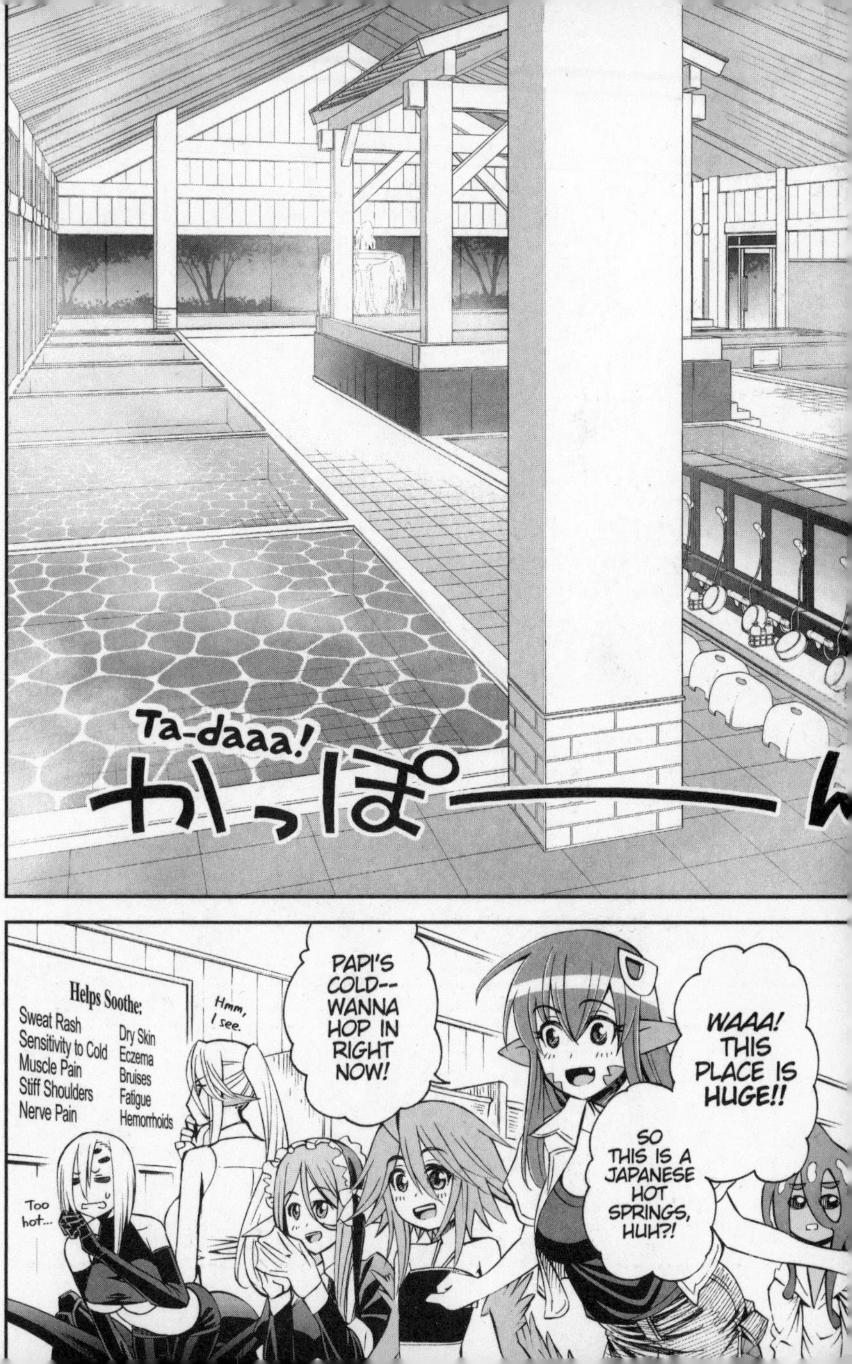
Ta-daaa!
かっぽー
WAAA! THIS PLACE IS HUGE!!
SO THIS IS A JAPANESE HOT SPRINGS, HUH?!
PAPI'S COLD--WANNA HOP IN RIGHT NOW!
Hmm, I see.
Helps Soothe:
Sweat Rash
Sensitivity to Cold
Muscle Pain
Stiff Shoulders
Nerve Pain
Dry Skin
Eczema
Bruises
Fatigue
Hemorrhoids
Too hot...

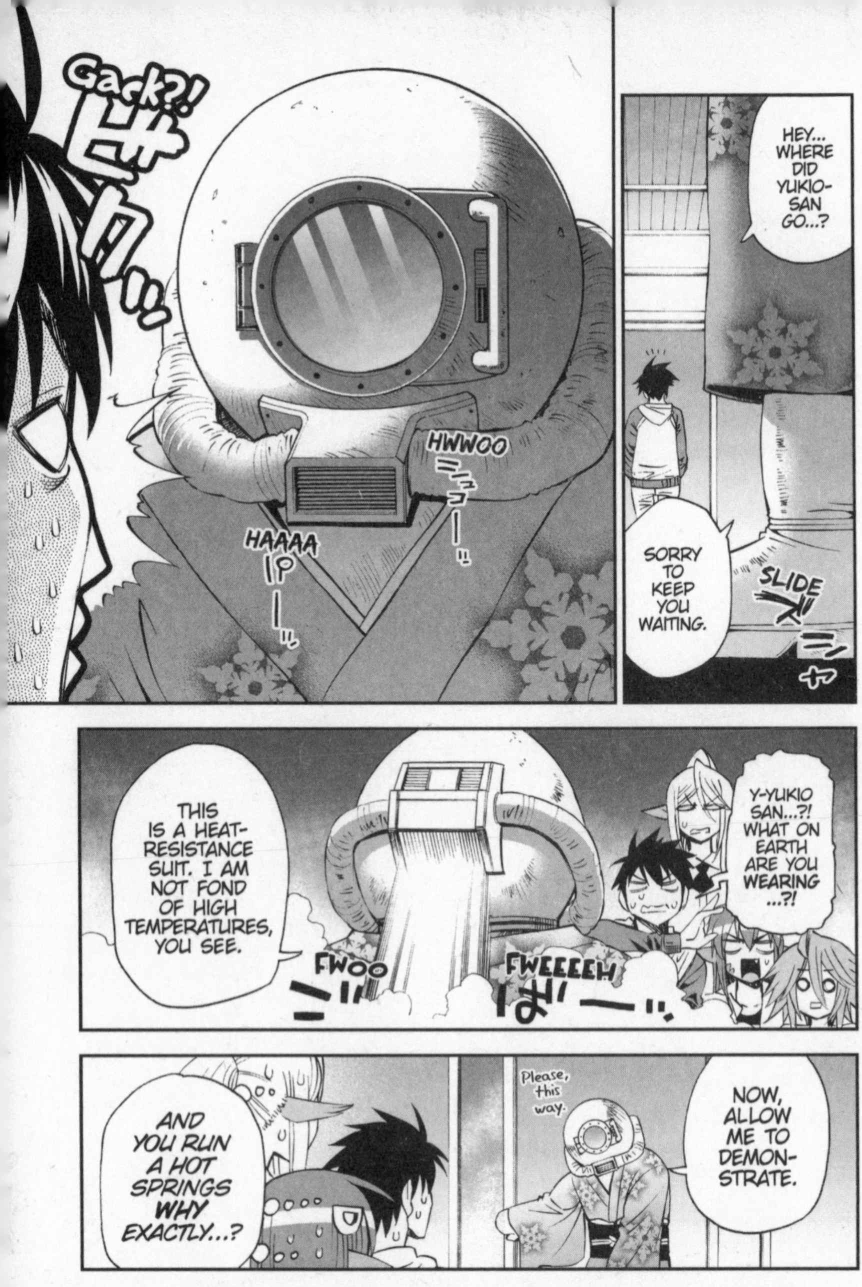
HEY... WHERE DID YUKIO-SAN GO...?
SORRY TO KEEP YOU WAITING.
SLIDE
HWWOO
HAAAA
Gack?!
Y-YUKIO SAN...?! WHAT ON EARTH ARE YOU WEARING...?!
FWEEEEEH
THIS IS A HEAT-RESISTANCE SUIT. I AM NOT FOND OF HIGH TEMPERATURES, YOU SEE.
FWOO
NOW, ALLOW ME TO DEMONSTRATE.
Please, this way.
AND YOU RUN A HOT SPRINGS WHY EXACTLY...?

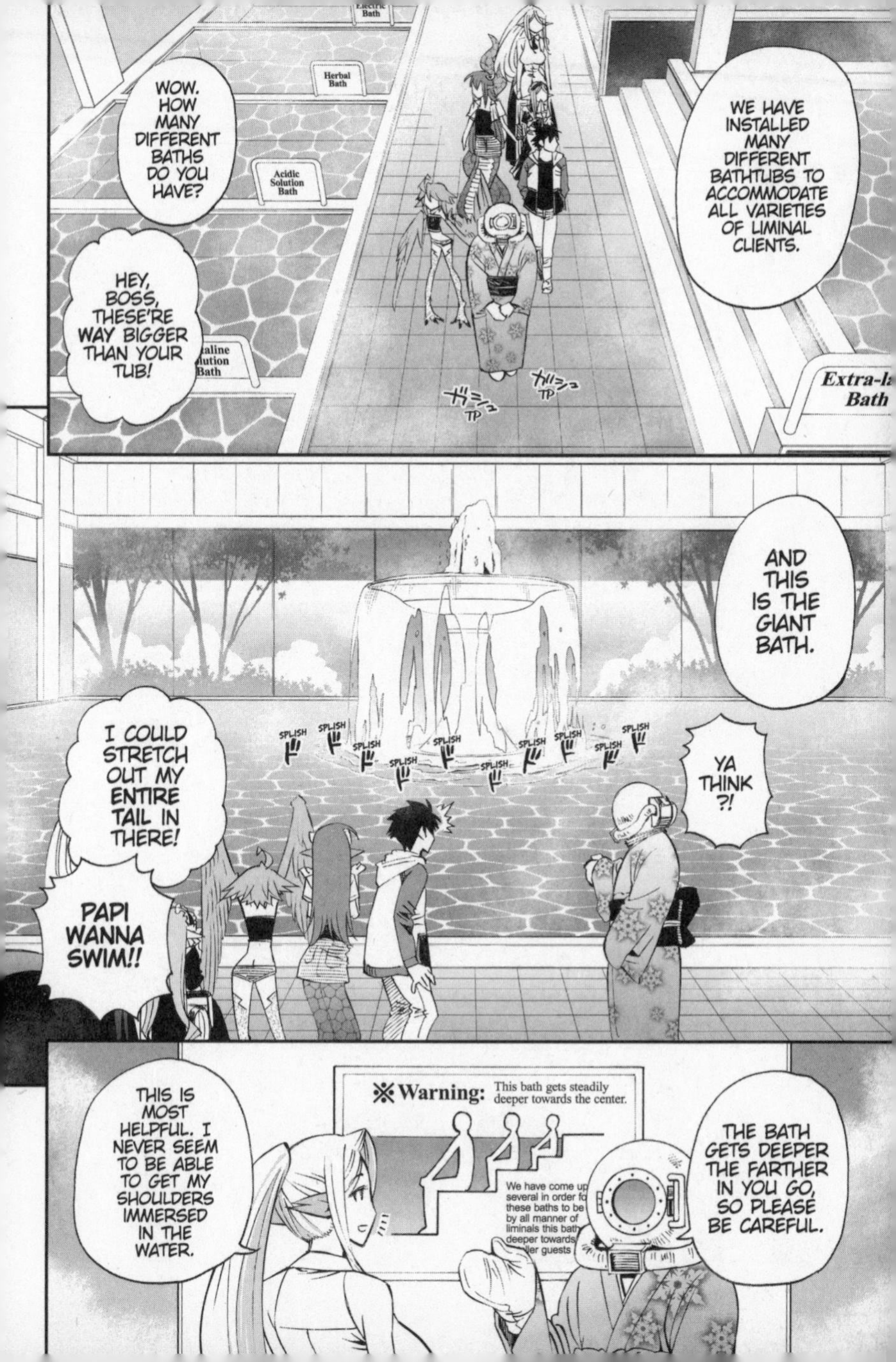
WE HAVE INSTALLED MANY DIFFERENT BATHTUBS TO ACCOMMODATE ALL VARIETIES OF LIMINAL CLIENTS.
Electric Bath
Herbal Bath
Acidic Solution Bath
WOW. HOW MANY DIFFERENT BATHS DO YOU HAVE?
HEY, BOSS, THESE'RE WAY BIGGER THAN YOUR TUB!
TP
TP
AND THIS IS THE GIANT BATH.
SPLISH SPLISH SPLISH SPLISH SPLISH SPLISH SPLISH SPLISH SPLISH SPLISH
I COULD STRETCH OUT MY ENTIRE TAIL IN THERE!
YA THINK?!
PAPI WANNA SWIM!!
THE BATH GETS DEEPER THE FARTHER IN YOU GO, SO PLEASE BE CAREFUL.
※Warning: This bath gets steadily deeper towards the center.
THIS IS MOST HELPFUL. I NEVER SEEM TO BE ABLE TO GET MY SHOULDERS IMMERSED IN THE WATER.

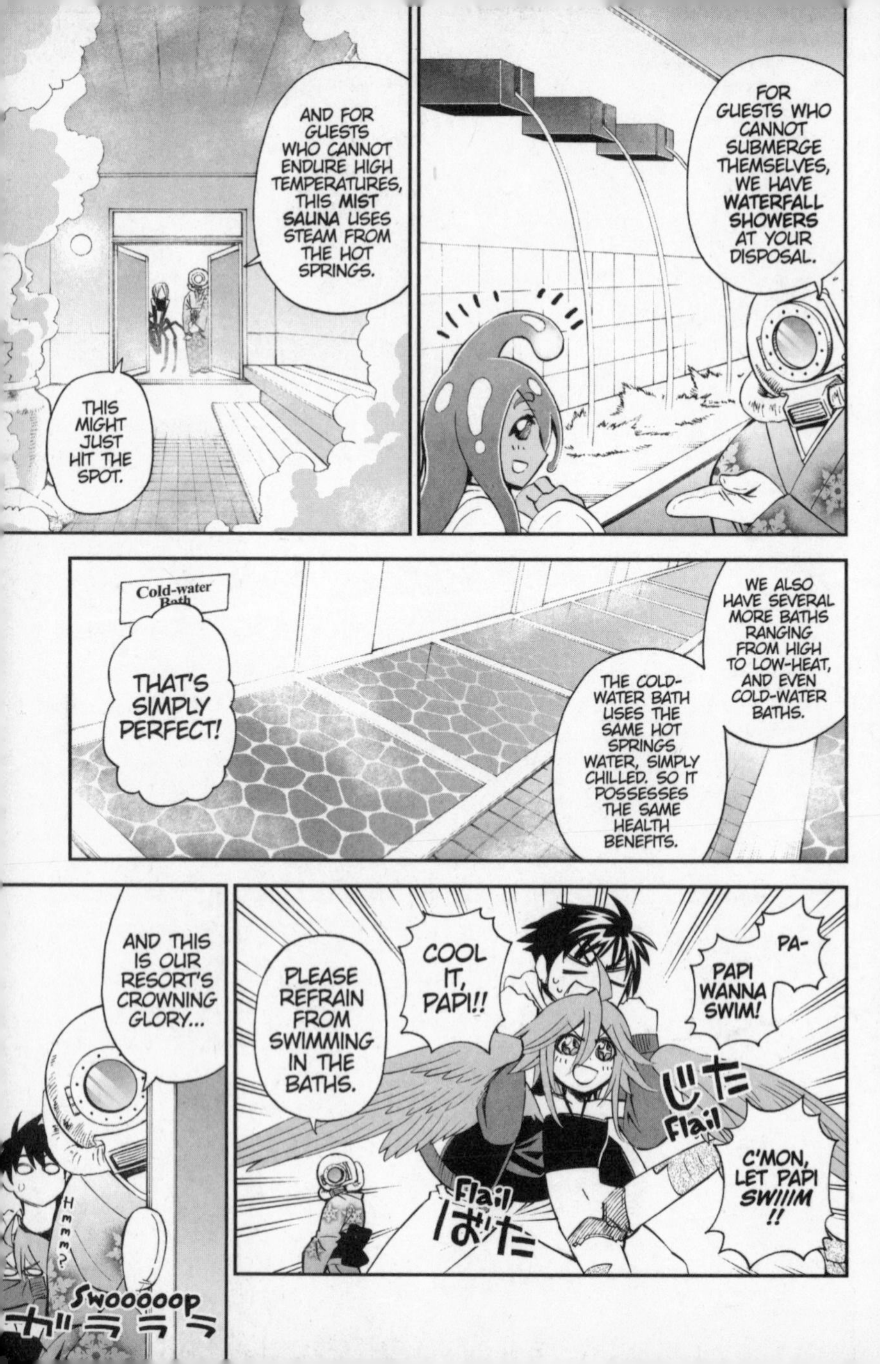
FOR GUESTS WHO CANNOT SUBMERGE THEMSELVES, WE HAVE WATERFALL SHOWERS AT YOUR DISPOSAL.
AND FOR GUESTS WHO CANNOT ENDURE HIGH TEMPERATURES, THIS MIST SAUNA USES STEAM FROM THE HOT SPRINGS.
THIS MIGHT JUST HIT THE SPOT.
WE ALSO HAVE SEVERAL MORE BATHS RANGING FROM HIGH TO LOW-HEAT, AND EVEN COLD-WATER BATHS.
THE COLD-WATER BATH USES THE SAME HOT SPRINGS WATER, SIMPLY CHILLED. SO IT POSSESSES THE SAME HEALTH BENEFITS.
Cold-water Bath
THAT'S SIMPLY PERFECT!
PA- PAPI WANNA SWIM!
COOL IT, PAPI!!
じた Flail
C'MON, LET PAPI SWIIIM!!
PLEASE REFRAIN FROM SWIMMING IN THE BATHS.
Flail ばた
AND THIS IS OUR RESORT'S CROWNING GLORY...
Hmmm?
Swoooop ガラララ

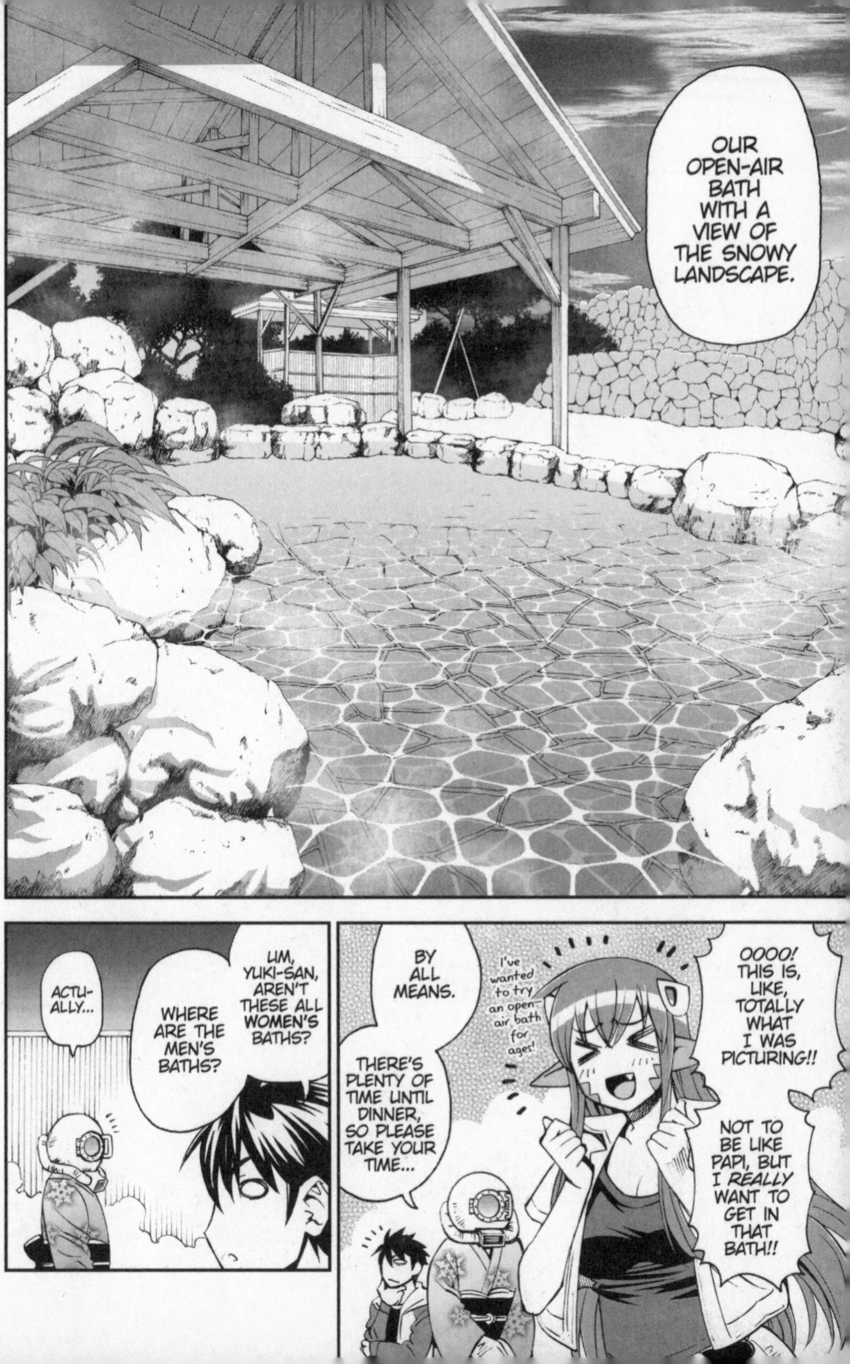
OUR OPEN-AIR BATH WITH A VIEW OF THE SNOWY LANDSCAPE.
OOOO! THIS IS, LIKE, TOTALLY WHAT I WAS PICTURING!!
NOT TO BE LIKE PAPI, BUT I *REALLY* WANT TO GET IN THAT BATH!!
I've wanted to try an open-air bath for ages!
BY ALL MEANS.
THERE'S PLENTY OF TIME UNTIL DINNER, SO PLEASE TAKE YOUR TIME...
UM, YUKI-SAN, AREN'T THESE ALL WOMEN'S BATHS?
WHERE ARE THE MEN'S BATHS?
ACTU-ALLY...

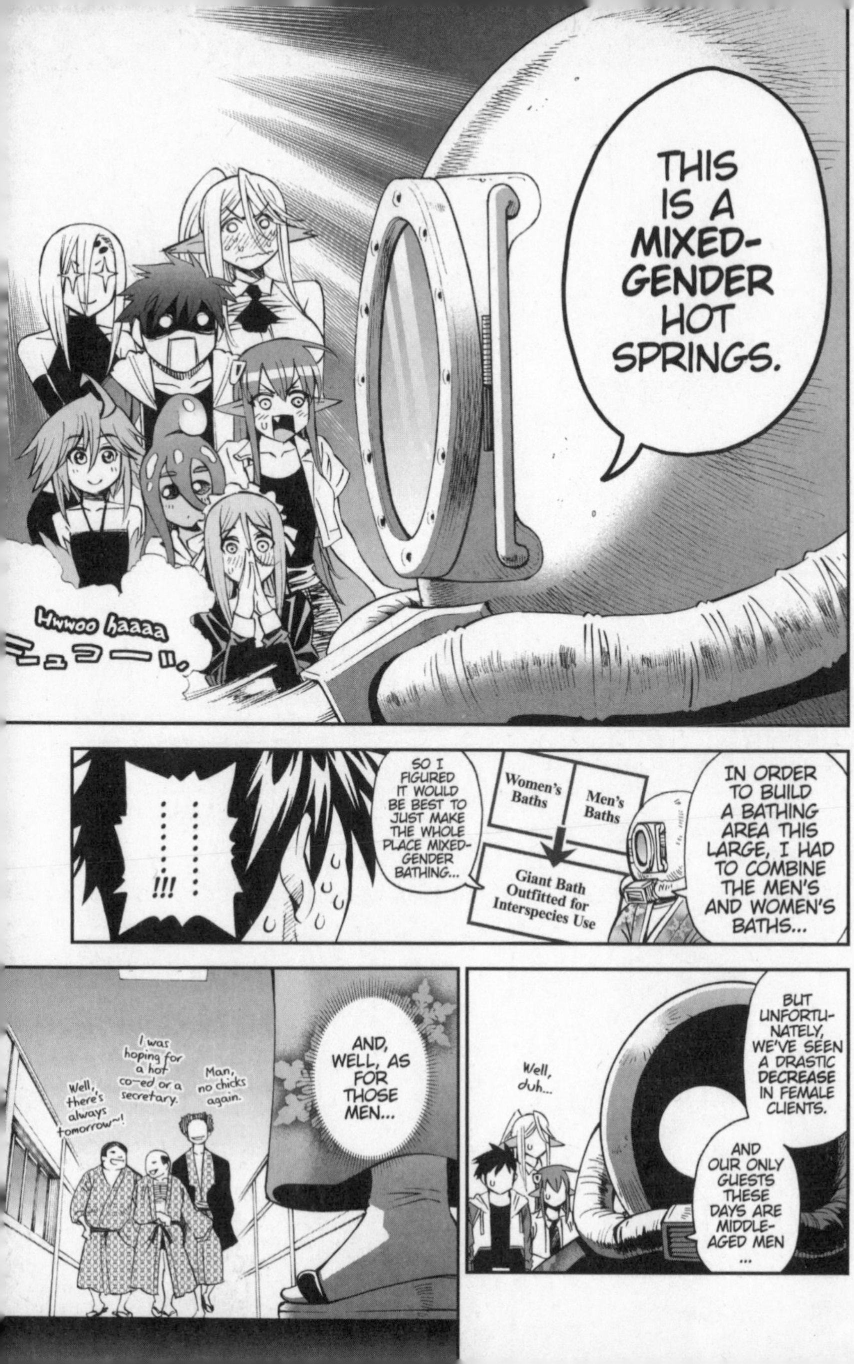
THIS IS A MIXED-GENDER HOT SPRINGS.
Hwwoo haaaa
IN ORDER TO BUILD A BATHING AREA THIS LARGE, I HAD TO COMBINE THE MEN'S AND WOMEN'S BATHS...
Men's Baths
Women's Baths
Giant Bath Outfitted for Interspecies Use
SO I FIGURED IT WOULD BE BEST TO JUST MAKE THE WHOLE PLACE MIXED-GENDER BATHING...
......!!!
BUT UNFORTUNATELY, WE'VE SEEN A DRASTIC DECREASE IN FEMALE CLIENTS.
Well, duh...
AND OUR ONLY GUESTS THESE DAYS ARE MIDDLE-AGED MEN...
AND, WELL, AS FOR THOSE MEN...
Man, no chicks again.
I was hoping for a hot co-ed or a secretary.
Well, there's always tomorrow~!

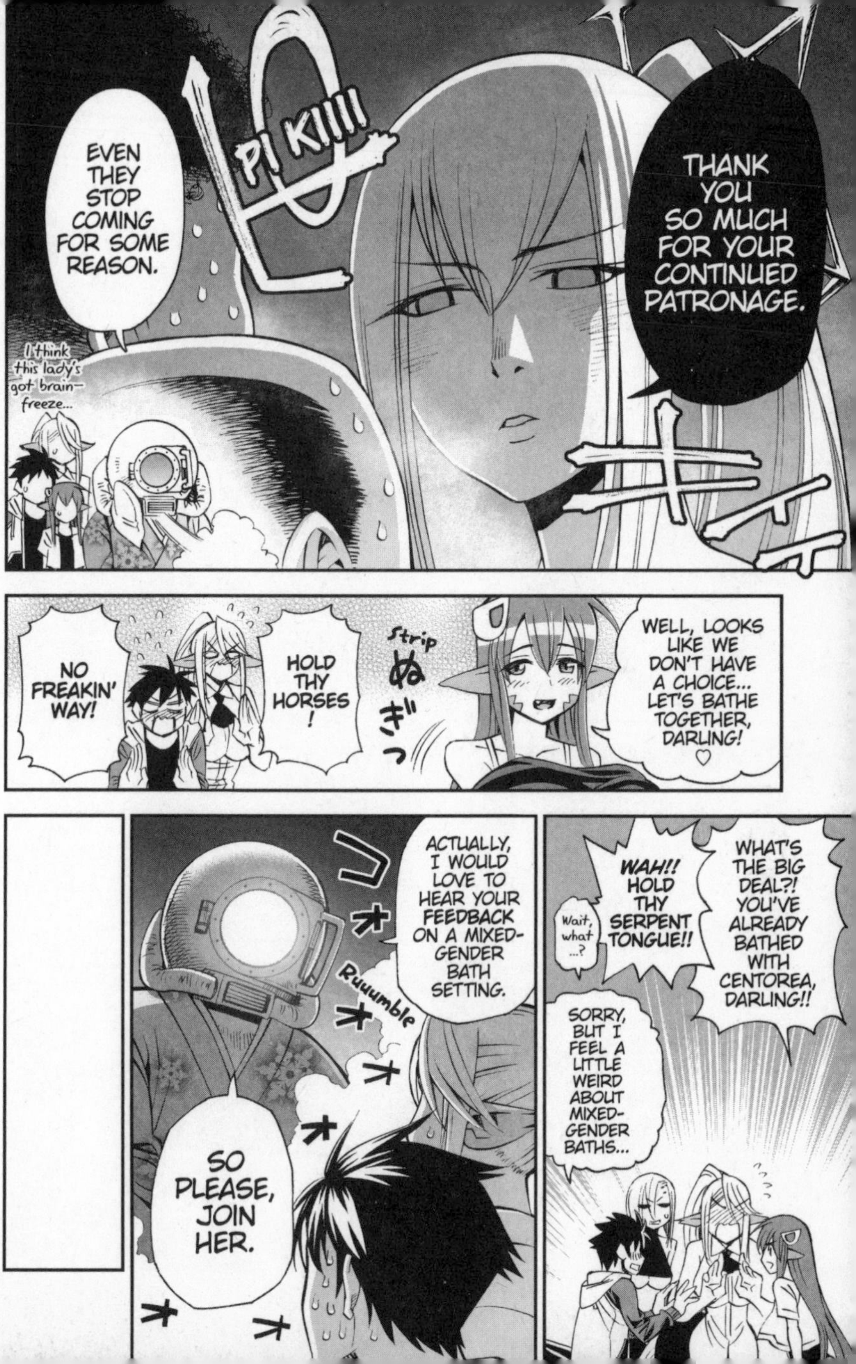
THANK YOU SO MUCH FOR YOUR CONTINUED PATRONAGE.
PI KIIII
EVEN THEY STOP COMING FOR SOME REASON.
I think this lady's got brain-freeze...
WELL, LOOKS LIKE WE DON'T HAVE A CHOICE... LET'S BATHE TOGETHER, DARLING! ♡
Strip
ぬぎっ
HOLD THY HORSES!
NO FREAKIN' WAY!
WHAT'S THE BIG DEAL?! YOU'VE ALREADY BATHED WITH CENTOREA, DARLING!!
WAH!! HOLD THY SERPENT TONGUE!!
Wait, what...?
SORRY, BUT I FEEL A LITTLE WEIRD ABOUT MIXED-GENDER BATHS...
ACTUALLY, I WOULD LOVE TO HEAR YOUR FEEDBACK ON A MIXED-GENDER BATH SETTING.
Ruuumble
SO PLEASE, JOIN HER.

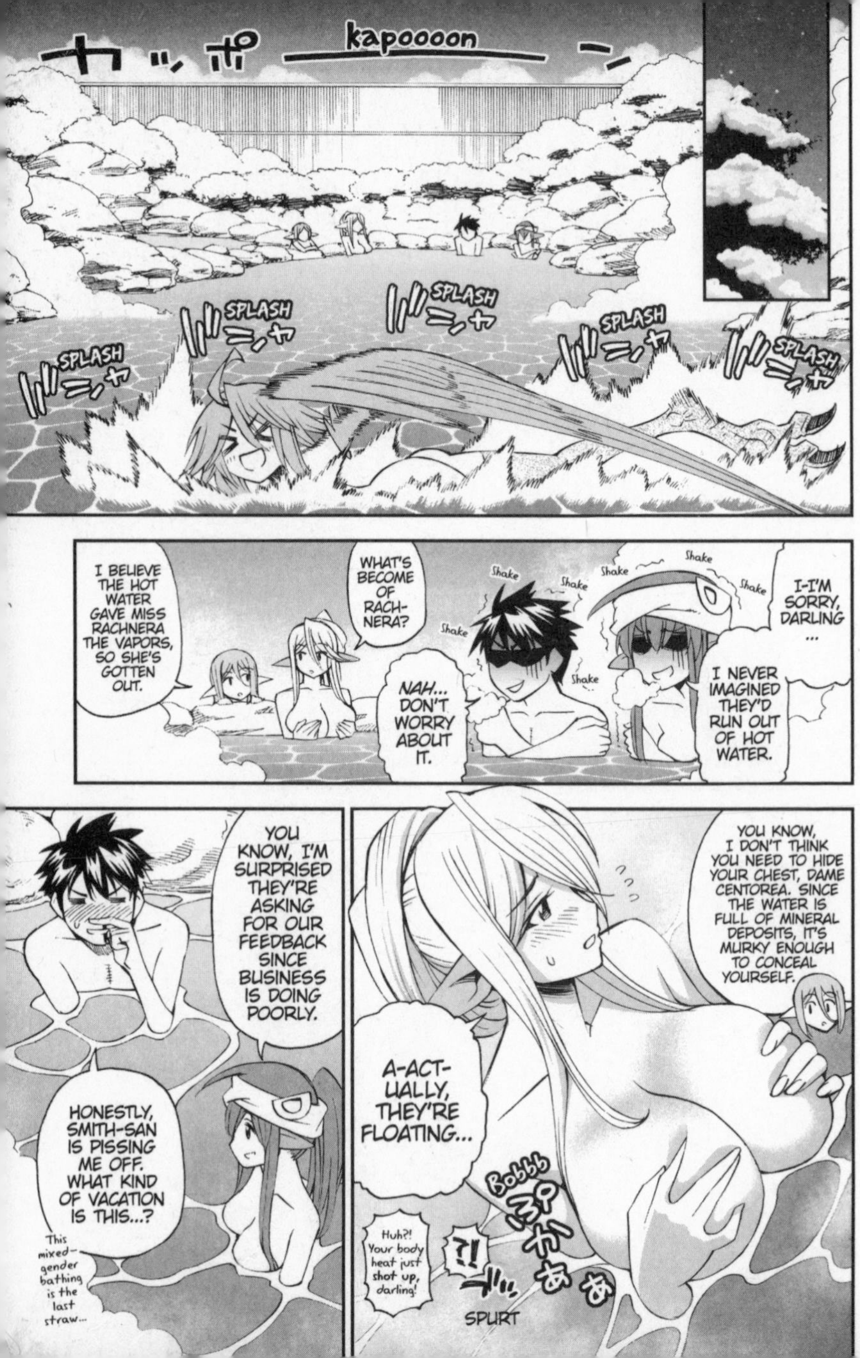
kapoooon
SPLASH
SPLASH
SPLASH
SPLASH
SPLASH
I-I'M SORRY, DARLING...
I NEVER IMAGINED THEY'D RUN OUT OF HOT WATER.
Shake Shake Shake Shake Shake Shake
NAH... DON'T WORRY ABOUT IT.
WHAT'S BECOME OF RACHNERA?
I BELIEVE THE HOT WATER GAVE MISS RACHNERA THE VAPORS, SO SHE'S GOTTEN OUT.
YOU KNOW, I DON'T THINK YOU NEED TO HIDE YOUR CHEST, DAME CENTOREA. SINCE THE WATER IS FULL OF MINERAL DEPOSITS, IT'S MURKY ENOUGH TO CONCEAL YOURSELF.
A-ACTUALLY, THEY'RE FLOATING...
Bobbb
?!
SPURT
Huh?! Your body heat just shot up, darling!
YOU KNOW, I'M SURPRISED THEY'RE ASKING FOR OUR FEEDBACK SINCE BUSINESS IS DOING POORLY.
HONESTLY, SMITH-SAN IS PISSING ME OFF. WHAT KIND OF VACATION IS THIS...?
This mixed-gender bathing is the last straw...

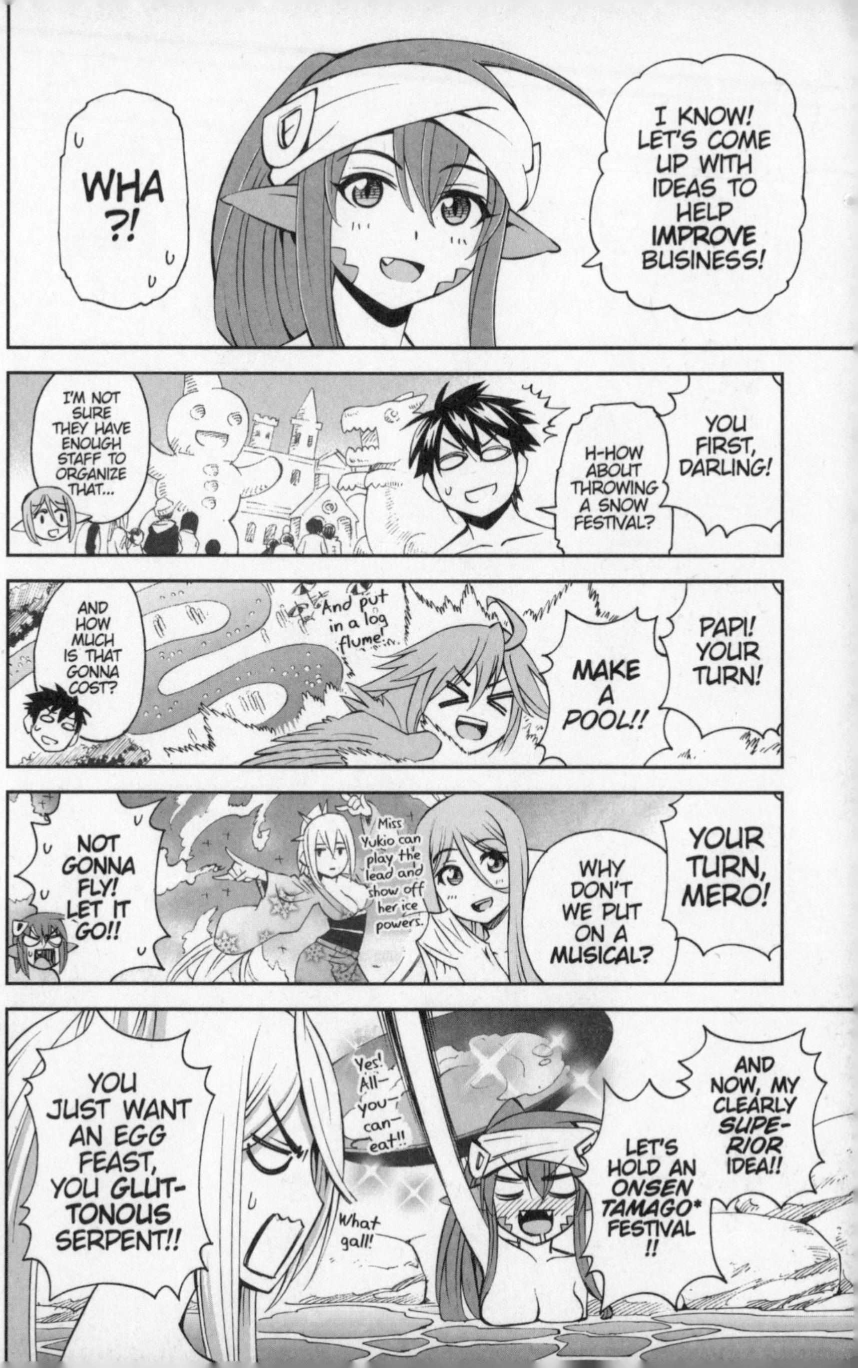
I KNOW! LET'S COME UP WITH IDEAS TO HELP IMPROVE BUSINESS!
WHA ?!
YOU FIRST, DARLING!
H-HOW ABOUT THROWING A SNOW FESTIVAL?
I'M NOT SURE THEY HAVE ENOUGH STAFF TO ORGANIZE THAT...
PAPI! YOUR TURN!
MAKE A POOL!!
And put in a log flume!
AND HOW MUCH IS THAT GONNA COST?
YOUR TURN, MERO!
WHY DON'T WE PUT ON A MUSICAL?
Miss Yukio can play the lead and show off her ice powers.
NOT GONNA FLY! LET IT GO!!
AND NOW, MY CLEARLY SUPER-RIOR IDEA!!
LET'S HOLD AN ONSEN TAMAGO* FESTIVAL !!
Yes! All-you-can-eat!!
What gall!
YOU JUST WANT AN EGG FEAST, YOU GLUT-TONOUS SERPENT!!

*Onsen tamago is a traditional Japanese egg dish, slow-cooked in the waters of hot springs.

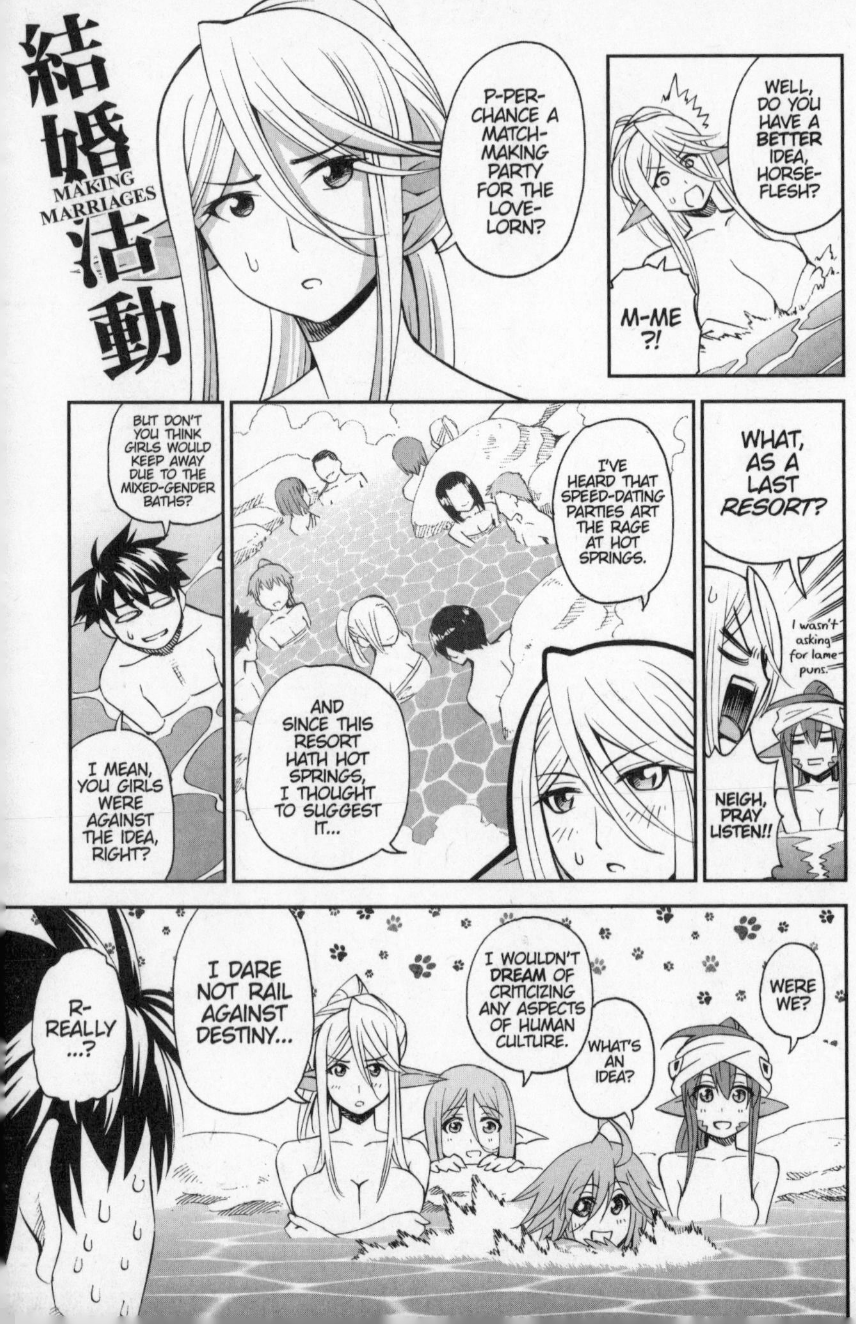
結婚活動
MAKING MARRIAGES
WELL, DO YOU HAVE A BETTER IDEA, HORSE-FLESH?
M-ME?!
P-PERCHANCE A MATCH-MAKING PARTY FOR THE LOVE-LORN?
WHAT, AS A LAST RESORT?
I wasn't asking for lame-puns.
NEIGH, PRAY LISTEN!!
I'VE HEARD THAT SPEED-DATING PARTIES ART THE RAGE AT HOT SPRINGS.
AND SINCE THIS RESORT HATH HOT SPRINGS, I THOUGHT TO SUGGEST IT...
BUT DON'T YOU THINK GIRLS WOULD KEEP AWAY DUE TO THE MIXED-GENDER BATHS?
I MEAN, YOU GIRLS WERE AGAINST THE IDEA, RIGHT?
WERE WE?
I WOULDN'T DREAM OF CRITICIZING ANY ASPECTS OF HUMAN CULTURE.
WHAT'S AN IDEA?
I DARE NOT RAIL AGAINST DESTINY...
R-REALLY ...?

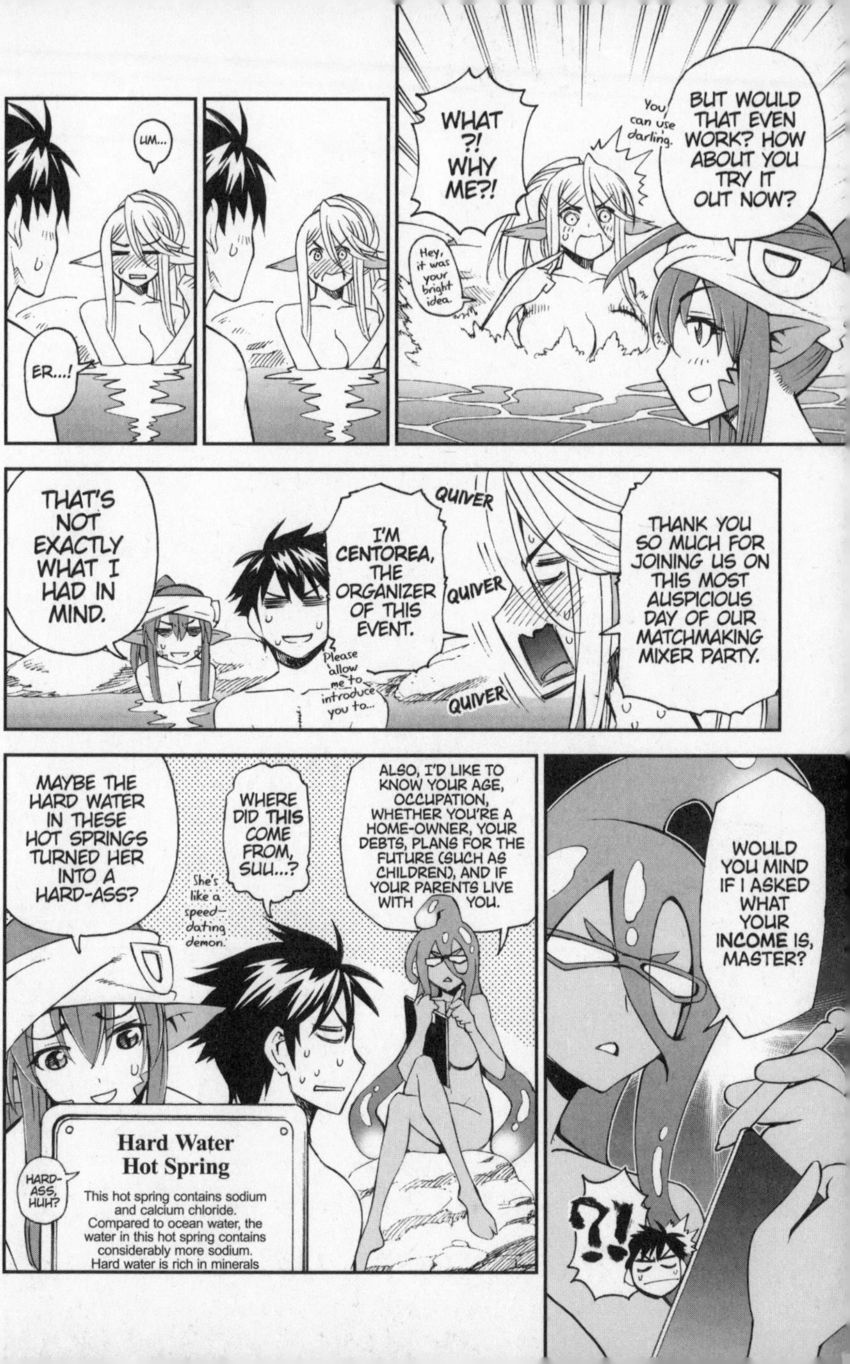
BUT WOULD THAT EVEN WORK? HOW ABOUT YOU TRY IT OUT NOW?
You can use darling.
WHAT?! WHY ME?!
Hey, it was your bright idea.
UM...
ER...!
THANK YOU SO MUCH FOR JOINING US ON THIS MOST AUSPICIOUS DAY OF OUR MATCHMAKING MIXER PARTY.
QUIVER
QUIVER
QUIVER
I'M CENTOREA, THE ORGANIZER OF THIS EVENT.
Please allow me to introduce you to...
THAT'S NOT EXACTLY WHAT I HAD IN MIND.
WOULD YOU MIND IF I ASKED WHAT YOUR INCOME IS, MASTER?
?!
ALSO, I'D LIKE TO KNOW YOUR AGE, OCCUPATION, WHETHER YOU'RE A HOME-OWNER, YOUR DEBTS, PLANS FOR THE FUTURE (SUCH AS CHILDREN), AND IF YOUR PARENTS LIVE WITH YOU.
WHERE DID THIS COME FROM, SUU...?
She's like a speed-dating demon.
MAYBE THE HARD WATER IN THESE HOT SPRINGS TURNED HER INTO A HARD-ASS?
Hard Water Hot Spring
This hot spring contains sodium and calcium chloride. Compared to ocean water, the water in this hot spring contains considerably more sodium. Hard water is rich in minerals
HARD-ASS, HUH?

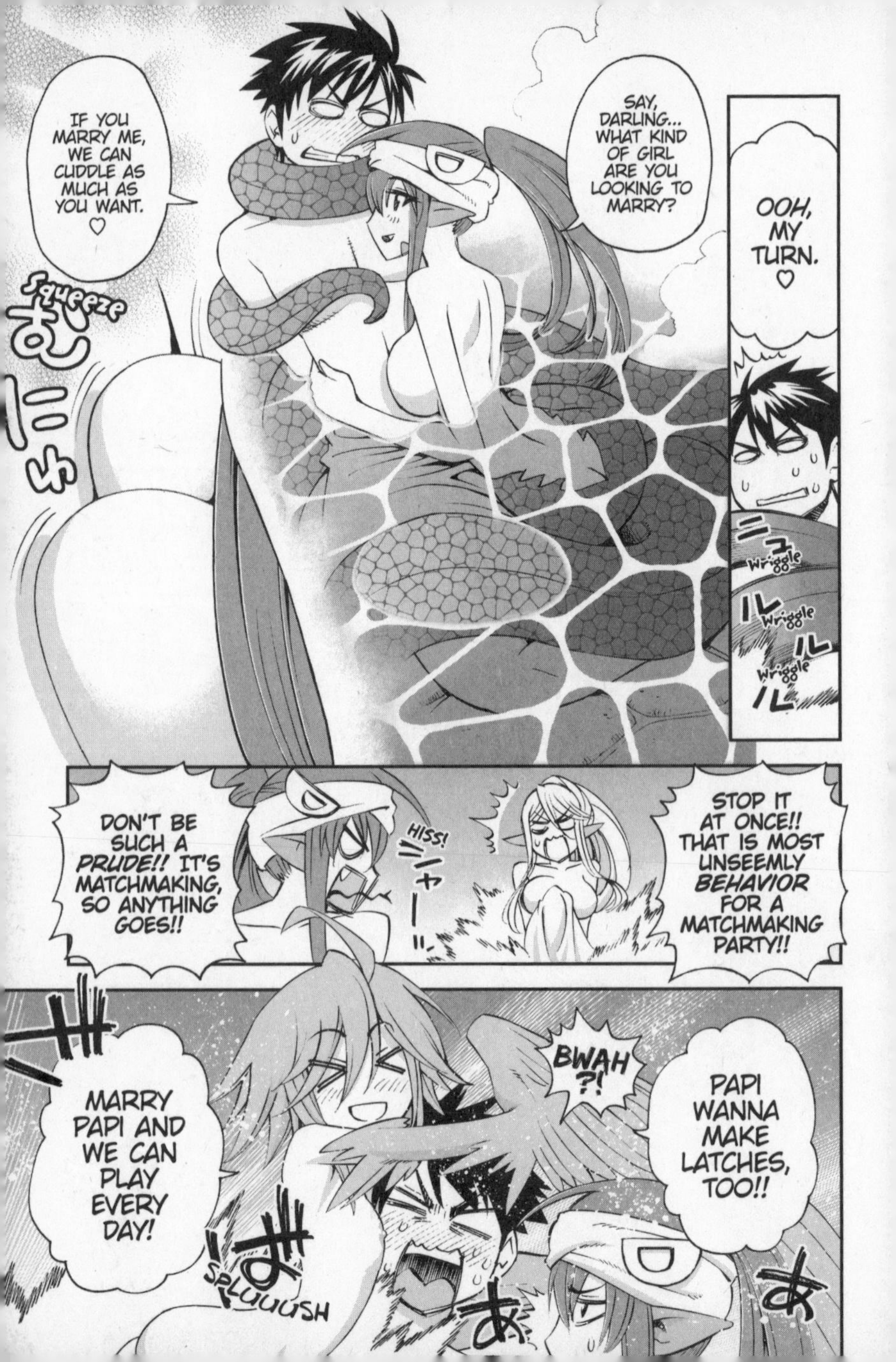
OOH, MY TURN. ♡
Wriggle
Wriggle
Wriggle
SAY, DARLING... WHAT KIND OF GIRL ARE YOU LOOKING TO MARRY?
IF YOU MARRY ME, WE CAN CUDDLE AS MUCH AS YOU WANT. ♡
Squeeze
STOP IT AT ONCE!! THAT IS MOST UNSEEMLY *BEHAVIOR* FOR A MATCHMAKING PARTY!!
HISS!
DON'T BE SUCH A *PRUDE!!* IT'S MATCHMAKING, SO ANYTHING GOES!!
PAPI WANNA MAKE LATCHES, TOO!!
BWAH ?!
MARRY PAPI AND WE CAN PLAY EVERY DAY!
SPLUUUSH

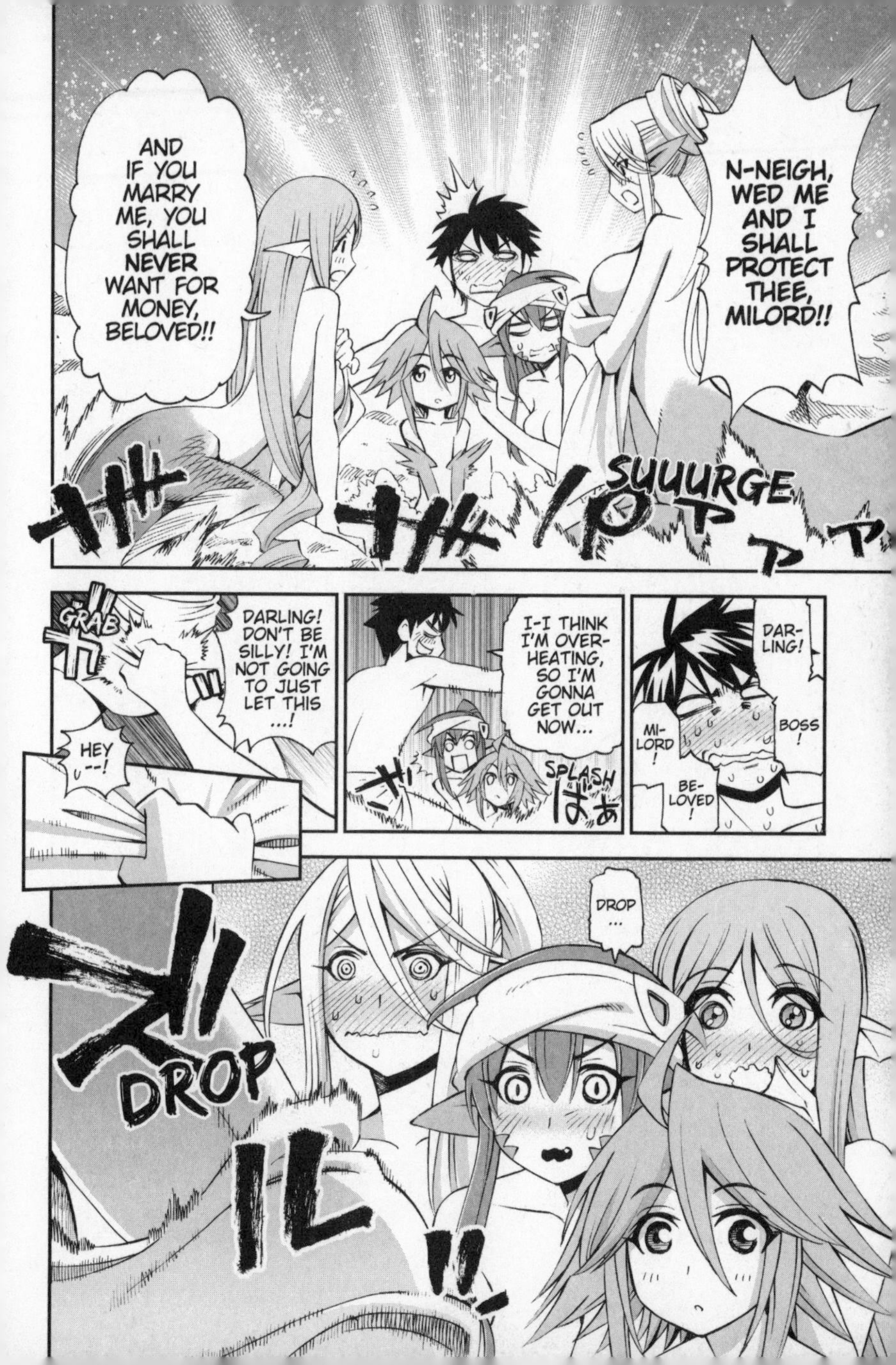
N-NEIGH, WED ME AND I SHALL PROTECT THEE, MILORD!!
AND IF YOU MARRY ME, YOU SHALL NEVER WANT FOR MONEY, BELOVED!!
SUUURGE
DAR-LING!
BOSS!
MI-LORD!
BE-LOVED!
I-I THINK I'M OVER-HEATING, SO I'M GONNA GET OUT NOW...
SPLASH
DARLING! DON'T BE SILLY! I'M NOT GOING TO JUST LET THIS ...!
GRAB
HEY --!
DROP ...
DROP

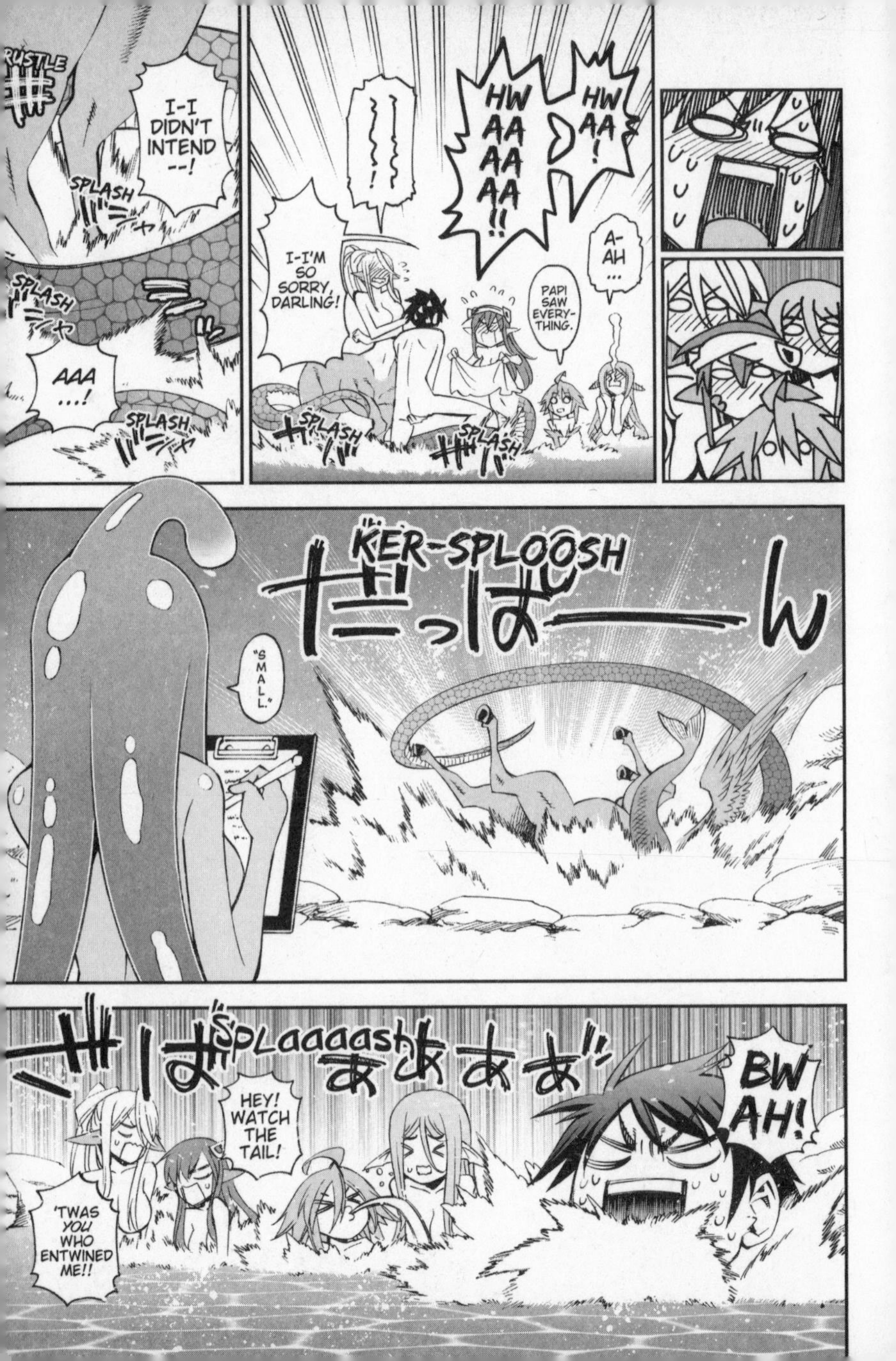
HWAA!
HWAAAAAAA!!
A-AH...
PAPI SAW EVERYTHING.
I-I'M SO SORRY, DARLING!
SPLASH
SPLASH
RUSTLE
I-I DIDN'T INTEND--!
SPLASH
SPLASH
AAA...!
SPLASH
KER-SPLOOSH
だっぱーーーん
"SMALL."
BWAH!
SPLAAAASH
ザばあああ!!
HEY! WATCH THE TAIL!
'TWAS YOU WHO ENTWINED ME!!

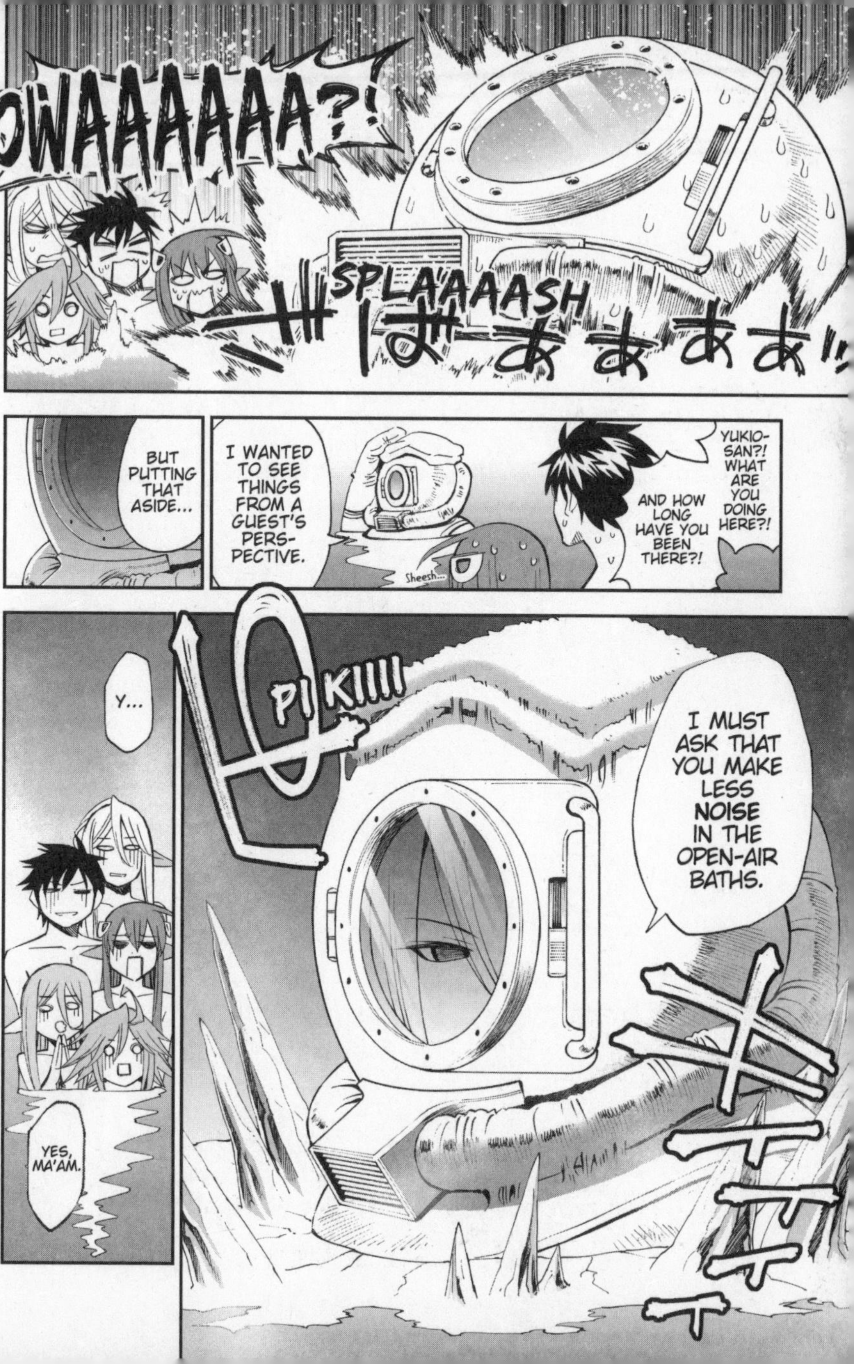
OWAAAAAA?!
SPLAAAASH
ばああああ!!
YUKIO-SAN?! WHAT ARE YOU DOING HERE?!
AND HOW LONG HAVE YOU BEEN THERE?!
I WANTED TO SEE THINGS FROM A GUEST'S PERSPECTIVE.
Sheesh...
BUT PUTTING THAT ASIDE...
PI KIIII
I MUST ASK THAT YOU MAKE LESS NOISE IN THE OPEN-AIR BATHS.
Y...
YES, MA'AM.

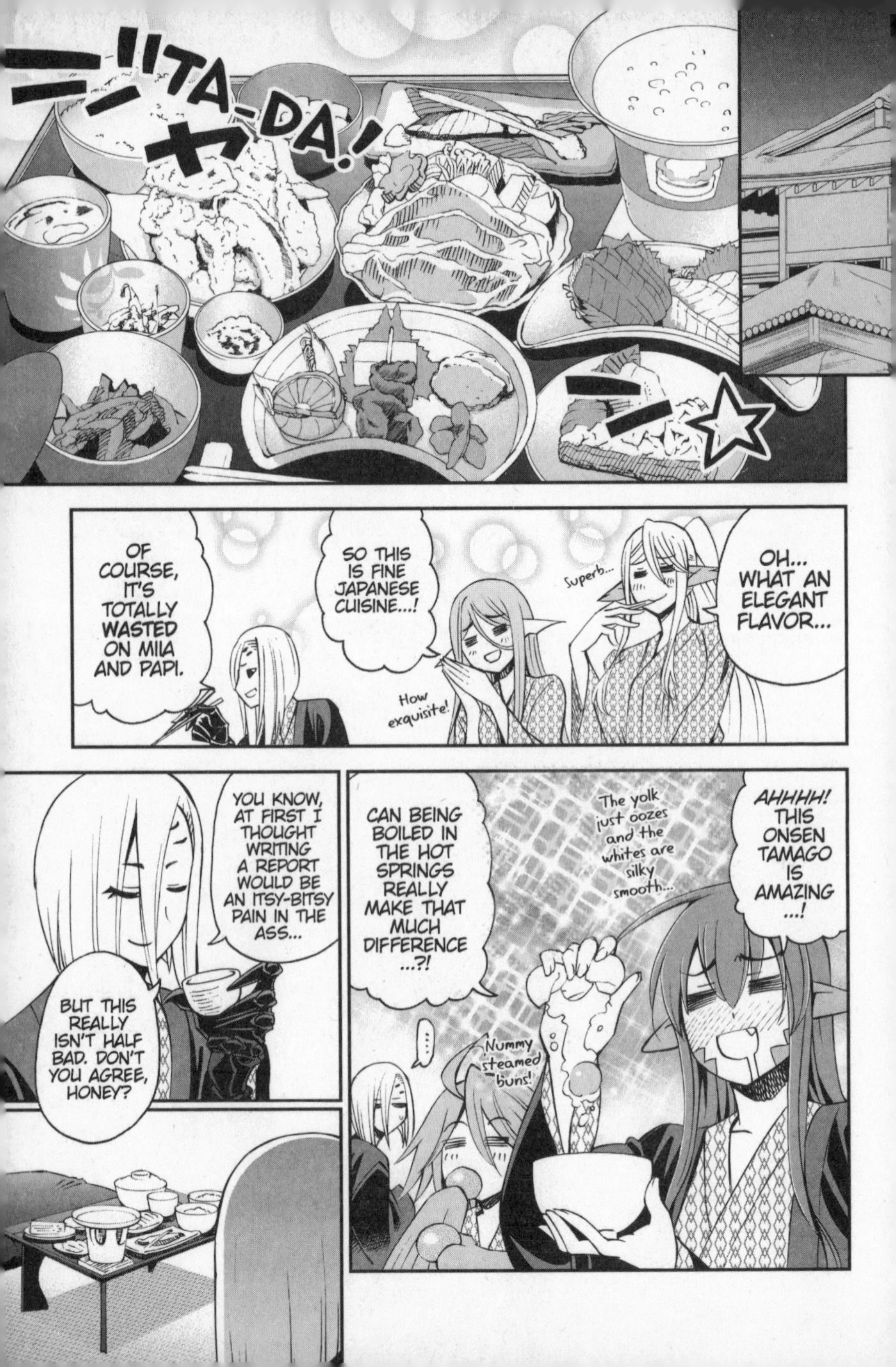
TA-DA!
OH... WHAT AN ELEGANT FLAVOR...
Superb...
SO THIS IS FINE JAPANESE CUISINE...!
How exquisite!
OF COURSE, IT'S TOTALLY WASTED ON MIIA AND PAPI.
AHHHH! THIS ONSEN TAMAGO IS AMAZING...!
The yolk just oozes and the whites are silky smooth...
CAN BEING BOILED IN THE HOT SPRINGS REALLY MAKE THAT MUCH DIFFERENCE...?!
Nummy steamed buns!
...
YOU KNOW, AT FIRST I THOUGHT WRITING A REPORT WOULD BE AN ITSY-BITSY PAIN IN THE ASS...
BUT THIS REALLY ISN'T HALF BAD. DON'T YOU AGREE, HONEY?

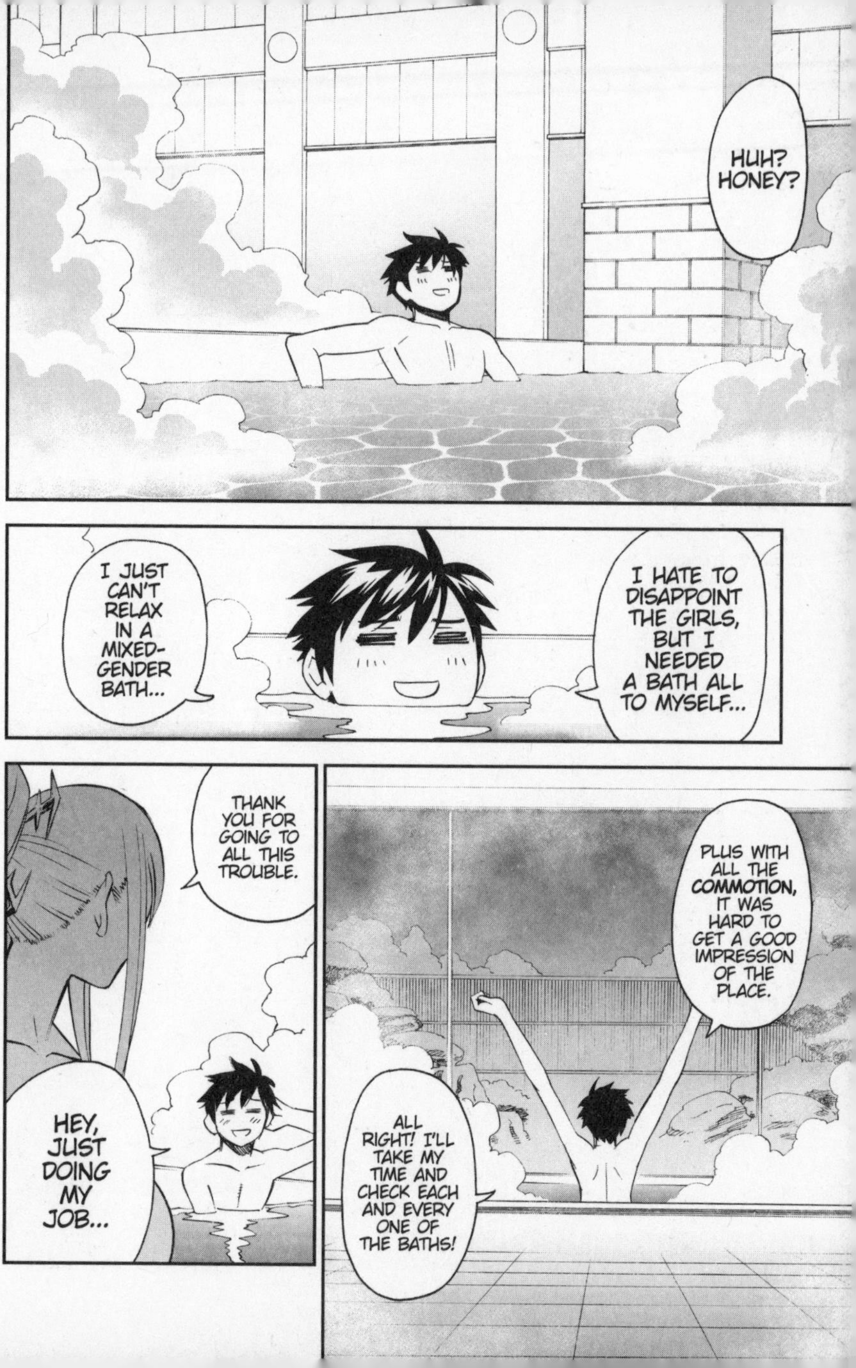
HUH? HONEY?
I HATE TO DISAPPOINT THE GIRLS, BUT I NEEDED A BATH ALL TO MYSELF...
I JUST CAN'T RELAX IN A MIXED-GENDER BATH...
PLUS WITH ALL THE COMMOTION, IT WAS HARD TO GET A GOOD IMPRESSION OF THE PLACE.
ALL RIGHT! I'LL TAKE MY TIME AND CHECK EACH AND EVERY ONE OF THE BATHS!
THANK YOU FOR GOING TO ALL THIS TROUBLE.
HEY, JUST DOING MY JOB...

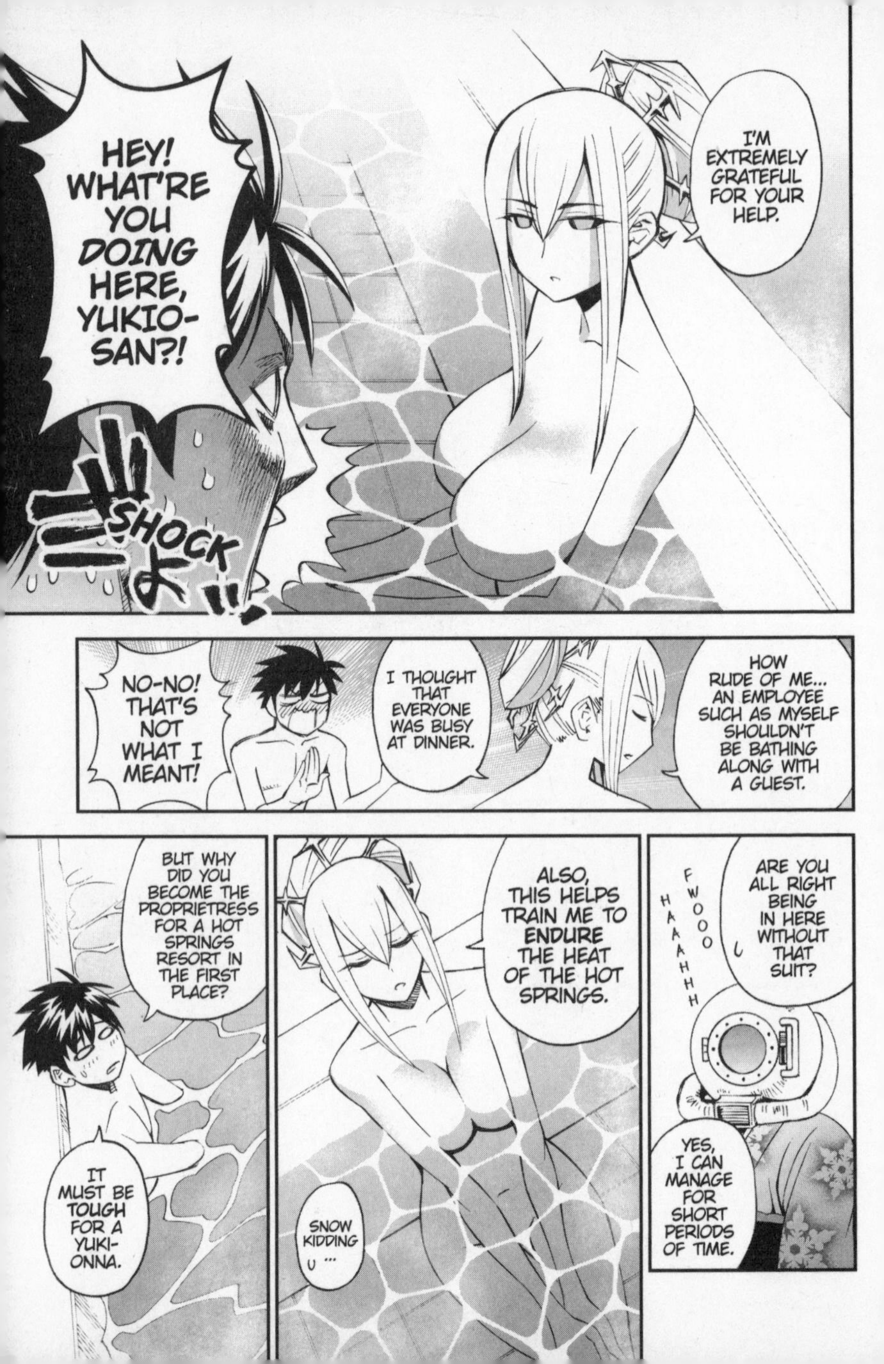
I'M EXTREMELY GRATEFUL FOR YOUR HELP.
HEY! WHAT'RE YOU DOING HERE, YUKIO-SAN?!
SHOCK
HOW RUDE OF ME... AN EMPLOYEE SUCH AS MYSELF SHOULDN'T BE BATHING ALONG WITH A GUEST.
I THOUGHT THAT EVERYONE WAS BUSY AT DINNER.
NO-NO! THAT'S NOT WHAT I MEANT!
ARE YOU ALL RIGHT BEING IN HERE WITHOUT THAT SUIT?
FWOOO
HAAAHHH
YES, I CAN MANAGE FOR SHORT PERIODS OF TIME.
ALSO, THIS HELPS TRAIN ME TO ENDURE THE HEAT OF THE HOT SPRINGS.
SNOW KIDDING ...
BUT WHY DID YOU BECOME THE PROPRIETRESS FOR A HOT SPRINGS RESORT IN THE FIRST PLACE?
IT MUST BE TOUGH FOR A YUKI-ONNA.

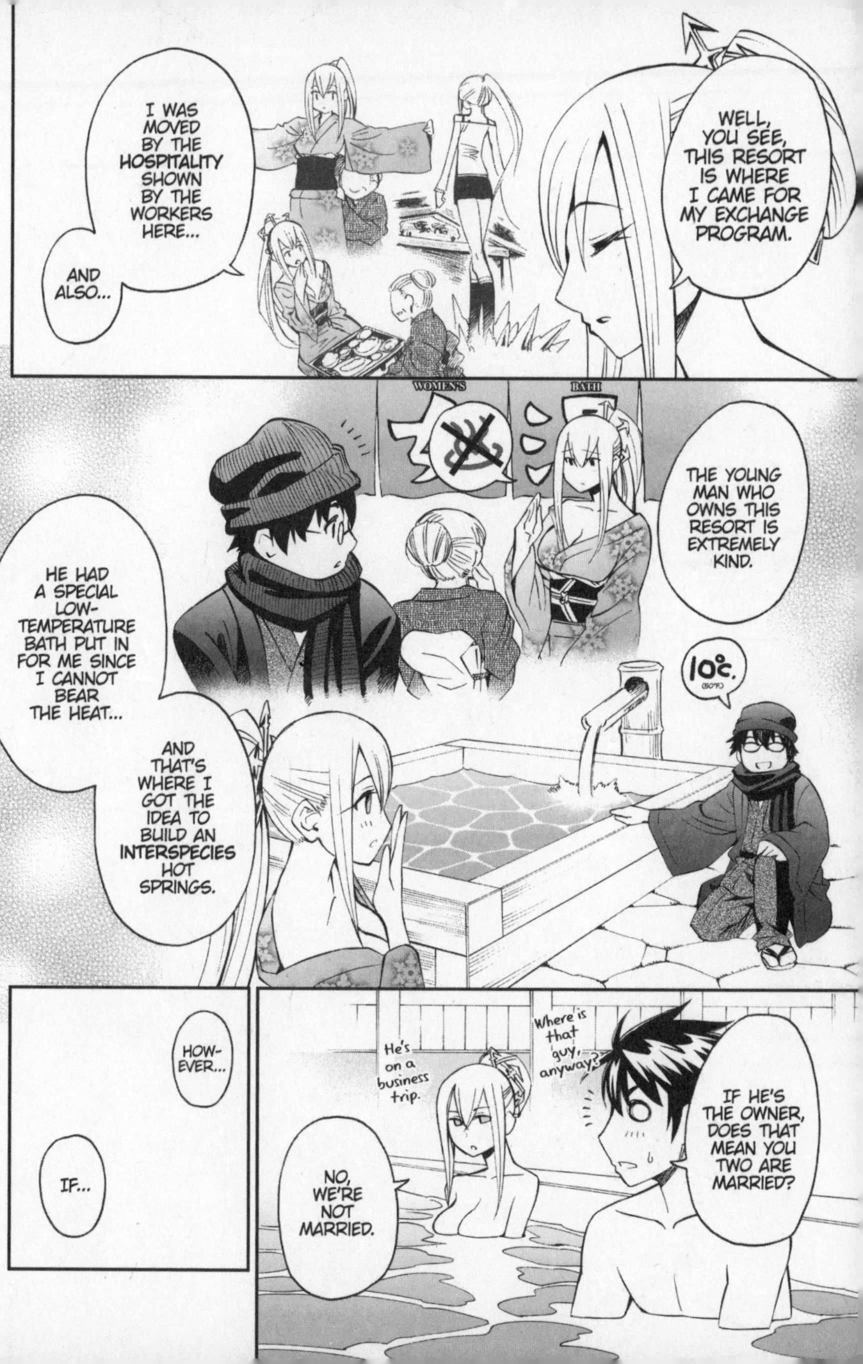
WELL, YOU SEE, THIS RESORT IS WHERE I CAME FOR MY EXCHANGE PROGRAM.
I WAS MOVED BY THE HOSPITALITY SHOWN BY THE WORKERS HERE...
AND ALSO...
WOMEN'S
BATH
THE YOUNG MAN WHO OWNS THIS RESORT IS EXTREMELY KIND.
HE HAD A SPECIAL LOW-TEMPERATURE BATH PUT IN FOR ME SINCE I CANNOT BEAR THE HEAT...
10°C. (50°F)
AND THAT'S WHERE I GOT THE IDEA TO BUILD AN INTERSPECIES HOT SPRINGS.
IF HE'S THE OWNER, DOES THAT MEAN YOU TWO ARE MARRIED?
Where is that guy, anyway?
He's on a business trip.
NO, WE'RE NOT MARRIED.
HOW-EVER...
IF...

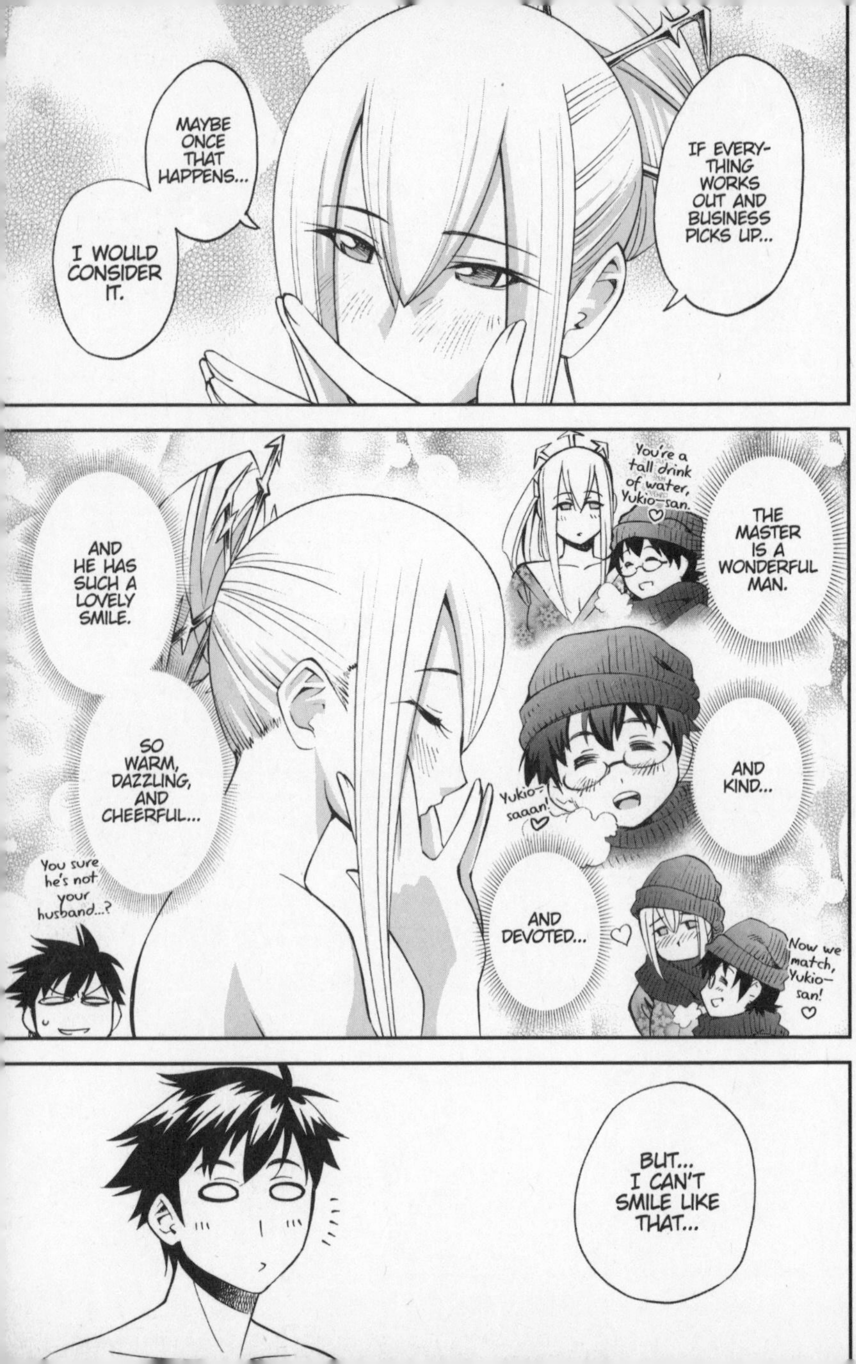
IF EVERYTHING WORKS OUT AND BUSINESS PICKS UP...
MAYBE ONCE THAT HAPPENS...
I WOULD CONSIDER IT.
You're a tall drink of water, Yukio-san. ♡
THE MASTER IS A WONDERFUL MAN.
AND HE HAS SUCH A LOVELY SMILE.
SO WARM, DAZZLING, AND CHEERFUL...
AND KIND...
Yukio-saaan! ♡
AND DEVOTED...
Now we match, Yukio-san! ♡
You sure he's not your husband...?
BUT... I CAN'T SMILE LIKE THAT...

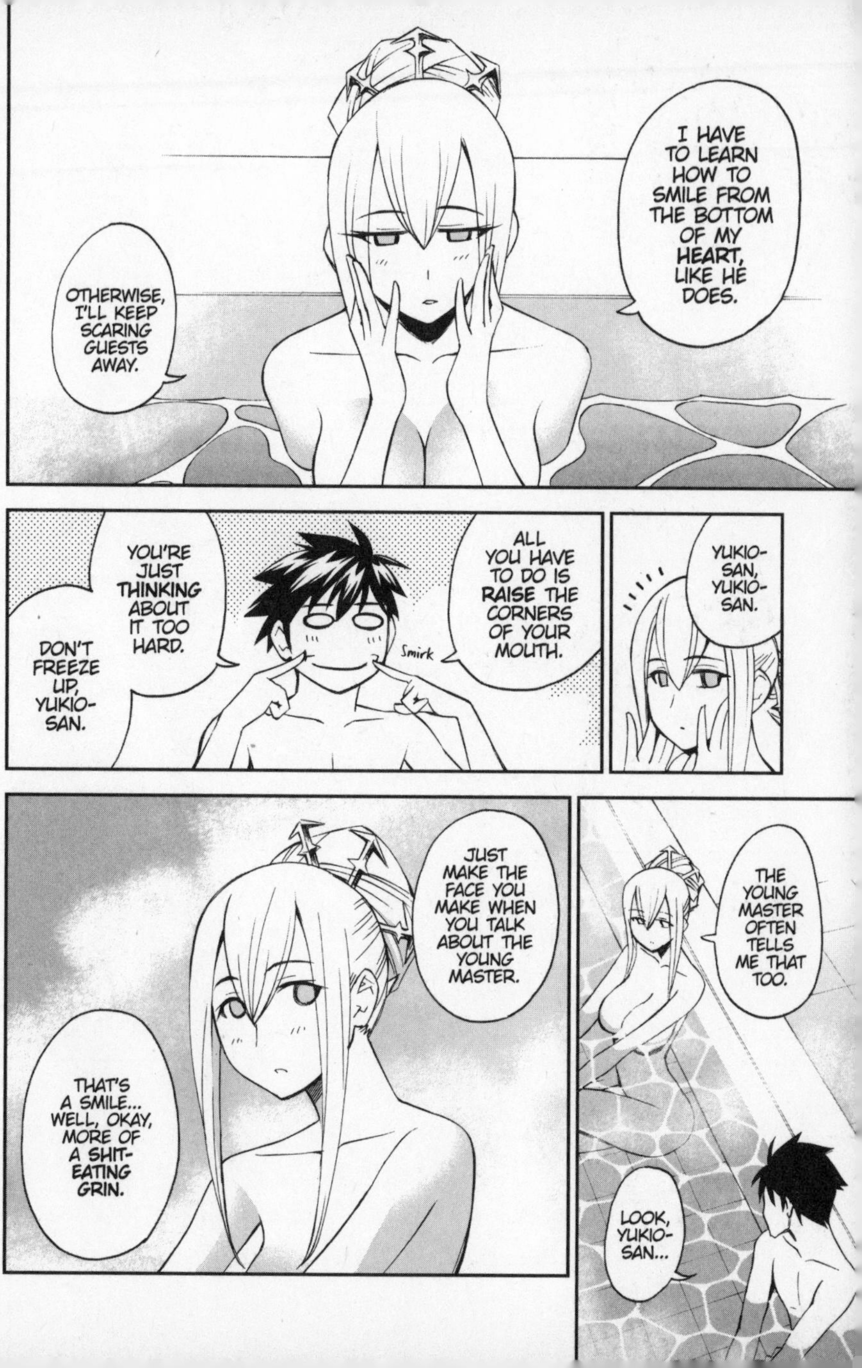
I HAVE TO LEARN HOW TO SMILE FROM THE BOTTOM OF MY HEART, LIKE HE DOES.
OTHERWISE, I'LL KEEP SCARING GUESTS AWAY.
YUKIO-SAN, YUKIO-SAN.
ALL YOU HAVE TO DO IS RAISE THE CORNERS OF YOUR MOUTH.
Smirk
YOU'RE JUST THINKING ABOUT IT TOO HARD.
DON'T FREEZE UP, YUKIO-SAN.
THE YOUNG MASTER OFTEN TELLS ME THAT TOO.
LOOK, YUKIO-SAN...
JUST MAKE THE FACE YOU MAKE WHEN YOU TALK ABOUT THE YOUNG MASTER.
THAT'S A SMILE... WELL, OKAY, MORE OF A SHIT-EATING GRIN.

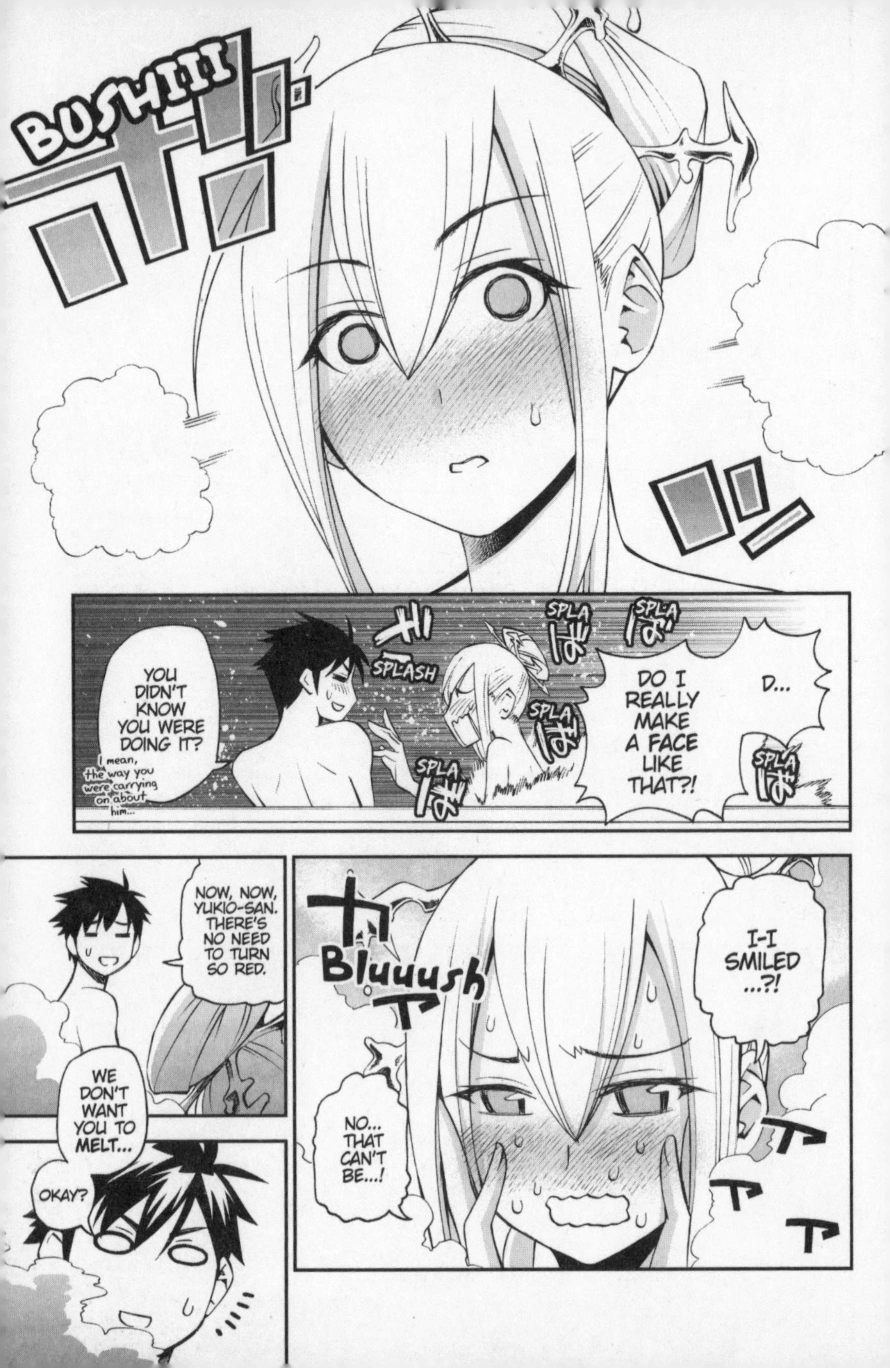
BUSHIII
D...
SPLA
SPLA
SPLA
DO I REALLY MAKE A FACE LIKE THAT?!
SPLA
SPLA
SPLASH
YOU DIDN'T KNOW YOU WERE DOING IT?
I mean, the way you were carrying on about him...
I-I SMILED ...?!
Bluuush
NO... THAT CAN'T BE...!
NOW, NOW, YUKIO-SAN. THERE'S NO NEED TO TURN SO RED.
WE DON'T WANT YOU TO MELT...
OKAY?

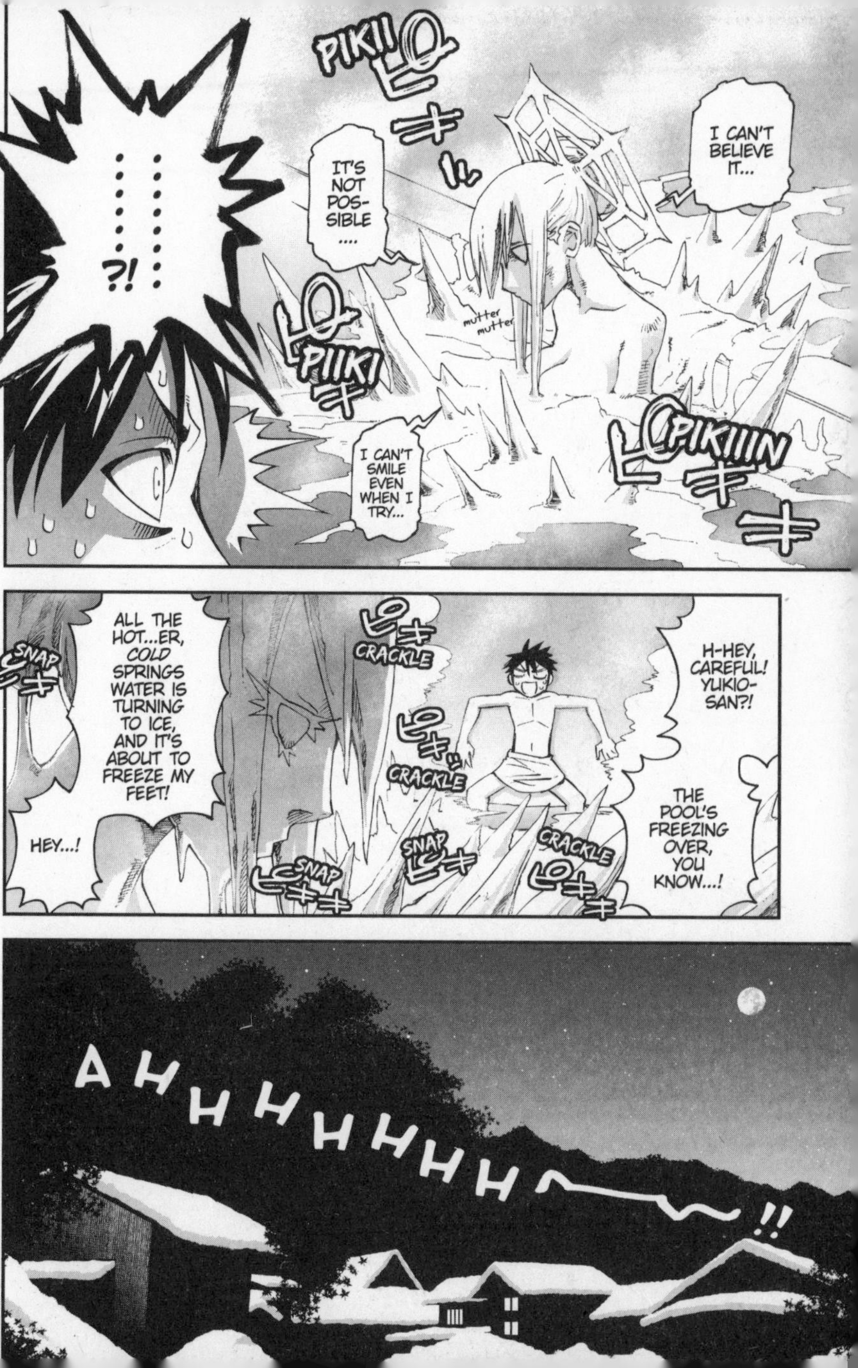

PIKII
I CAN'T BELIEVE IT...
IT'S NOT POSSIBLE ....
mutter mutter
PIIKI
PIKIIIN
I CAN'T SMILE EVEN WHEN I TRY...
......?!
H-HEY, CAREFUL! YUKIO-SAN?!
THE POOL'S FREEZING OVER, YOU KNOW...!
CRACKLE
CRACKLE
CRACKLE
SNAP
SNAP
ALL THE HOT...ER, COLD SPRINGS WATER IS TURNING TO ICE, AND IT'S ABOUT TO FREEZE MY FEET!
SNAP
HEY...!
AHHHHHHH~~!!

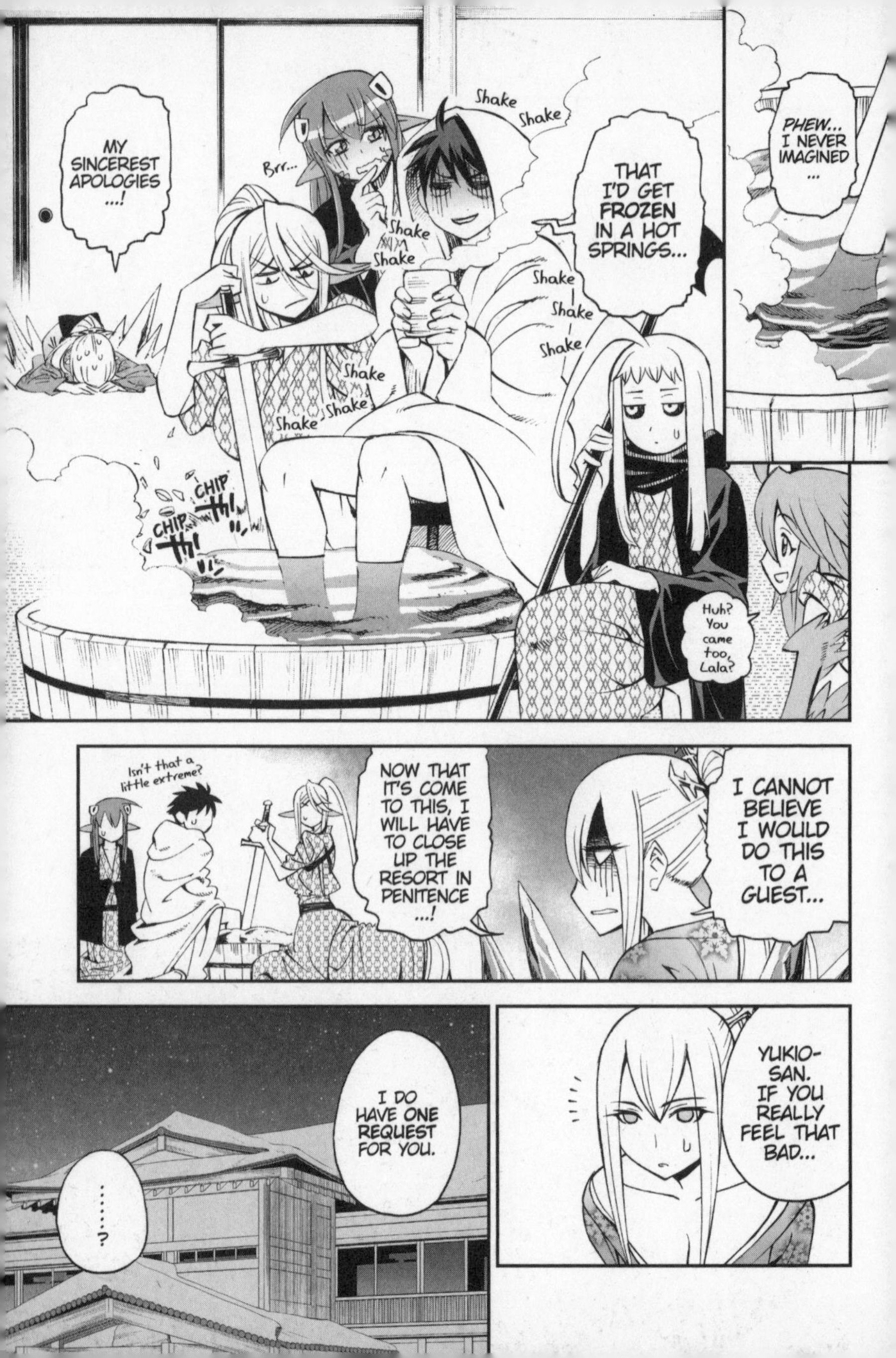
PHEW... I NEVER IMAGINED ...
THAT I'D GET FROZEN IN A HOT SPRINGS...
Shake Shake
Shake Shake Shake
Brrr...
Shake Shake
Shake Shake Shake
MY SINCEREST APOLOGIES ...!
CHIP CHIP
Huh? You came too, Lala?
I CANNOT BELIEVE I WOULD DO THIS TO A GUEST...
NOW THAT IT'S COME TO THIS, I WILL HAVE TO CLOSE UP THE RESORT IN PENITENCE ...!
Isn't that a little extreme?
YUKIO-SAN. IF YOU REALLY FEEL THAT BAD...
I DO HAVE ONE REQUEST FOR YOU.
......?

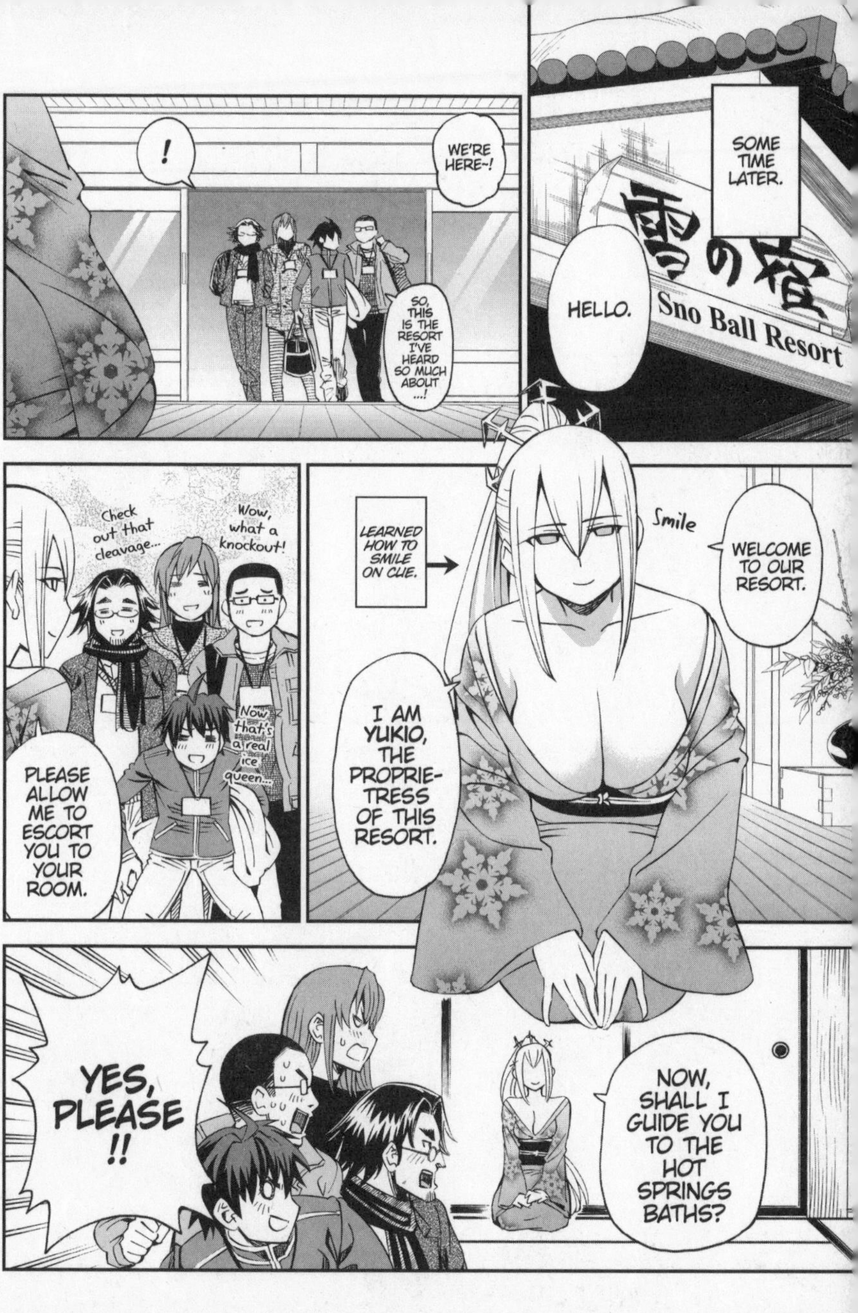
SOME TIME LATER.
雪の宿
Sno Ball Resort
HELLO.
WE'RE HERE~!
SO, THIS IS THE RESORT I'VE HEARD SO MUCH ABOUT ...!
!
Smile
WELCOME TO OUR RESORT.
I AM YUKIO, THE PROPRIE-TRESS OF THIS RESORT.
LEARNED HOW TO SMILE ON CUE.
Wow, what a knockout!
Check out that cleavage...
Now that's a real ice queen...
PLEASE ALLOW ME TO ESCORT YOU TO YOUR ROOM.
NOW, SHALL I GUIDE YOU TO THE HOT SPRINGS BATHS?
YES, PLEASE !!

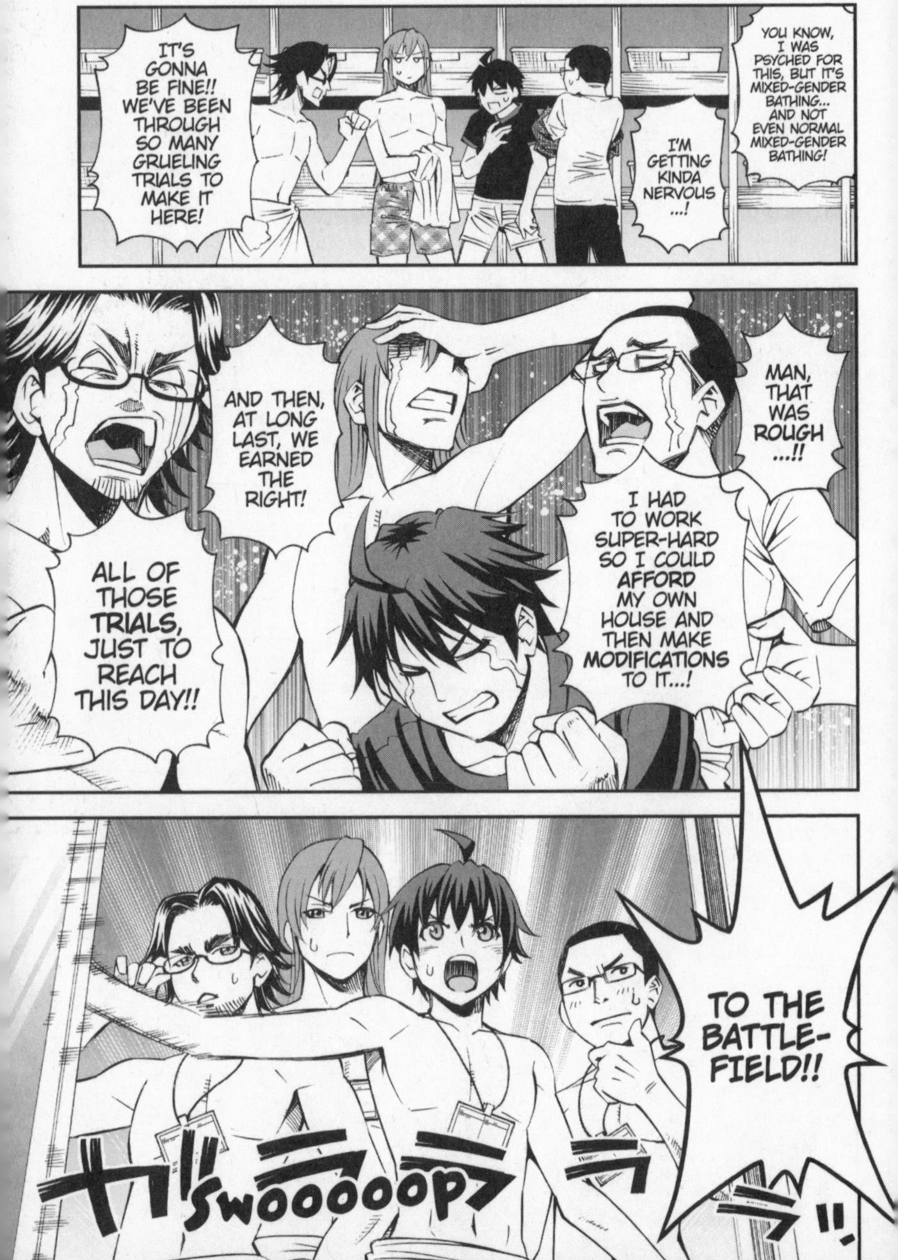
YOU KNOW, I WAS PSYCHED FOR THIS, BUT IT'S MIXED-GENDER BATHING... AND NOT EVEN NORMAL MIXED-GENDER BATHING!
I'M GETTING KINDA NERVOUS ...!
IT'S GONNA BE FINE!! WE'VE BEEN THROUGH SO MANY GRUELING TRIALS TO MAKE IT HERE!
MAN, THAT WAS ROUGH ...!!
AND THEN, AT LONG LAST, WE EARNED THE RIGHT!
I HAD TO WORK SUPER-HARD SO I COULD AFFORD MY OWN HOUSE AND THEN MAKE MODIFICATIONS TO IT...!
ALL OF THOSE TRIALS, JUST TO REACH THIS DAY!!
TO THE BATTLE-FIELD!!
SWOOOOOP

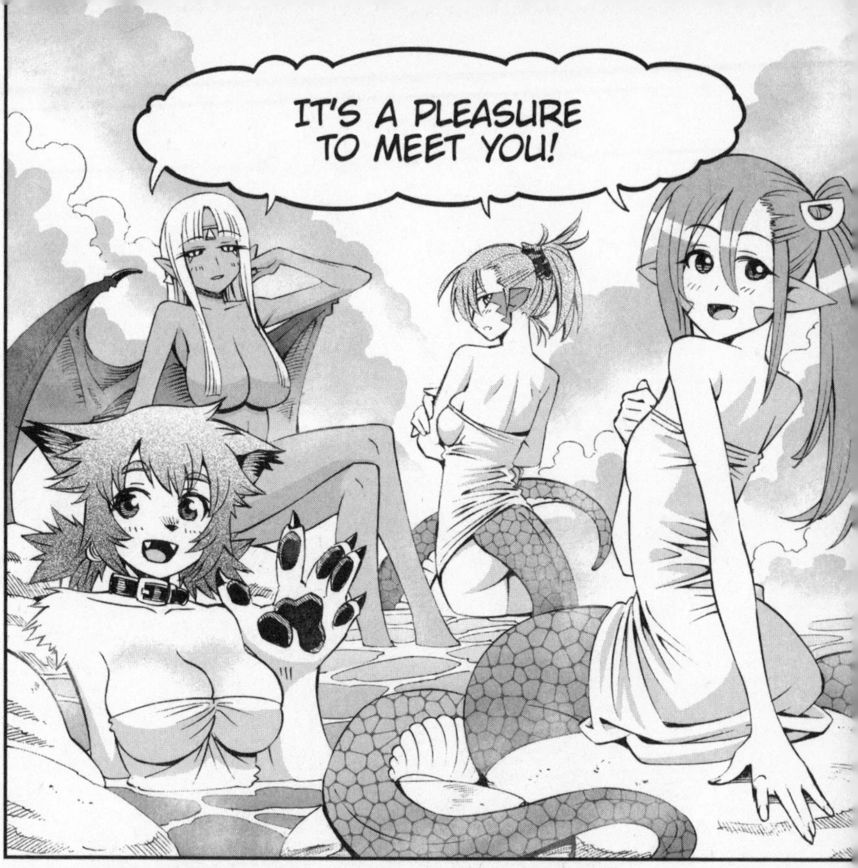
IT'S A PLEASURE TO MEET YOU!

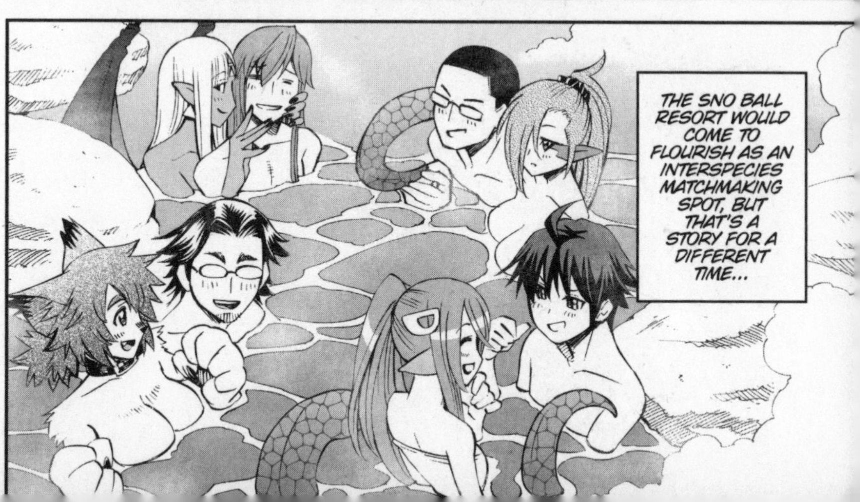
THE SNO BALL RESORT WOULD COME TO FLOURISH AS AN INTERSPECIES MATCHMAKING SPOT, BUT THAT'S A STORY FOR A DIFFERENT TIME...

Monster Musume

Everyday Life with Monster Girls

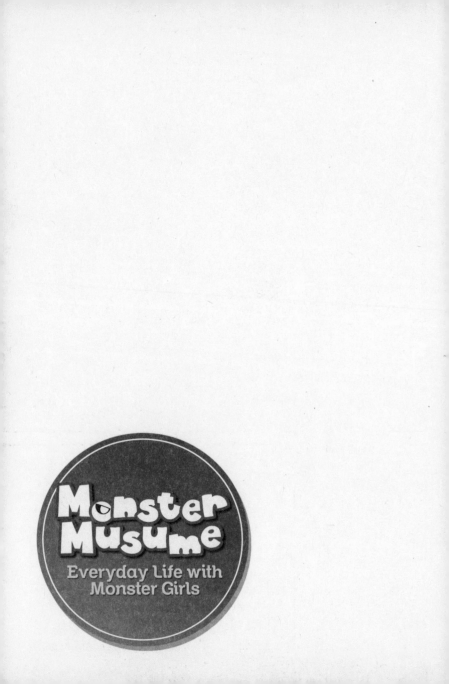

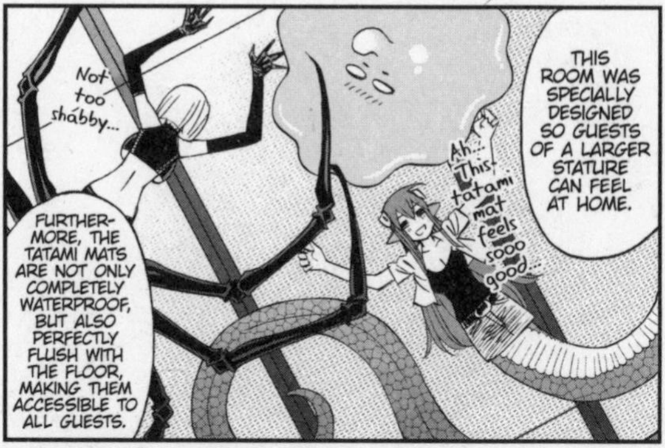
THIS ROOM WAS SPECIALLY DESIGNED SO GUESTS OF A LARGER STATURE CAN FEEL AT HOME.
Ah... This tatami mat feels sooo good...
Not too shabby...
FURTHER-MORE, THE TATAMI MATS ARE NOT ONLY COMPLETELY WATERPROOF, BUT ALSO PERFECTLY FLUSH WITH THE FLOOR, MAKING THEM ACCESSIBLE TO ALL GUESTS.

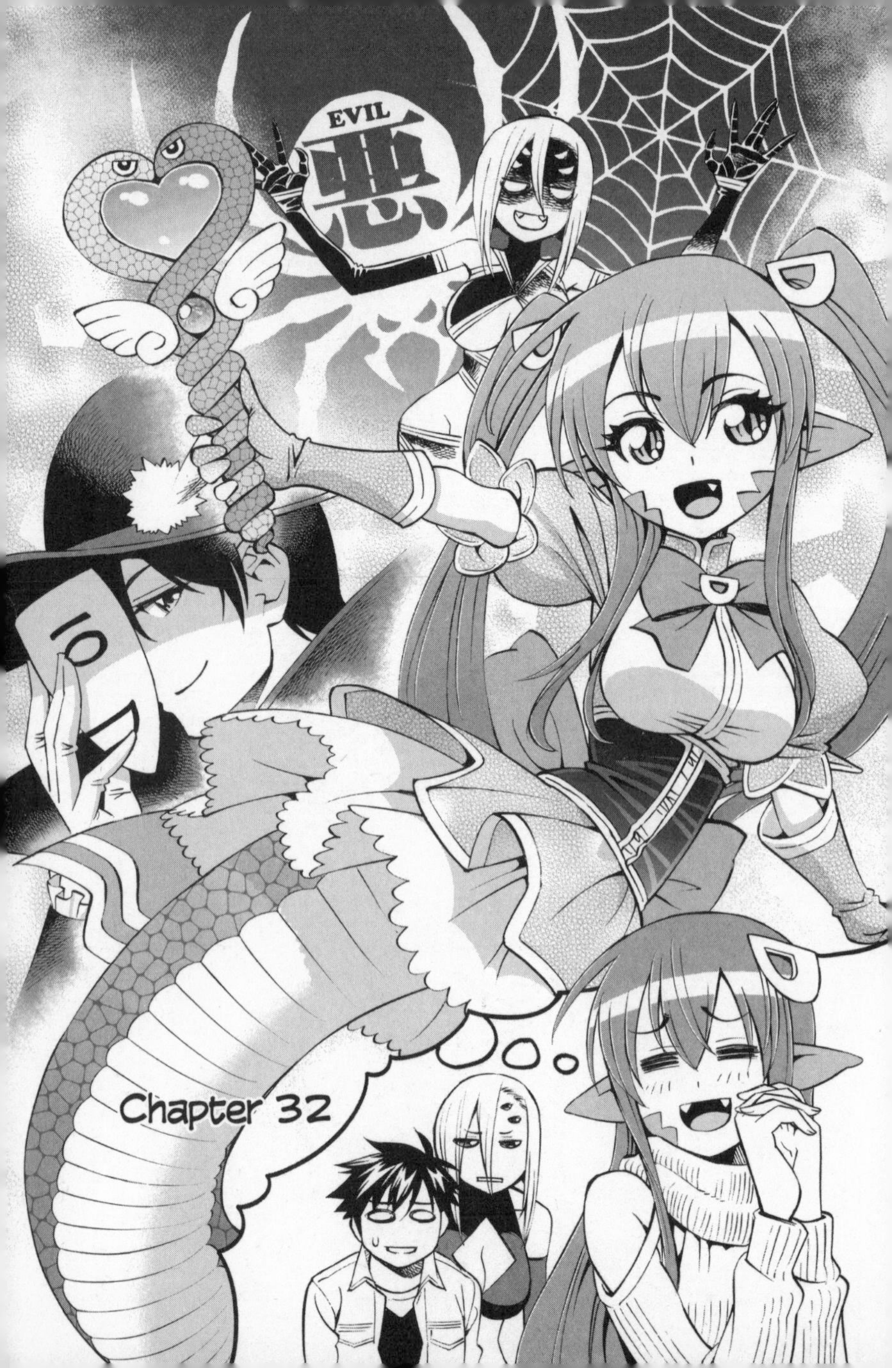
EVIL
悪
Chapter 32

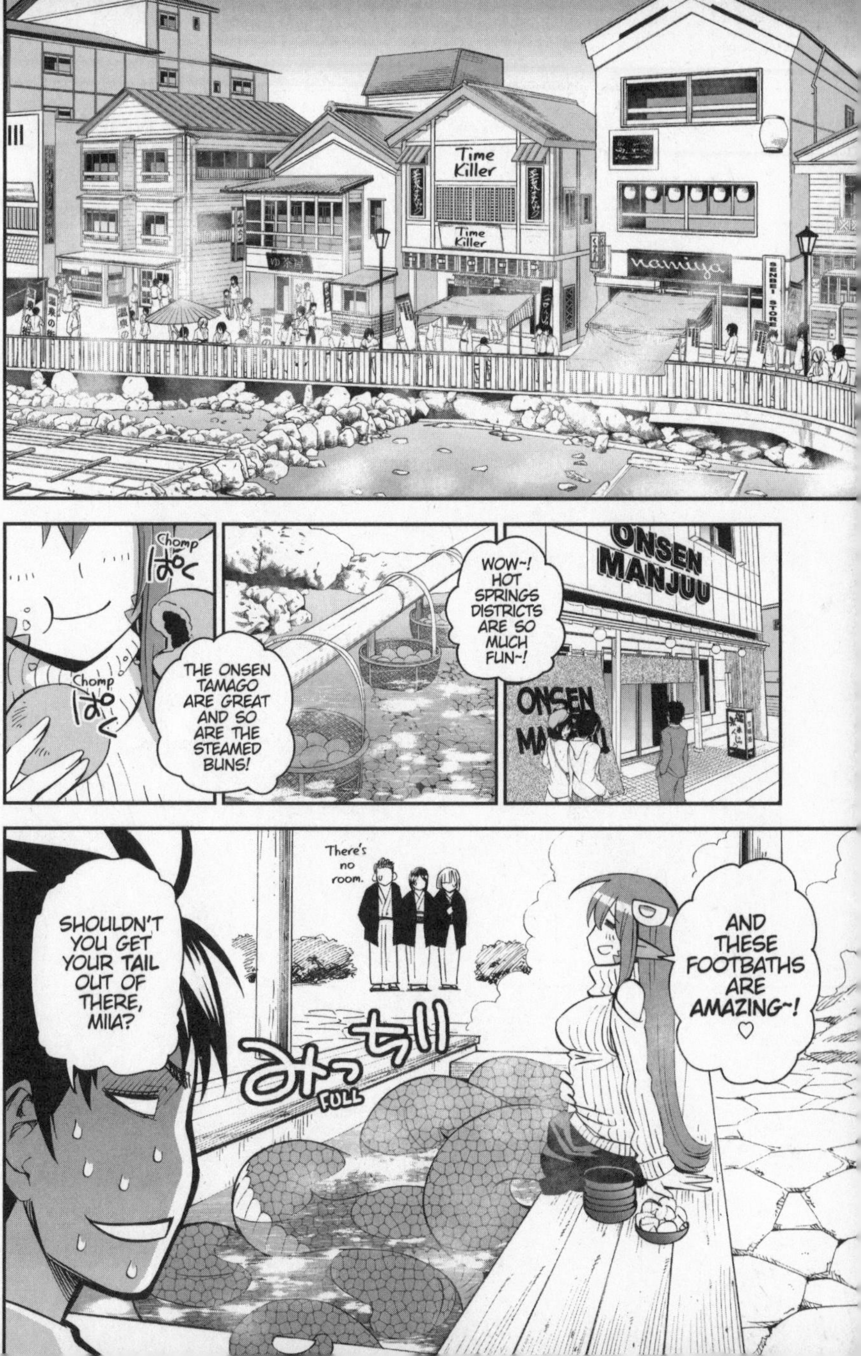
Time Killer
Time Killer
naniya
SENBEI STORE
ONSEN MANJUU
WOW~! HOT SPRINGS DISTRICTS ARE SO MUCH FUN~!
THE ONSEN TAMAGO ARE GREAT AND SO ARE THE STEAMED BUNS!
Chomp ぱく
Chomp ぱく
AND THESE FOOTBATHS ARE AMAZING~! ♡
There's no room.
みっちり FULL
SHOULDN'T YOU GET YOUR TAIL OUT OF THERE, MIIA?

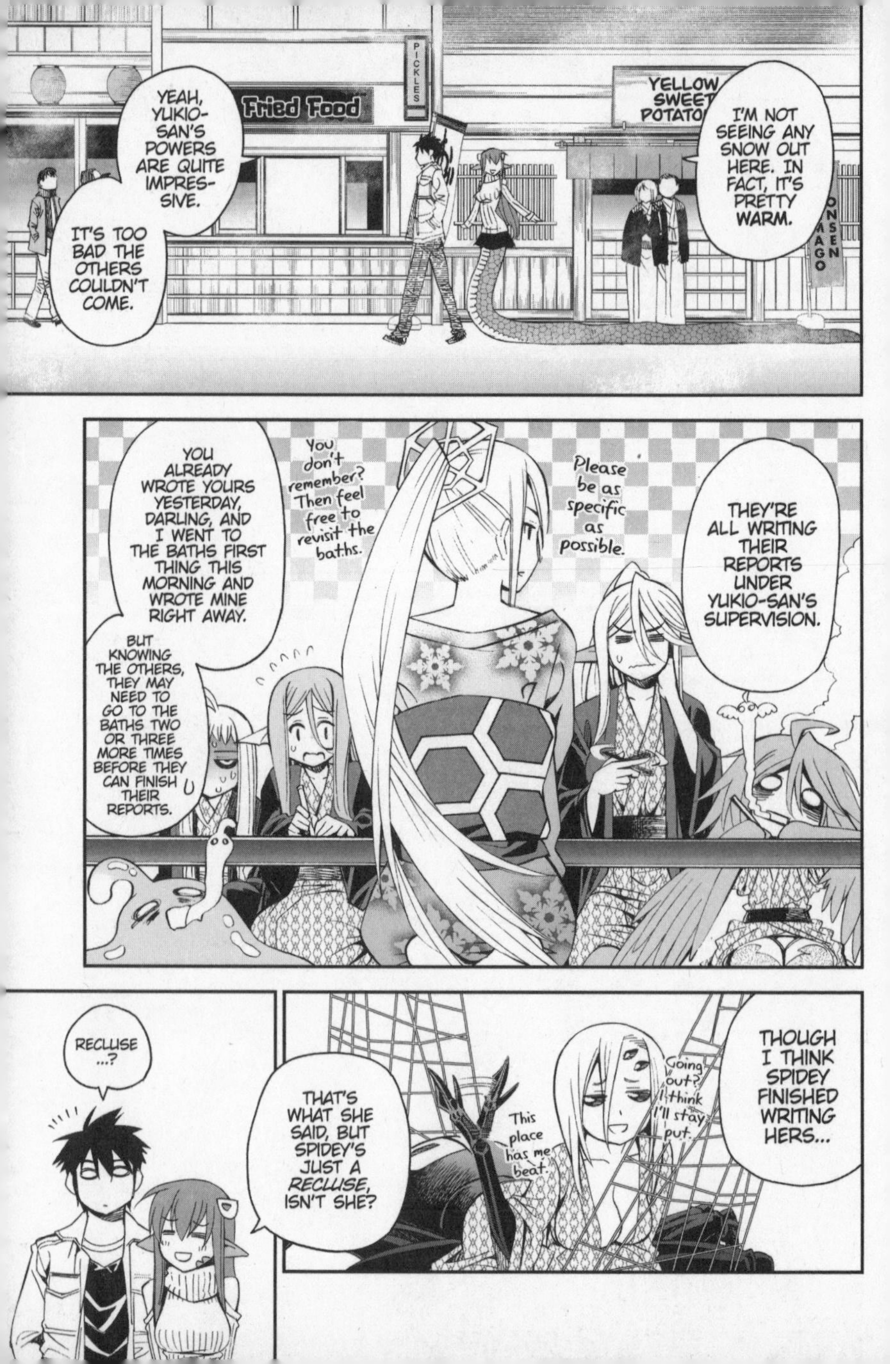

YELLOW SWEET POTATO
PICKLES
Fried Food
I'M NOT SEEING ANY SNOW OUT HERE. IN FACT, IT'S PRETTY WARM.
YEAH, YUKIO-SAN'S POWERS ARE QUITE IMPRESSIVE.
IT'S TOO BAD THE OTHERS COULDN'T COME.
THEY'RE ALL WRITING THEIR REPORTS UNDER YUKIO-SAN'S SUPERVISION.
Please be as specific as possible.
You don't remember? Then feel free to revisit the baths.
YOU ALREADY WROTE YOURS YESTERDAY, DARLING, AND I WENT TO THE BATHS FIRST THING THIS MORNING AND WROTE MINE RIGHT AWAY.
BUT KNOWING THE OTHERS, THEY MAY NEED TO GO TO THE BATHS TWO OR THREE MORE TIMES BEFORE THEY CAN FINISH THEIR REPORTS.
THOUGH I THINK SPIDEY FINISHED WRITING HERS...
Going out? I think I'll stay put.
This place has me beat.
THAT'S WHAT SHE SAID, BUT SPIDEY'S JUST A *RECLUSE*, ISN'T SHE?
RECLUSE ...?

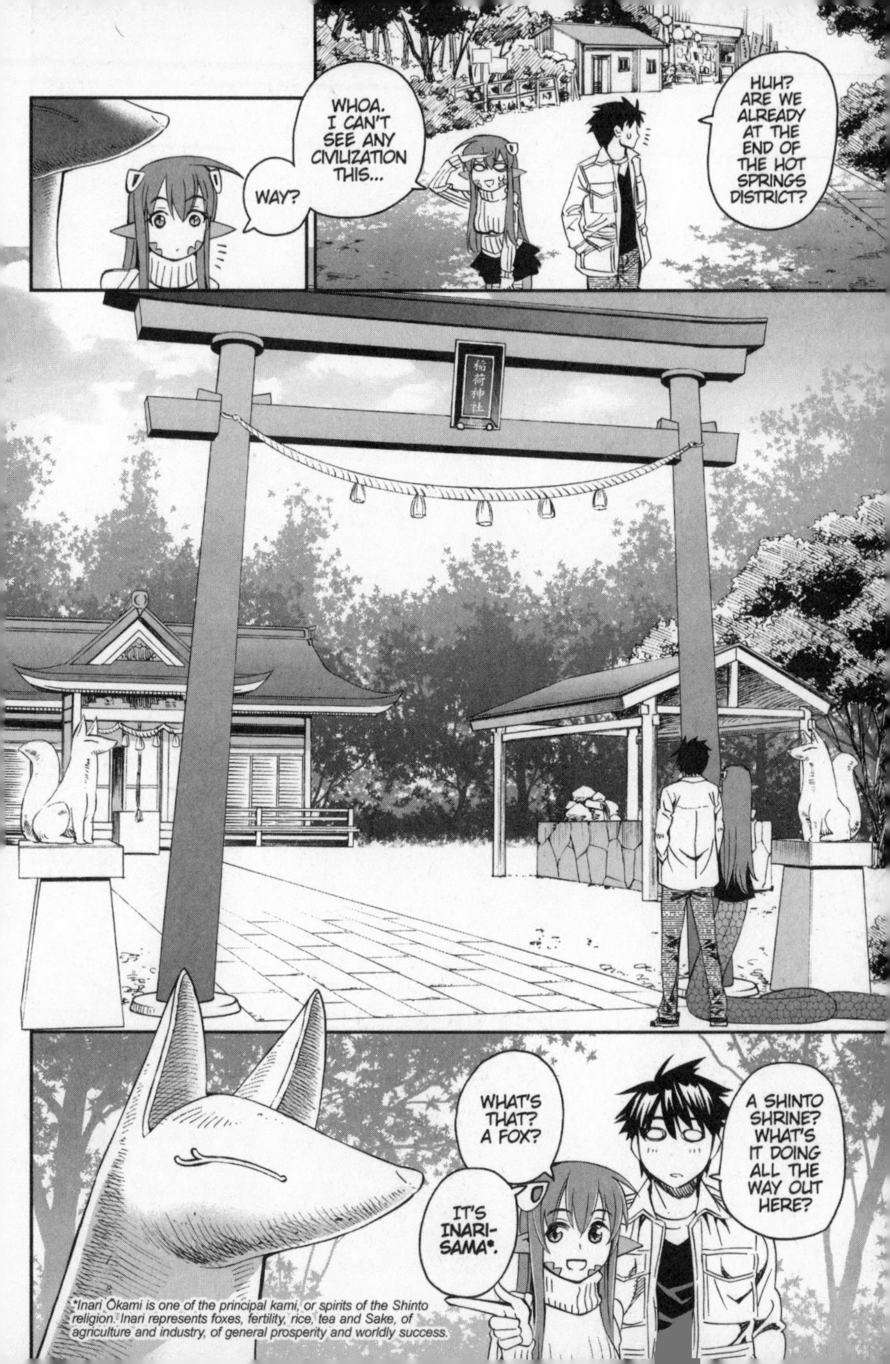
HUH? ARE WE ALREADY AT THE END OF THE HOT SPRINGS DISTRICT?
WHOA. I CAN'T SEE ANY CIVILIZATION THIS...
WAY?
稲荷神社
A SHINTO SHRINE? WHAT'S IT DOING ALL THE WAY OUT HERE?
WHAT'S THAT? A FOX?
IT'S INARI-SAMA*.

*Inari Ōkami is one of the principal kami, or spirits of the Shinto religion. Inari represents foxes, fertility, rice, tea and Sake, of agriculture and industry, of general prosperity and worldly success.

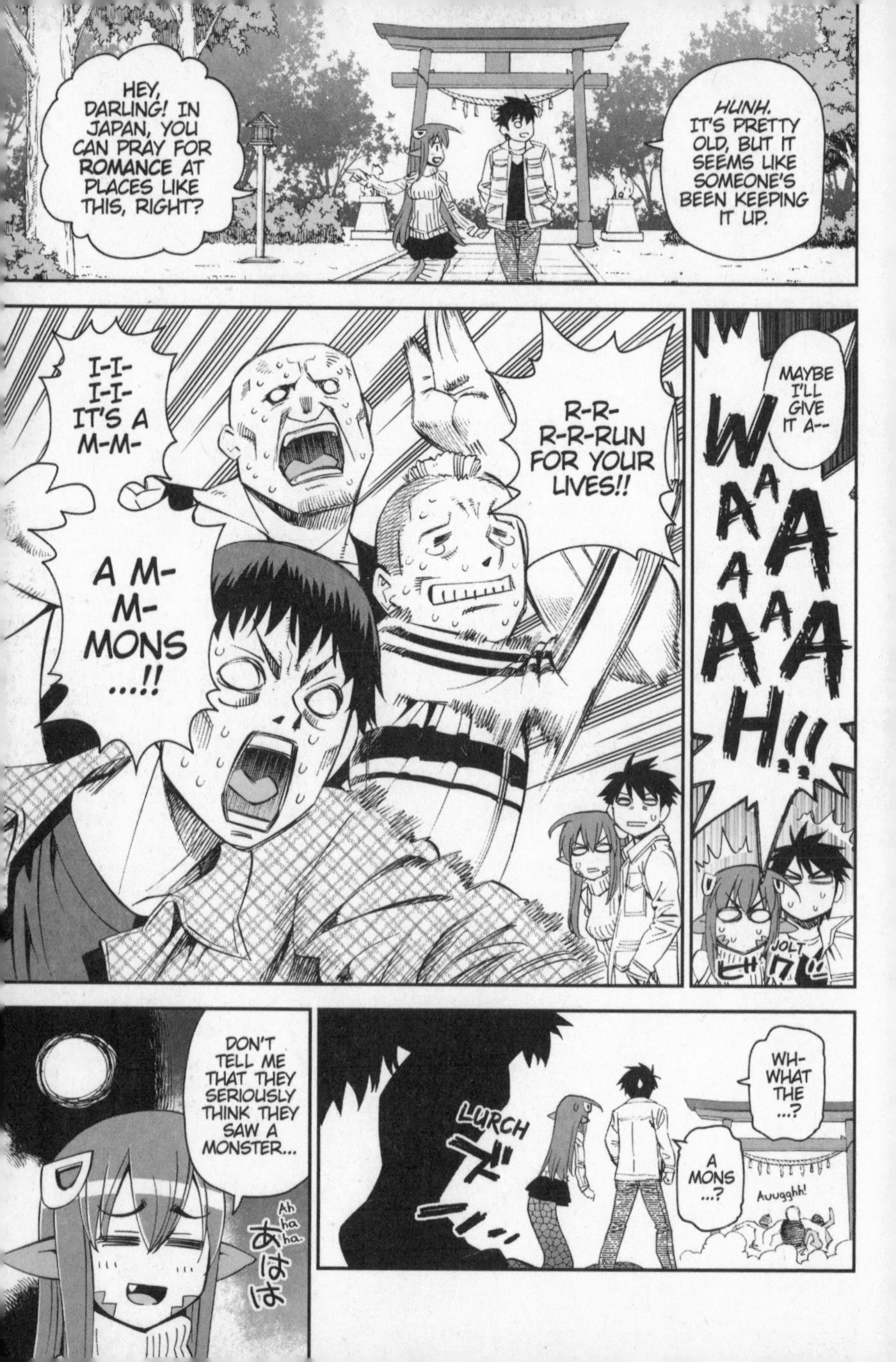
HUNH. IT'S PRETTY OLD, BUT IT SEEMS LIKE SOMEONE'S BEEN KEEPING IT UP.
HEY, DARLING! IN JAPAN, YOU CAN PRAY FOR ROMANCE AT PLACES LIKE THIS, RIGHT?
MAYBE I'LL GIVE IT A--
WAAAAAAAAH!!
JOLT
R-R-R-R-RUN FOR YOUR LIVES!!
I-I-I-I-IT'S A M-M-
A M-M-MONS...!!
WH-WHAT THE...?
A MONS...?
Auugghh!
LURCH
DON'T TELL ME THAT THEY SERIOUSLY THINK THEY SAW A MONSTER...
Ah ha ha.
あはは

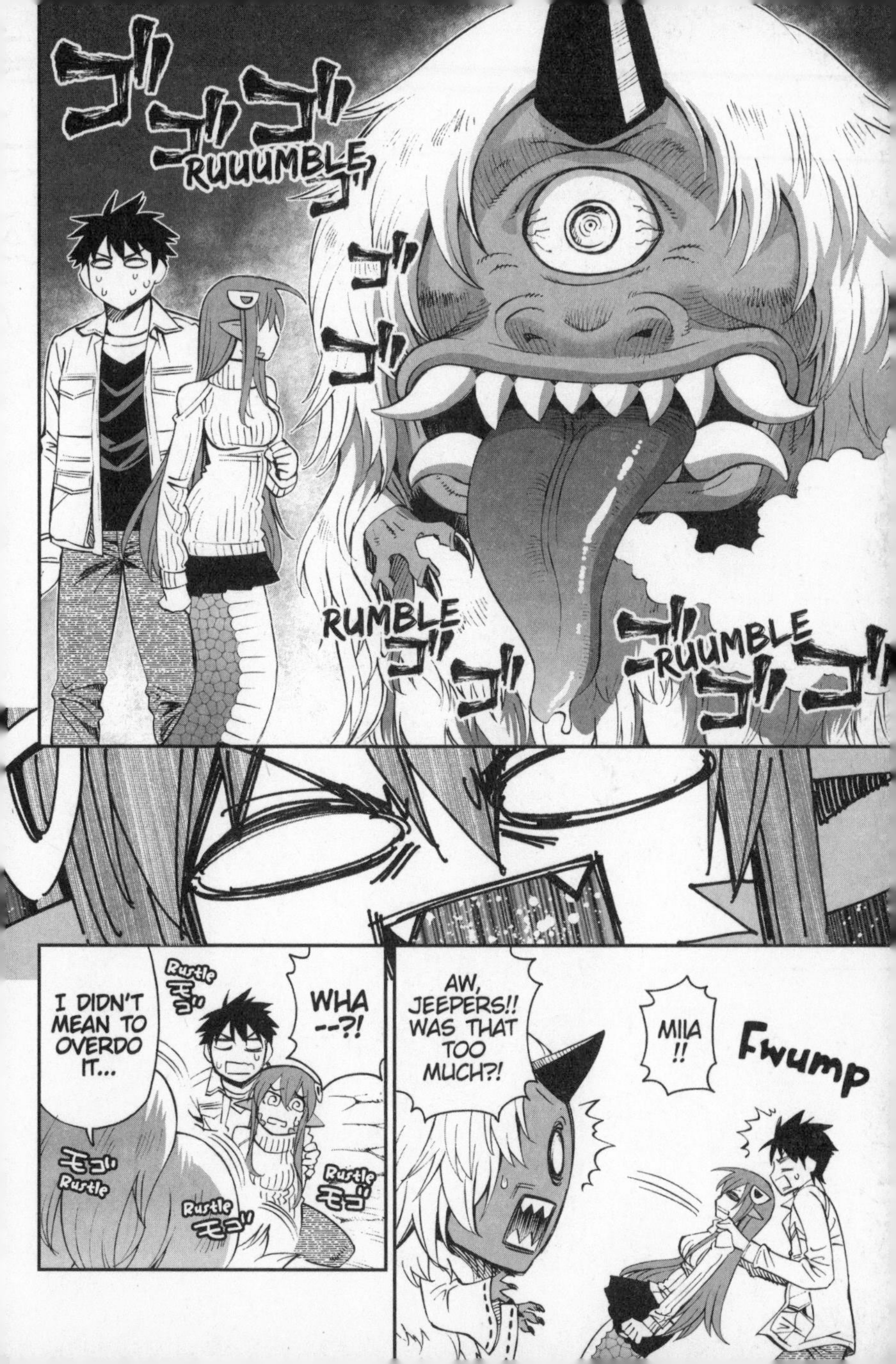
ゴゴゴ
RUUUMBLE
RUMBLE
RUUMBLE
Fwump
MIIA !!
AW, JEEPERS!! WAS THAT TOO MUCH?!
WHA --?!
Rustle
I DIDN'T MEAN TO OVERDO IT...
Rustle
Rustle
Rustle

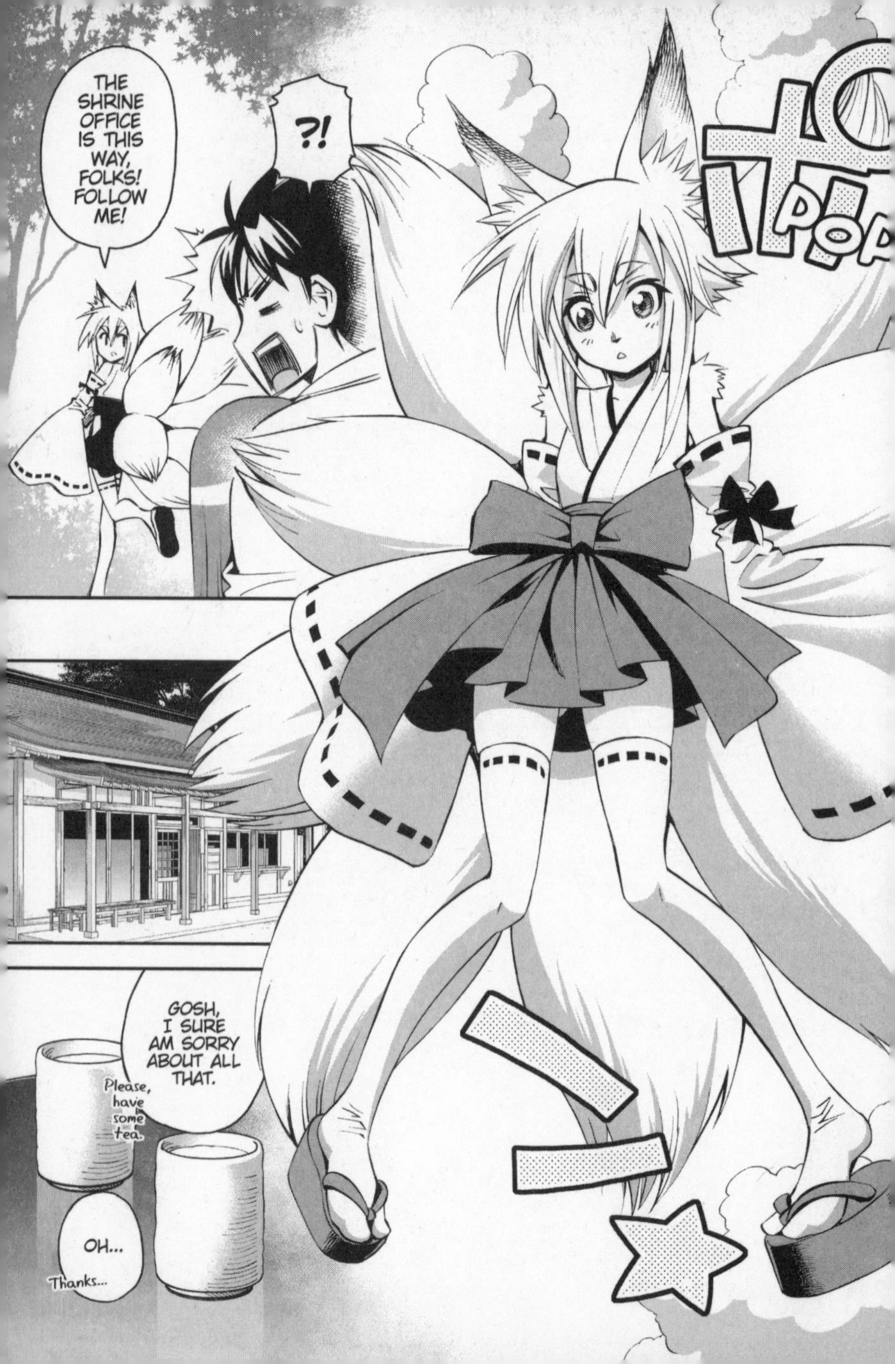
POP
?!
THE SHRINE OFFICE IS THIS WAY, FOLKS! FOLLOW ME!
GOSH, I SURE AM SORRY ABOUT ALL THAT.
Please, have some tea.
OH...
Thanks...

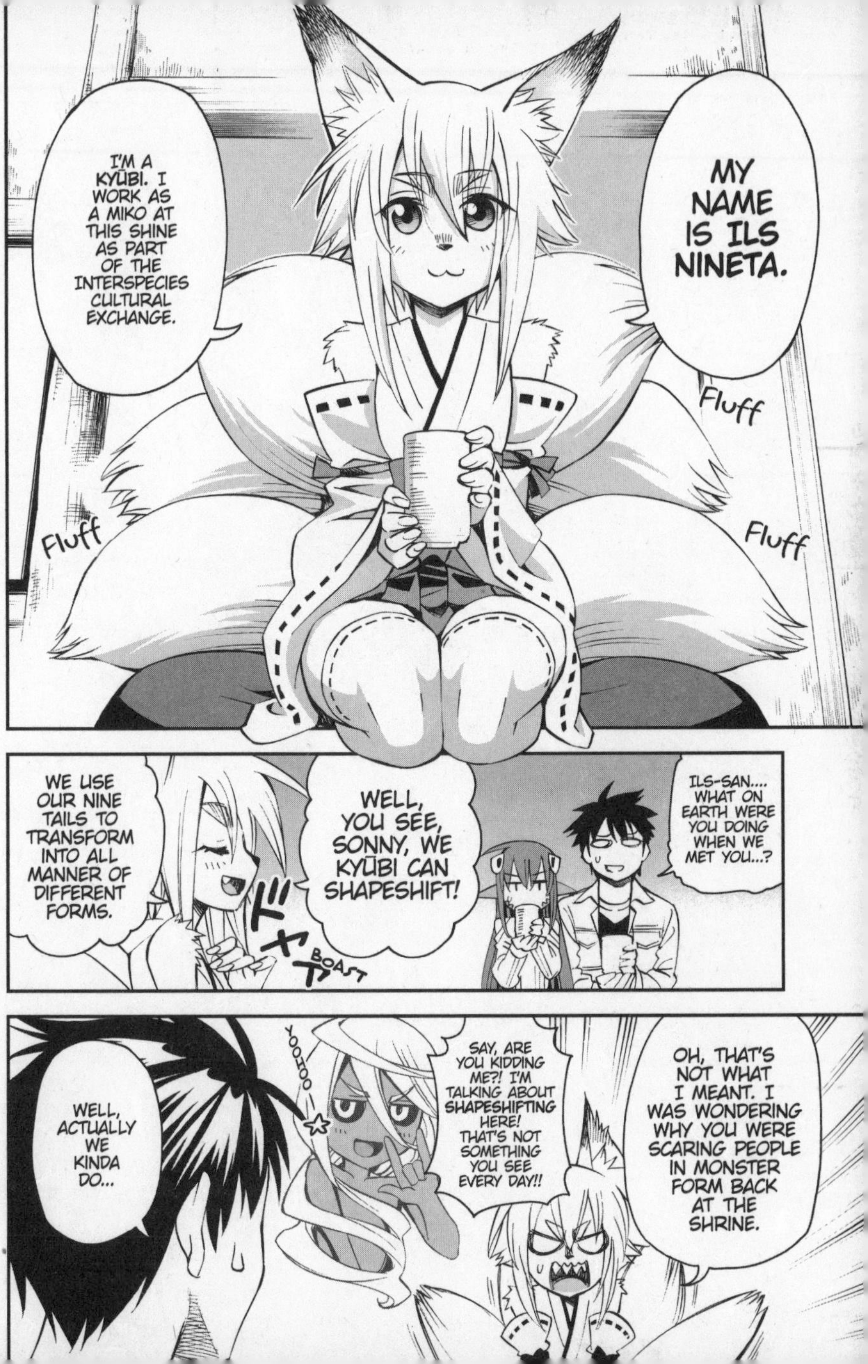
MY NAME IS ILS NINETA.
I'M A KYŪBI. I WORK AS A MIKO AT THIS SHINE AS PART OF THE INTERSPECIES CULTURAL EXCHANGE.
Fluff
Fluff
Fluff
ILS-SAN.... WHAT ON EARTH WERE YOU DOING WHEN WE MET YOU...?
WELL, YOU SEE, SONNY, WE KYŪBI CAN SHAPESHIFT!
WE USE OUR NINE TAILS TO TRANSFORM INTO ALL MANNER OF DIFFERENT FORMS.
BOAST
OH, THAT'S NOT WHAT I MEANT. I WAS WONDERING WHY YOU WERE SCARING PEOPLE IN MONSTER FORM BACK AT THE SHRINE.
SAY, ARE YOU KIDDING ME?! I'M TALKING ABOUT SHAPESHIFTING HERE! THAT'S NOT SOMETHING YOU SEE EVERY DAY!!
YOOHOO
WELL, ACTUALLY WE KINDA DO...

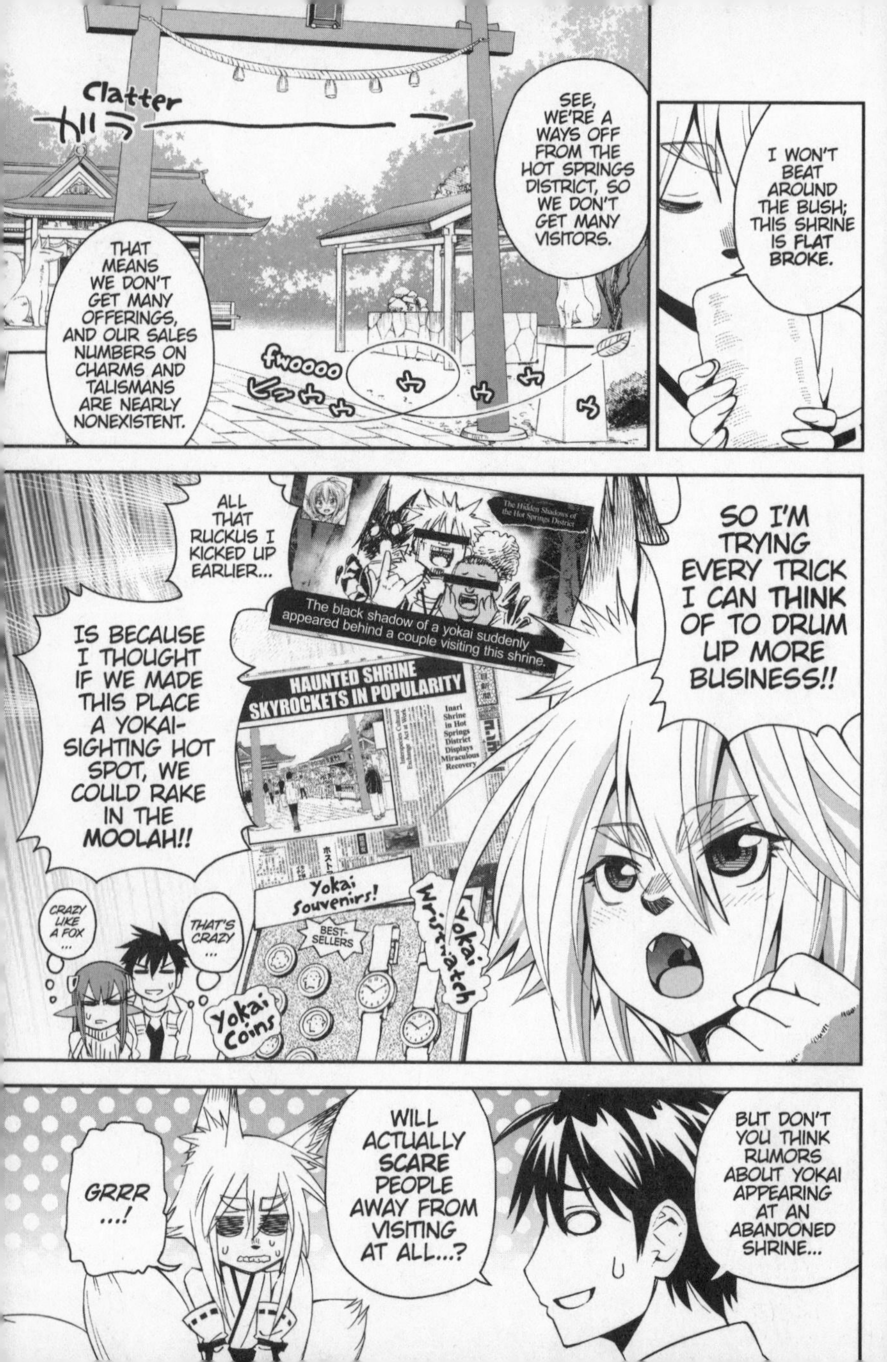
I WON'T BEAT AROUND THE BUSH; THIS SHRINE IS FLAT BROKE.
SEE, WE'RE A WAYS OFF FROM THE HOT SPRINGS DISTRICT, SO WE DON'T GET MANY VISITORS.
Clatter
THAT MEANS WE DON'T GET MANY OFFERINGS, AND OUR SALES NUMBERS ON CHARMS AND TALISMANS ARE NEARLY NONEXISTENT.
fwoooo
SO I'M TRYING EVERY TRICK I CAN THINK OF TO DRUM UP MORE BUSINESS!!
ALL THAT RUCKUS I KICKED UP EARLIER...
The Hidden Shadows of the Hot Springs District
The black shadow of a yokai suddenly appeared behind a couple visiting this shrine.
IS BECAUSE I THOUGHT IF WE MADE THIS PLACE A YOKAI-SIGHTING HOT SPOT, WE COULD RAKE IN THE MOOLAH!!
HAUNTED SHRINE SKYROCKETS IN POPULARITY
Interspecies Cultural Exchange Act at Work
Inari Shrine in Hot Springs District Displays Miraculous Recovery
Yokai Souvenirs!
BEST-SELLERS
Yokai Wristwatch
Yokai Coins
THAT'S CRAZY ...
CRAZY LIKE A FOX ...
BUT DON'T YOU THINK RUMORS ABOUT YOKAI APPEARING AT AN ABANDONED SHRINE...
WILL ACTUALLY SCARE PEOPLE AWAY FROM VISITING AT ALL...?
GRRR ...!

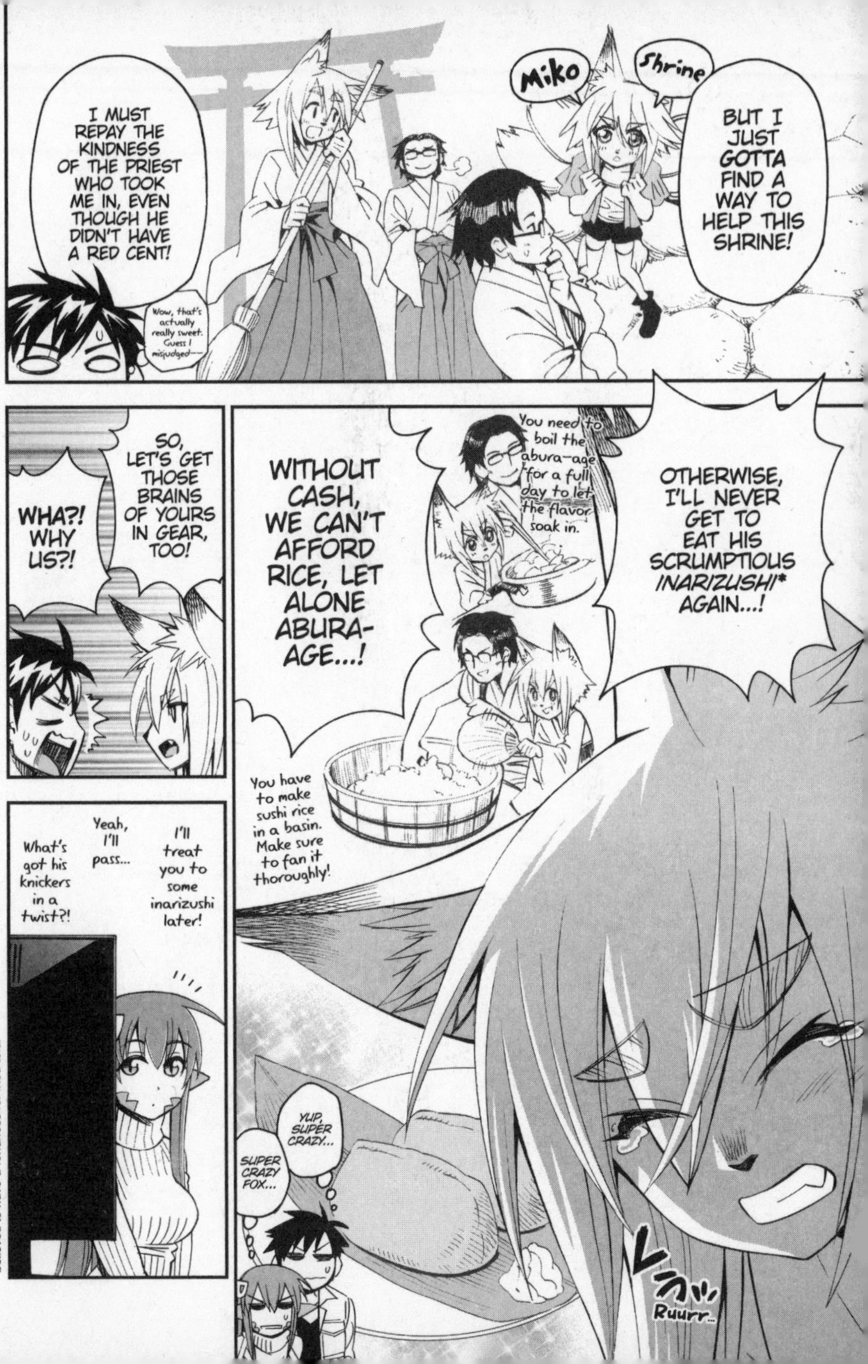
Miko
Shrine
BUT I JUST GOTTA FIND A WAY TO HELP THIS SHRINE!
I MUST REPAY THE KINDNESS OF THE PRIEST WHO TOOK ME IN, EVEN THOUGH HE DIDN'T HAVE A RED CENT!
Wow, that's actually really sweet. Guess I misjudged—
OTHERWISE, I'LL NEVER GET TO EAT HIS SCRUMPTIOUS INARIZUSHI* AGAIN...!
You need to boil the abura-age for a full day to let the flavor soak in.
WITHOUT CASH, WE CAN'T AFFORD RICE, LET ALONE ABURA-AGE...!
You have to make sushi rice in a basin. Make sure to fan it thoroughly!
YUP, SUPER CRAZY...
SUPER CRAZY FOX...
Ruurr...
SO, LET'S GET THOSE BRAINS OF YOURS IN GEAR, TOO!
WHA?! WHY US?!
I'll treat you to some inarizushi later!
Yeah, I'll pass...
What's got his knickers in a twist?!

sushi rice alone. It is named after the Shinto kami Inari, who is believed to have a fondness for fried tofu.

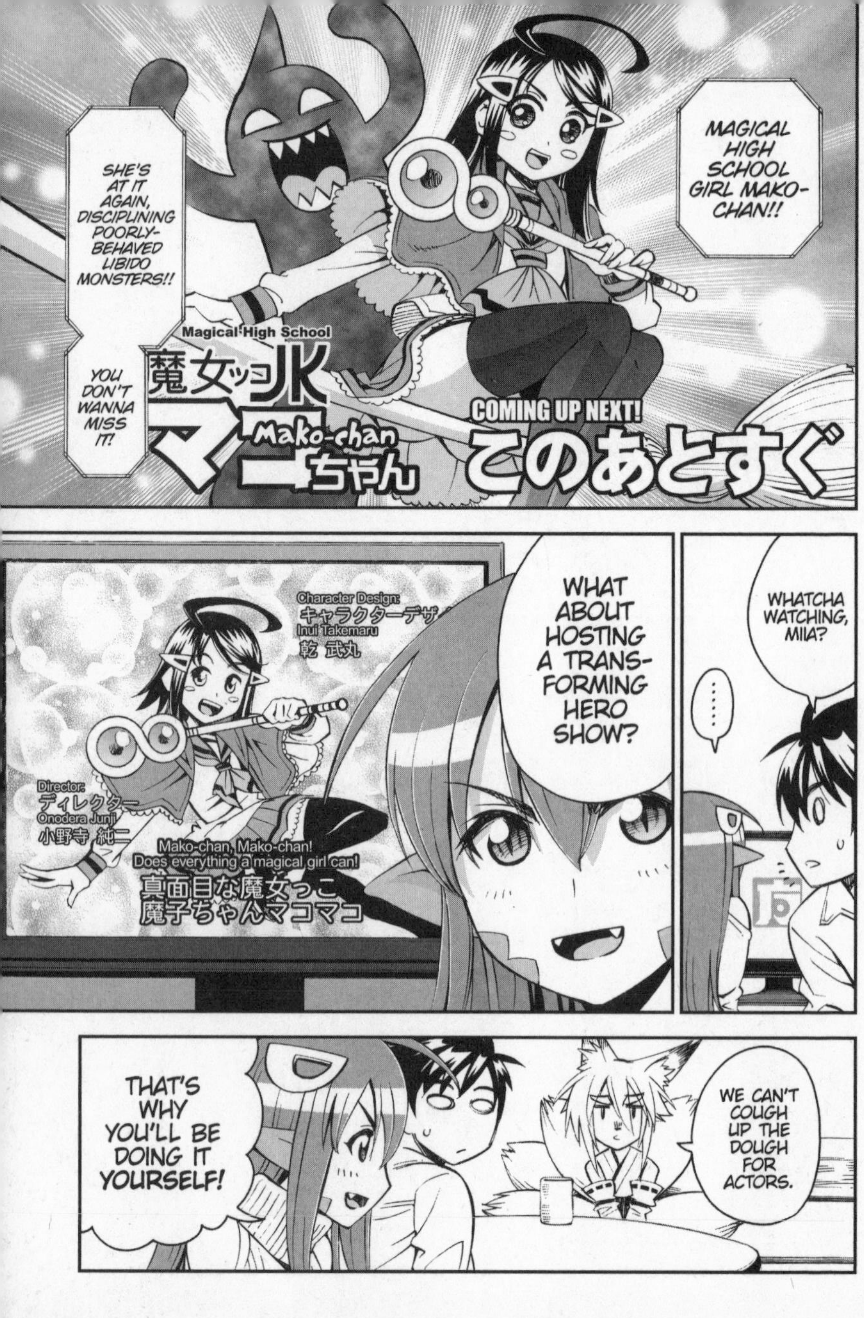
MAGICAL HIGH SCHOOL GIRL MAKO-CHAN!!
SHE'S AT IT AGAIN, DISCIPLINING POORLY-BEHAVED LIBIDO MONSTERS!!
Magical High School
魔女ッコJK マコちゃん
Mako-chan
COMING UP NEXT!
てのあとすぐ
YOU DON'T WANNA MISS IT!
WHATCHA WATCHING, MIIA?
……
WHAT ABOUT HOSTING A TRANS-FORMING HERO SHOW?
Character Design:
キャラクターデザ
Inui Takemaru
乾 武丸
Director:
ディレクター
Onodera Junji
小野寺 純二
Mako-chan, Mako-chan! Does everything a magical girl can!
真面目な魔女っこ
魔子ちゃんマコマコ
WE CAN'T COUGH UP THE DOUGH FOR ACTORS.
THAT'S WHY YOU'LL BE DOING IT YOURSELF!

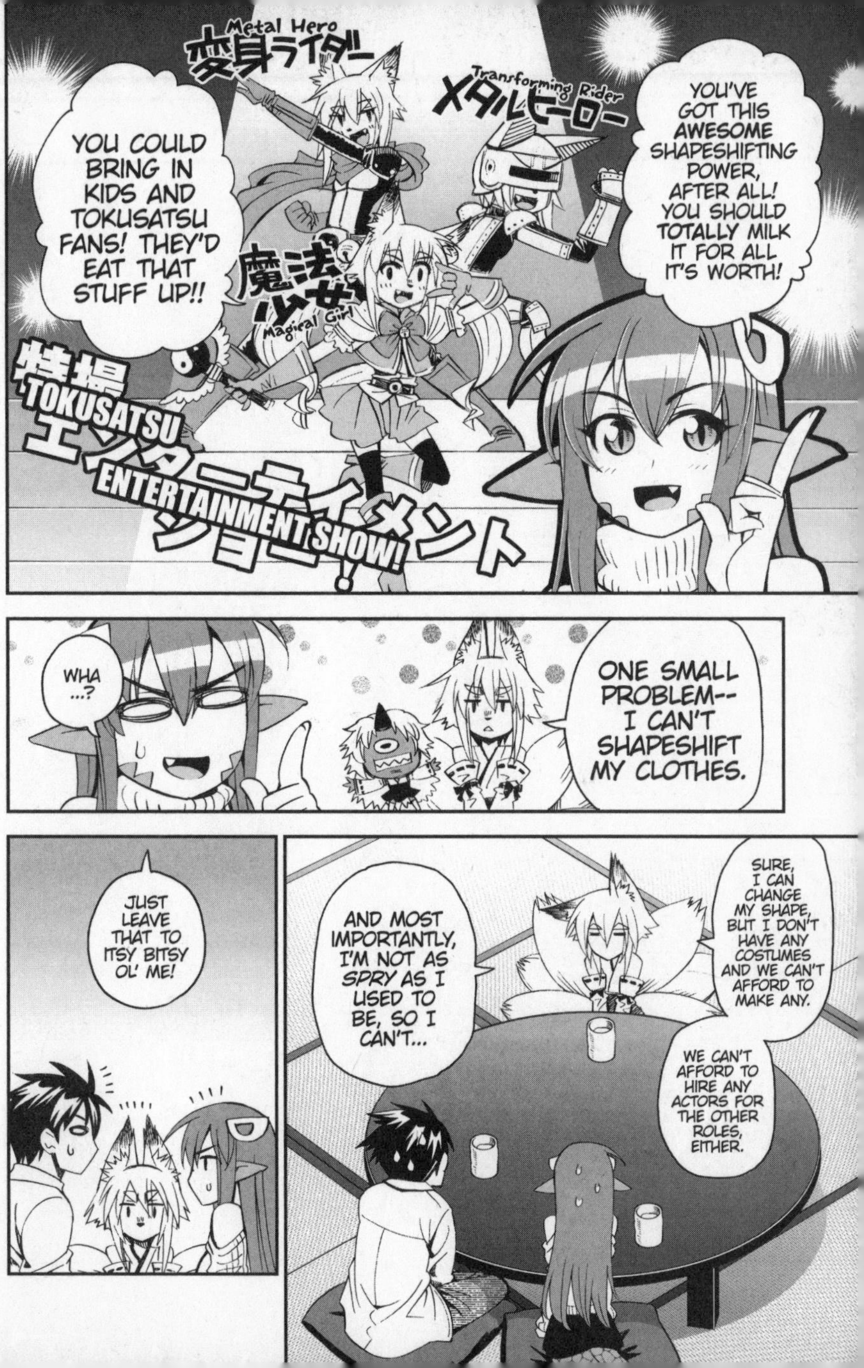
YOU'VE GOT THIS AWESOME SHAPESHIFTING POWER, AFTER ALL! YOU SHOULD TOTALLY MILK IT FOR ALL IT'S WORTH!
Transforming Rider
メタルヒーロー
Metal Hero
変身ライダー
魔法少女
Magical Girl
YOU COULD BRING IN KIDS AND TOKUSATSU FANS! THEY'D EAT THAT STUFF UP!!
特撮エンターテイメントショー!
TOKUSATSU ENTERTAINMENT SHOW!
ONE SMALL PROBLEM-- I CAN'T SHAPESHIFT MY CLOTHES.
WHA ...?
SURE, I CAN CHANGE MY SHAPE, BUT I DON'T HAVE ANY COSTUMES AND WE CAN'T AFFORD TO MAKE ANY.
WE CAN'T AFFORD TO HIRE ANY ACTORS FOR THE OTHER ROLES, EITHER.
AND MOST IMPORTANTLY, I'M NOT AS SPRY AS I USED TO BE, SO I CAN'T...
JUST LEAVE THAT TO ITSY BITSY OL' ME!

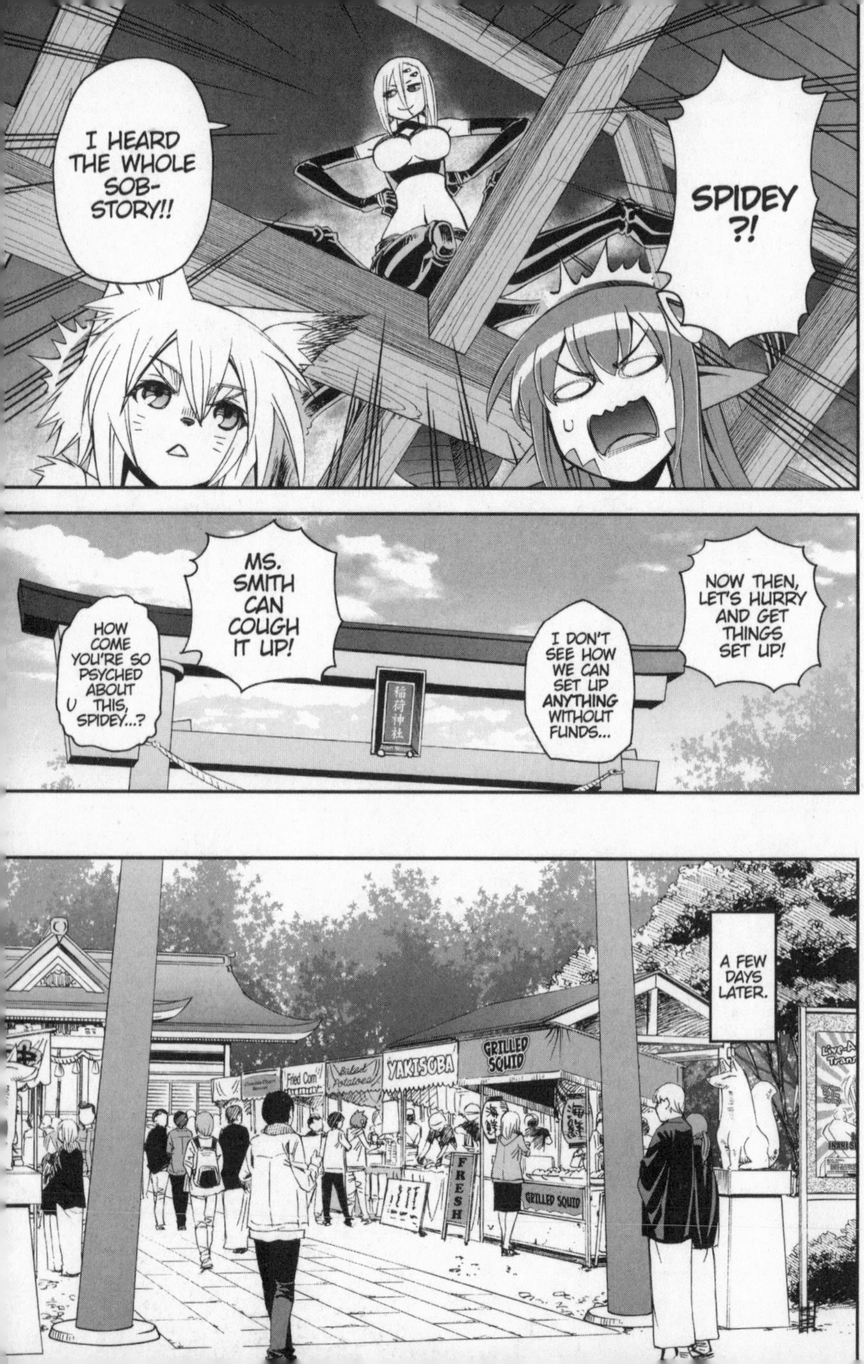
SPIDEY ?!
I HEARD THE WHOLE SOB-STORY!!
NOW THEN, LET'S HURRY AND GET THINGS SET UP!
I DON'T SEE HOW WE CAN SET UP ANYTHING WITHOUT FUNDS...
MS. SMITH CAN COUGH IT UP!
HOW COME YOU'RE SO PSYCHED ABOUT THIS, SPIDEY...?
A FEW DAYS LATER.
GRILLED SQUID
YAKISOBA
Baked Potatoes
Fried Corn
FRESH
GRILLED SQUID

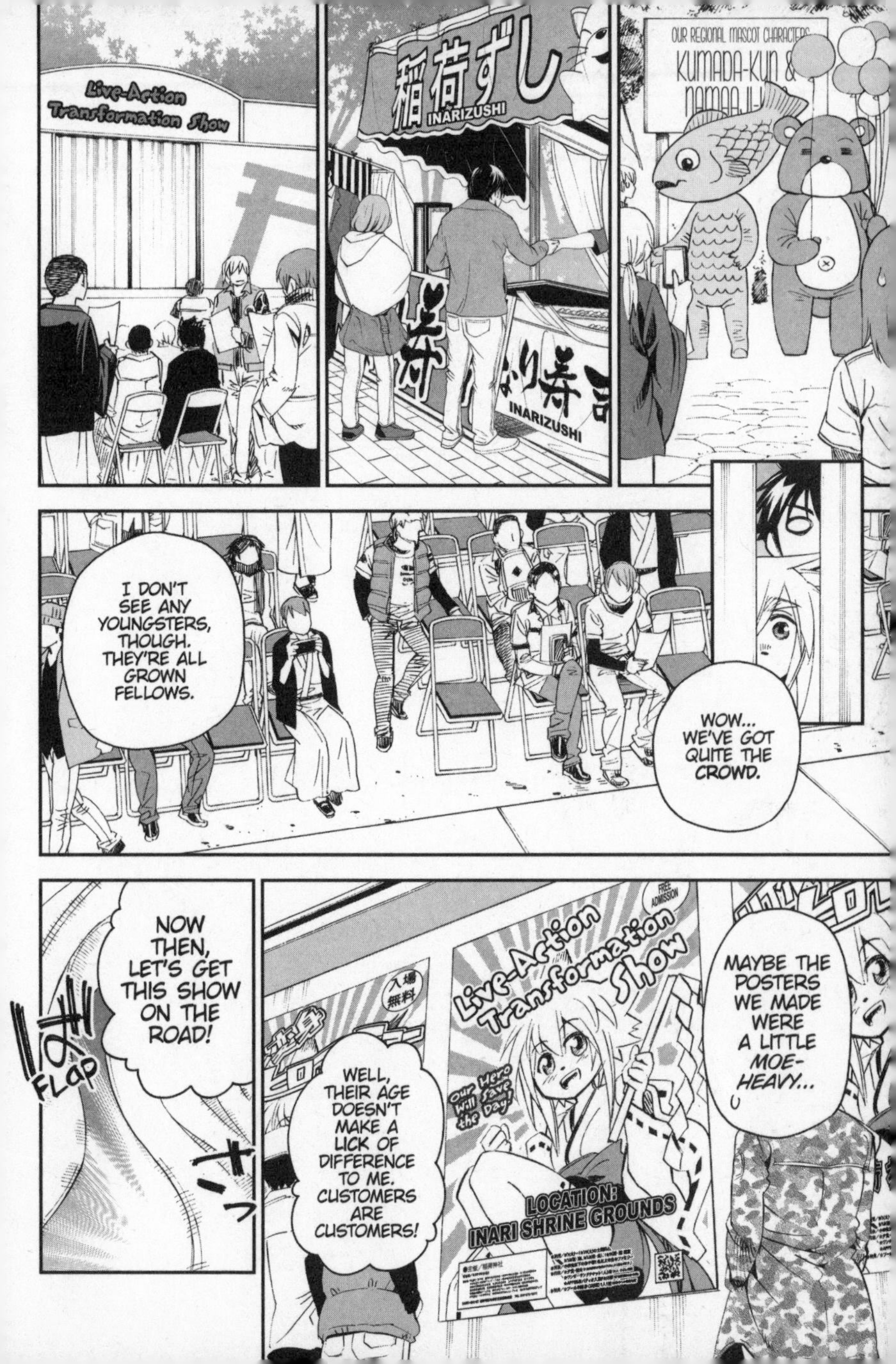
OUR REGIONAL MASCOT CHARACTERS
KUMADA-KUN &
稲荷ずし
INARIZUSHI
INARIZUSHI
Live-Action Transformation Show
WOW... WE'VE GOT QUITE THE CROWD.
I DON'T SEE ANY YOUNGSTERS, THOUGH. THEY'RE ALL GROWN FELLOWS.
MAYBE THE POSTERS WE MADE WERE A LITTLE MOE-HEAVY...
FREE ADMISSION
Live-Action Transformation Show
入場無料
Our Hero Will Save the Day!
LOCATION: INARI SHRINE GROUNDS
WELL, THEIR AGE DOESN'T MAKE A LICK OF DIFFERENCE TO ME. CUSTOMERS ARE CUSTOMERS!
NOW THEN, LET'S GET THIS SHOW ON THE ROAD!
FLAP

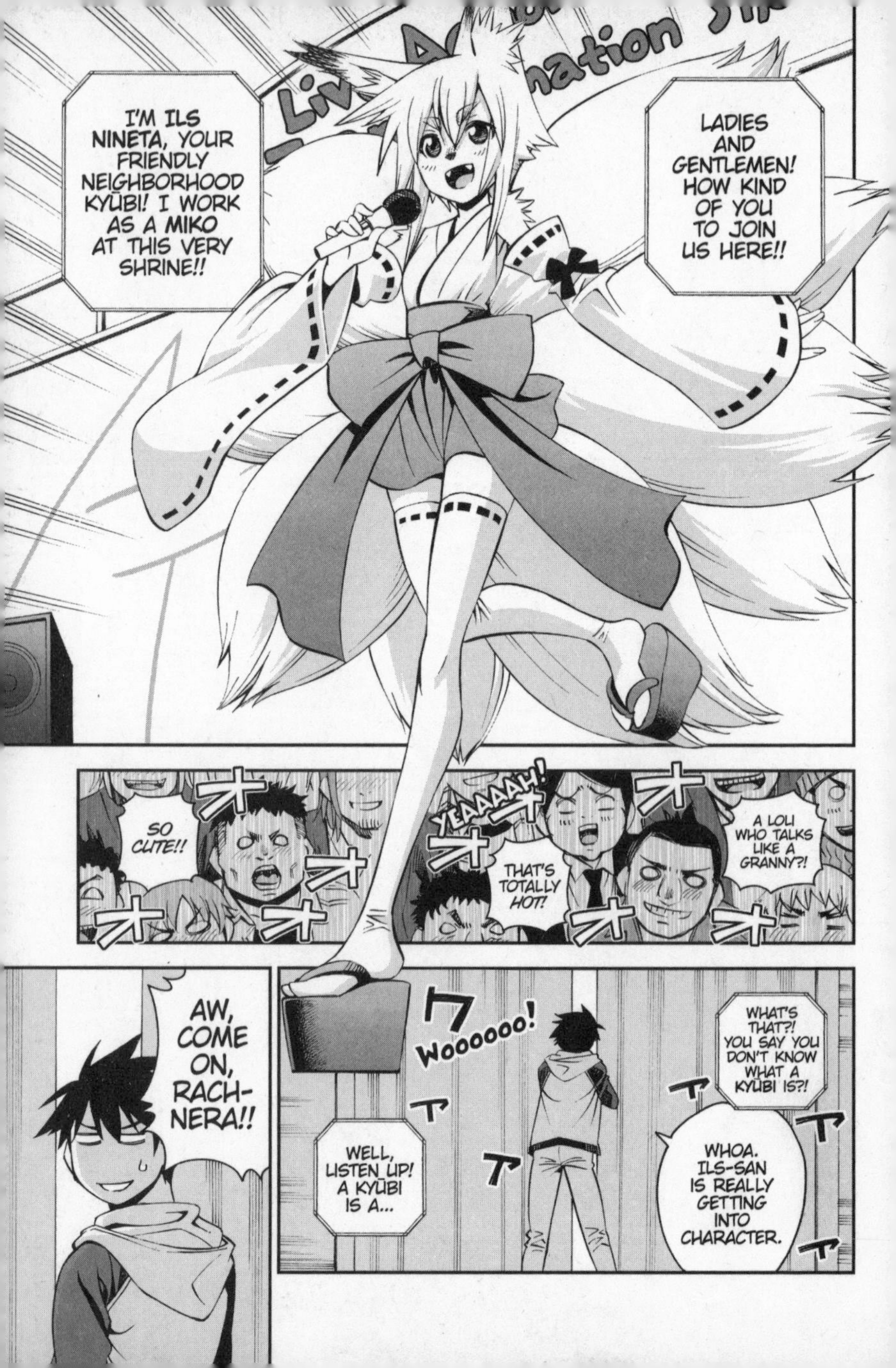
LADIES AND GENTLEMEN! HOW KIND OF YOU TO JOIN US HERE!!
I'M ILS NINETA, YOUR FRIENDLY NEIGHBORHOOD KYŪBI! I WORK AS A MIKO AT THIS VERY SHRINE!!
A LOLI WHO TALKS LIKE A GRANNY?!
THAT'S TOTALLY HOT!
YEAAAAH!
SO CUTE!!
WHAT'S THAT?! YOU SAY YOU DON'T KNOW WHAT A KYŪBI IS?!
WHOA. ILS-SAN IS REALLY GETTING INTO CHARACTER.
WELL, LISTEN UP! A KYŪBI IS A...
WOOOOOO!
AW, COME ON, RACHNERA!!

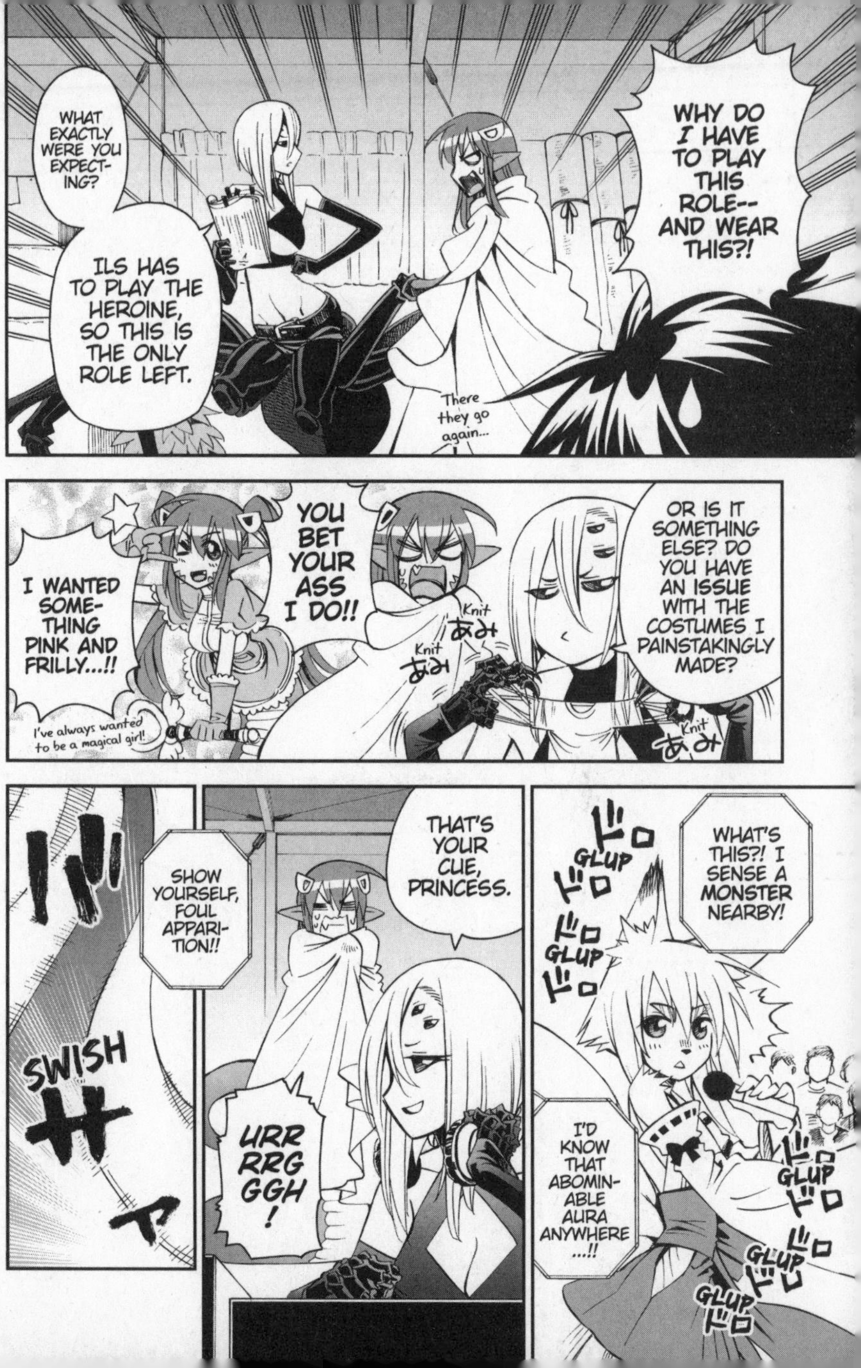
WHY DO I HAVE TO PLAY THIS ROLE-- AND WEAR THIS?!
There they go again...
WHAT EXACTLY WERE YOU EXPECTING?
ILS HAS TO PLAY THE HEROINE, SO THIS IS THE ONLY ROLE LEFT.
OR IS IT SOMETHING ELSE? DO YOU HAVE AN ISSUE WITH THE COSTUMES I PAINSTAKINGLY MADE?
Knit あみ
Knit あみ
Knit あみ
YOU BET YOUR ASS I DO!!
I WANTED SOMETHING PINK AND FRILLY...!!
I've always wanted to be a magical girl!
WHAT'S THIS?! I SENSE A MONSTER NEARBY!
GLUP ドロ
GLUP ドロ
GLUP ドロ
I'D KNOW THAT ABOMINABLE AURA ANYWHERE...!!
GLUP ドロ
GLUP ドロ
GLUP ドロ
THAT'S YOUR CUE, PRINCESS.
SHOW YOURSELF, FOUL APPARITION!!
URRRRGGGH!
SWISH
サッ

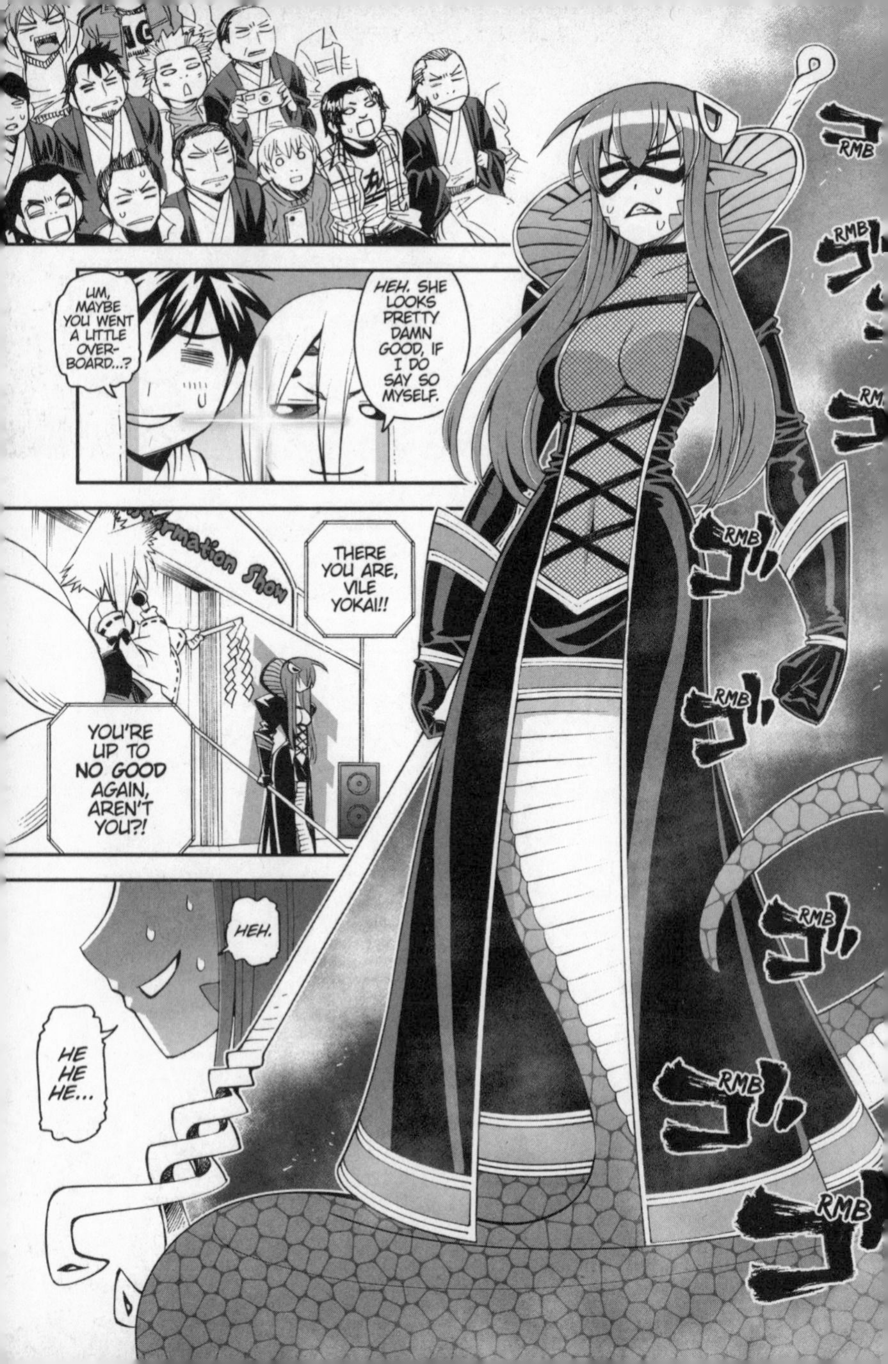
RMB
RMB
RM
RMB
RMB
RMB
RMB
RMB
HEH. SHE LOOKS PRETTY DAMN GOOD, IF I DO SAY SO MYSELF.
UM, MAYBE YOU WENT A LITTLE OVER-BOARD...?
rmation Show
THERE YOU ARE, VILE YOKAI!!
YOU'RE UP TO NO GOOD AGAIN, AREN'T YOU?!
HEH.
HE HE HE...

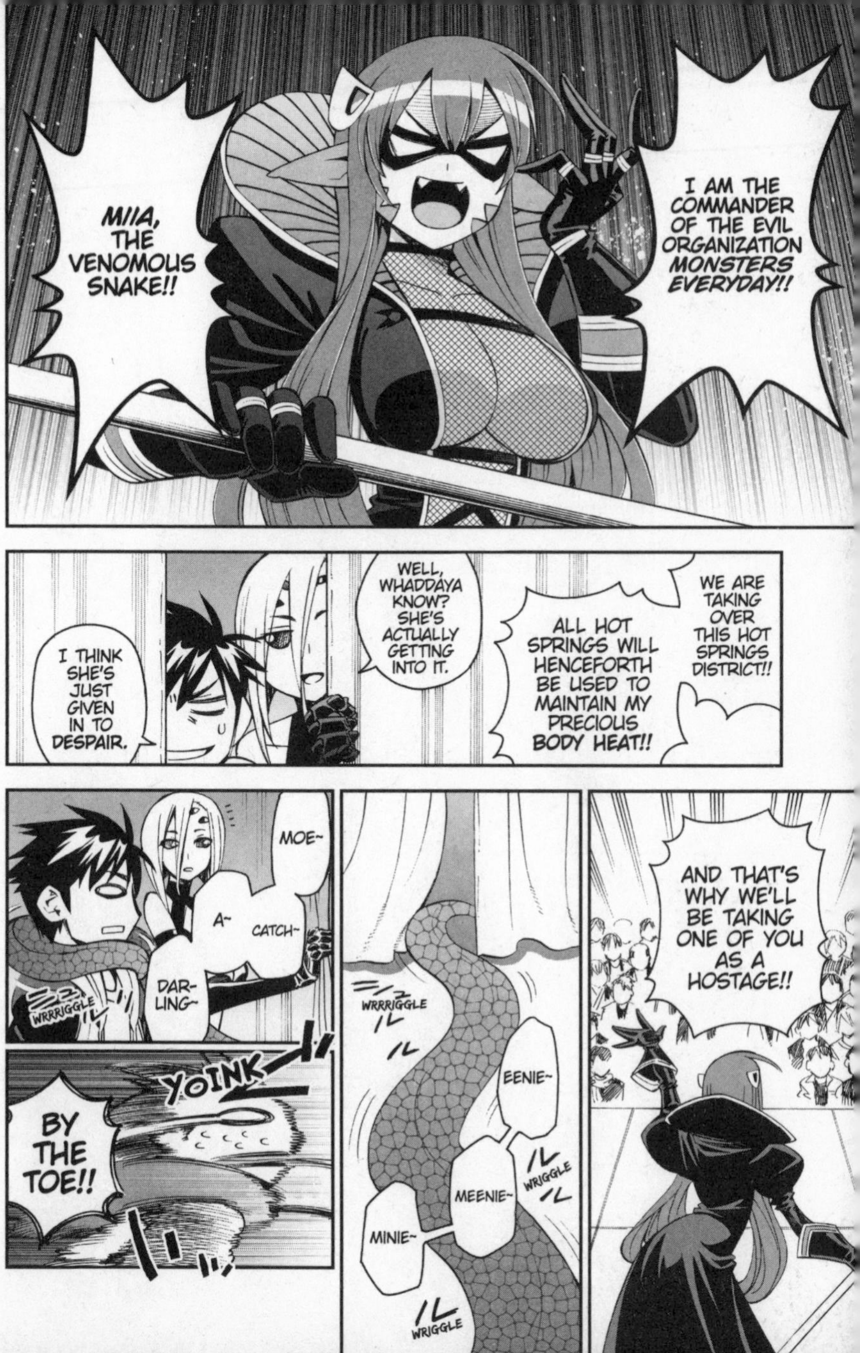
I AM THE COMMANDER OF THE EVIL ORGANIZATION *MONSTERS EVERYDAY!!*
MIIA, THE VENOMOUS SNAKE!!
WE ARE TAKING OVER THIS HOT SPRINGS DISTRICT!!
ALL HOT SPRINGS WILL HENCEFORTH BE USED TO MAINTAIN MY PRECIOUS BODY HEAT!!
WELL, WHADDAYA KNOW? SHE'S ACTUALLY GETTING INTO IT.
I THINK SHE'S JUST GIVEN IN TO DESPAIR.
AND THAT'S WHY WE'LL BE TAKING ONE OF YOU AS A HOSTAGE!!
WRRRIGGLE
EENIE~
WRIGGLE
MEENIE~
MINIE~
WRIGGLE
MOE~
CATCH~
A~
DAR-LING~
WRRRIGGLE
YOINK
BY THE TOE!!

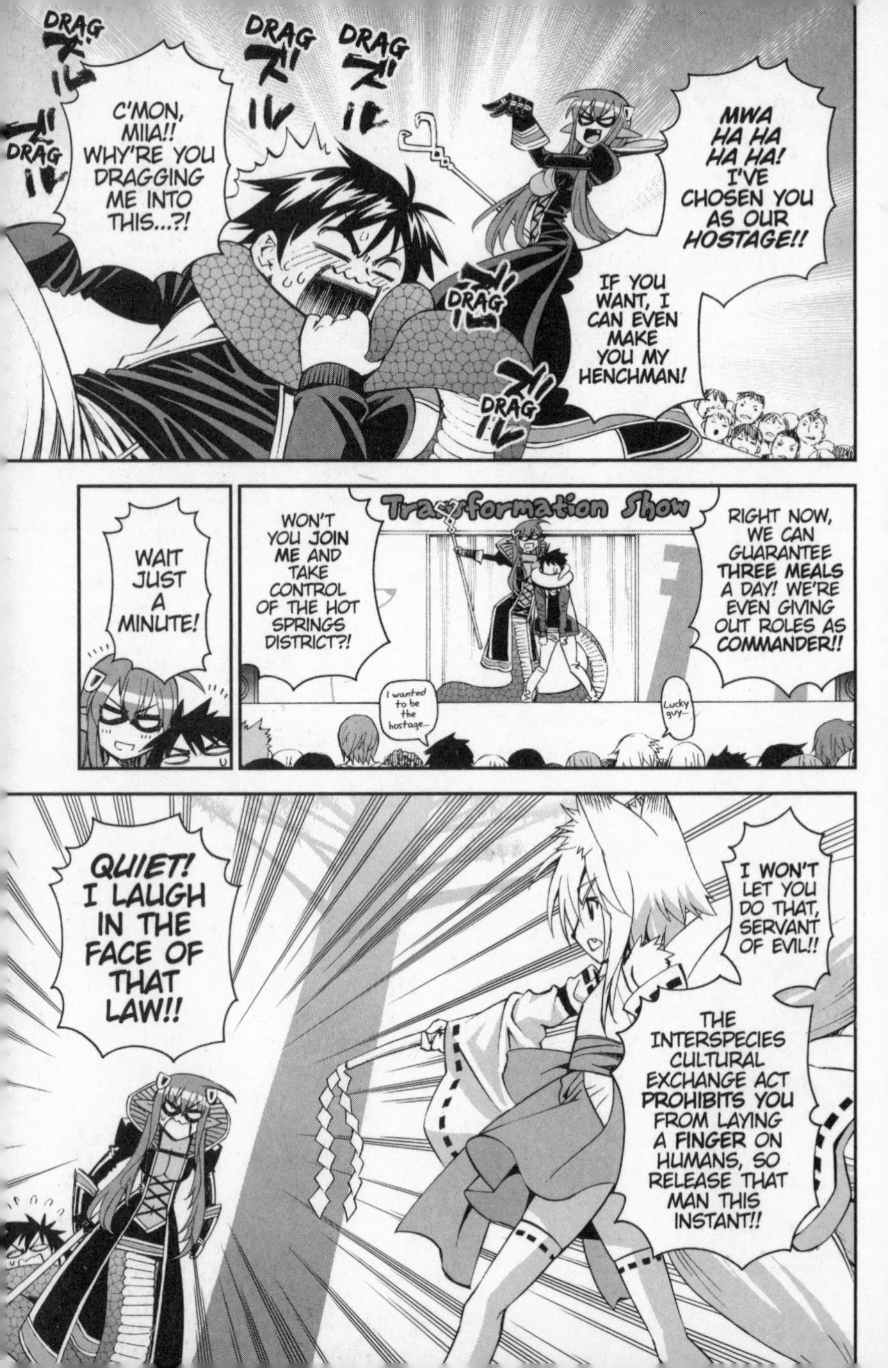

MWA HA HA HA HA! I'VE CHOSEN YOU AS OUR HOSTAGE!!
IF YOU WANT, I CAN EVEN MAKE YOU MY HENCHMAN!
DRAG
DRAG
DRAG
DRAG
C'MON, MIIA!! WHY'RE YOU DRAGGING ME INTO THIS...?!
DRAG
DRAG
Transformation Show
RIGHT NOW, WE CAN GUARANTEE THREE MEALS A DAY! WE'RE EVEN GIVING OUT ROLES AS COMMANDER!!
WON'T YOU JOIN ME AND TAKE CONTROL OF THE HOT SPRINGS DISTRICT?!
Lucky guy...
I wanted to be the hostage...
WAIT JUST A MINUTE!
I WON'T LET YOU DO THAT, SERVANT OF EVIL!!
THE INTERSPECIES CULTURAL EXCHANGE ACT PROHIBITS YOU FROM LAYING A FINGER ON HUMANS, SO RELEASE THAT MAN THIS INSTANT!!
QUIET! I LAUGH IN THE FACE OF THAT LAW!!

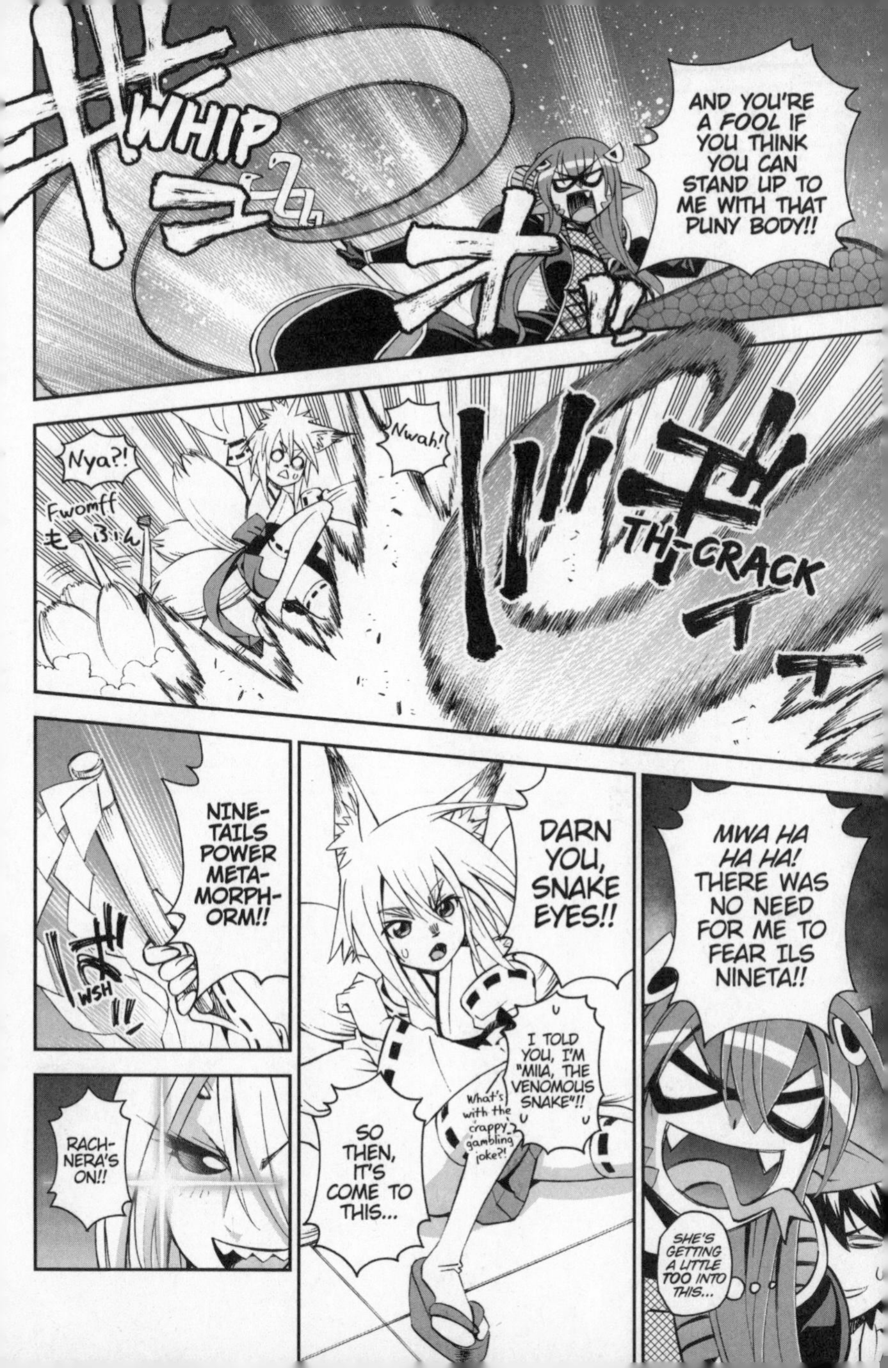
AND YOU'RE A FOOL IF YOU THINK YOU CAN STAND UP TO ME WITH THAT PUNY BODY!!
WHIP
TH-CRACK
Nwah!
Nya?!
Fwomff
もふぃん
MWA HA HA HA! THERE WAS NO NEED FOR ME TO FEAR ILS NINETA!!
SHE'S GETTING A LITTLE TOO INTO THIS...
DARN YOU, SNAKE EYES!!
I TOLD YOU, I'M "MIIA, THE VENOMOUS SNAKE"!!
What's with the crappy gambling joke?!
SO THEN, IT'S COME TO THIS...
NINE-TAILS POWER META-MORPHORM!!
WSH
RACHNERA'S ON!!

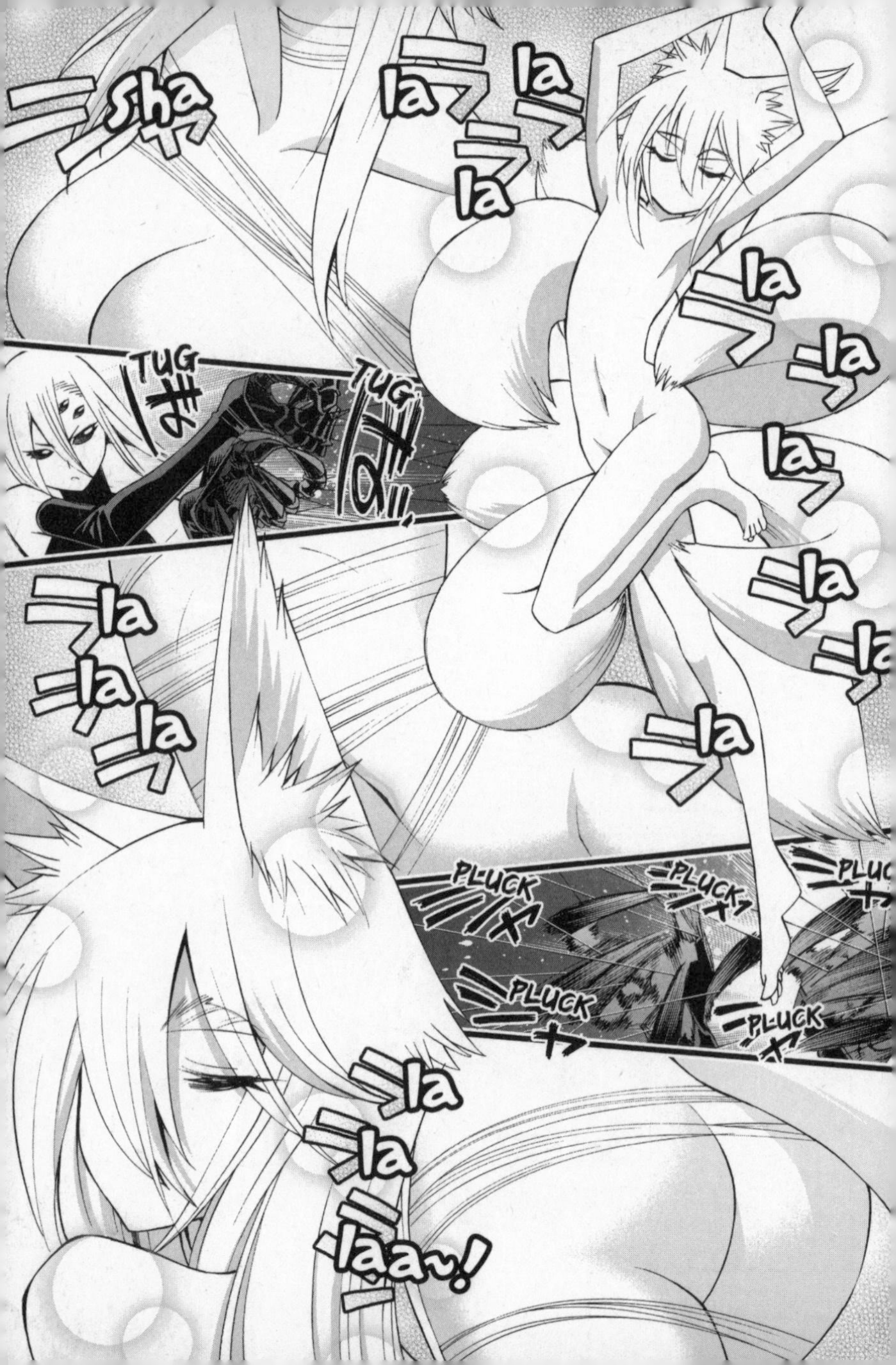
la
la
la
la
la
la
la
la
la
la
sha
TUG
TUG
la
la
la
PLUCK
PLUCK
PLUCK
PLUCK
la
la
laaa~!

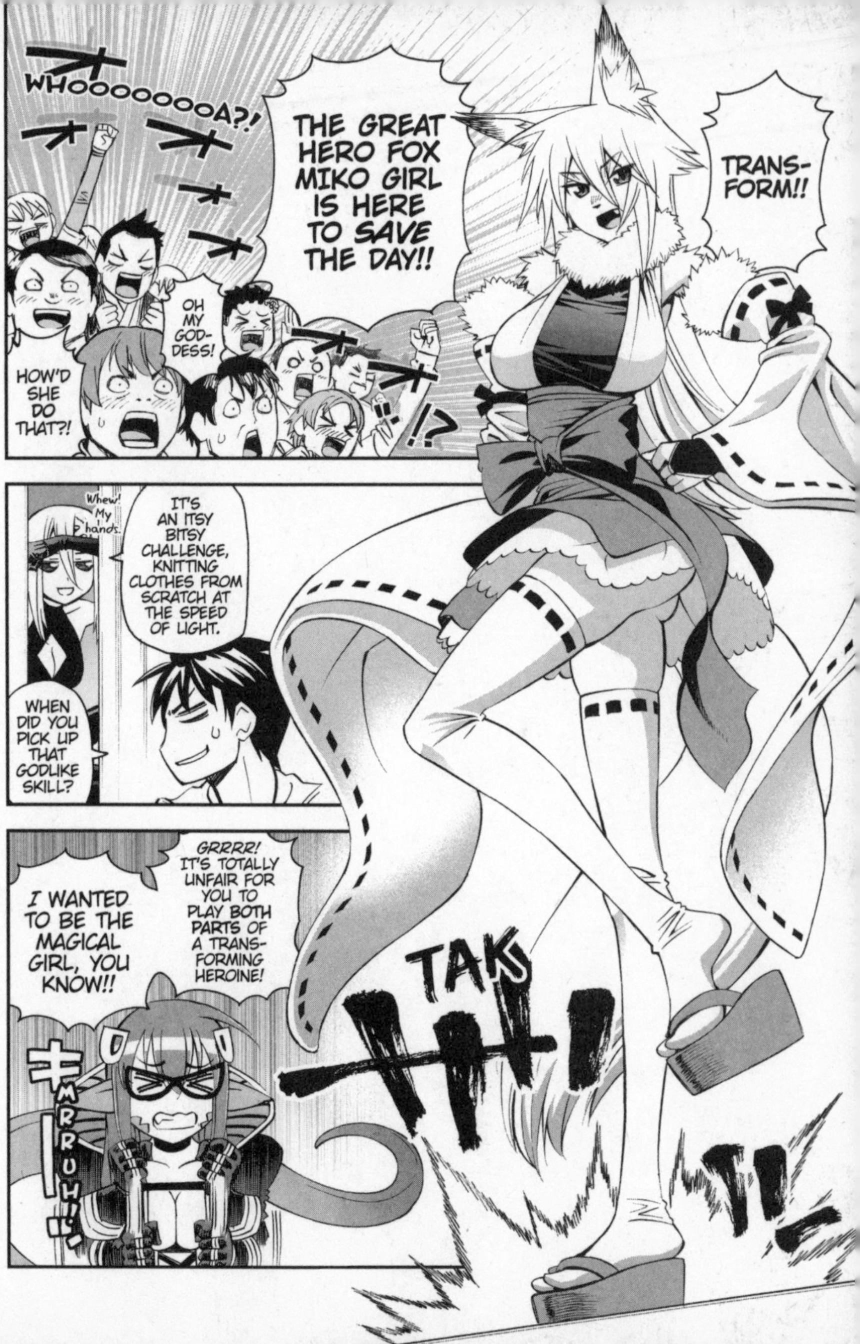
TRANS-FORM!!
THE GREAT HERO FOX MIKO GIRL IS HERE TO SAVE THE DAY!!
WHOOOOOOOA?!
OH MY GOD-DESS!
HOW'D SHE DO THAT?!
!?
IT'S AN ITSY BITSY CHALLENGE, KNITTING CLOTHES FROM SCRATCH AT THE SPEED OF LIGHT.
Whew! My hands.
WHEN DID YOU PICK UP THAT GODLIKE SKILL?
GRRRR! IT'S TOTALLY UNFAIR FOR YOU TO PLAY BOTH PARTS OF A TRANS-FORMING HEROINE!
I WANTED TO BE THE MAGICAL GIRL, YOU KNOW!!
MRRUH!!
TAK

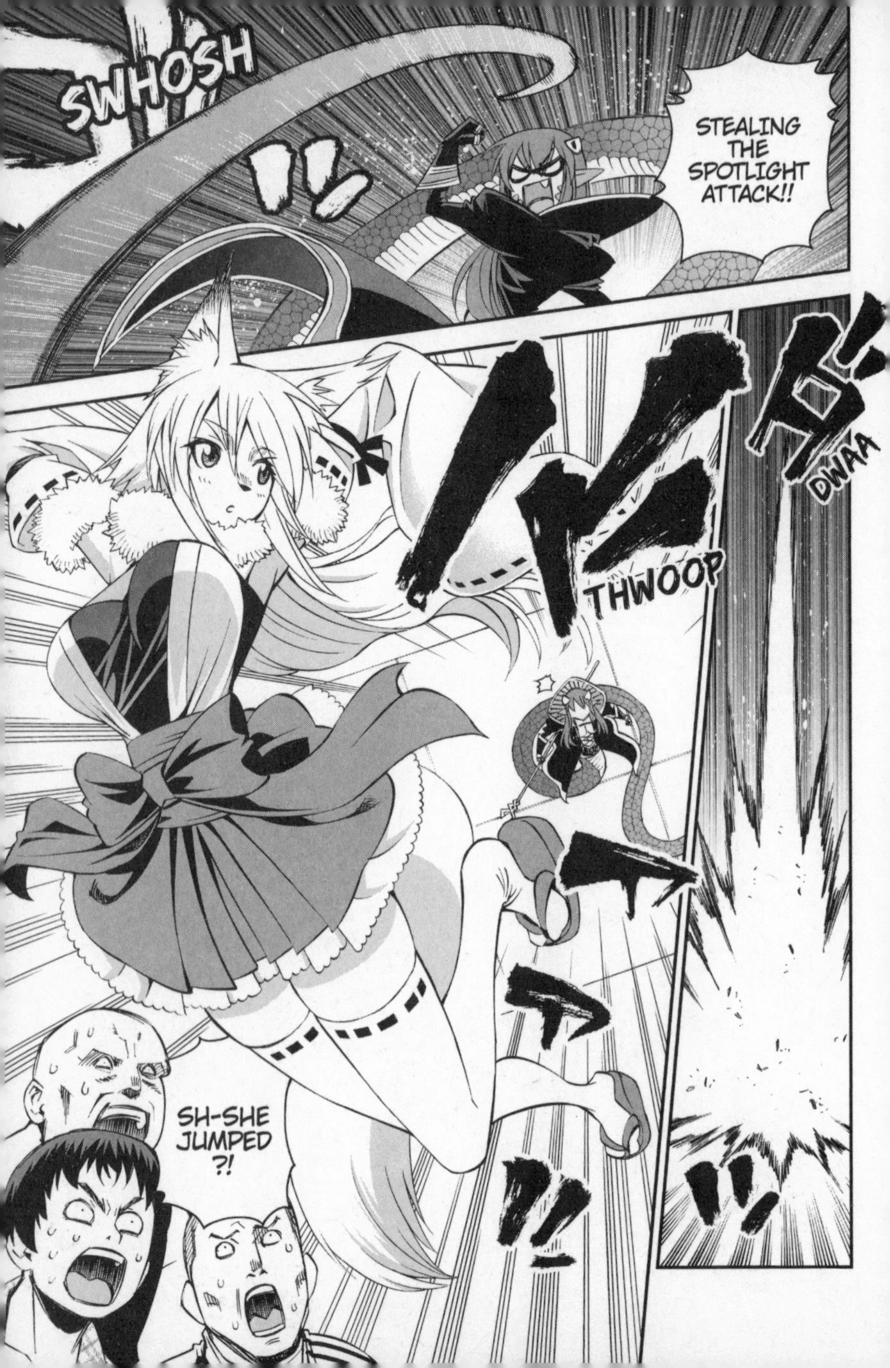
STEALING THE SPOTLIGHT ATTACK!!
SWHOSH
!!
DWAA
THWOOP
SH-SHE JUMPED ?!
!!
!!

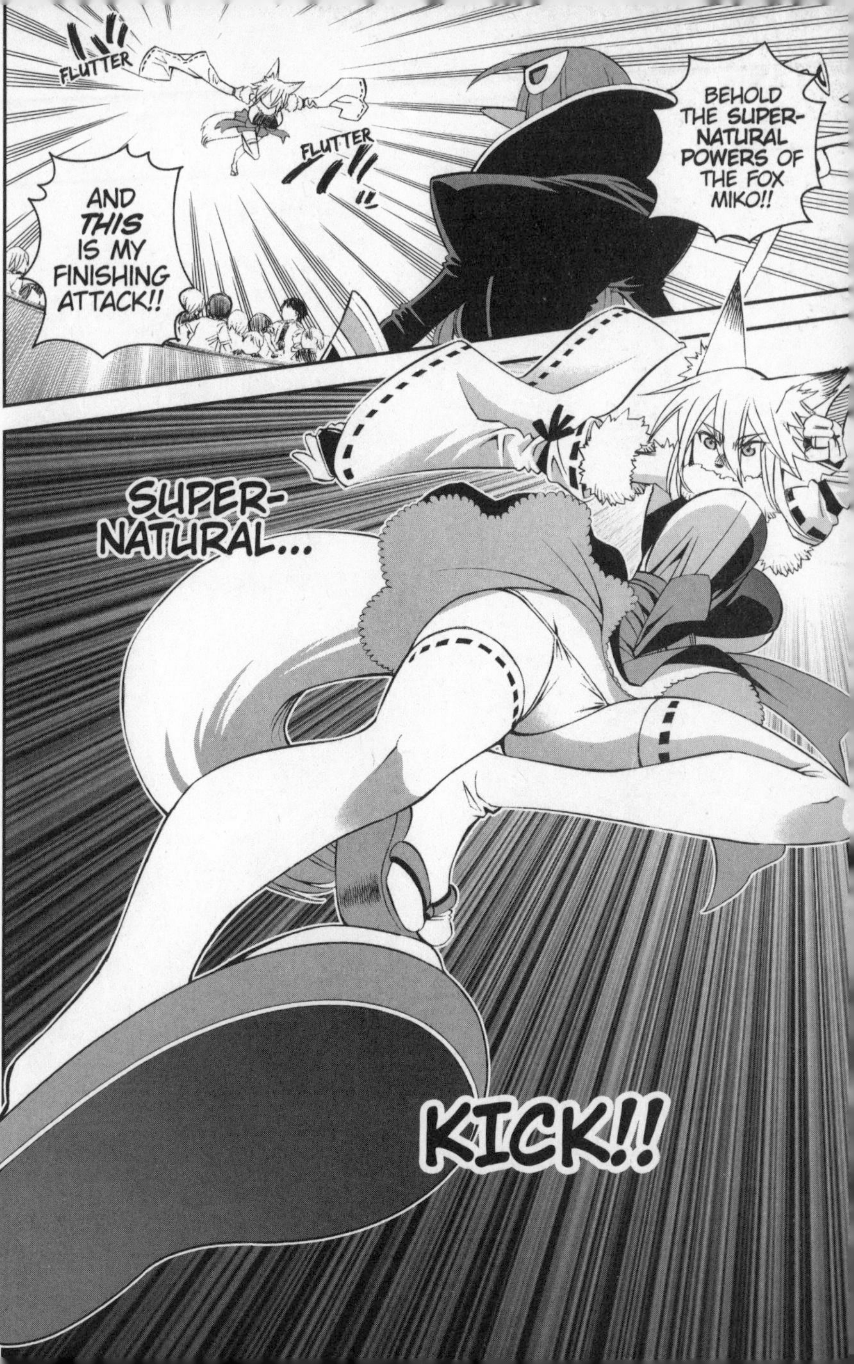
BEHOLD THE SUPER-NATURAL POWERS OF THE FOX MIKO!!
FLUTTER
FLUTTER
AND *THIS* IS MY FINISHING ATTACK!!
SUPER-NATURAL...
KICK!!

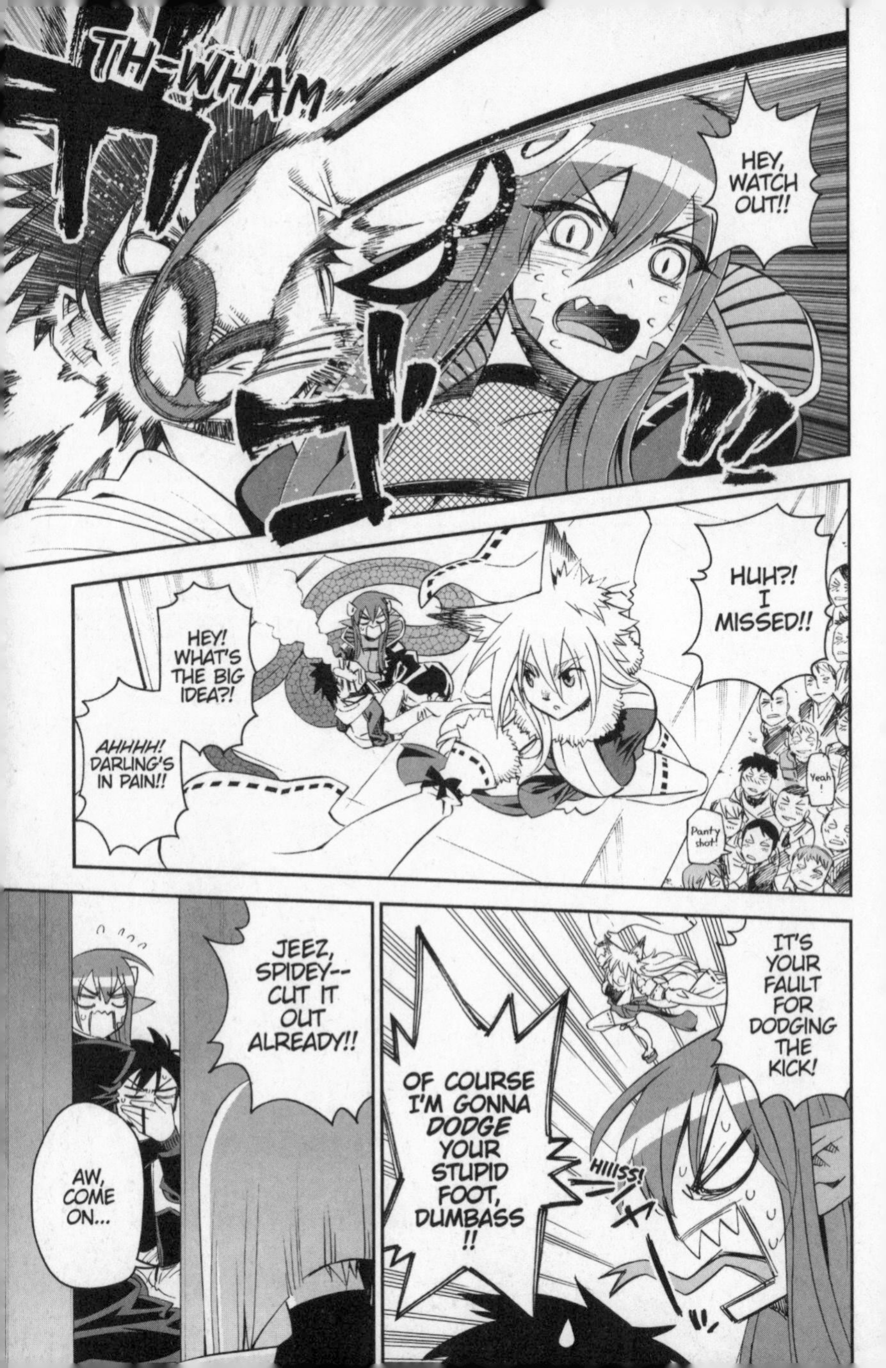
HEY, WATCH OUT!!
TH-WHAM
HUH?! I MISSED!!
Yeah!
Panty shot!
HEY! WHAT'S THE BIG IDEA?!
AHHHH! DARLING'S IN PAIN!!
IT'S YOUR FAULT FOR DODGING THE KICK!
OF COURSE I'M GONNA DODGE YOUR STUPID FOOT, DUMBASS!!
HIIISS!
JEEZ, SPIDEY-- CUT IT OUT ALREADY!!
AW, COME ON...

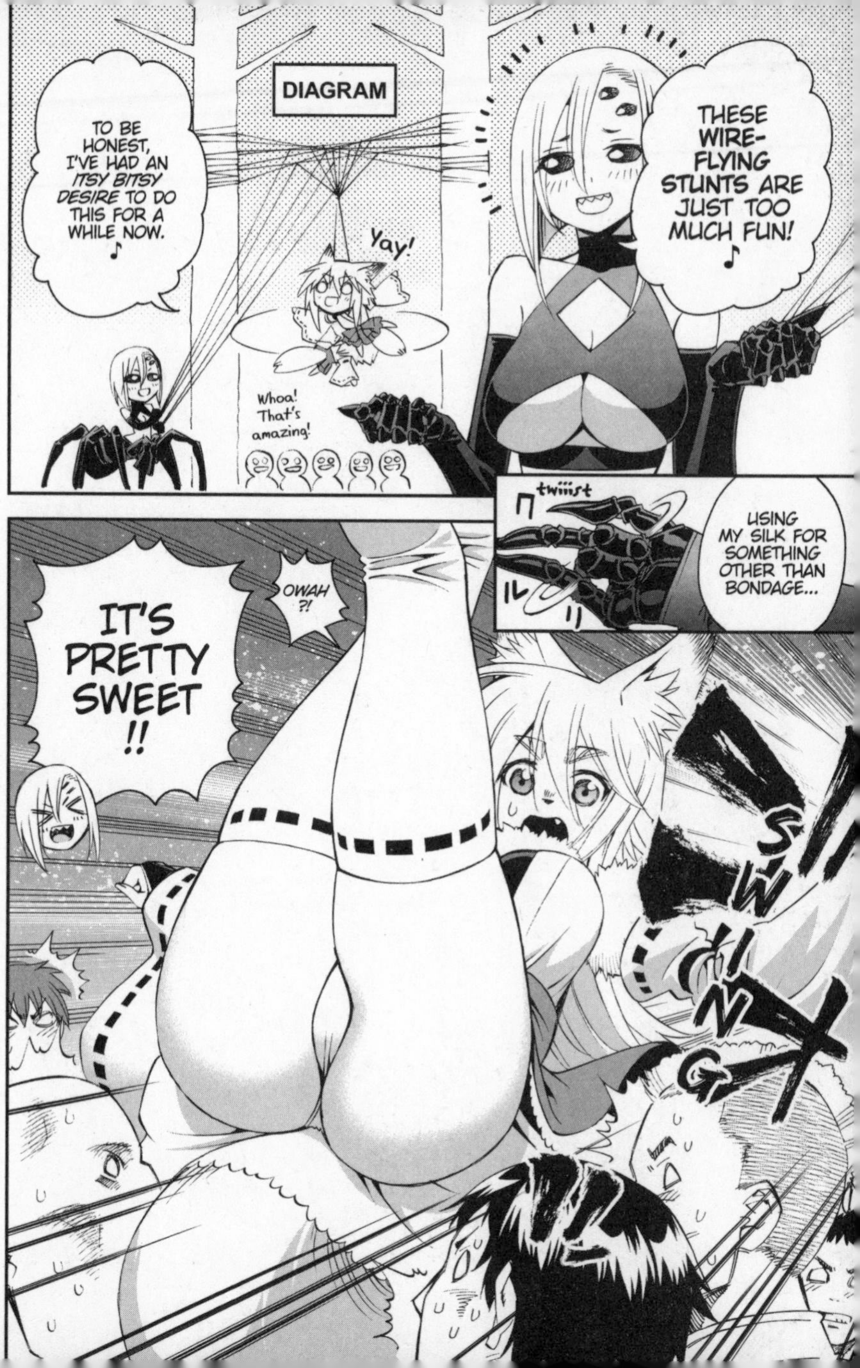
THESE WIRE-FLYING STUNTS ARE JUST TOO MUCH FUN! ♪
DIAGRAM
TO BE HONEST, I'VE HAD AN *ITSY BITSY DESIRE* TO DO THIS FOR A WHILE NOW. ♪
Yay!
Whoa! That's amazing!
twiiist
クルリ
USING MY SILK FOR SOMETHING OTHER THAN BONDAGE...
IT'S PRETTY SWEET !!
OWAH ?!
SWING

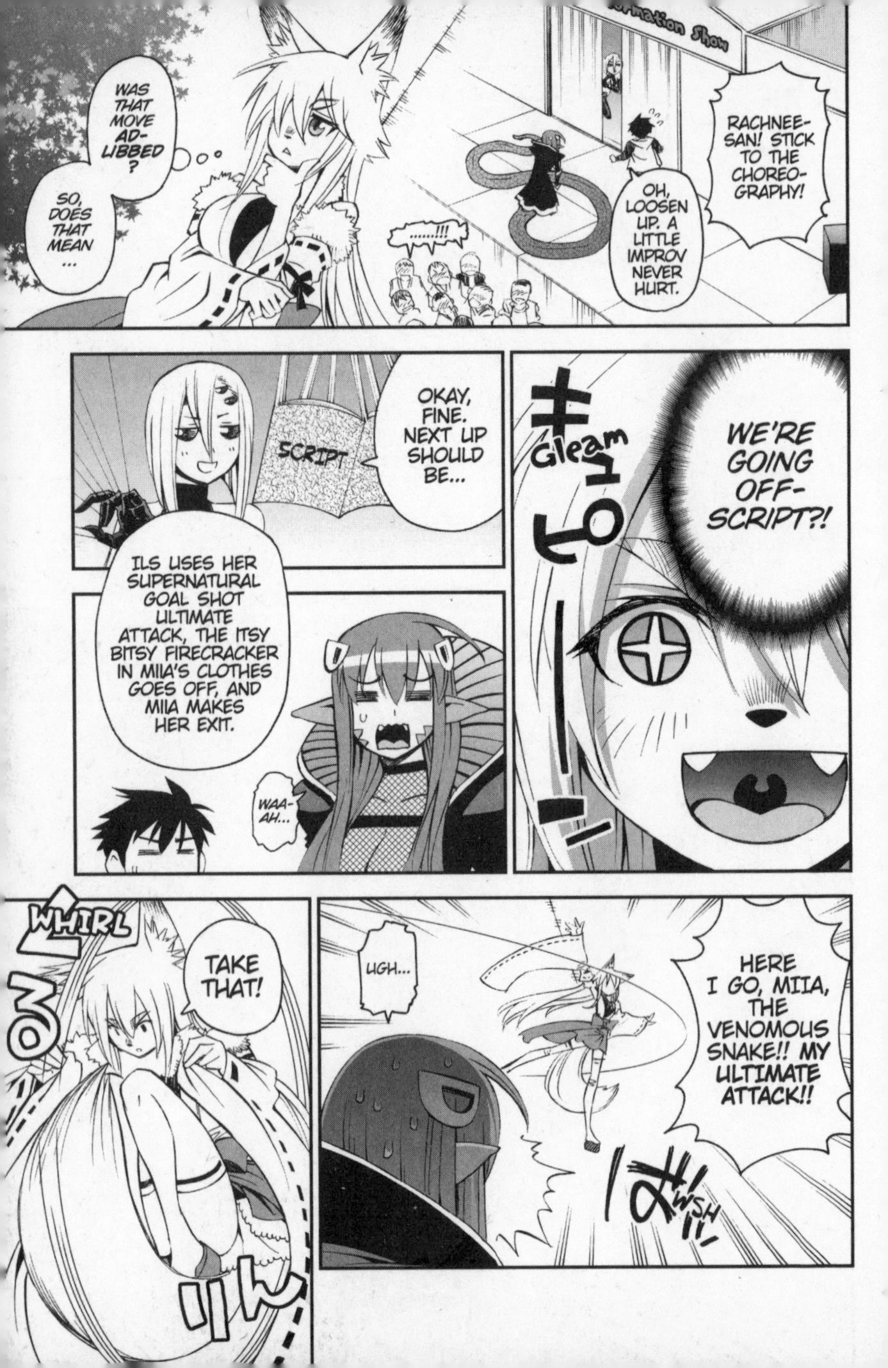
formation Show
RACHNEE-SAN! STICK TO THE CHOREOGRAPHY!
OH, LOOSEN UP. A LITTLE IMPROV NEVER HURT.
......!!!
WAS THAT MOVE AD-LIBBED?
SO, DOES THAT MEAN ...
Gleam
WE'RE GOING OFF-SCRIPT?!
OKAY, FINE. NEXT UP SHOULD BE...
SCRIPT
ILS USES HER SUPERNATURAL GOAL SHOT ULTIMATE ATTACK, THE ITSY BITSY FIRECRACKER IN MIIA'S CLOTHES GOES OFF, AND MIIA MAKES HER EXIT.
WAA-AH...
HERE I GO, MIIA, THE VENOMOUS SNAKE!! MY ULTIMATE ATTACK!!
UGH...
WSH
WHIRL
TAKE THAT!

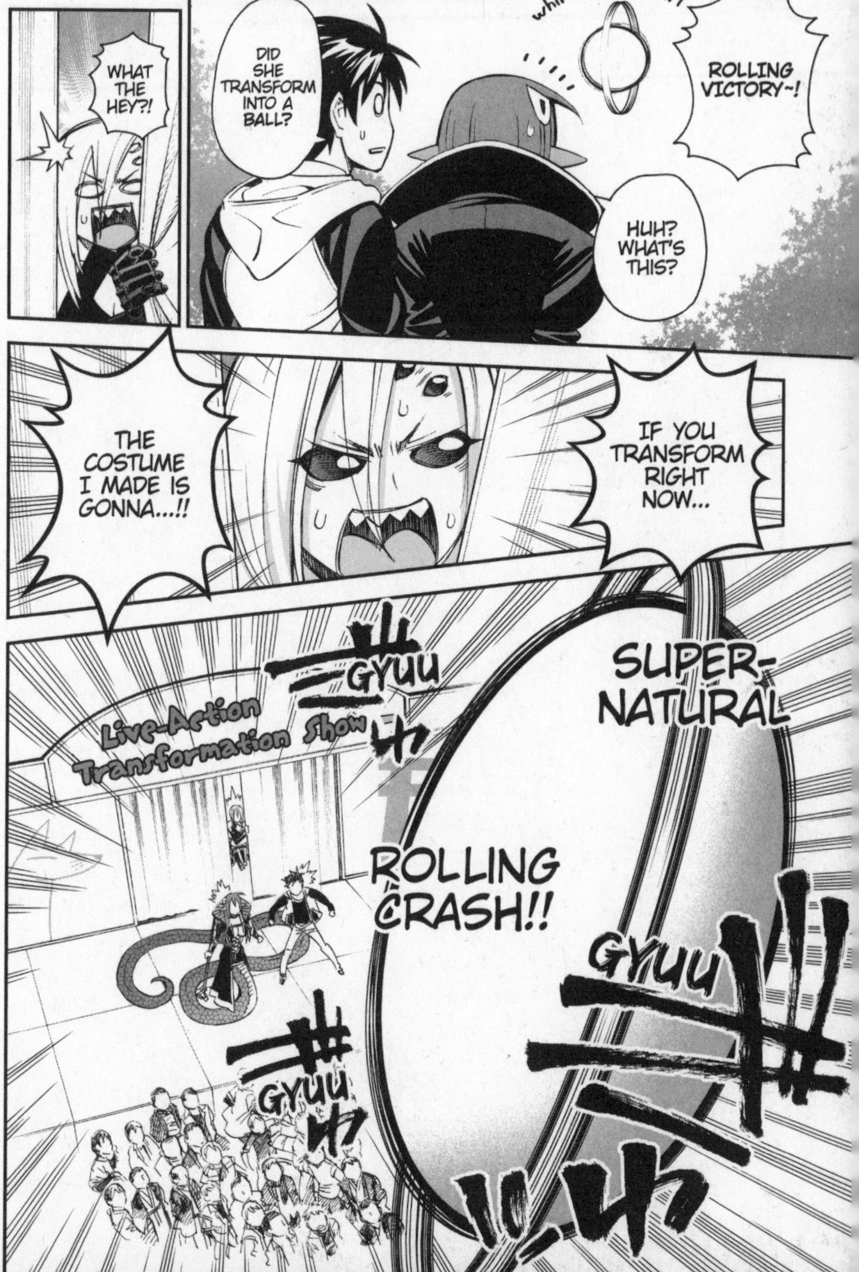
whirl whirl whiiirl
ROLLING VICTORY~!
HUH? WHAT'S THIS?
DID SHE TRANSFORM INTO A BALL?
WHAT THE HEY?!
IF YOU TRANSFORM RIGHT NOW...
THE COSTUME I MADE IS GONNA...!!
SUPER-NATURAL
ROLLING CRASH!!
GYUU
GYUU
Live-Action Transformation Show
GYUU

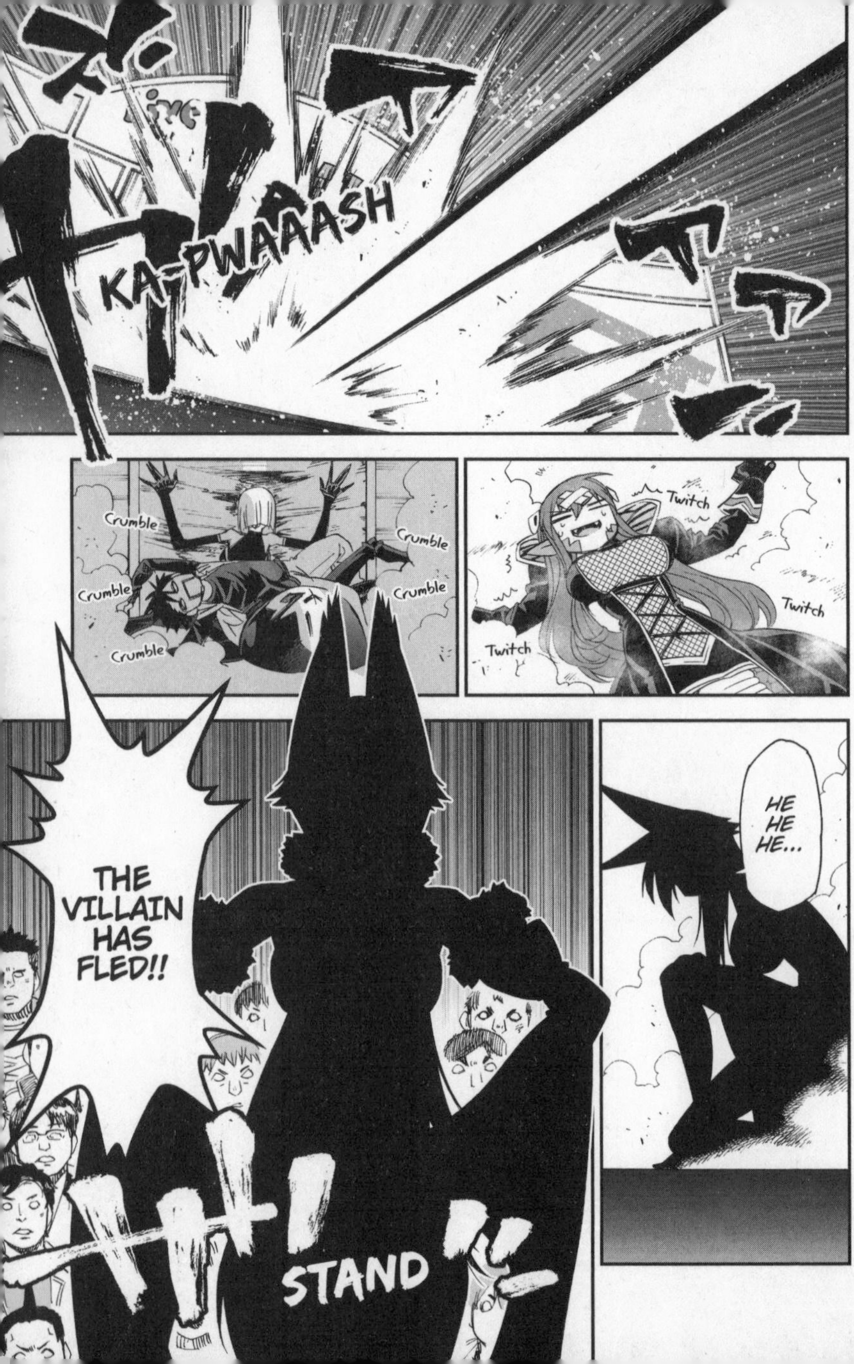
KA-PWAAASH
Twitch
Twitch
Twitch
Crumble
Crumble
Crumble
Crumble
Crumble
HE HE HE...
THE VILLAIN HAS FLED!!
STAND

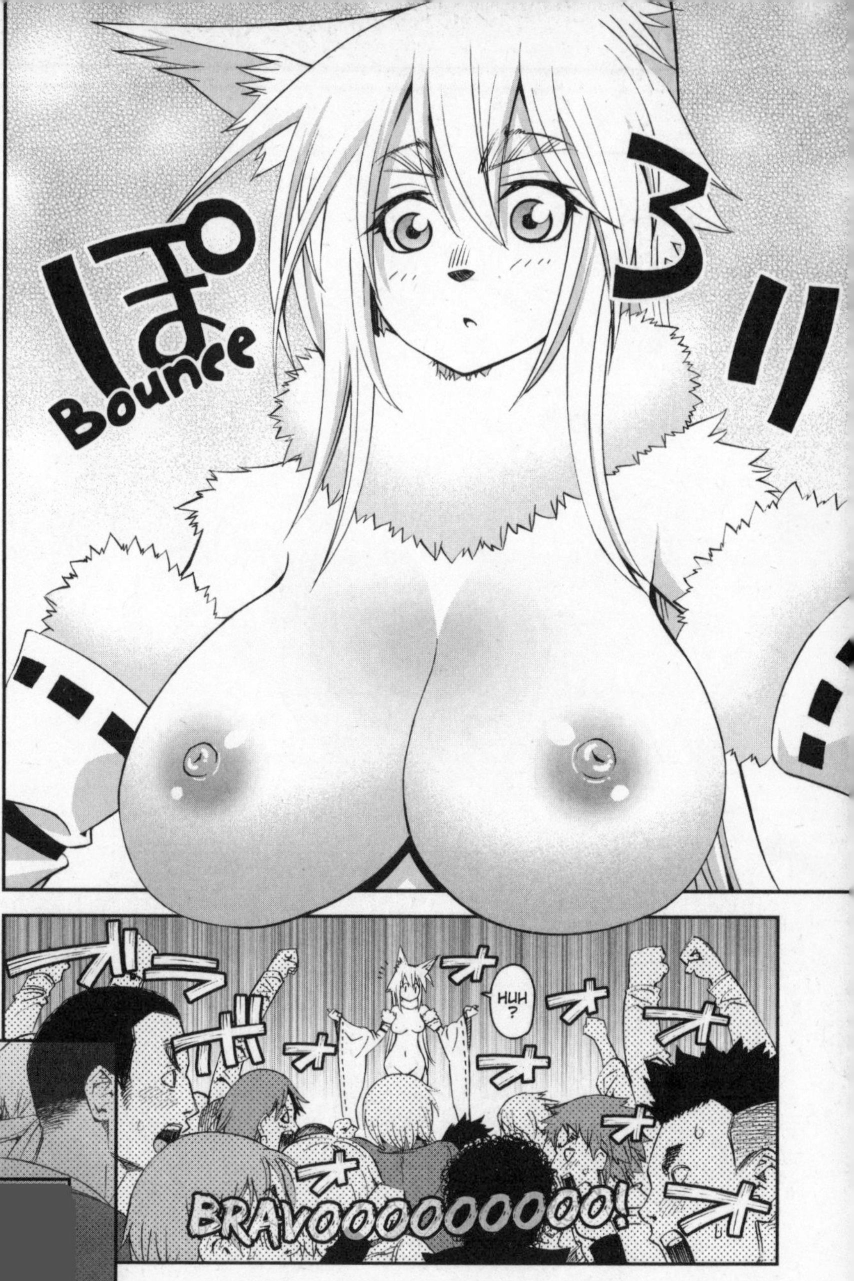
ぷる
Bounce
HUH?
BRAVOOOOOOOOOOO!

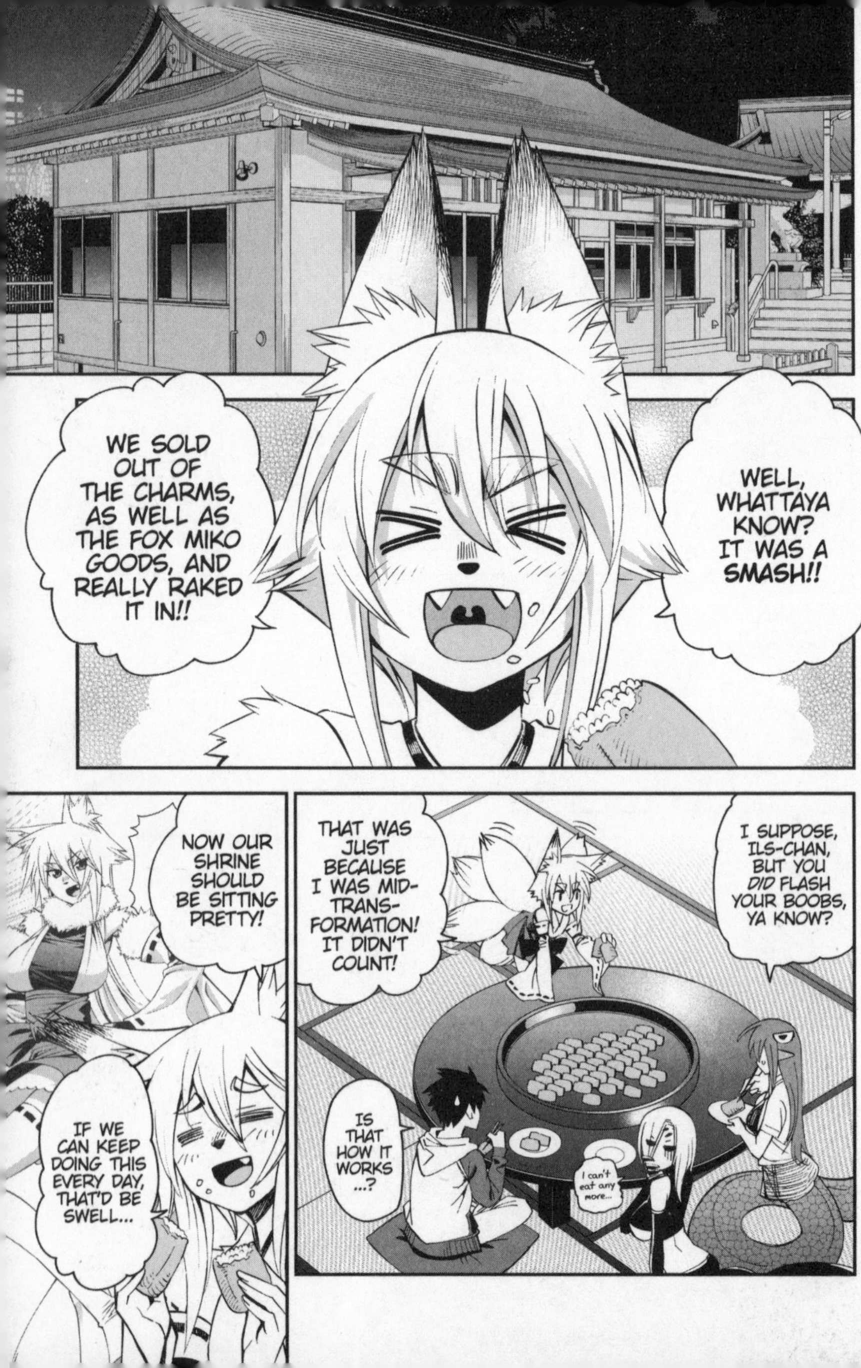
WELL, WHATTAYA KNOW? IT WAS A SMASH!!
WE SOLD OUT OF THE CHARMS, AS WELL AS THE FOX MIKO GOODS, AND REALLY RAKED IT IN!!
I SUPPOSE, ILS-CHAN, BUT YOU *DID* FLASH YOUR BOOBS, YA KNOW?
THAT WAS JUST BECAUSE I WAS MID-TRANSFORMATION! IT DIDN'T COUNT!
I can't eat any more...
IS THAT HOW IT WORKS ...?
NOW OUR SHRINE SHOULD BE SITTING PRETTY!
IF WE CAN KEEP DOING THIS EVERY DAY, THAT'D BE SWELL...

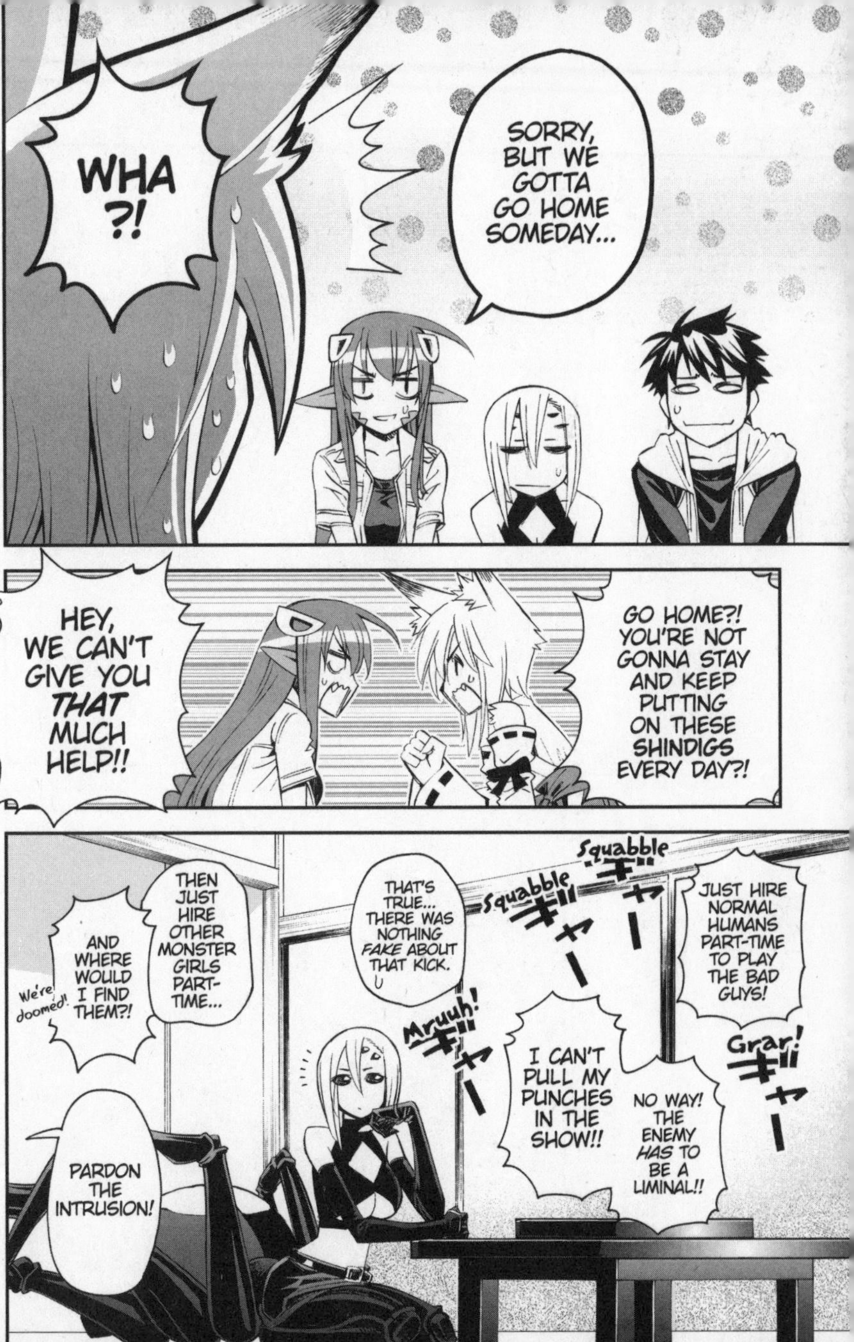
SORRY, BUT WE GOTTA GO HOME SOMEDAY...
WHA ?!
GO HOME?! YOU'RE NOT GONNA STAY AND KEEP PUTTING ON THESE SHINDIGS EVERY DAY?!
HEY, WE CAN'T GIVE YOU *THAT* MUCH HELP!!
JUST HIRE NORMAL HUMANS PART-TIME TO PLAY THE BAD GUYS!
Squabble
Squabble
THAT'S TRUE... THERE WAS NOTHING *FAKE* ABOUT THAT KICK.
THEN JUST HIRE OTHER MONSTER GIRLS PART-TIME...
AND WHERE WOULD I FIND THEM?!
We're doomed!
Grar!
NO WAY! THE ENEMY *HAS* TO BE A LIMINAL!!
I CAN'T PULL MY PUNCHES IN THE SHOW!!
Mruuh!
PARDON THE INTRUSION!

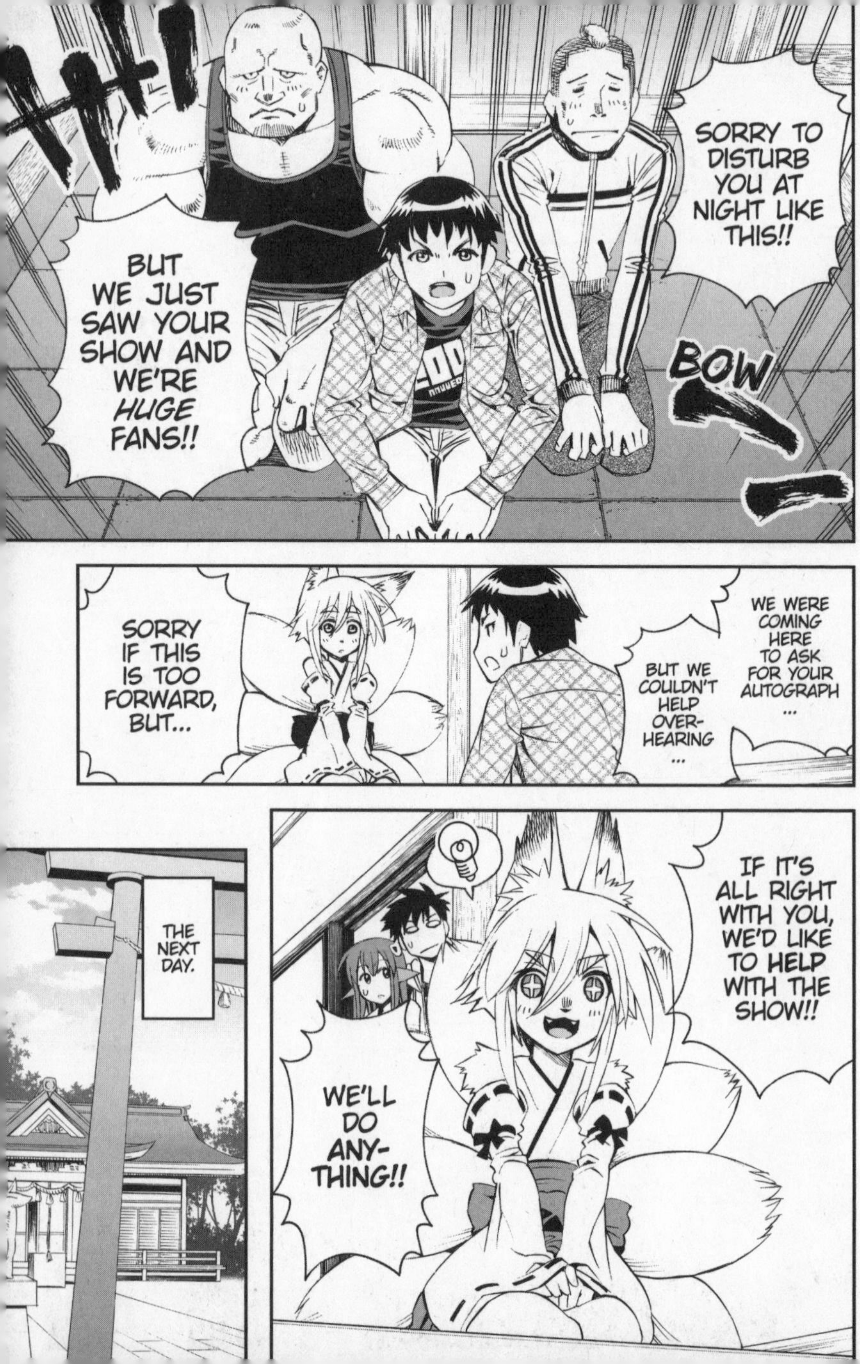
SORRY TO DISTURB YOU AT NIGHT LIKE THIS!!
BOW
BUT WE JUST SAW YOUR SHOW AND WE'RE *HUGE* FANS!!
WE WERE COMING HERE TO ASK FOR YOUR AUTOGRAPH ...
BUT WE COULDN'T HELP OVER-HEARING ...
SORRY IF THIS IS TOO FORWARD, BUT...
IF IT'S ALL RIGHT WITH YOU, WE'D LIKE TO HELP WITH THE SHOW!!
WE'LL DO ANY-THING!!
THE NEXT DAY.

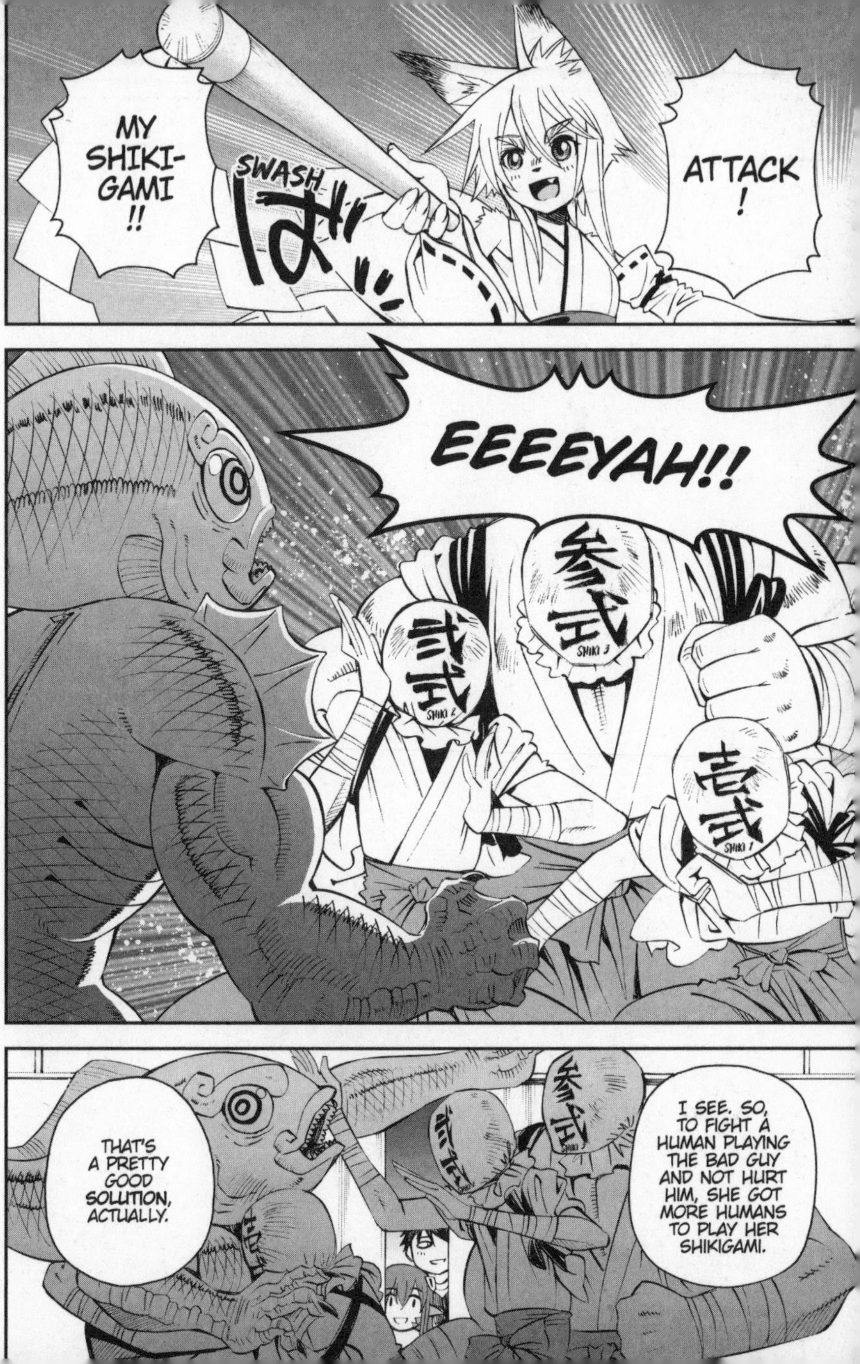
ATTACK!
MY SHIKIGAMI!!
SWASH
ば
EEEEYAH!!!
参式
SHIKI 3
弐式
SHIKI 2
壱式
SHIKI 1
I SEE. SO, TO FIGHT A HUMAN PLAYING THE BAD GUY AND NOT HURT HIM, SHE GOT MORE HUMANS TO PLAY HER SHIKIGAMI.
THAT'S A PRETTY GOOD SOLUTION, ACTUALLY.

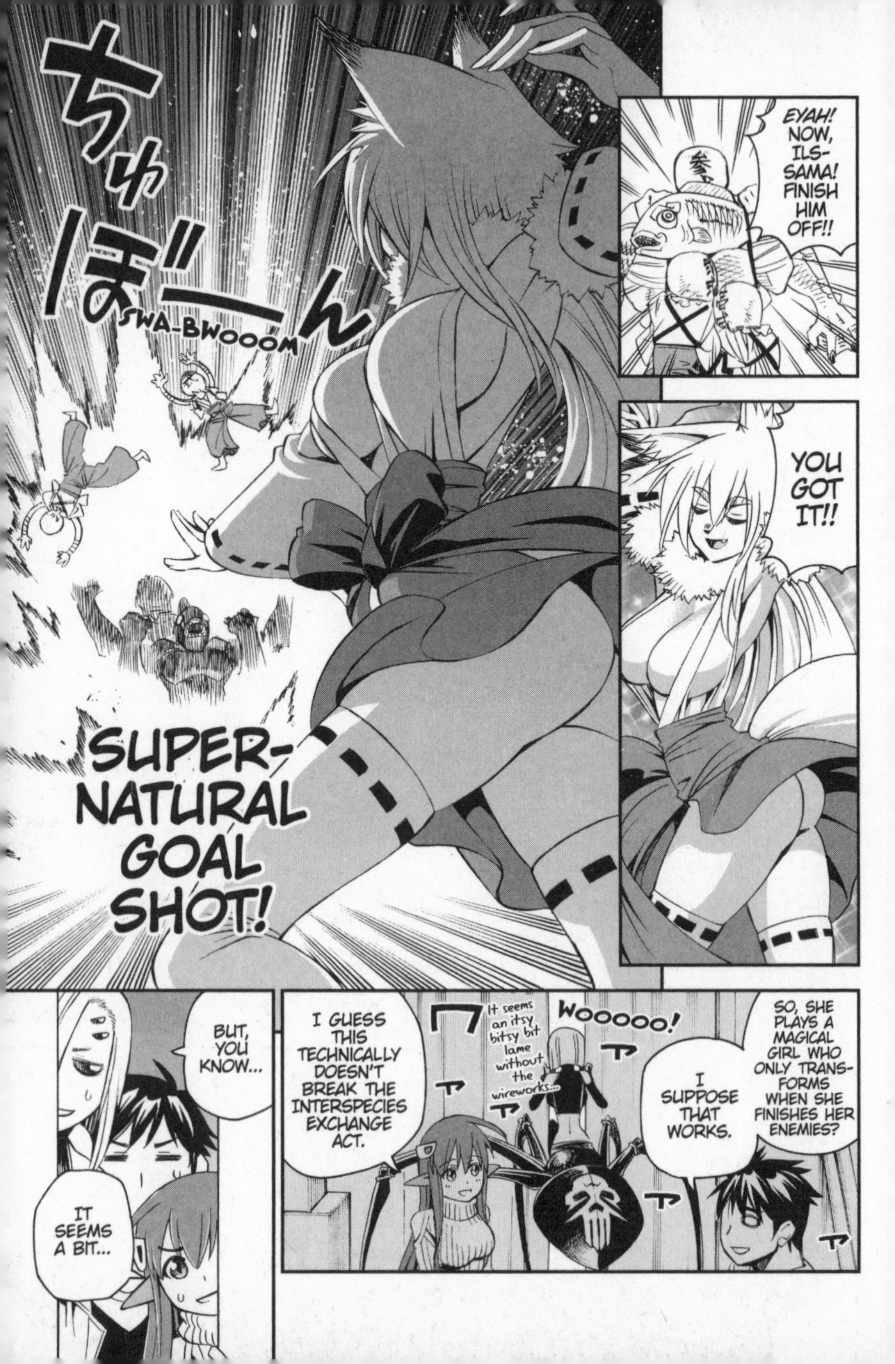
EYAH! NOW, ILS-SAMA! FINISH HIM OFF!!
YOU GOT IT!!
ちゅぽーん
SWA-BWOOOOM
SUPER-NATURAL GOAL SHOT!
SO, SHE PLAYS A MAGICAL GIRL WHO ONLY TRANS-FORMS WHEN SHE FINISHES HER ENEMIES?
I SUPPOSE THAT WORKS.
WOOOOO!
It seems an itsy bitsy bit lame without the wireworks...
I GUESS THIS TECHNICALLY DOESN'T BREAK THE INTERSPECIES EXCHANGE ACT.
BUT, YOU KNOW...
IT SEEMS A BIT...

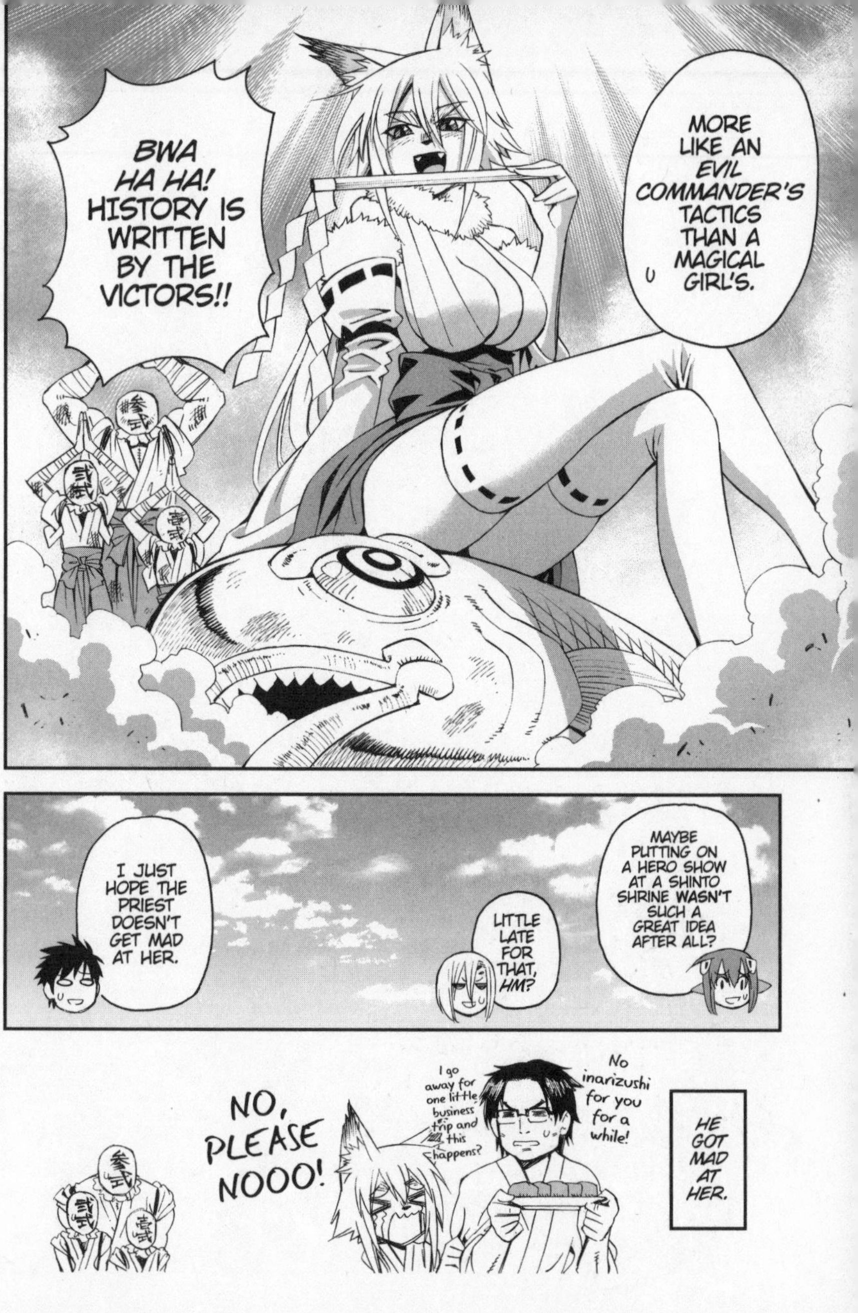
MORE LIKE AN EVIL COMMANDER'S TACTICS THAN A MAGICAL GIRL'S.
BWA HA HA! HISTORY IS WRITTEN BY THE VICTORS!!
MAYBE PUTTING ON A HERO SHOW AT A SHINTO SHRINE WASN'T SUCH A GREAT IDEA AFTER ALL?
LITTLE LATE FOR THAT, HM?
I JUST HOPE THE PRIEST DOESN'T GET MAD AT HER.
HE GOT MAD AT HER.
No inarizushi for you for a while!
I go away for one little business trip and this happens?
NO, PLEASE NOOO!

Monster Musume

Everyday Life with Monster Girls

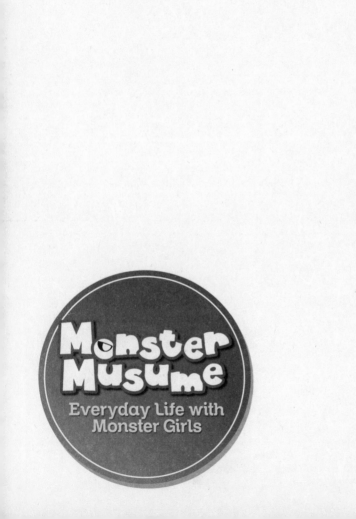

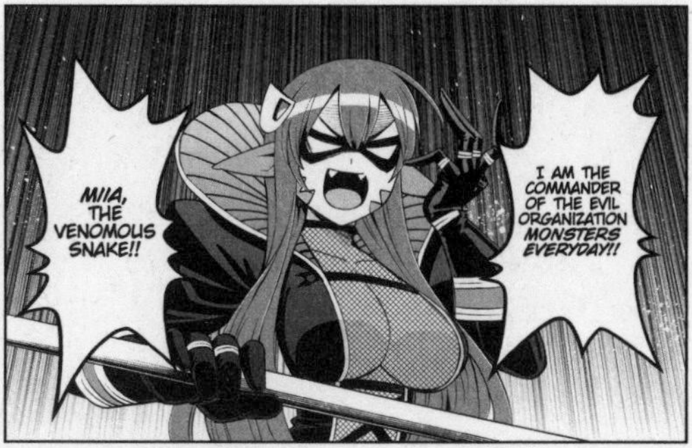
I AM THE COMMANDER OF THE EVIL ORGANIZATION *MONSTERS EVERYDAY!!*
MIIA, THE VENOMOUS SNAKE!!

Chapter 33

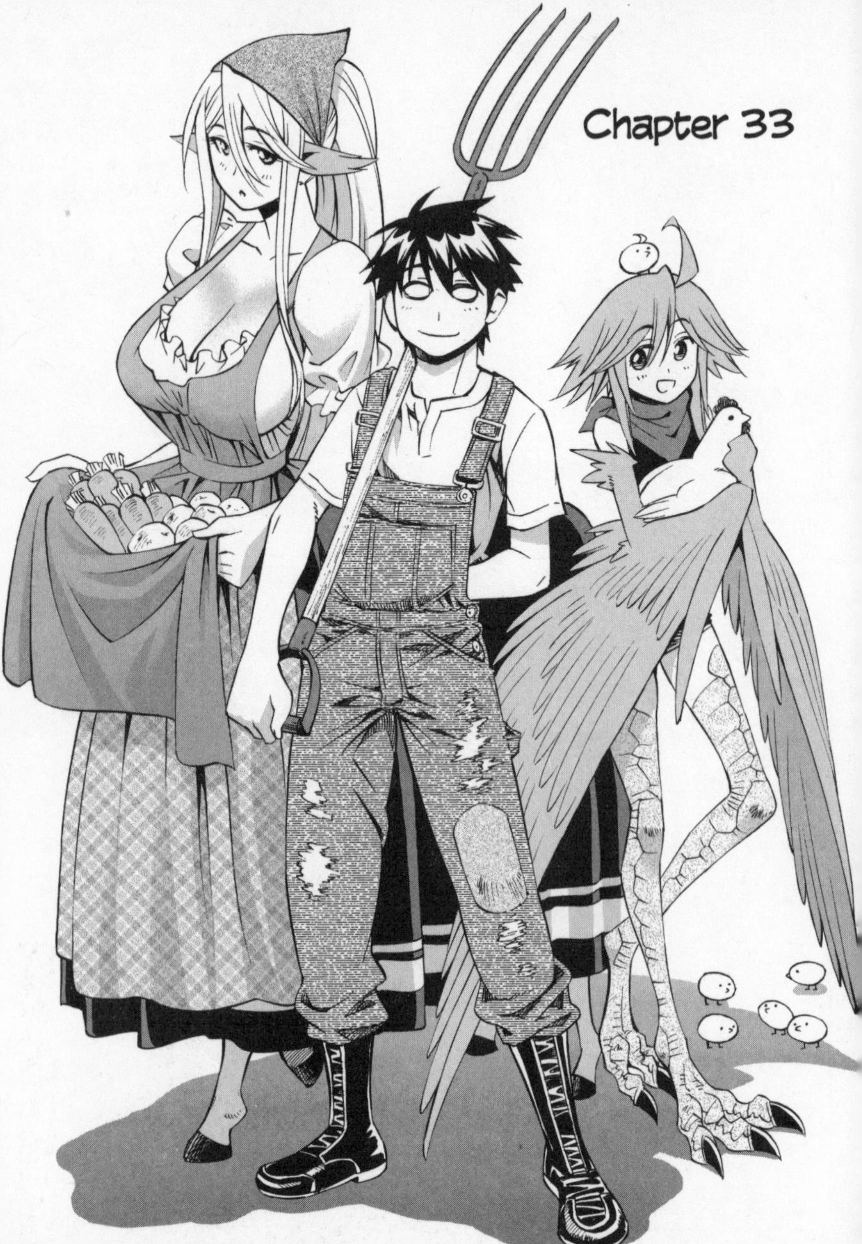

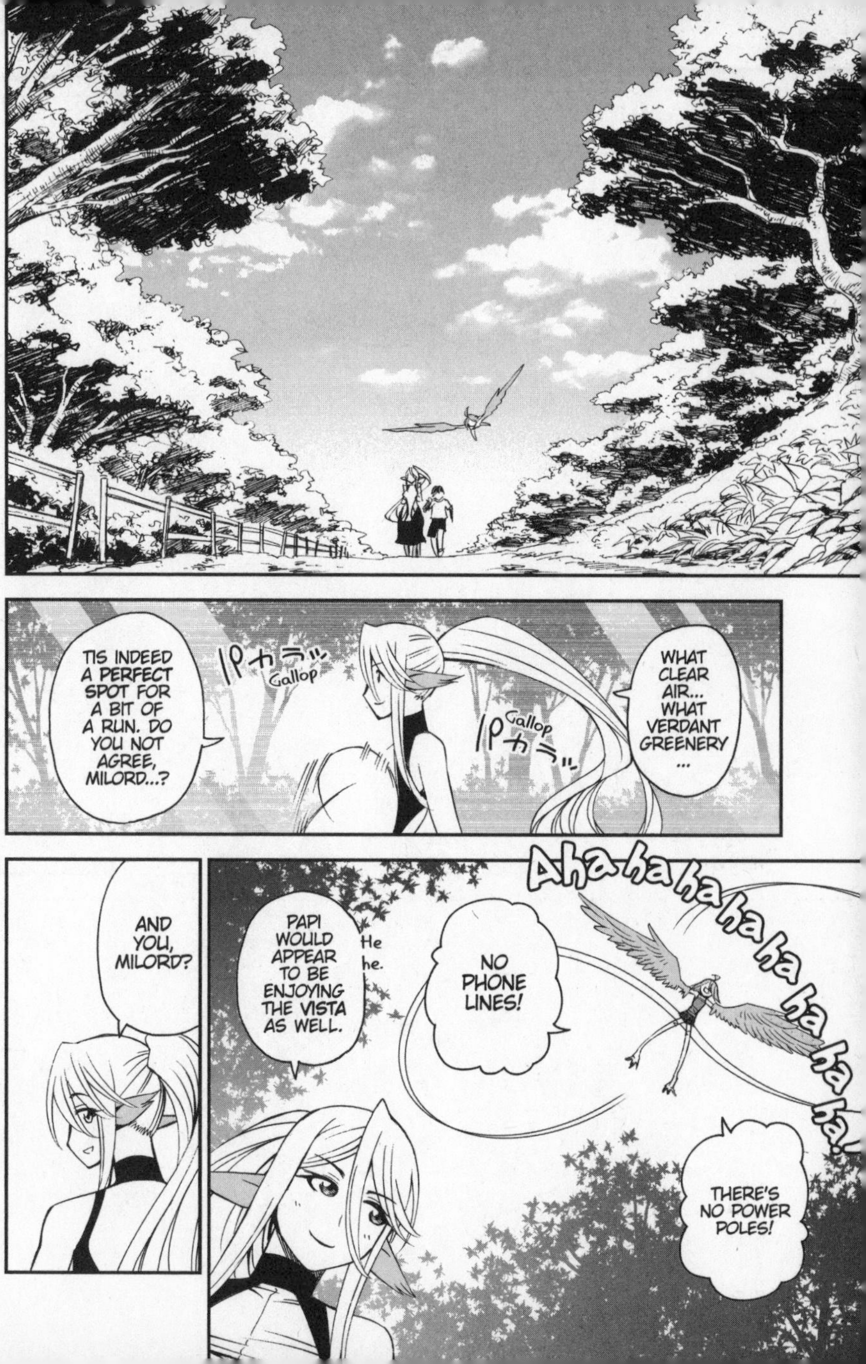
WHAT CLEAR AIR... WHAT VERDANT GREENERY ...
パカラッ Gallop
パカラッ Gallop
TIS INDEED A PERFECT SPOT FOR A BIT OF A RUN. DO YOU NOT AGREE, MILORD...?
Aha ha ha ha ha ha ha ha ha!
NO PHONE LINES!
THERE'S NO POWER POLES!
He he.
PAPI WOULD APPEAR TO BE ENJOYING THE VISTA AS WELL.
AND YOU, MILORD?

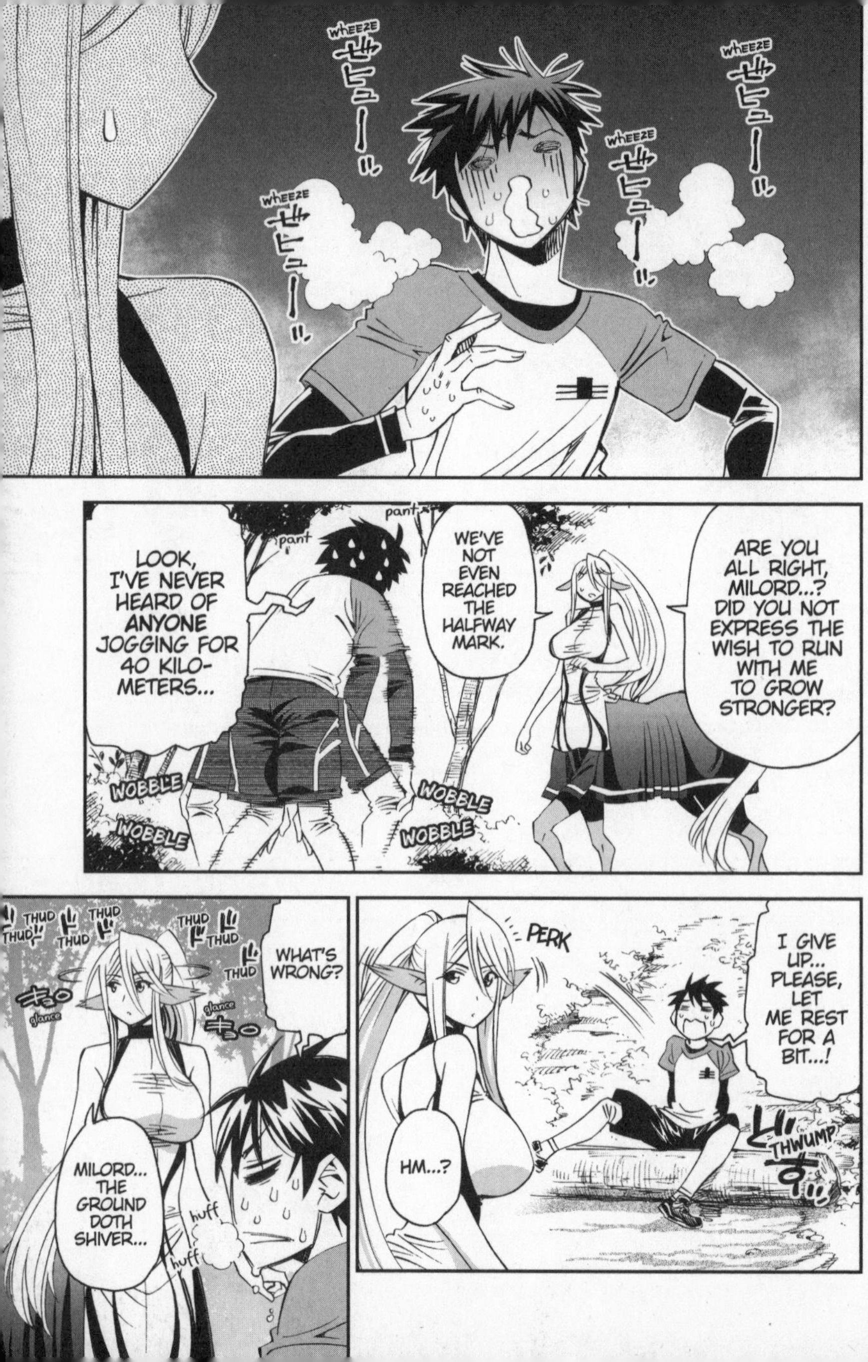
wheeze
wheeze
wheeze
wheeze
ARE YOU ALL RIGHT, MILORD...? DID YOU NOT EXPRESS THE WISH TO RUN WITH ME TO GROW STRONGER?
WE'VE NOT EVEN REACHED THE HALFWAY MARK.
pant
pant
LOOK, I'VE NEVER HEARD OF ANYONE JOGGING FOR 40 KILO-METERS...
WOBBLE
WOBBLE
WOBBLE
WOBBLE
I GIVE UP... PLEASE, LET ME REST FOR A BIT...!
THWUMP
PERK
HM...?
WHAT'S WRONG?
THUD
THUD
THUD
THUD
THUD
THUD
glance
glance
MILORD... THE GROUND DOTH SHIVER...
huff
huff

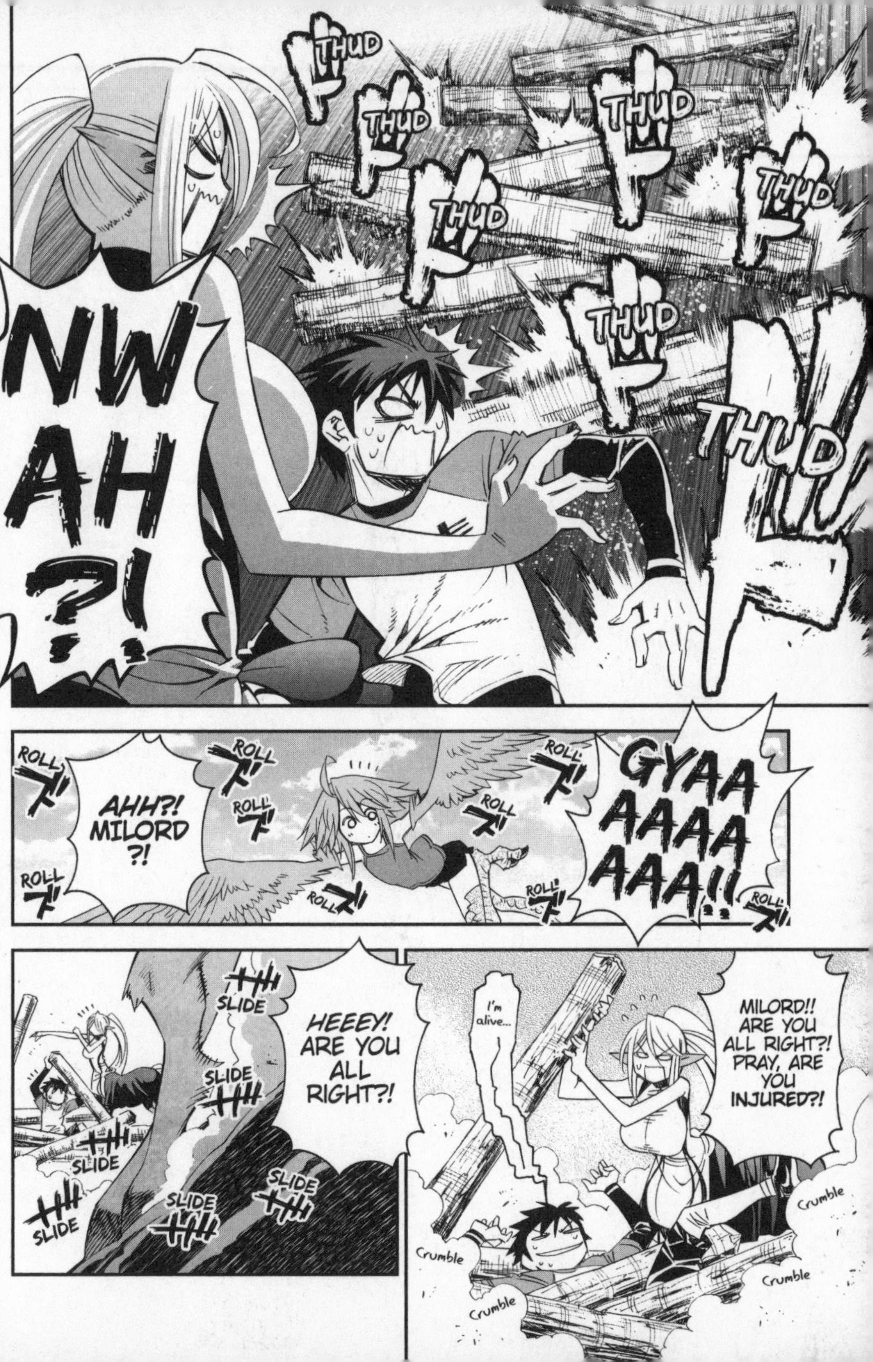
THUD
THUD
THUD
THUD
THUD
THUD
THUD
NWAH?!
GYAAAAAAAAA!!
ROLL
ROLL
ROLL
ROLL
ROLL
AHH?! MILORD?!
ROLL
ROLL
ROLL
MILORD!! ARE YOU ALL RIGHT?! PRAY, ARE YOU INJURED?!
I'm alive...
Crumble
Crumble
Crumble
Crumble
HEEEY! ARE YOU ALL RIGHT?!
SLIDE
SLIDE
SLIDE
SLIDE
SLIDE
SLIDE

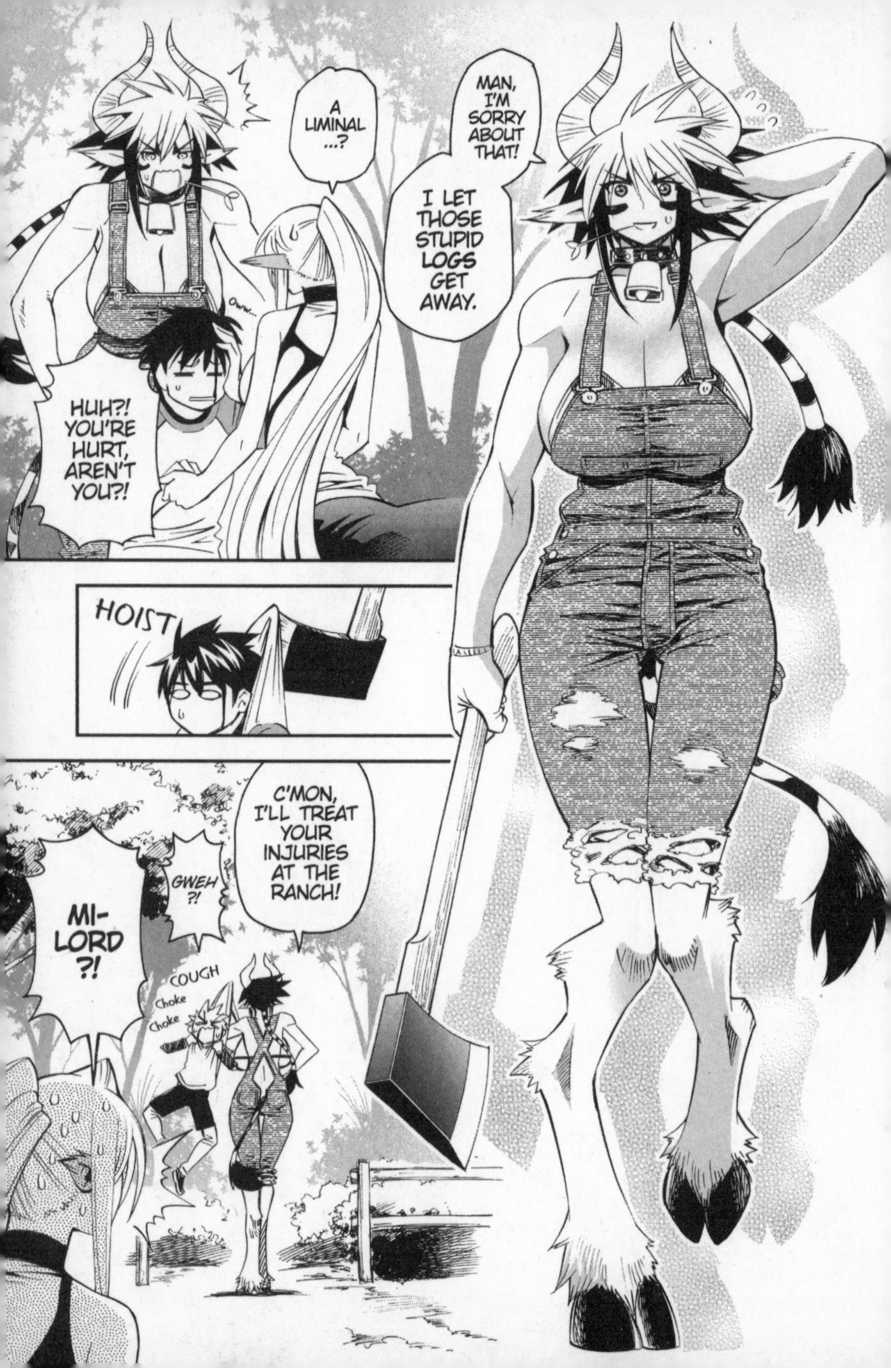
MAN, I'M SORRY ABOUT THAT!
I LET THOSE STUPID LOGS GET AWAY.
A LIMINAL ...?
Oww...
HUH?! YOU'RE HURT, AREN'T YOU?!
HOIST
C'MON, I'LL TREAT YOUR INJURIES AT THE RANCH!
GWEH ?!
MI-LORD ?!
COUGH
Choke
Choke

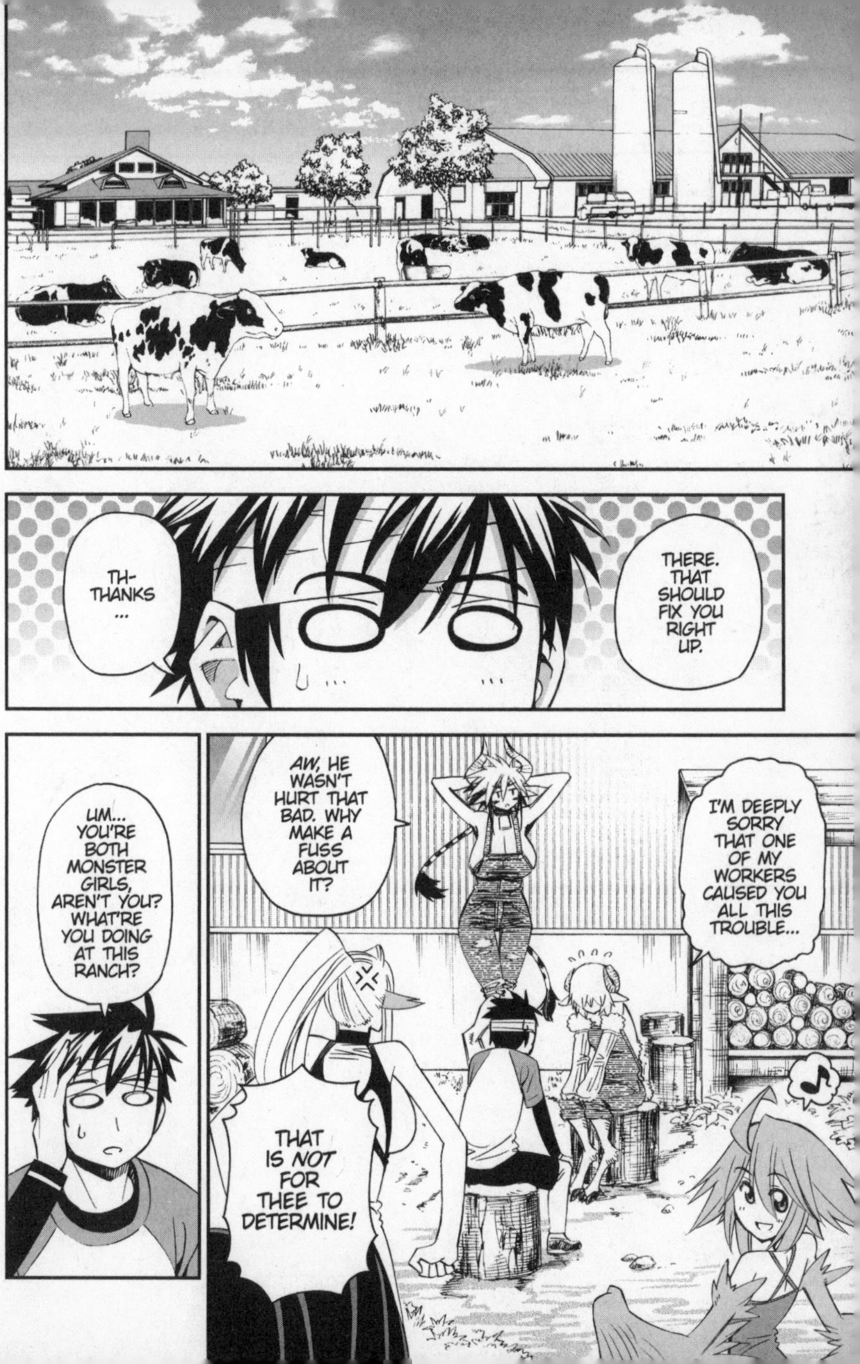
THERE. THAT SHOULD FIX YOU RIGHT UP.
TH-THANKS ...
I'M DEEPLY SORRY THAT ONE OF MY WORKERS CAUSED YOU ALL THIS TROUBLE...
AW, HE WASN'T HURT THAT BAD. WHY MAKE A FUSS ABOUT IT?
THAT IS *NOT* FOR THEE TO DETERMINE!
UM... YOU'RE BOTH MONSTER GIRLS, AREN'T YOU? WHAT'RE YOU DOING AT THIS RANCH?

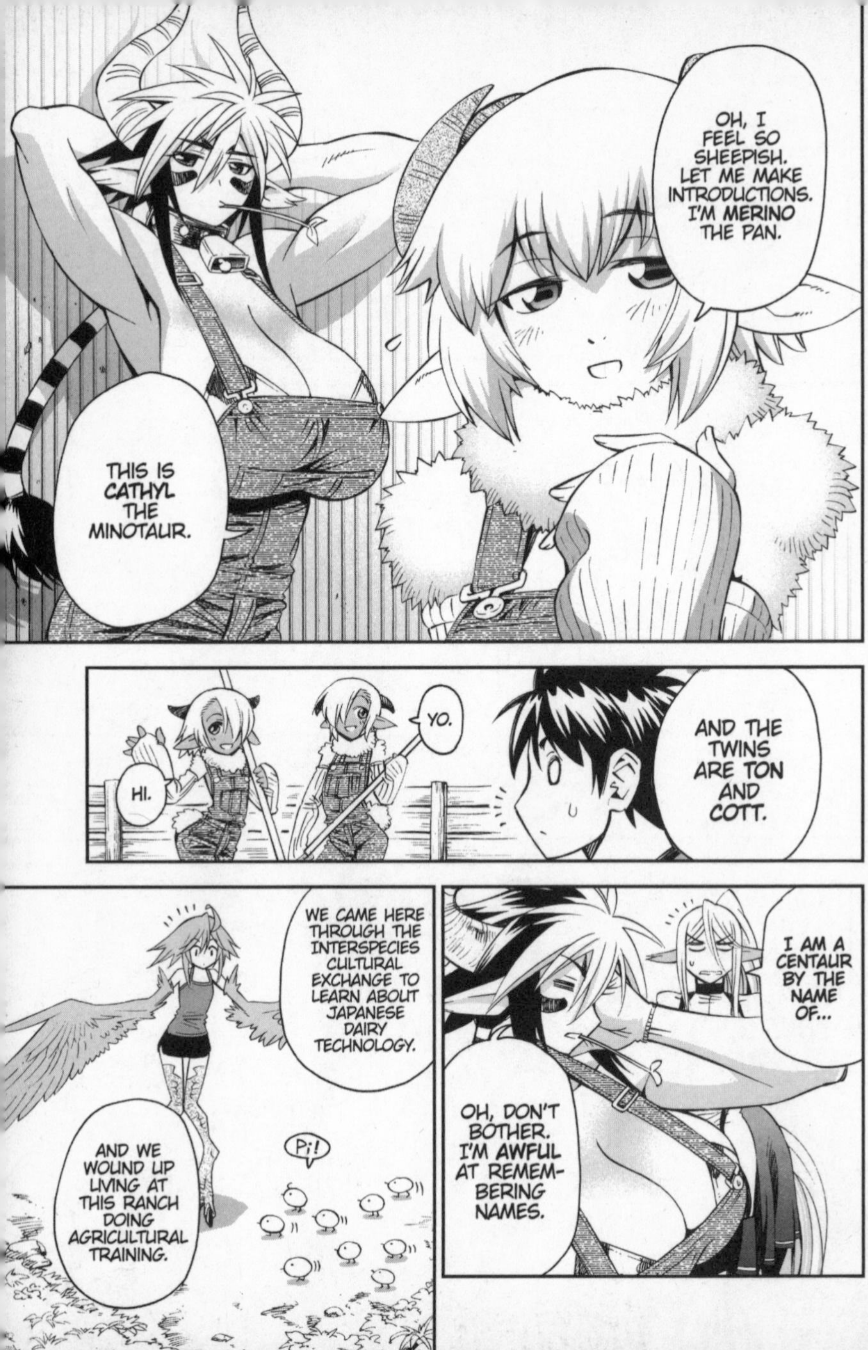
OH, I FEEL SO SHEEPISH. LET ME MAKE INTRODUCTIONS. I'M MERINO THE PAN.
THIS IS CATHYL THE MINOTAUR.
AND THE TWINS ARE TON AND COTT.
YO.
HI.
I AM A CENTAUR BY THE NAME OF...
OH, DON'T BOTHER. I'M AWFUL AT REMEMBERING NAMES.
WE CAME HERE THROUGH THE INTERSPECIES CULTURAL EXCHANGE TO LEARN ABOUT JAPANESE DAIRY TECHNOLOGY.
Pi!
AND WE WOUND UP LIVING AT THIS RANCH DOING AGRICULTURAL TRAINING.

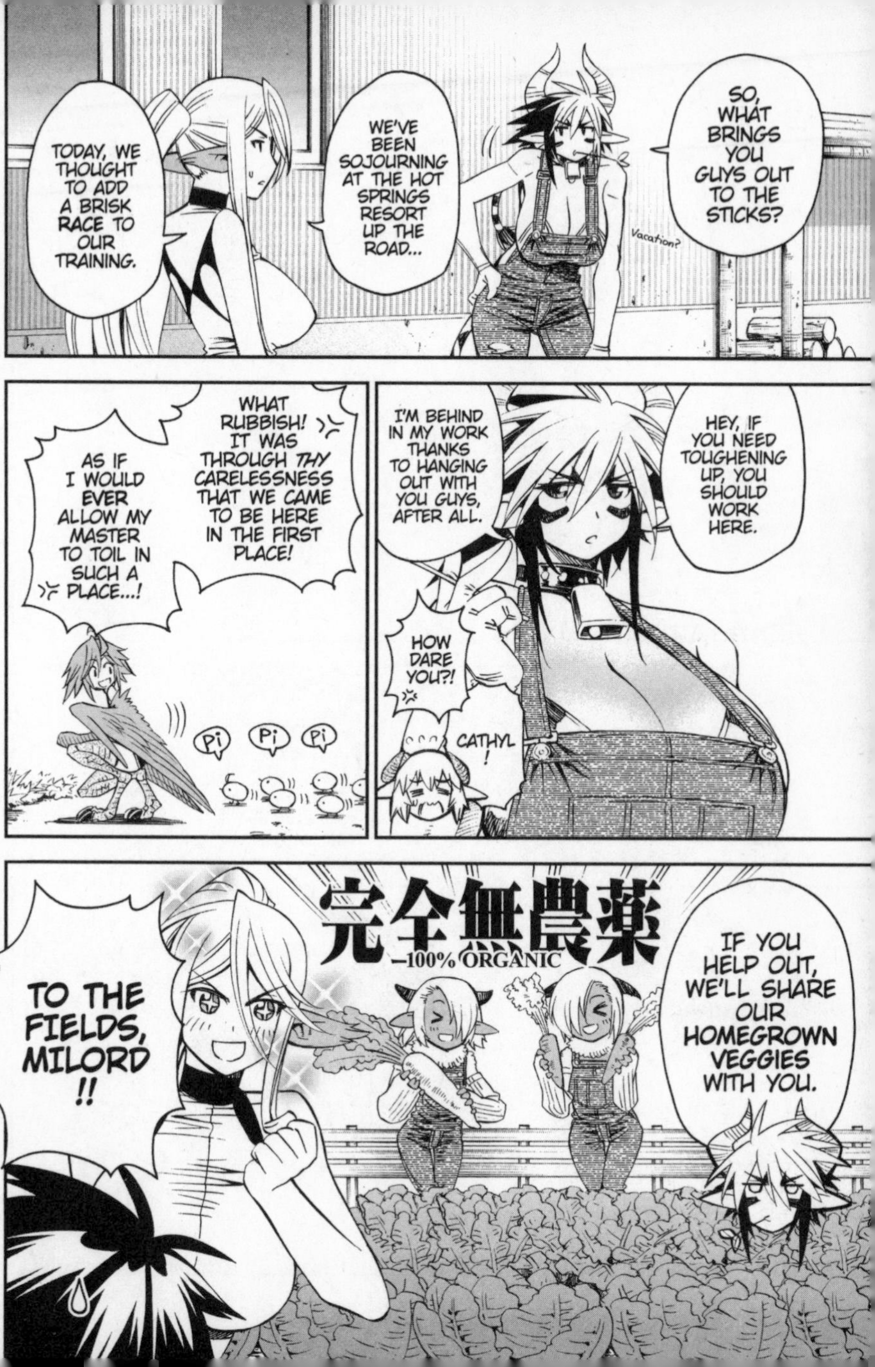

SO, WHAT BRINGS YOU GUYS OUT TO THE STICKS?
Vacation?
WE'VE BEEN SOJOURNING AT THE HOT SPRINGS RESORT UP THE ROAD...
TODAY, WE THOUGHT TO ADD A BRISK RACE TO OUR TRAINING.
HEY, IF YOU NEED TOUGHENING UP, YOU SHOULD WORK HERE.
I'M BEHIND IN MY WORK THANKS TO HANGING OUT WITH YOU GUYS, AFTER ALL.
HOW DARE YOU?!
CATHYL!
WHAT RUBBISH! IT WAS THROUGH *THY* CARELESSNESS THAT WE CAME TO BE HERE IN THE FIRST PLACE!
AS IF I WOULD EVER ALLOW MY MASTER TO TOIL IN SUCH A PLACE...!
Pi
Pi
Pi
IF YOU HELP OUT, WE'LL SHARE OUR HOMEGROWN VEGGIES WITH YOU.
完全無農薬
—100% ORGANIC
TO THE FIELDS, MILORD!!

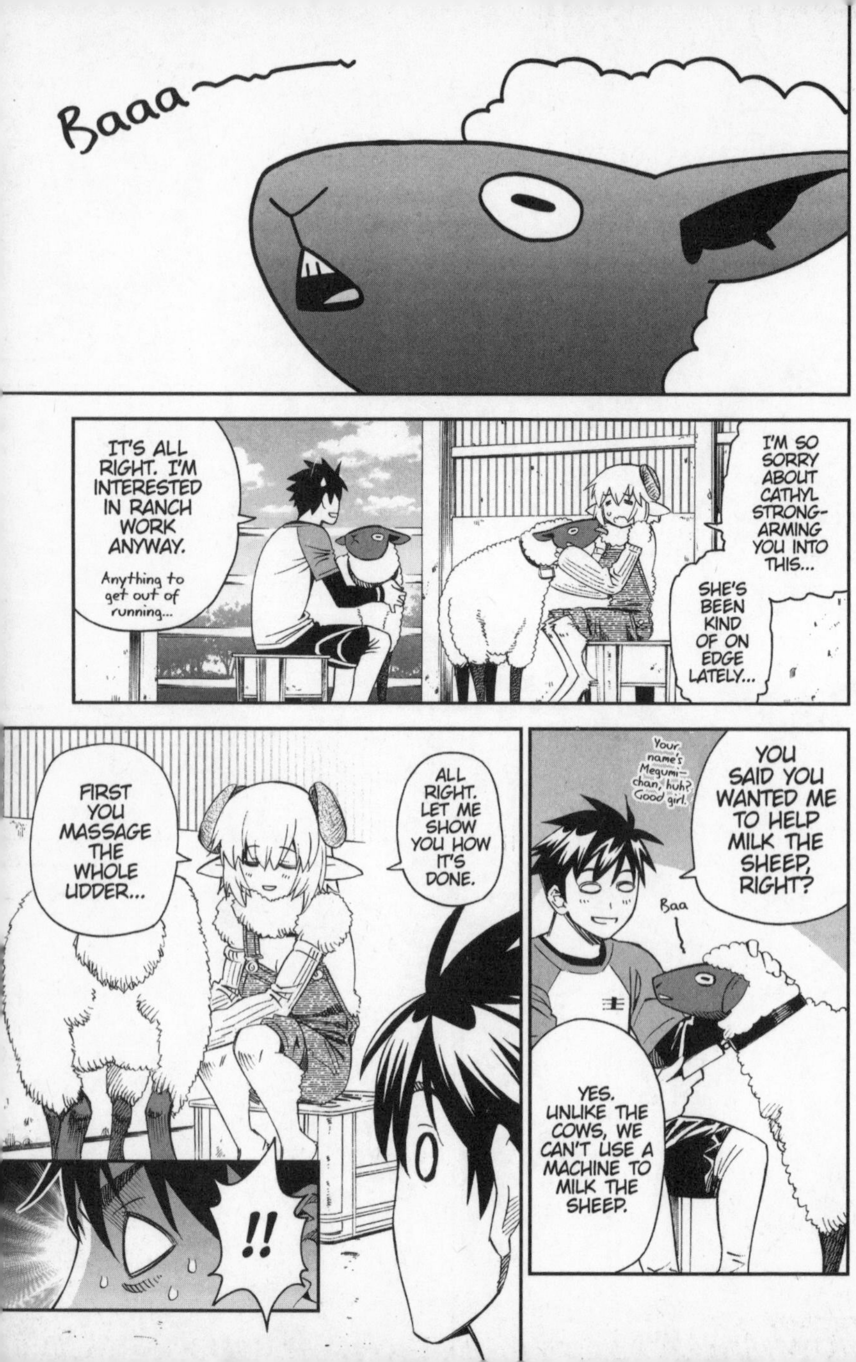
Baaa
I'M SO SORRY ABOUT CATHYL STRONG-ARMING YOU INTO THIS...
SHE'S BEEN KIND OF ON EDGE LATELY...
IT'S ALL RIGHT. I'M INTERESTED IN RANCH WORK ANYWAY.
Anything to get out of running...
YOU SAID YOU WANTED ME TO HELP MILK THE SHEEP, RIGHT?
Your name's Megumi-chan, huh? Good girl.
Baa
YES. UNLIKE THE COWS, WE CAN'T USE A MACHINE TO MILK THE SHEEP.
ALL RIGHT. LET ME SHOW YOU HOW IT'S DONE.
FIRST YOU MASSAGE THE WHOLE UDDER...
!!

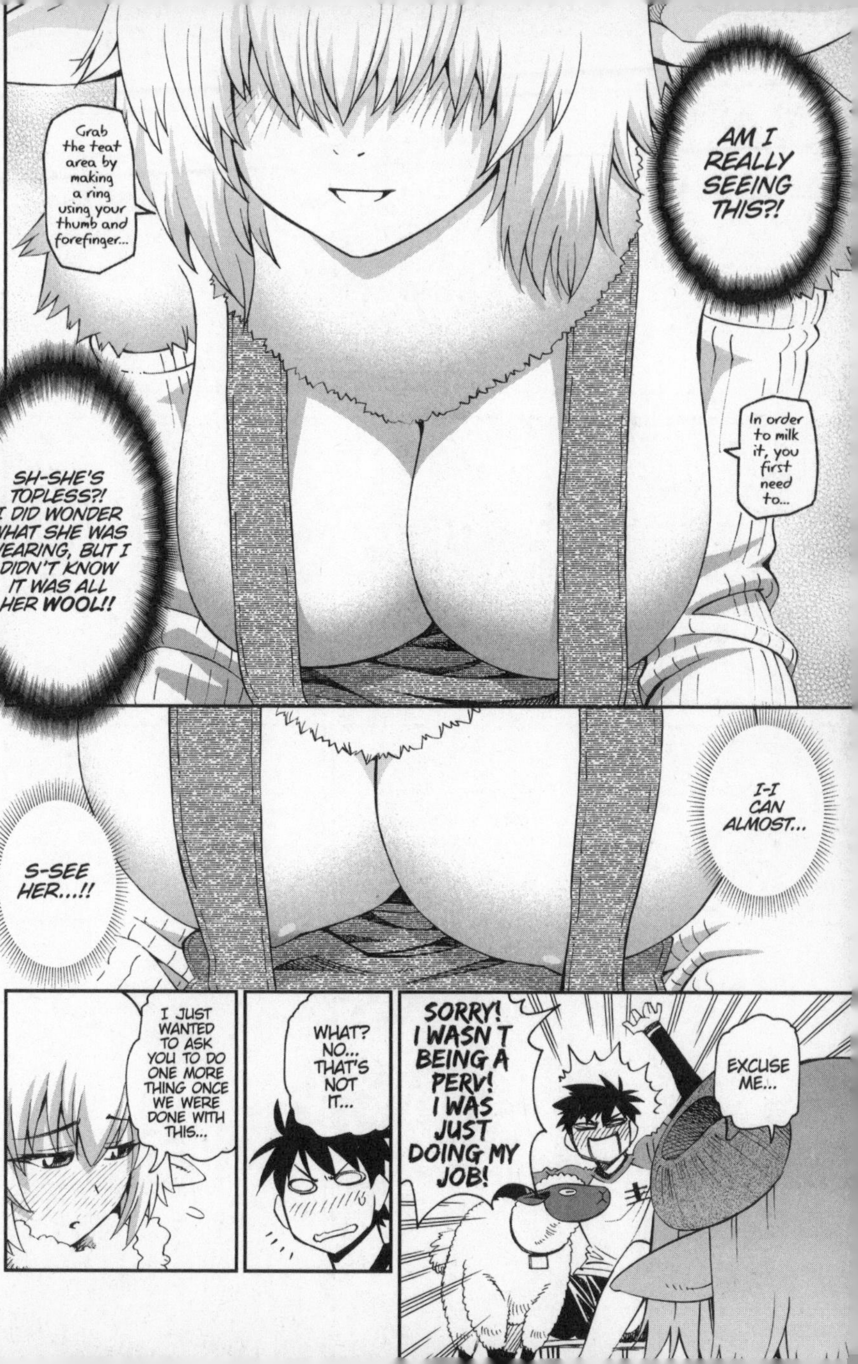
AM I REALLY SEEING THIS?!
Grab the teat area by making a ring using your thumb and forefinger...
In order to milk it, you first need to...
SH-SHE'S TOPLESS?! I DID WONDER WHAT SHE WAS WEARING, BUT I DIDN'T KNOW IT WAS ALL HER WOOL!!
I-I CAN ALMOST...
S-SEE HER...!!
EXCUSE ME...
SORRY! I WASN T BEING A PERV! I WAS JUST DOING MY JOB!
WHAT? NO... THAT'S NOT IT...
I JUST WANTED TO ASK YOU TO DO ONE MORE THING ONCE WE WERE DONE WITH THIS...

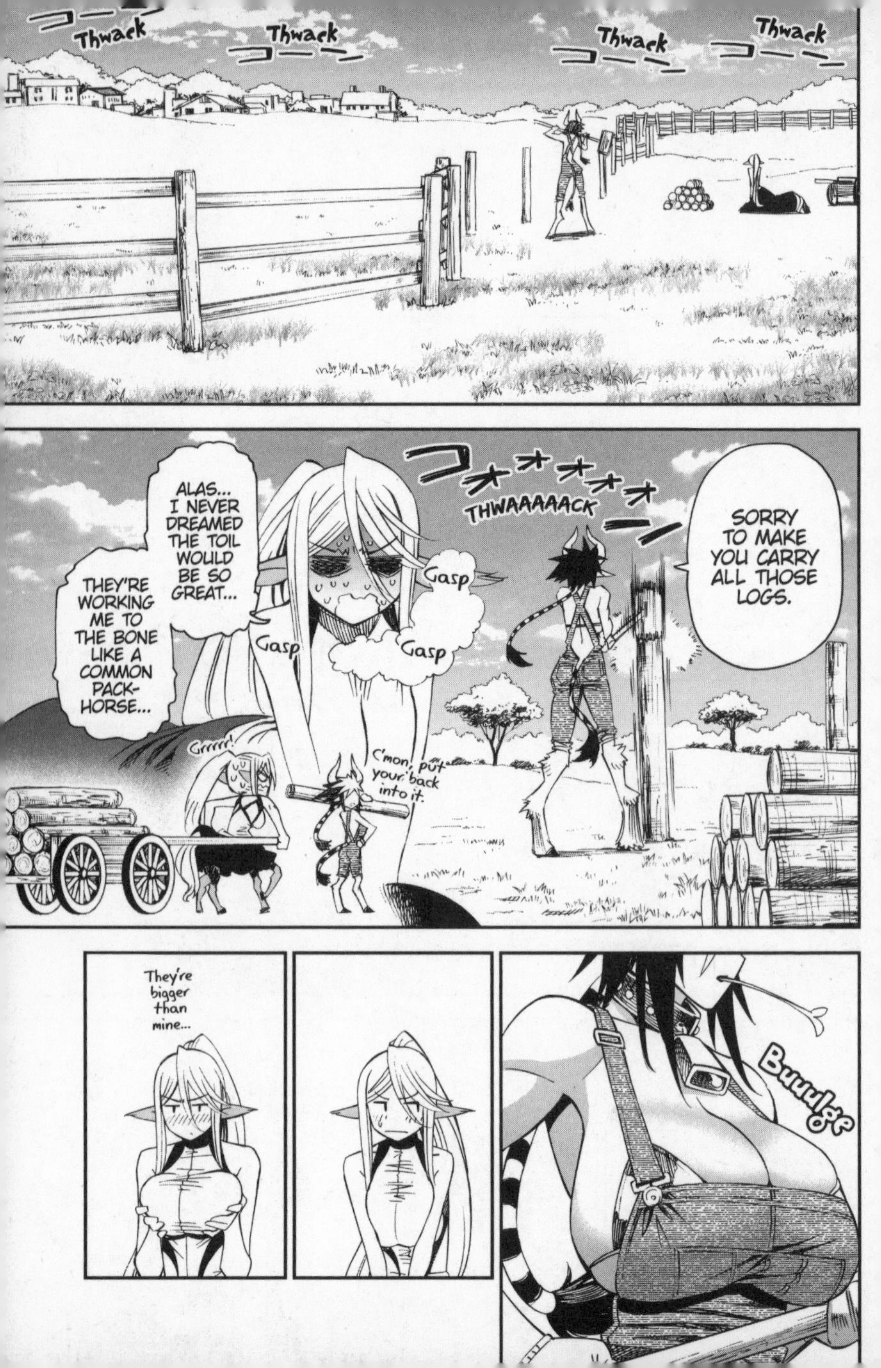
Thwack
Thwack
Thwack
Thwack
SORRY TO MAKE YOU CARRY ALL THOSE LOGS.
THWAAAAACK
ALAS... I NEVER DREAMED THE TOIL WOULD BE SO GREAT...
THEY'RE WORKING ME TO THE BONE LIKE A COMMON PACK-HORSE...
Gasp
Gasp
Gasp
C'mon, put your back into it.
Grrrrr!
Buuulge
They're bigger than mine...

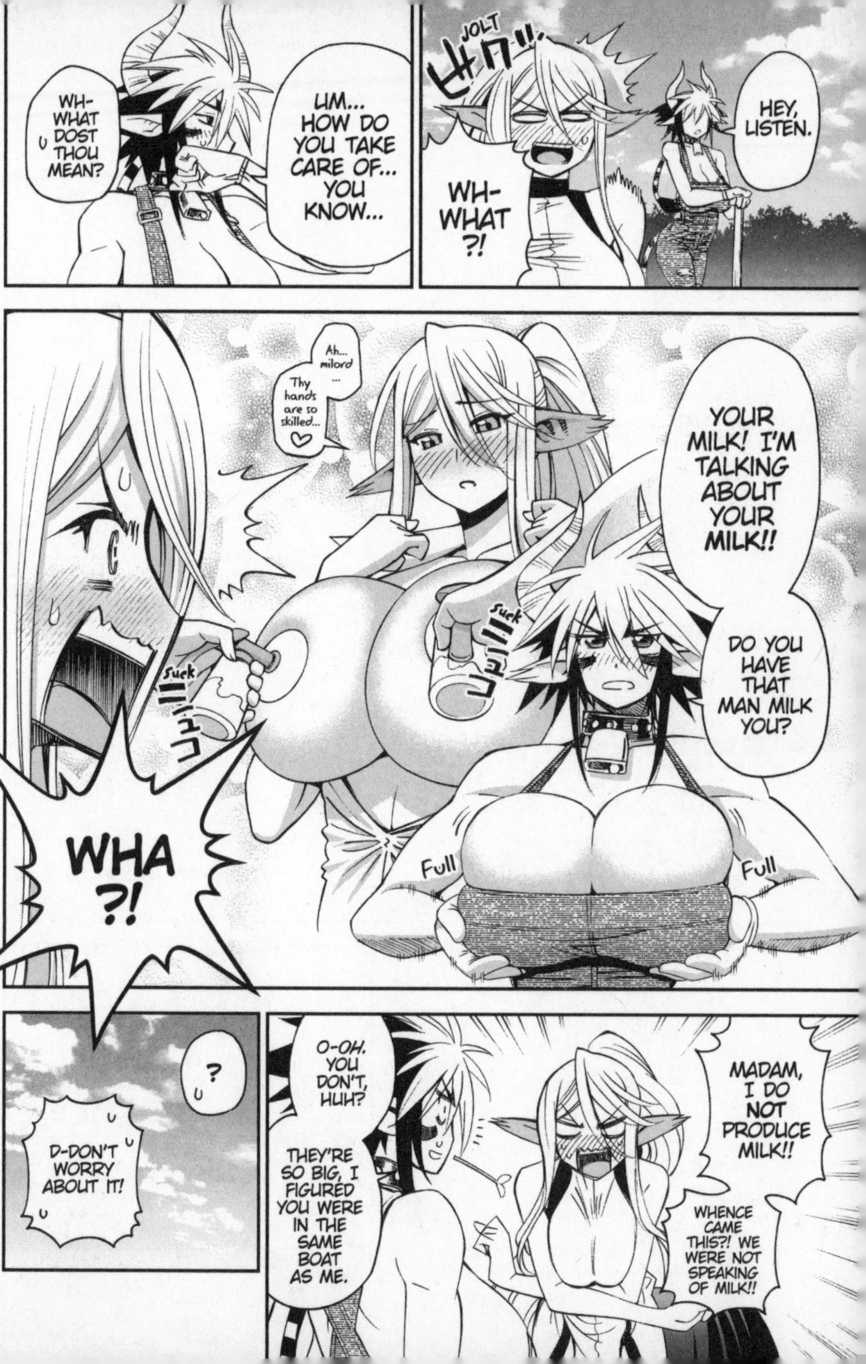
HEY, LISTEN.
JOLT
WH-WHAT?!
UM... HOW DO YOU TAKE CARE OF... YOU KNOW...
WH-WHAT DOST THOU MEAN?
YOUR MILK! I'M TALKING ABOUT YOUR MILK!!
DO YOU HAVE THAT MAN MILK YOU?
Ah... milord ...
Thy hands are so skilled...
Suck
Suck
Full
Full
WHA?!
MADAM, I DO NOT PRODUCE MILK!!
WHENCE CAME THIS?! WE WERE NOT SPEAKING OF MILK!!
O-OH. YOU DON'T, HUH?
THEY'RE SO BIG, I FIGURED YOU WERE IN THE SAME BOAT AS ME.
?
D-DON'T WORRY ABOUT IT!

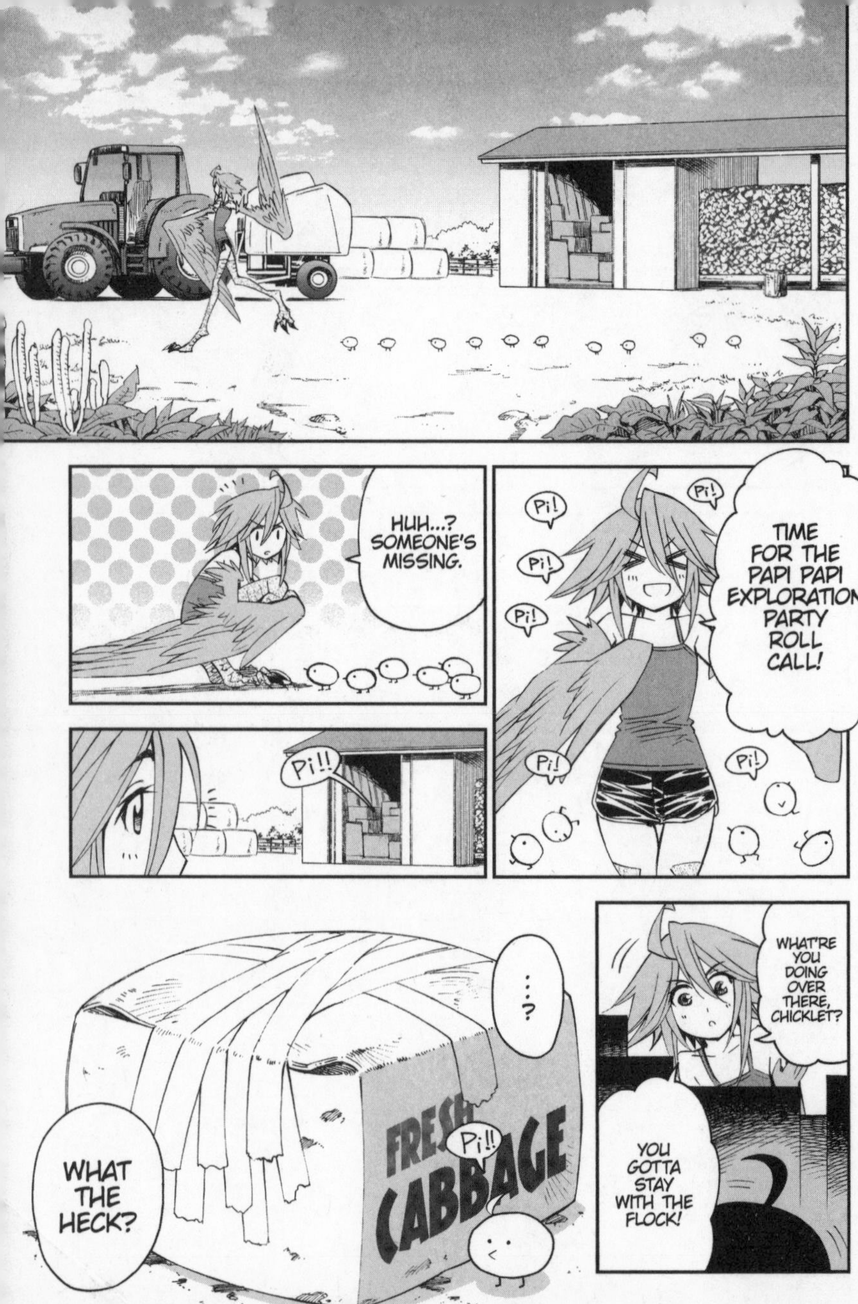
Pi!
Pi!
Pi!
Pi!
TIME FOR THE PAPI PAPI EXPLORATION PARTY ROLL CALL!
Pi!
Pi!
HUH...? SOMEONE'S MISSING.
Pi!!
WHAT'RE YOU DOING OVER THERE, CHICKLET?
YOU GOTTA STAY WITH THE FLOCK!
...?
FRESH CABBAGE
Pi!!
WHAT THE HECK?

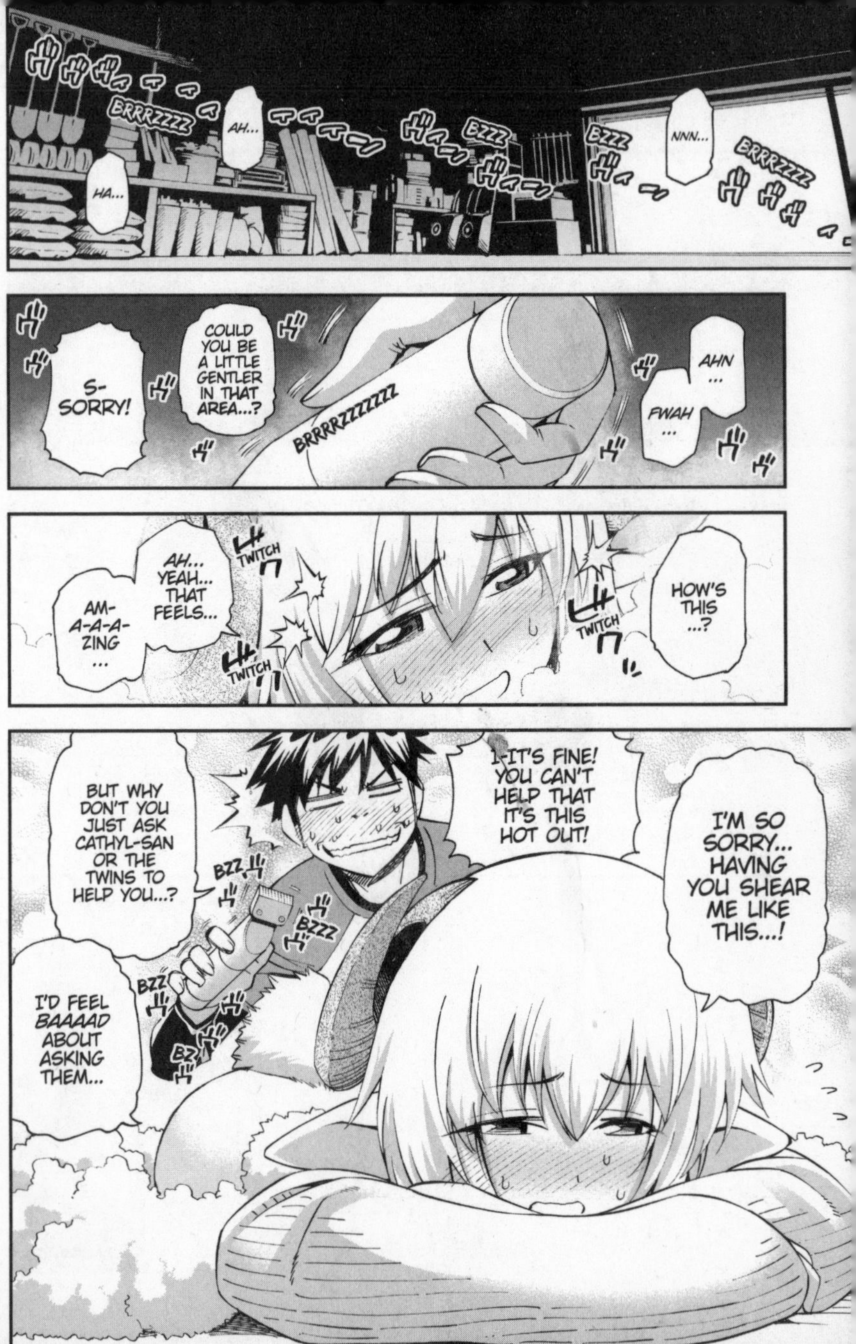
BRRRZZZZ
NNN...
BZZZ
BZZZ
AH...
BRRRZZZZ
HA...
AHN... FWAH...
COULD YOU BE A LITTLE GENTLER IN THAT AREA...?
BRRRRZZZZZZZ
S-SORRY!
HOW'S THIS...?
TWITCH
TWITCH
AH... YEAH... THAT FEELS...
TWITCH
AM-A-A-A-ZING...
I'M SO SORRY... HAVING YOU SHEAR ME LIKE THIS...!
I-IT'S FINE! YOU CAN'T HELP THAT IT'S THIS HOT OUT!
BUT WHY DON'T YOU JUST ASK CATHYL-SAN OR THE TWINS TO HELP YOU...?
BZZ
BZZZ
BZZ
BZ
I'D FEEL BAAAAD ABOUT ASKING THEM...

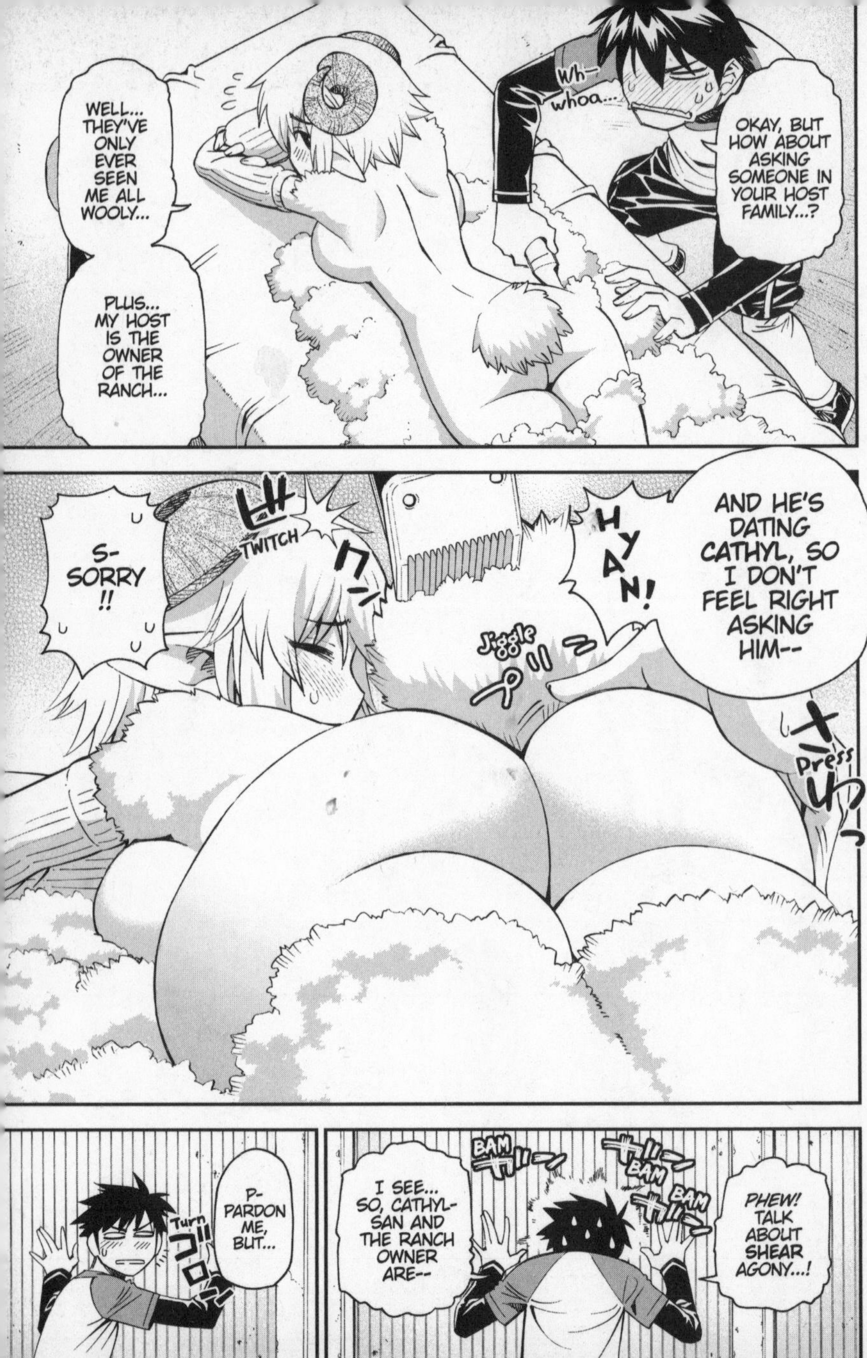
OKAY, BUT HOW ABOUT ASKING SOMEONE IN YOUR HOST FAMILY...?
Wh- whoa...
WELL... THEY'VE ONLY EVER SEEN ME ALL WOOLY...
PLUS... MY HOST IS THE OWNER OF THE RANCH...
AND HE'S DATING CATHYL, SO I DON'T FEEL RIGHT ASKING HIM--
Press
HYAN!
Jiggle
TWITCH
S-SORRY!!
PHEW! TALK ABOUT SHEAR AGONY...!
BAM
BAM
BAM
I SEE... SO, CATHYL-SAN AND THE RANCH OWNER ARE--
P-PARDON ME, BUT...
Turn

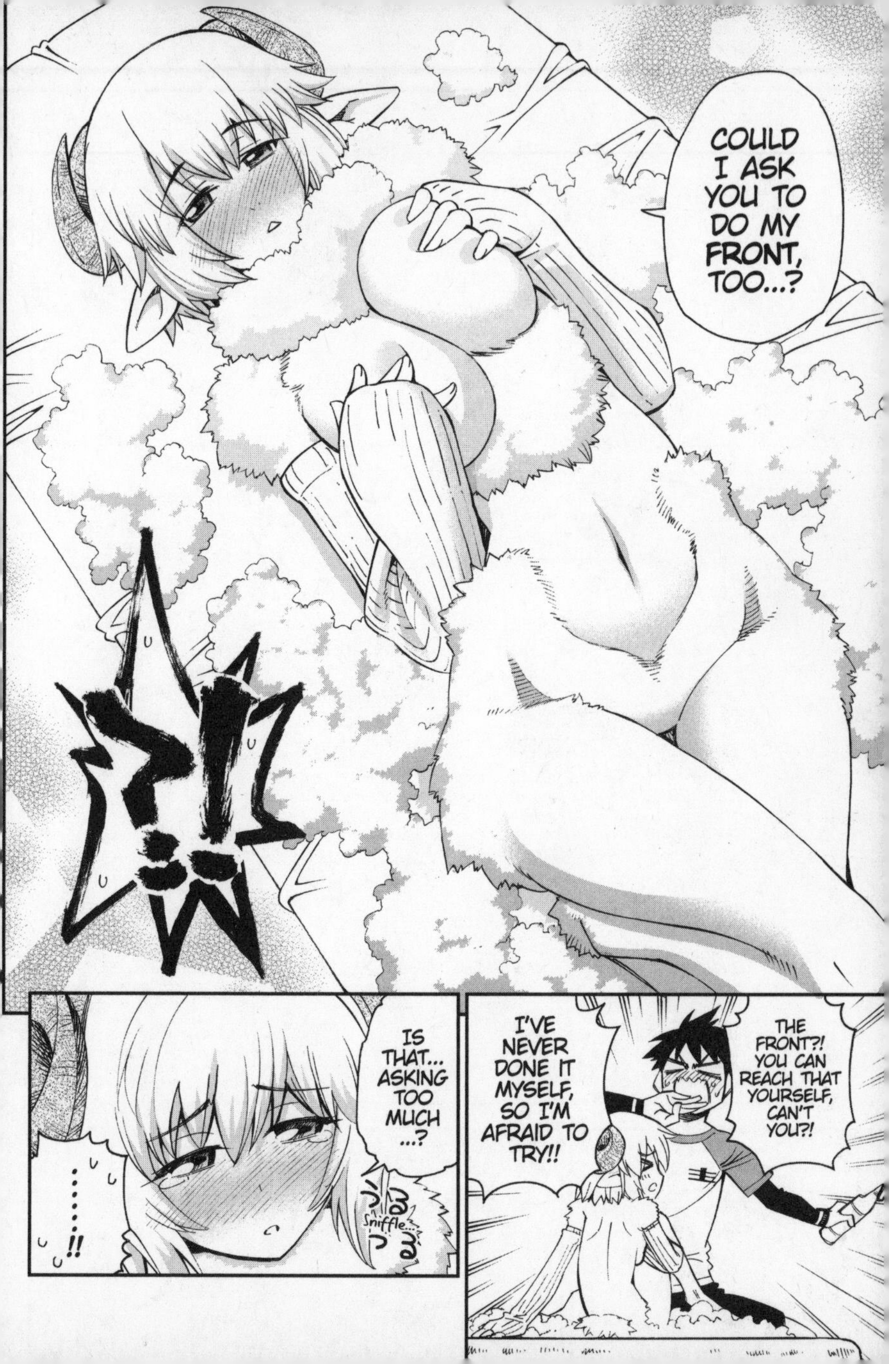
COULD I ASK YOU TO DO MY FRONT, TOO...?
?!
THE FRONT?! YOU CAN REACH THAT YOURSELF, CAN'T YOU?!
I'VE NEVER DONE IT MYSELF, SO I'M AFRAID TO TRY!!
IS THAT... ASKING TOO MUCH ...?
Sniffle...
......!!

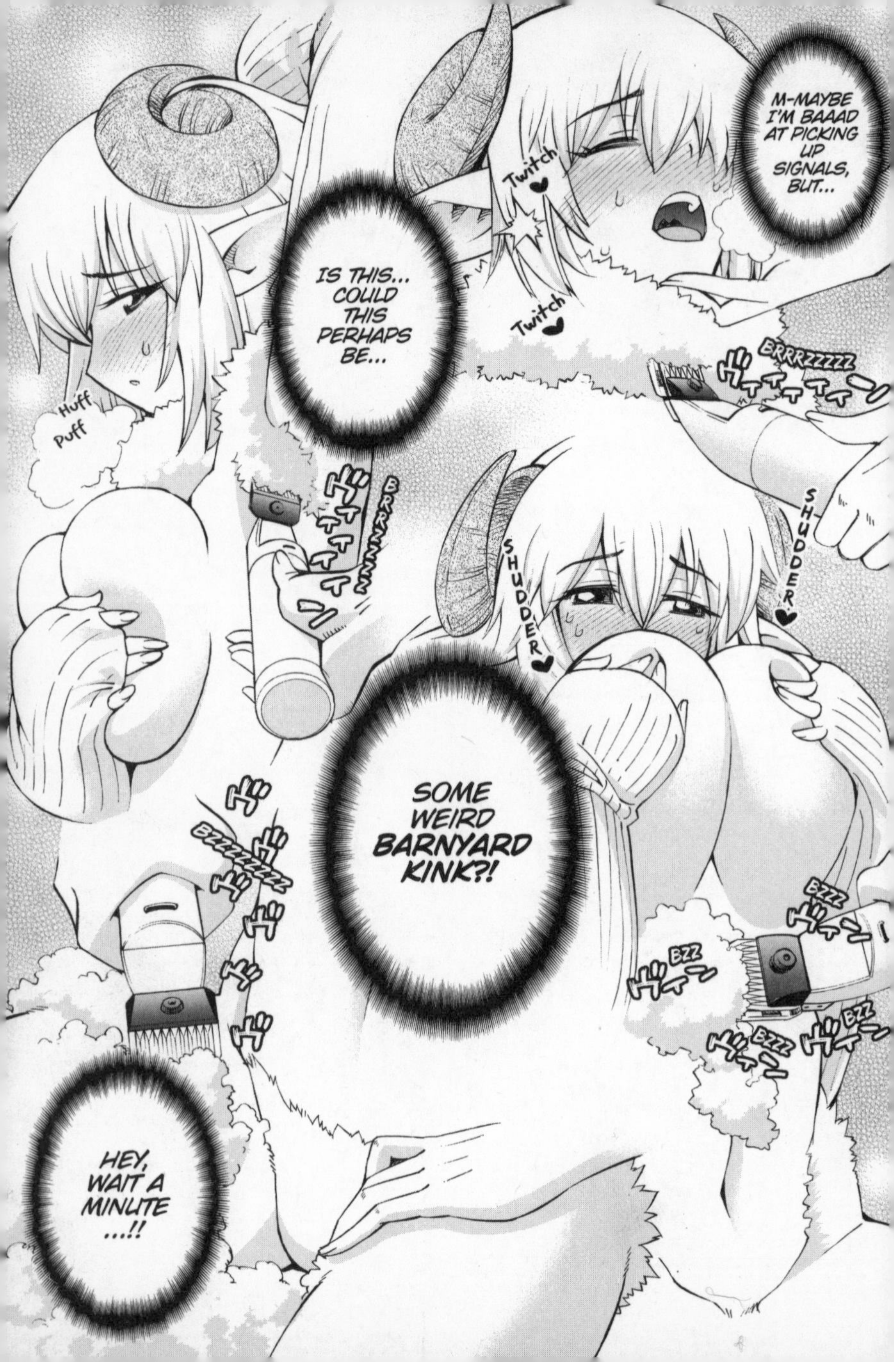

M-MAYBE I'M BAAAD AT PICKING UP SIGNALS, BUT...
Twitch
Twitch
BRRRZZZZZ
IS THIS... COULD THIS PERHAPS BE...
Huff Puff
BRRRZZZZZ
SHUDDER
SHUDDER
SOME WEIRD BARNYARD KINK?!
BZZZ
BZZ
BZZZ
BZZ
BZZZZZZZZZ
HEY, WAIT A MINUTE ...!!

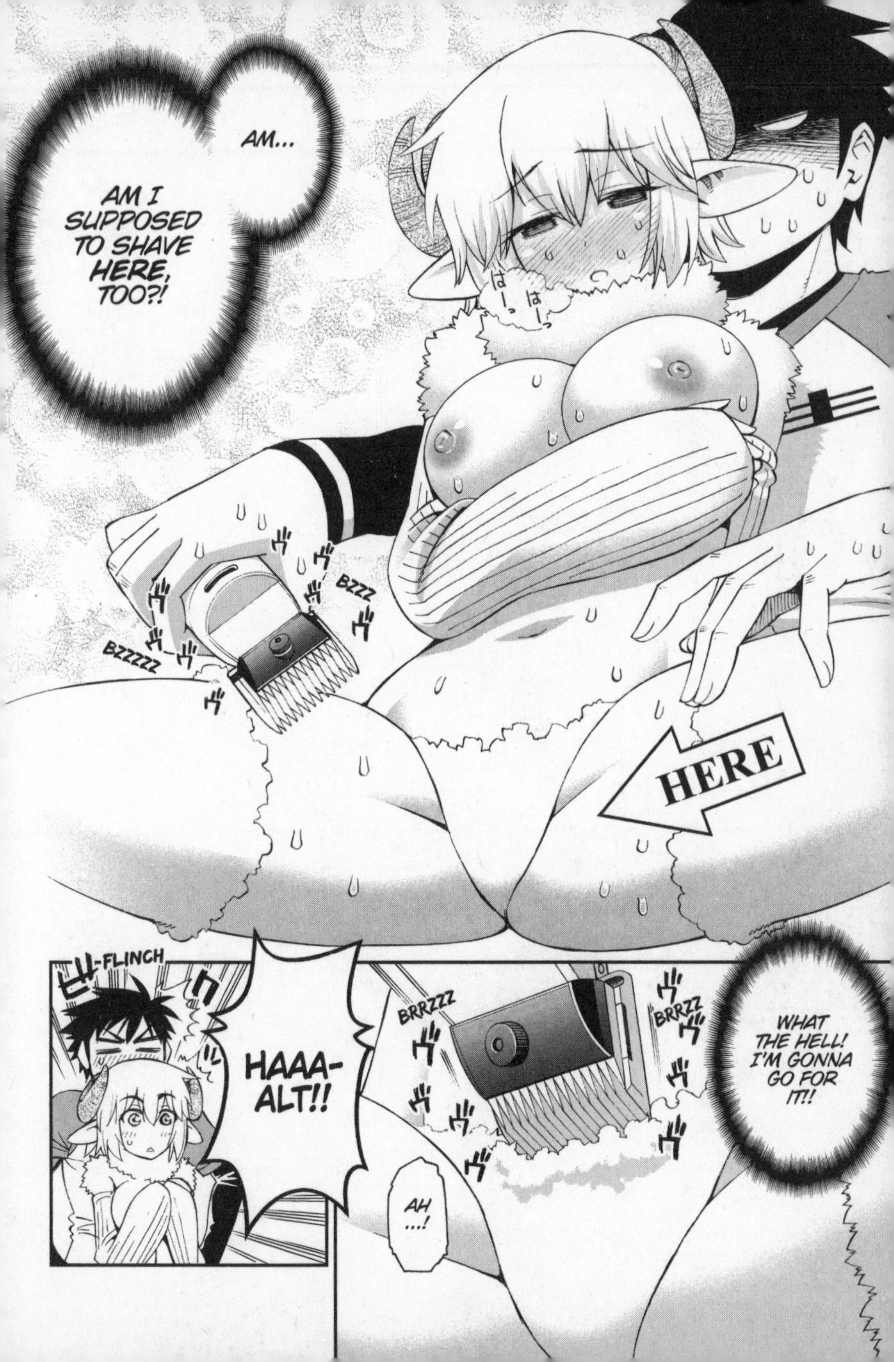
AM...
AM I SUPPOSED TO SHAVE HERE, TOO?!
はーっ はーっ
BZZZ
BZZZZZ
HERE
WHAT THE HELL! I'M GONNA GO FOR IT!!
BRRZZZ
BRRZZZ
AH ...!
HAAA-ALT!!
-FLINCH

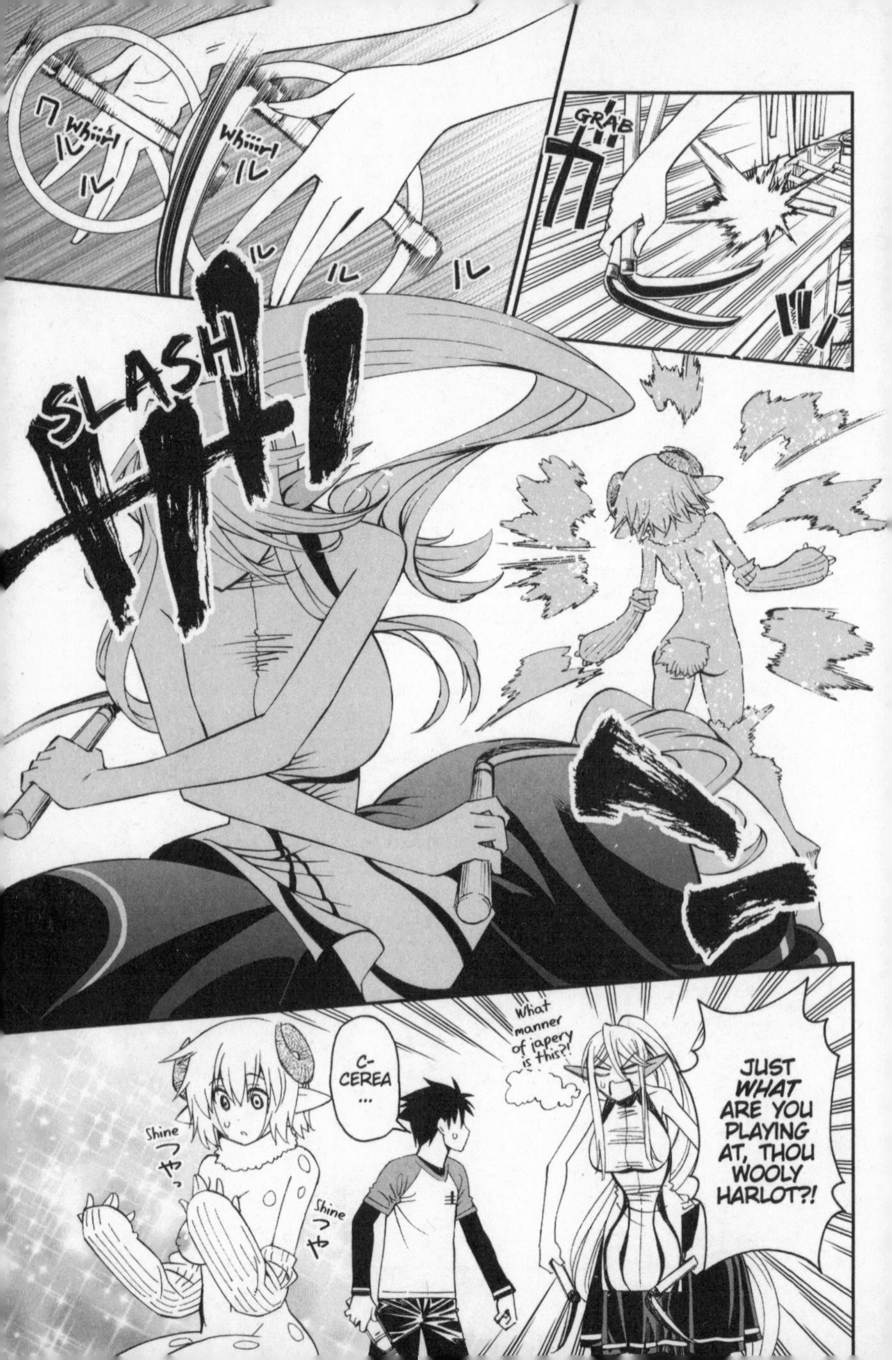
GRAB
カッ
Whirl
ワルル
Whirl
ルルルル
SLASH
JUST WHAT ARE YOU PLAYING AT, THOU WOOLY HARLOT?!
What manner of japery is this?!
C-CEREA ...
Shine
つやっ
Shine
つや

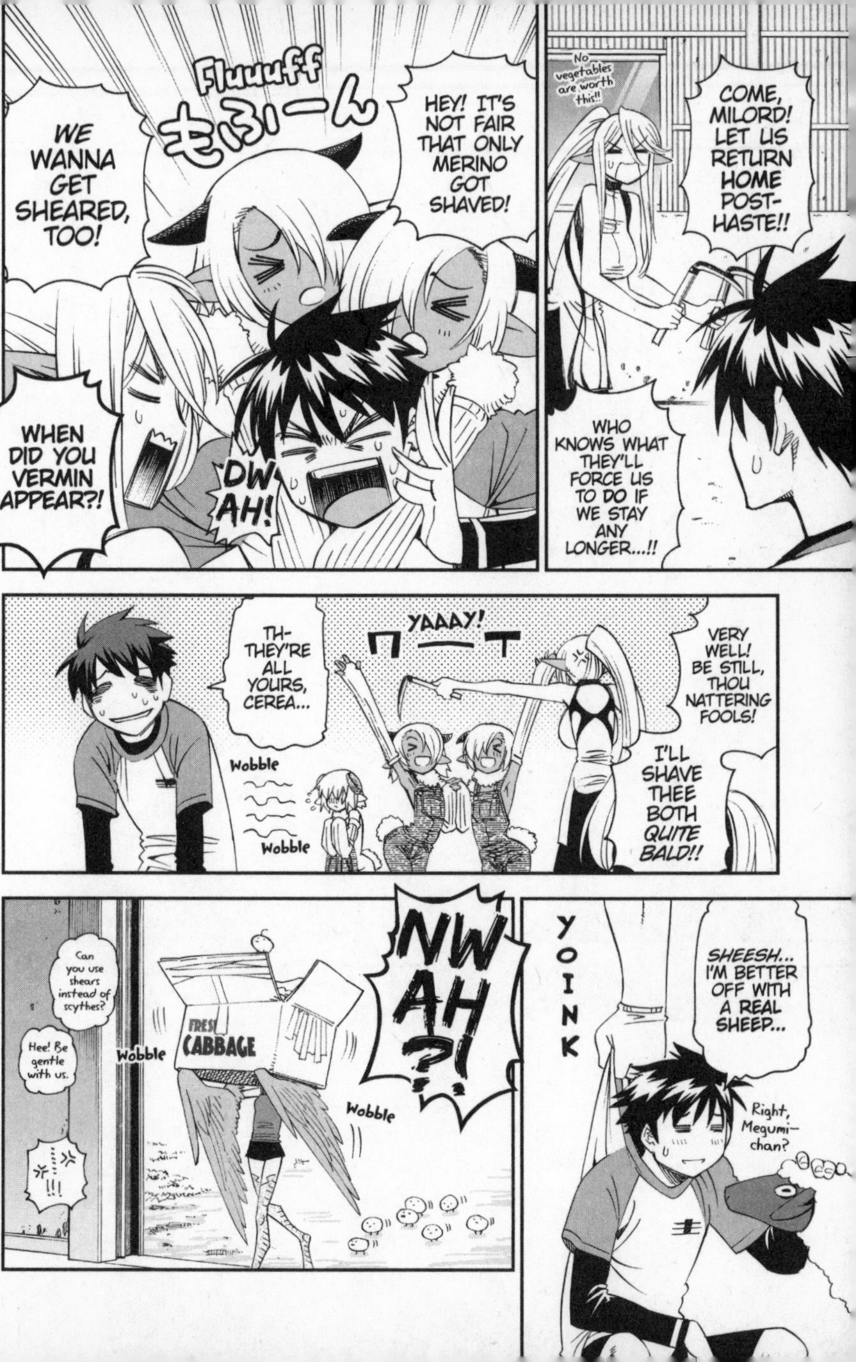
No vegetables are worth this!!
COME, MILORD! LET US RETURN HOME POST-HASTE!!
WHO KNOWS WHAT THEY'LL FORCE US TO DO IF WE STAY ANY LONGER...!!
HEY! IT'S NOT FAIR THAT ONLY MERINO GOT SHAVED!
Fluuuff
もふーん
WE WANNA GET SHEARED, TOO!
DWAH!
WHEN DID YOU VERMIN APPEAR?!
VERY WELL! BE STILL, THOU NATTERING FOOLS!
I'LL SHAVE THEE BOTH QUITE BALD!!
YAAAY!
ワーイ
TH-THEY'RE ALL YOURS, CEREA...
Wobble
Wobble
YOINK
SHEESH... I'M BETTER OFF WITH A REAL SHEEP...
Right, Megumi-chan?
NWAH?!
Can you use shears instead of scythes?
Hee! Be gentle with us.
FRESH CABBAGE
Wobble
Wobble
...!!!

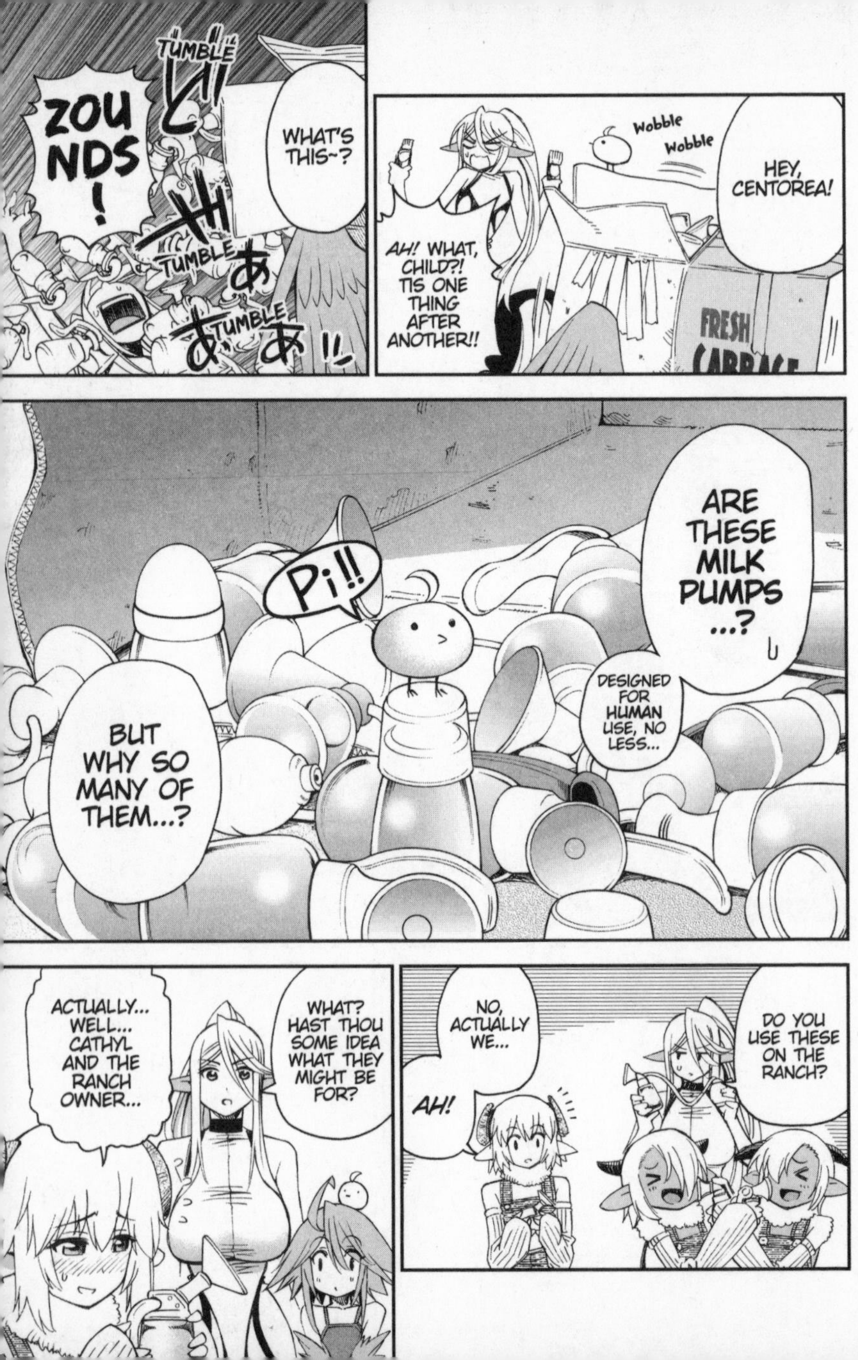
HEY, CENTOREA!
Wobble
Wobble
AH! WHAT, CHILD?! TIS ONE THING AFTER ANOTHER!!
FRESH CABBAGE
WHAT'S THIS~?
TUMBLE
ZOUNDS!
TUMBLE
TUMBLE
ARE THESE MILK PUMPS ...?
DESIGNED FOR HUMAN USE, NO LESS...
Pi!!
BUT WHY SO MANY OF THEM...?
DO YOU USE THESE ON THE RANCH?
NO, ACTUALLY WE...
AH!
WHAT? HAST THOU SOME IDEA WHAT THEY MIGHT BE FOR?
ACTUALLY... WELL... CATHYL AND THE RANCH OWNER...

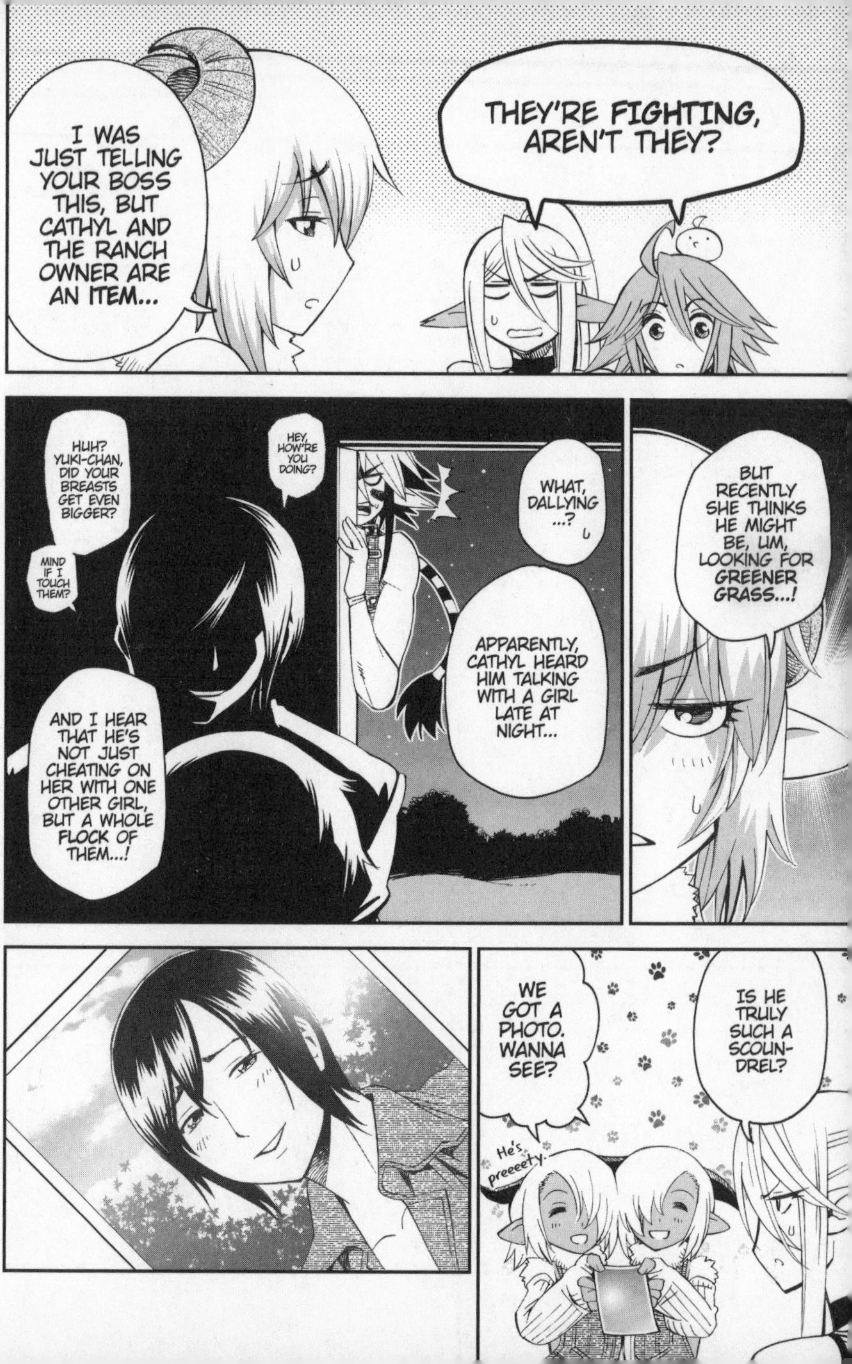
THEY'RE FIGHTING, AREN'T THEY?
I WAS JUST TELLING YOUR BOSS THIS, BUT CATHYL AND THE RANCH OWNER ARE AN ITEM...
BUT RECENTLY SHE THINKS HE MIGHT BE, UM, LOOKING FOR GREENER GRASS...!
WHAT, DALLYING...?
APPARENTLY, CATHYL HEARD HIM TALKING WITH A GIRL LATE AT NIGHT...
HEY, HOW'RE YOU DOING?
HUH? YUKI-CHAN, DID YOUR BREASTS GET EVEN BIGGER?
MIND IF I TOUCH THEM?
AND I HEAR THAT HE'S NOT JUST CHEATING ON HER WITH ONE OTHER GIRL, BUT A WHOLE FLOCK OF THEM...!
IS HE TRULY SUCH A SCOUN-DREL?
WE GOT A PHOTO. WANNA SEE?
He's preeeety.

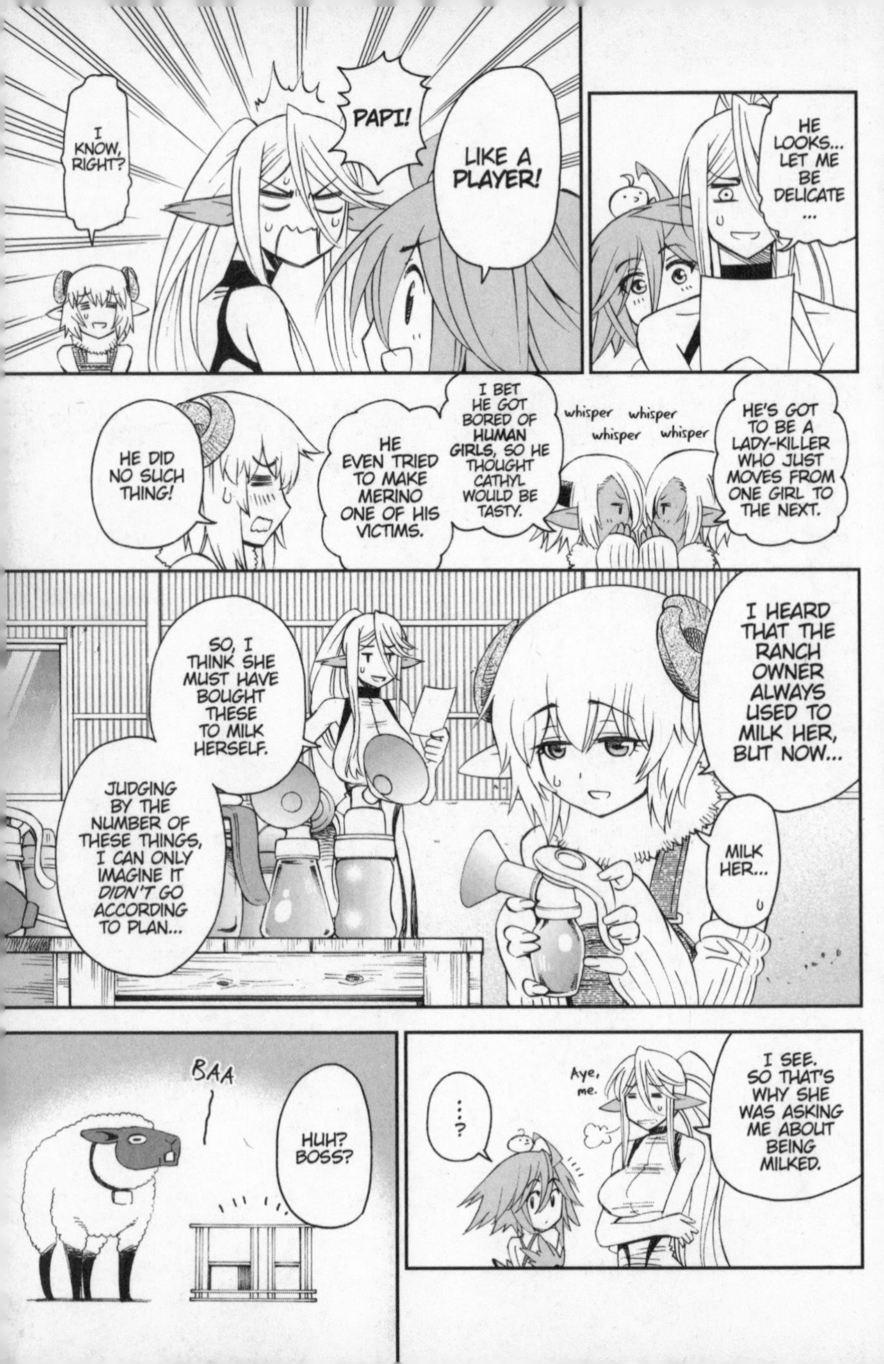

HE LOOKS... LET ME BE DELICATE ...
LIKE A PLAYER!
PAPI!
I KNOW, RIGHT?
HE'S GOT TO BE A LADY-KILLER WHO JUST MOVES FROM ONE GIRL TO THE NEXT.
whisper whisper whisper whisper
I BET HE GOT BORED OF HUMAN GIRLS, SO HE THOUGHT CATHYL WOULD BE TASTY.
HE EVEN TRIED TO MAKE MERINO ONE OF HIS VICTIMS.
HE DID NO SUCH THING!
I HEARD THAT THE RANCH OWNER ALWAYS USED TO MILK HER, BUT NOW...
MILK HER...
SO, I THINK SHE MUST HAVE BOUGHT THESE TO MILK HERSELF.
JUDGING BY THE NUMBER OF THESE THINGS, I CAN ONLY IMAGINE IT *DIDN'T* GO ACCORDING TO PLAN...
I SEE. SO THAT'S WHY SHE WAS ASKING ME ABOUT BEING MILKED.
Aye, me.
...?
HUH? BOSS?
BAA

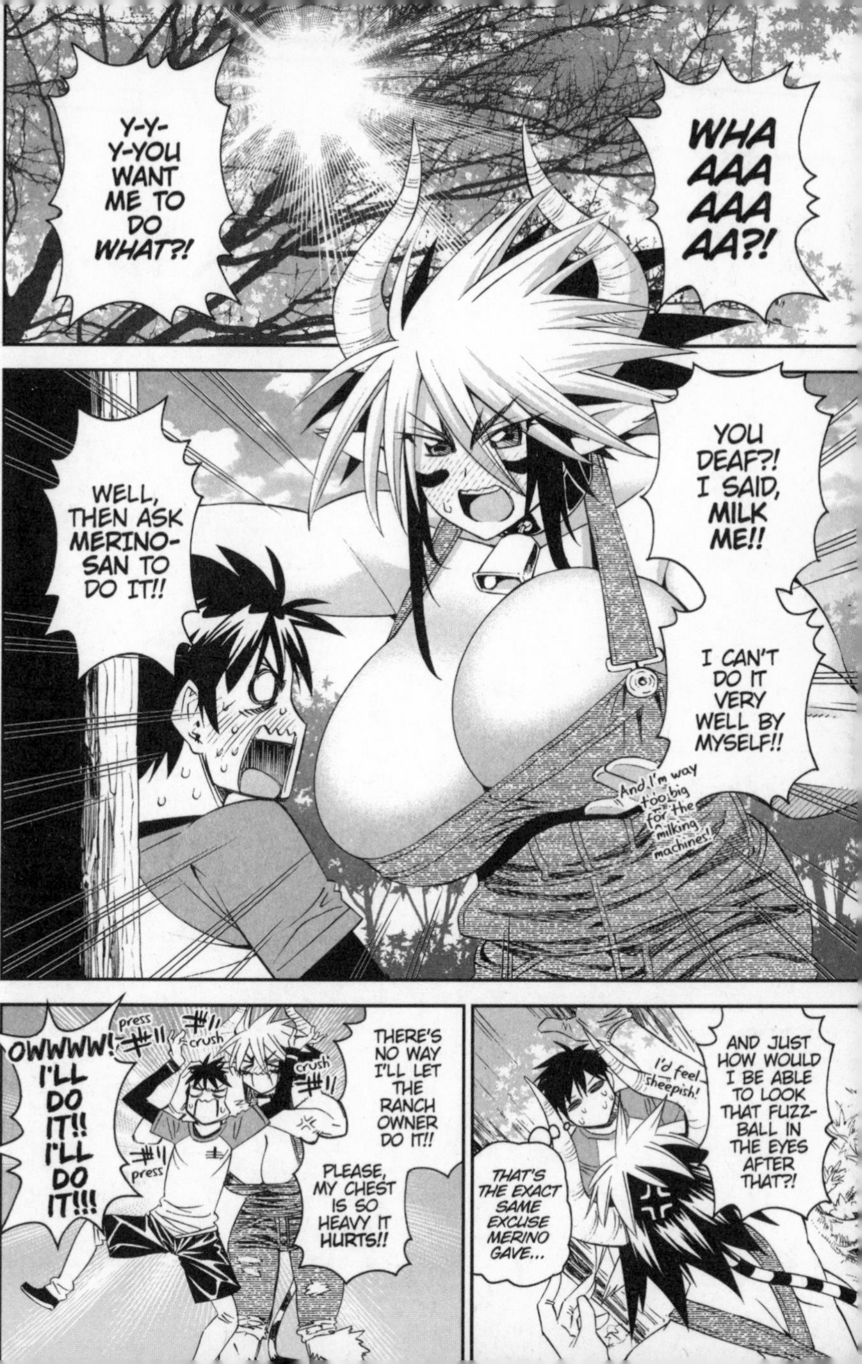
WHA AAA AAA AA?!
Y-Y-Y-YOU WANT ME TO DO WHAT?!
YOU DEAF?! I SAID, MILK ME!!
I CAN'T DO IT VERY WELL BY MYSELF!!
And I'm way too big for the milking machines!
WELL, THEN ASK MERINO-SAN TO DO IT!!
AND JUST HOW WOULD I BE ABLE TO LOOK THAT FUZZ-BALL IN THE EYES AFTER THAT?!
I'd feel sheepish!
THAT'S THE EXACT SAME EXCUSE MERINO GAVE...
THERE'S NO WAY I'LL LET THE RANCH OWNER DO IT!!
PLEASE, MY CHEST IS SO HEAVY IT HURTS!!
press
crush
crush
press
OWWWW! I'LL DO IT!! I'LL DO IT!!!

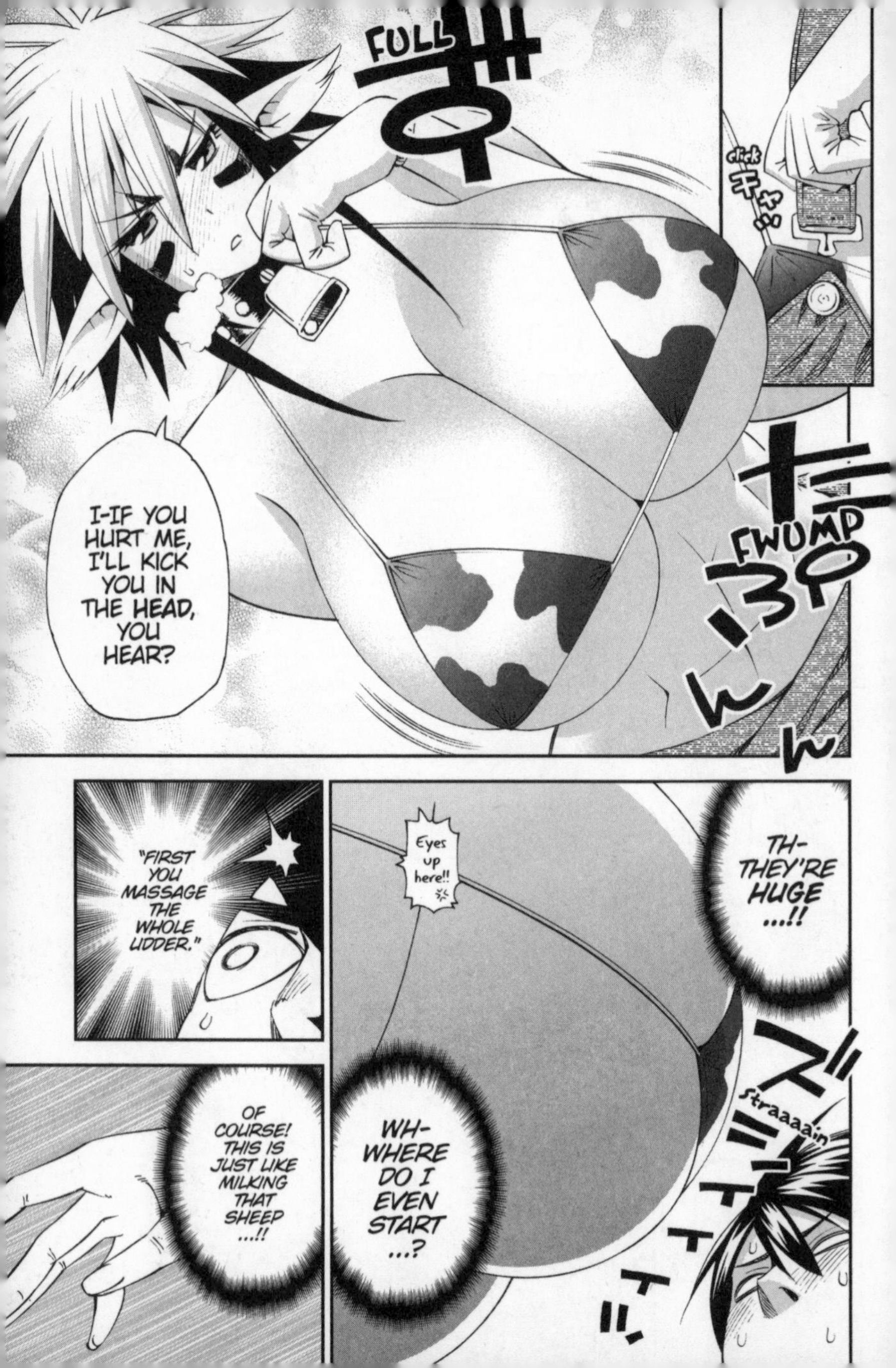
click
FULL
FWUMP
I-IF YOU HURT ME, I'LL KICK YOU IN THE HEAD, YOU HEAR?
TH-THEY'RE HUGE ...!!
Eyes up here!!
Straaaain
WH-WHERE DO I EVEN START ...?
"FIRST YOU MASSAGE THE WHOLE UDDER."
OF COURSE! THIS IS JUST LIKE MILKING THAT SHEEP ...!!

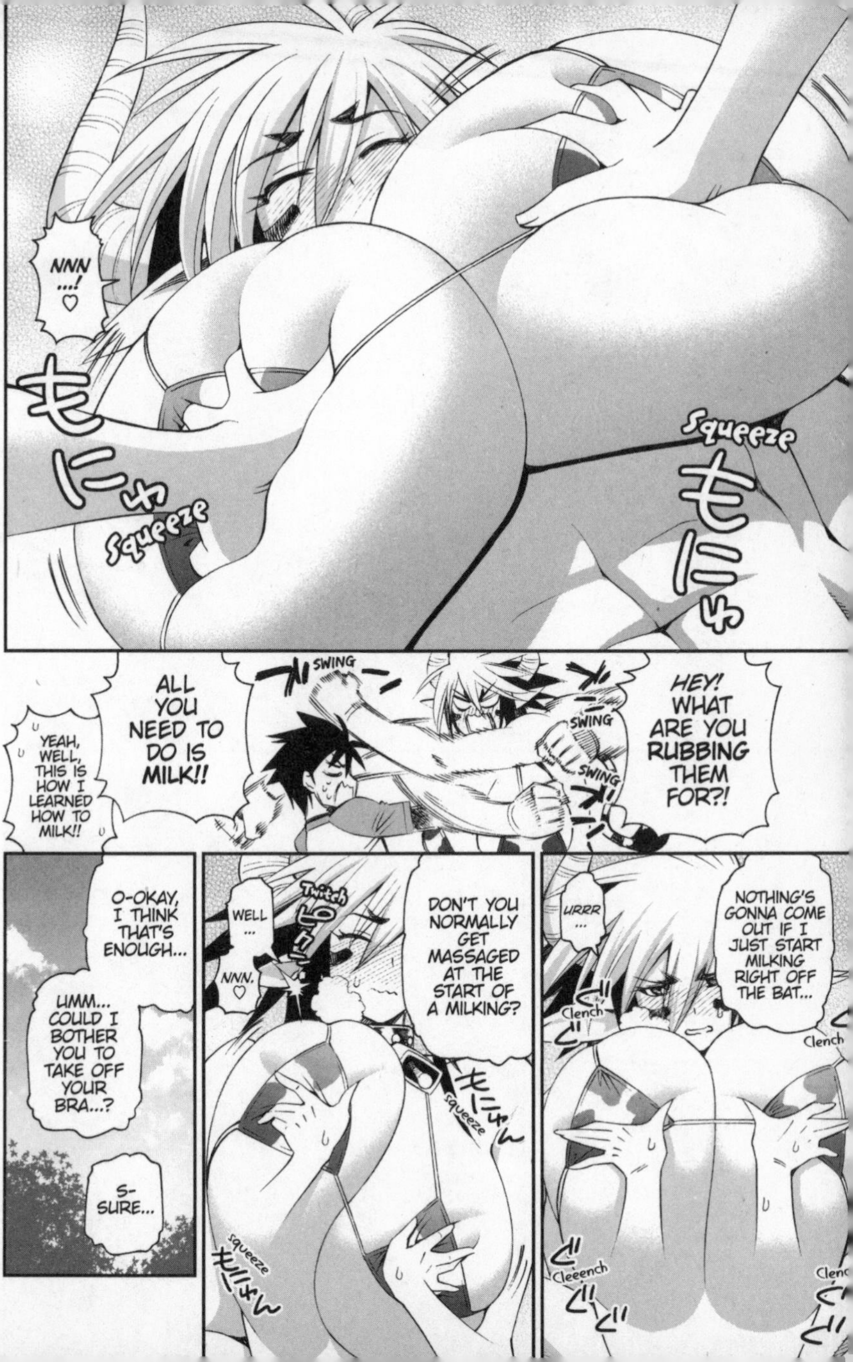
Squeeze
もにゅ
NNN ...! ♡
もにゅ
squeeze
HEY! WHAT ARE YOU RUBBING THEM FOR?!
SWING
SWING
SWING
ALL YOU NEED TO DO IS MILK!!
YEAH, WELL, THIS IS HOW I LEARNED HOW TO MILK!!
NOTHING'S GONNA COME OUT IF I JUST START MILKING RIGHT OFF THE BAT...
URRR ...
Clench
Clench
Cleeench
Clench
DON'T YOU NORMALLY GET MASSAGED AT THE START OF A MILKING?
WELL ...
Twitch
NNN. ♡
squeeze
squeeze
O-OKAY, I THINK THAT'S ENOUGH...
UMM... COULD I BOTHER YOU TO TAKE OFF YOUR BRA...?
S-SURE...

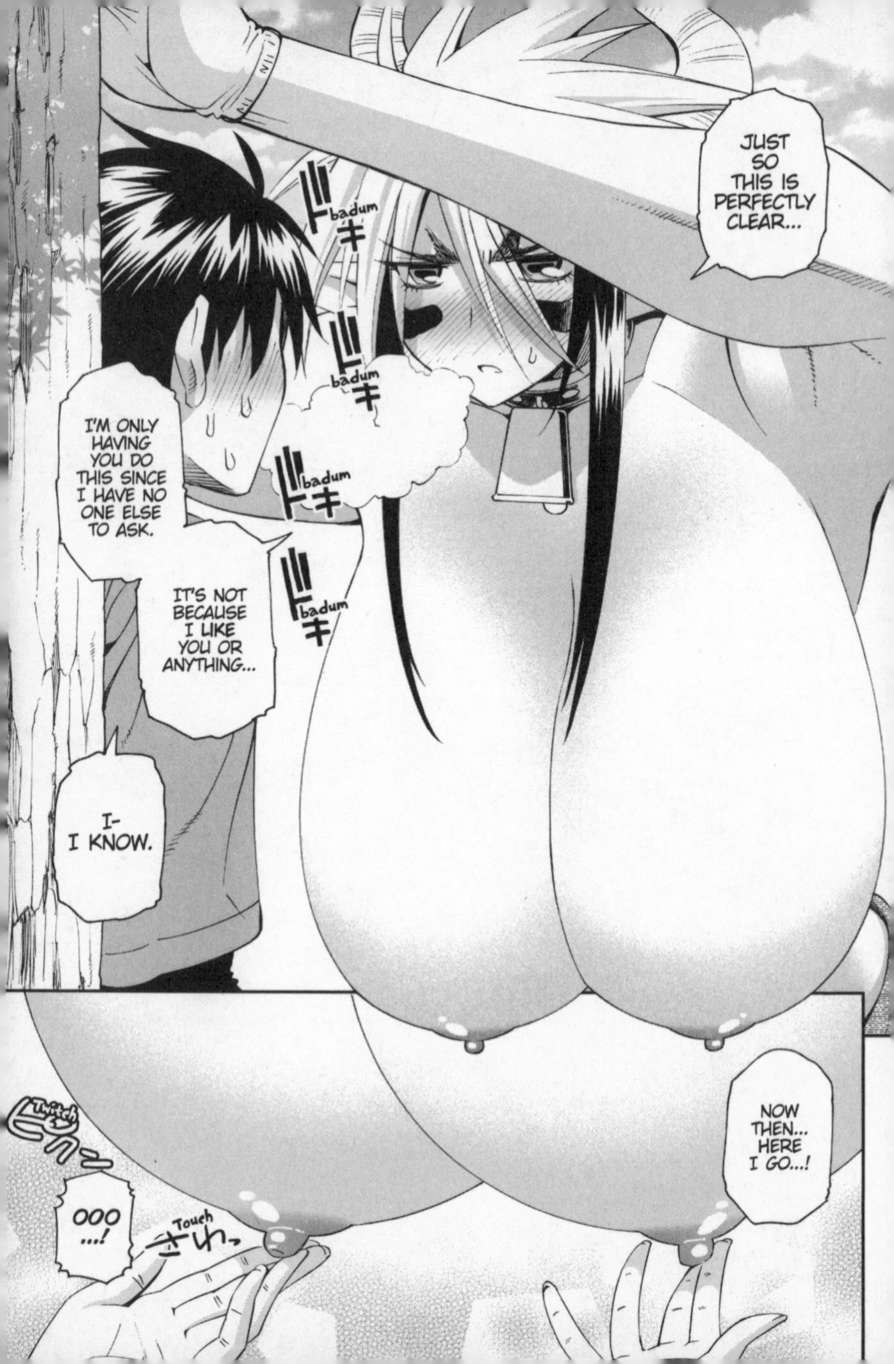
JUST SO THIS IS PERFECTLY CLEAR...
ドキ badum
ドキ badum
ドキ badum
ドキ badum
I'M ONLY HAVING YOU DO THIS SINCE I HAVE NO ONE ELSE TO ASK.
IT'S NOT BECAUSE I LIKE YOU OR ANYTHING...
I- I KNOW.
NOW THEN... HERE I GO...!
さわっ Touch
ビクン Twitch
OOO...!

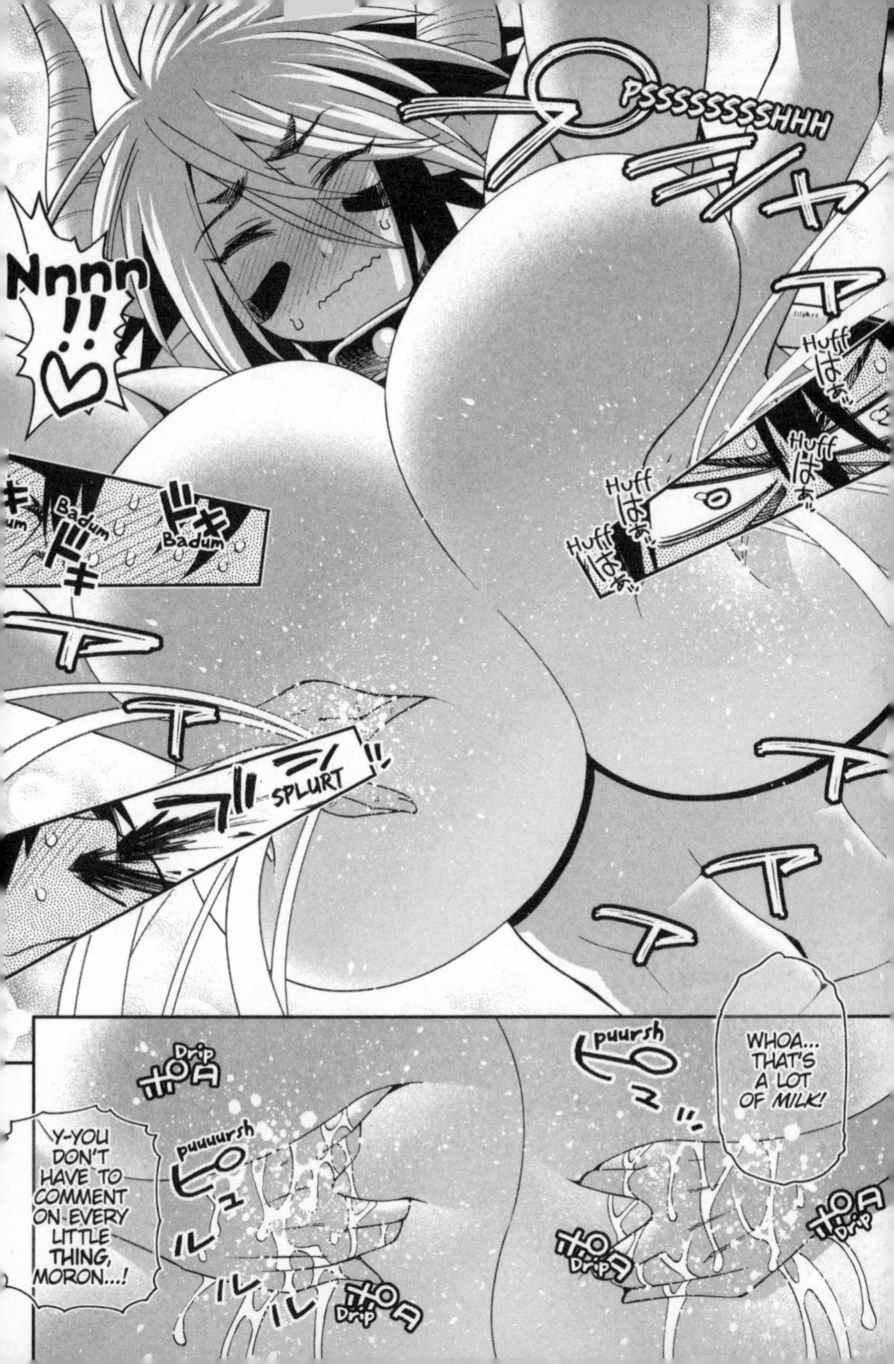
PSSSSSSSSHHH
Huff はぁ
Huff はぁ
Huff はぁ
Huff はぁ
Nnnn!!♡
Badum ドキ
Badum ドキ
SPLURT
WHOA... THAT'S A LOT OF MILK!
Drip ポタ
Drip ポタ
puursh
Drip ポタ
puuuursh
Y-YOU DON'T HAVE TO COMMENT ON EVERY LITTLE THING, MORON...!

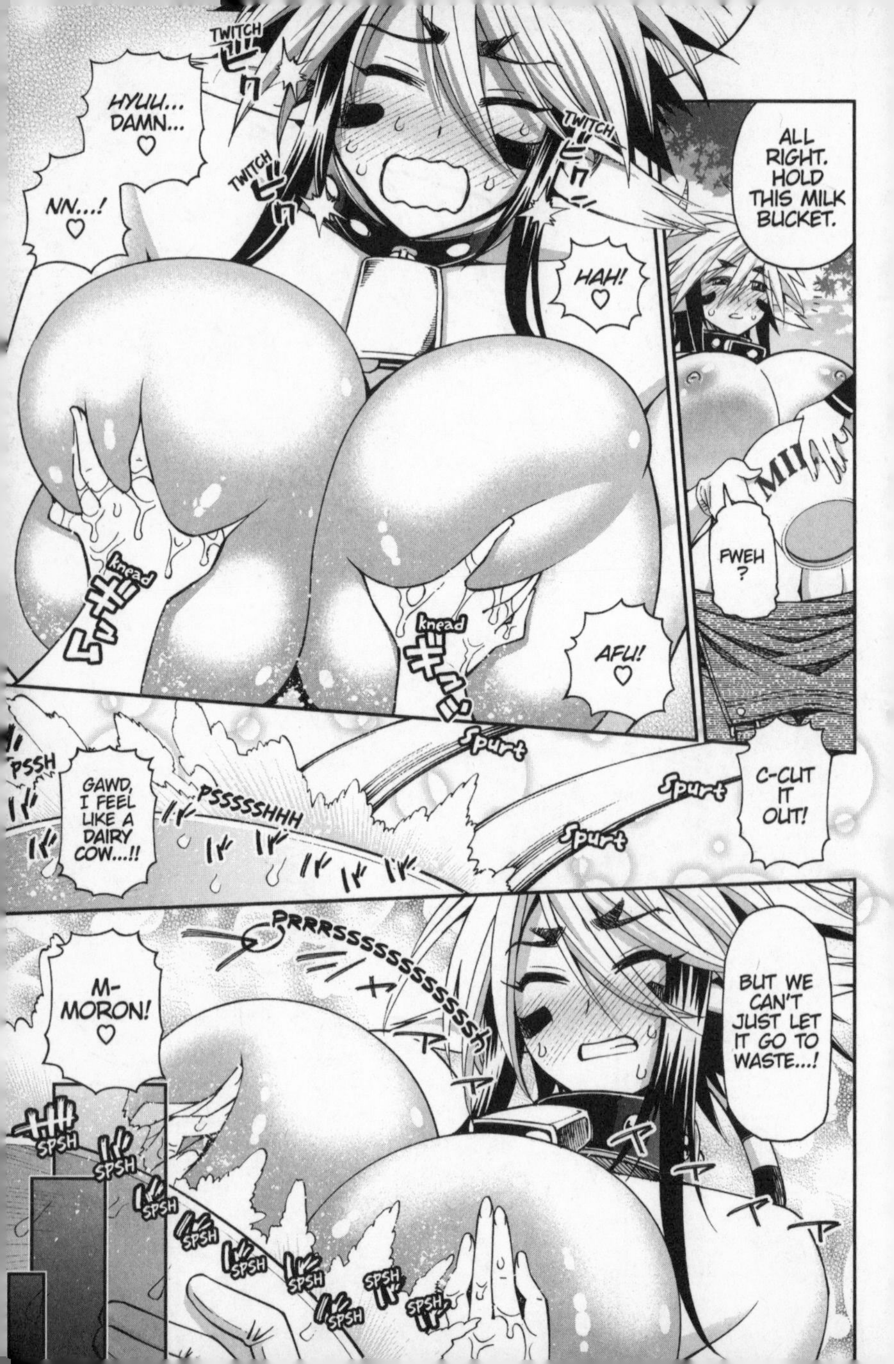

ALL RIGHT. HOLD THIS MILK BUCKET.
FWEH?
TWITCH
HYUU... DAMN... ♡
TWITCH
TWITCH
NN...! ♡
HAH! ♡
knead
knead
AFU! ♡
C-CUT IT OUT!
Spurt
Spurt
Spurt
PSSSSSHHH
GAWD, I FEEL LIKE A DAIRY COW...!!
PSSH
BUT WE CAN'T JUST LET IT GO TO WASTE...!
PRRRSSSSSSSSSSSSSSSSSt
M-MORON! ♡
SPSH
SPSH
SPSH
SPSH
SPSH
SPSH
SPSH
SPSH
SPSH

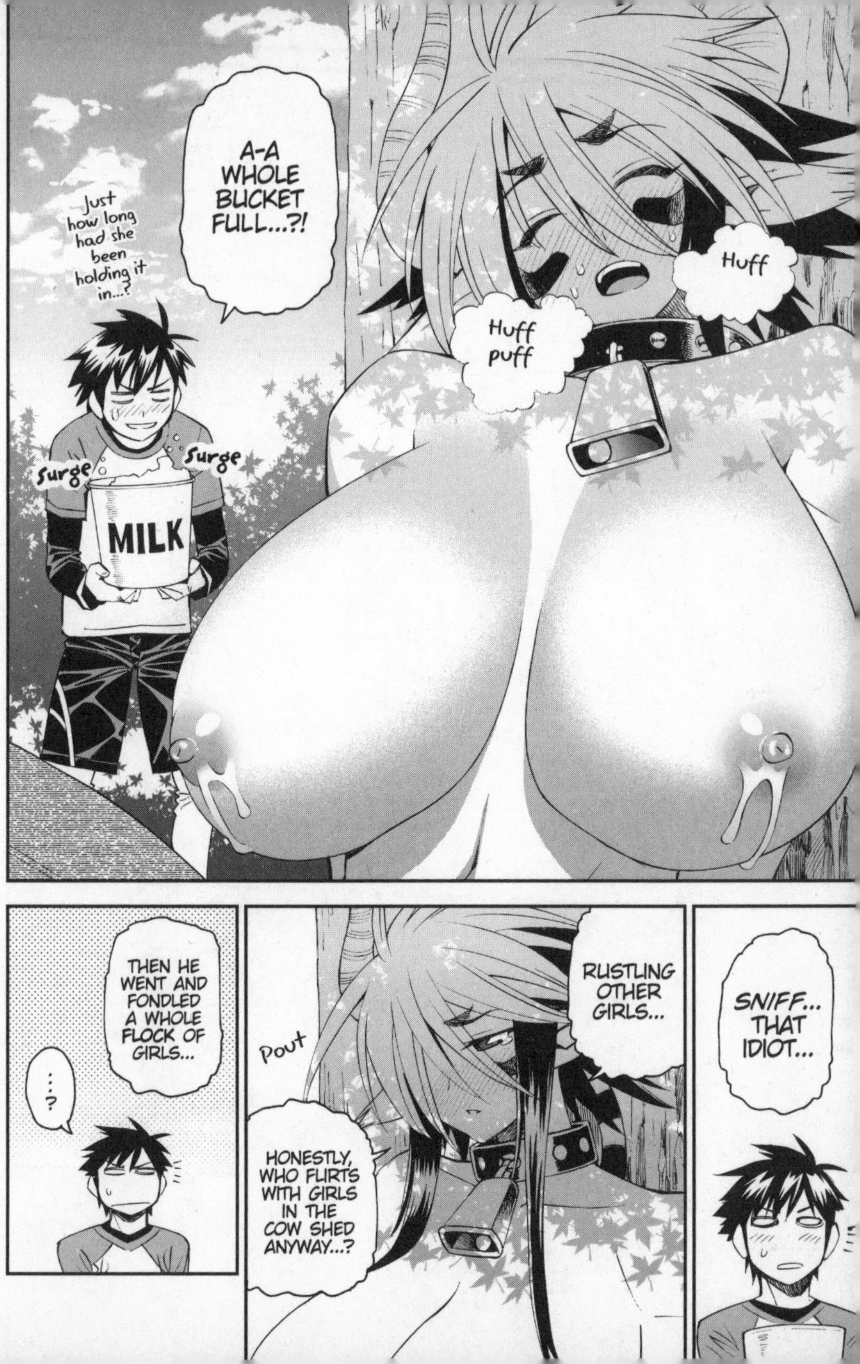
Huff
Huff puff
A-A WHOLE BUCKET FULL...?!
Just how long had she been holding it in...?
Surge
Surge
MILK
SNIFF... THAT IDIOT...
RUSTLING OTHER GIRLS...
Pout
HONESTLY, WHO FLIRTS WITH GIRLS IN THE COW SHED ANYWAY...?
THEN HE WENT AND FONDLED A WHOLE FLOCK OF GIRLS...
...?

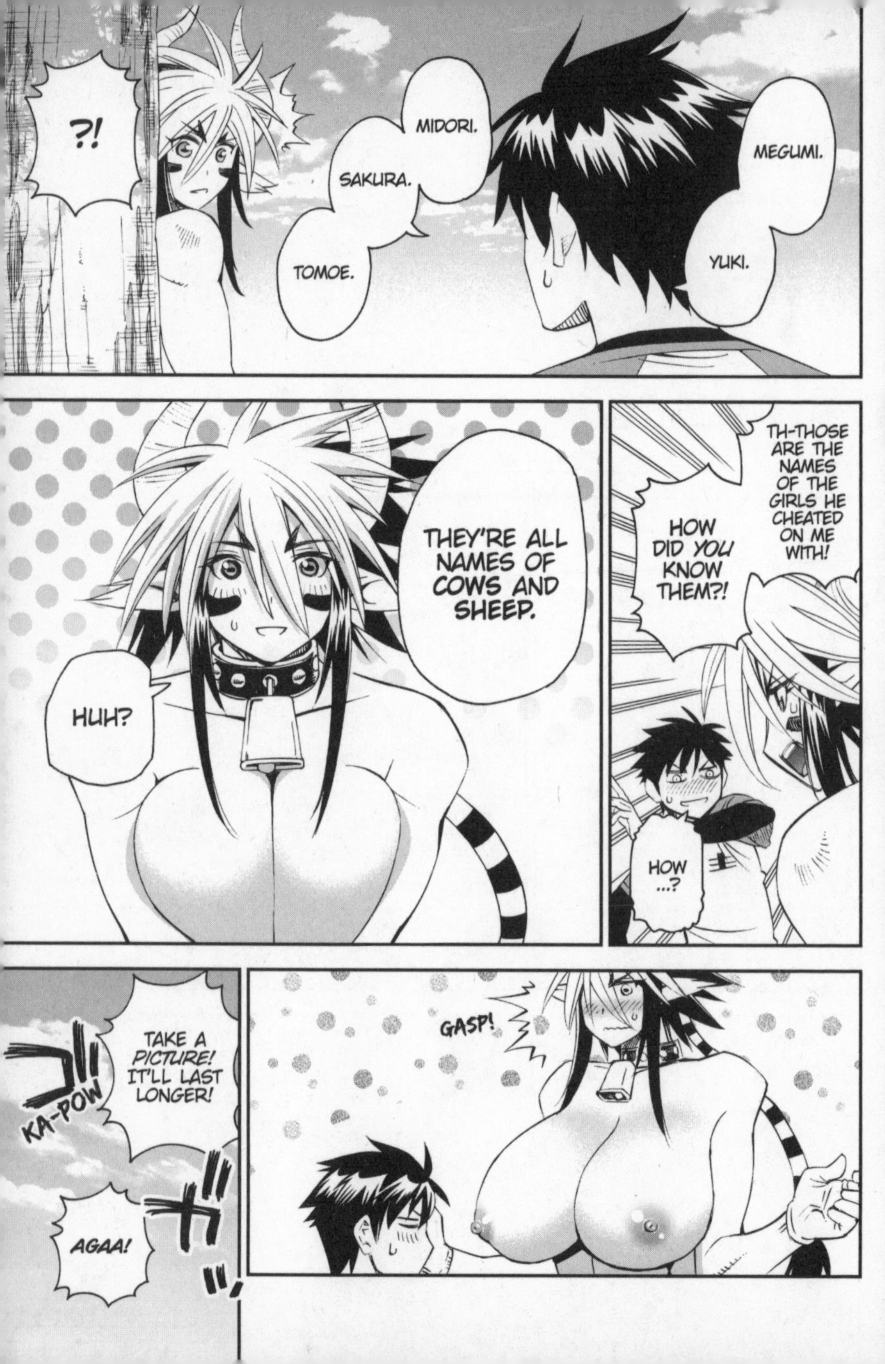
MEGUMI.
YUKI.
MIDORI.
SAKURA.
TOMOE.
?!
TH-THOSE ARE THE NAMES OF THE GIRLS HE CHEATED ON ME WITH!
HOW DID YOU KNOW THEM?!
HOW ...?
THEY'RE ALL NAMES OF COWS AND SHEEP.
HUH?
GASP!
TAKE A PICTURE! IT'LL LAST LONGER!
KA-POW
AGAA!

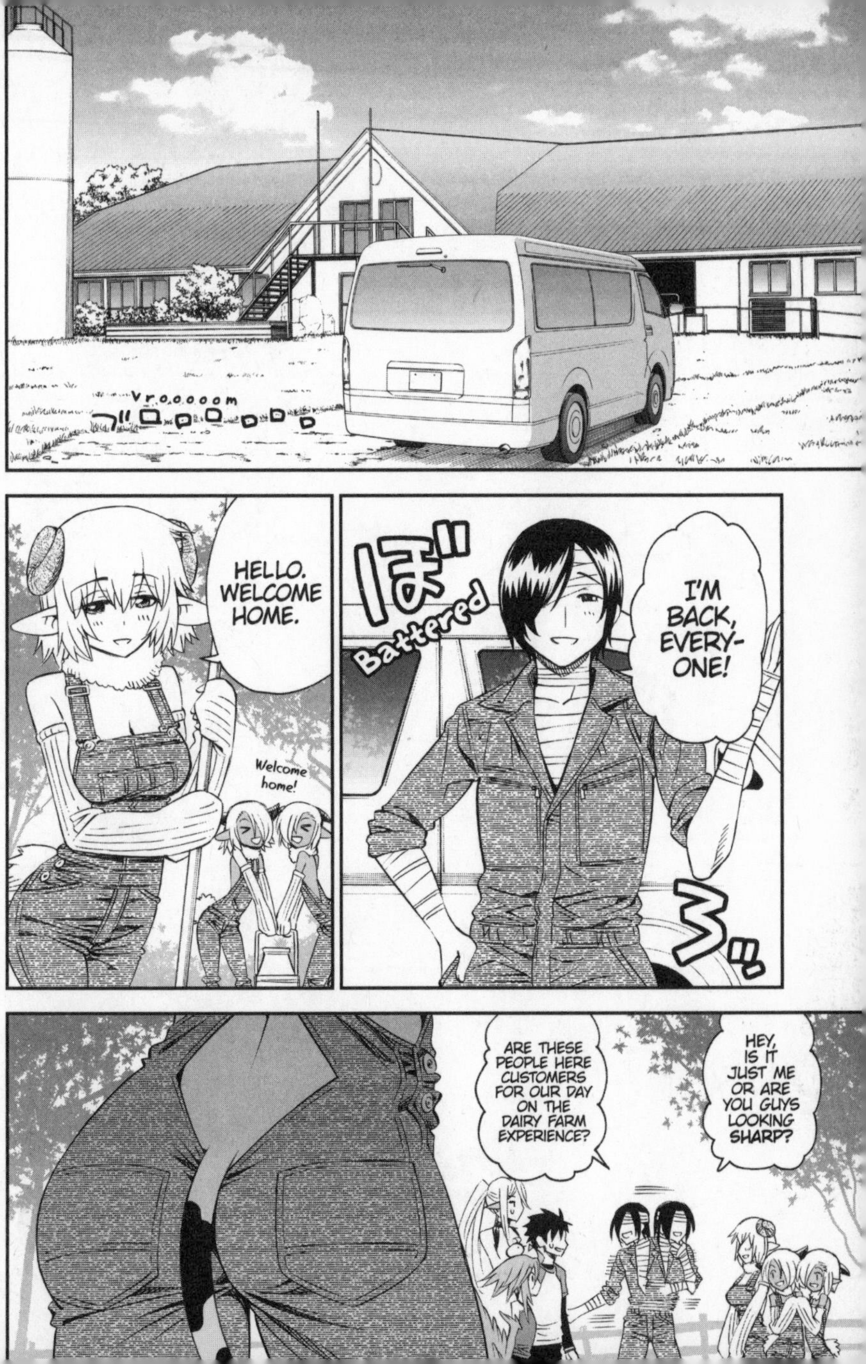
Vrooooom
ブロロロロロロロ
I'M BACK, EVERY-ONE!
ぼ
Battered
ろ
HELLO. WELCOME HOME.
Welcome home!
HEY, IS IT JUST ME OR ARE YOU GUYS LOOKING SHARP?
ARE THESE PEOPLE HERE CUSTOMERS FOR OUR DAY ON THE DAIRY FARM EXPERIENCE?

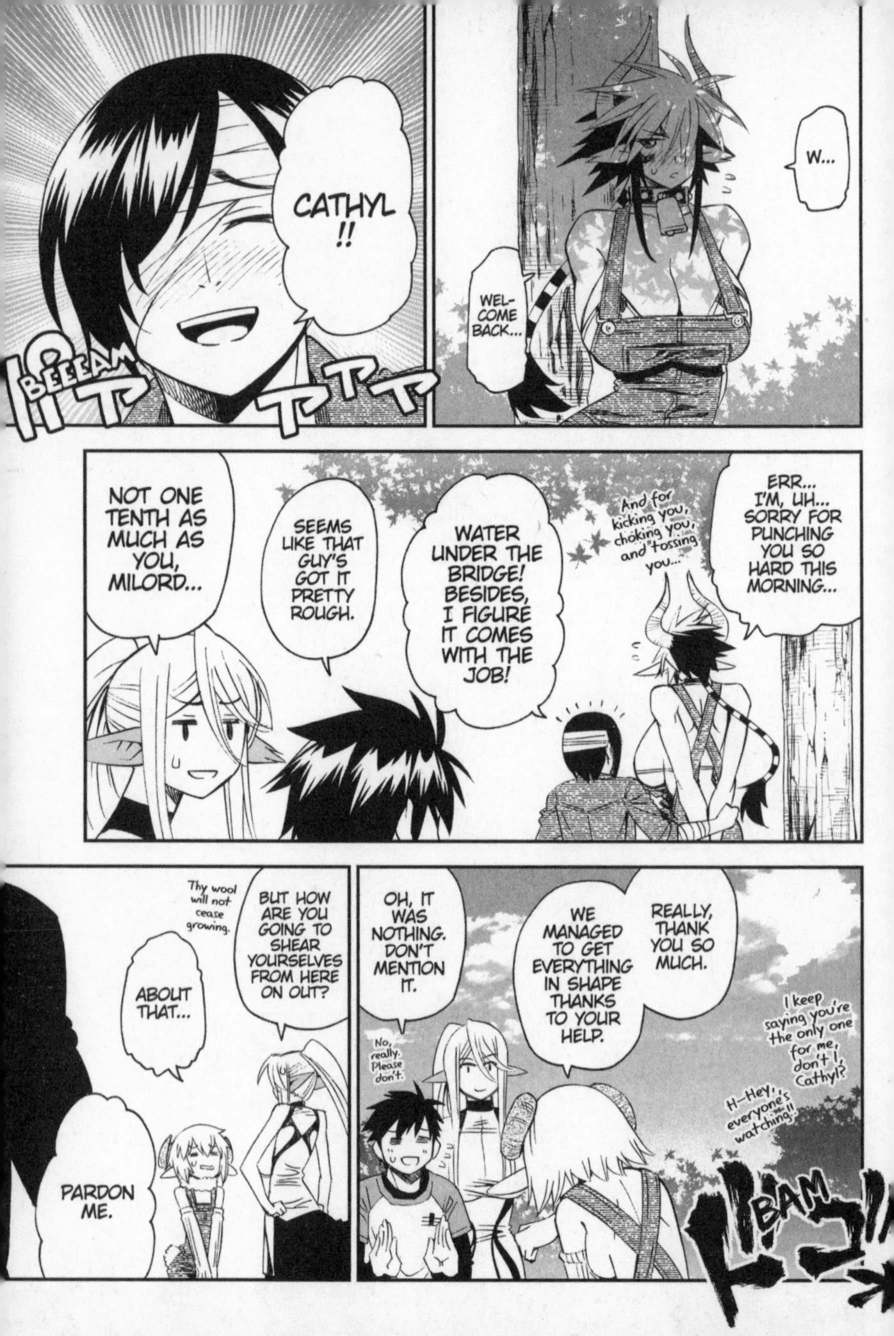
W...
WEL-COME BACK...
CATHYL!!
BEEEAM
ERR... I'M, UH... SORRY FOR PUNCHING YOU SO HARD THIS MORNING...
And for kicking you, choking you, and tossing you...
WATER UNDER THE BRIDGE! BESIDES, I FIGURE IT COMES WITH THE JOB!
SEEMS LIKE THAT GUY'S GOT IT PRETTY ROUGH.
NOT ONE TENTH AS MUCH AS YOU, MILORD...
REALLY, THANK YOU SO MUCH.
WE MANAGED TO GET EVERYTHING IN SHAPE THANKS TO YOUR HELP.
OH, IT WAS NOTHING. DON'T MENTION IT.
No, really. Please don't.
I keep saying you're the only one for me, don't I, Cathyl!?
H-Hey, everyone's watching!!
BAM
BUT HOW ARE YOU GOING TO SHEAR YOURSELVES FROM HERE ON OUT?
Thy wool will not cease growing.
ABOUT THAT...
PARDON ME.

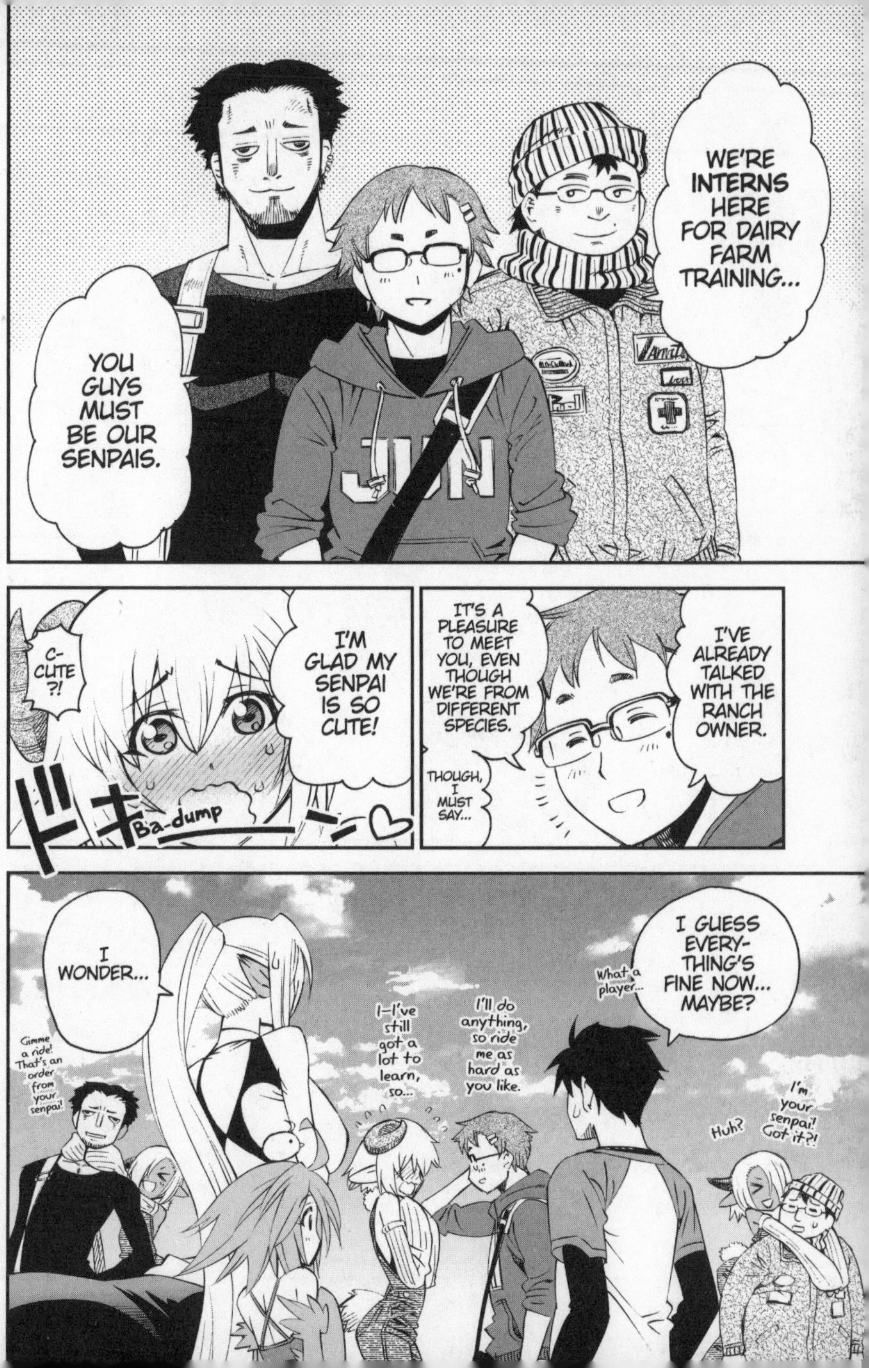
WE'RE INTERNS HERE FOR DAIRY FARM TRAINING...
YOU GUYS MUST BE OUR SENPAIS.
I'VE ALREADY TALKED WITH THE RANCH OWNER.
IT'S A PLEASURE TO MEET YOU, EVEN THOUGH WE'RE FROM DIFFERENT SPECIES.
THOUGH, I MUST SAY...
I'M GLAD MY SENPAI IS SO CUTE!
C-CUTE?!
ドキ
Ba-dump
I GUESS EVERY-THING'S FINE NOW... MAYBE?
What a player...
I'm your senpai! Got it?!
Huh?
I'll do anything, so ride me as hard as you like.
I-I've still got a lot to learn, so...
I WONDER...
Gimme a ride! That's an order from your senpai!

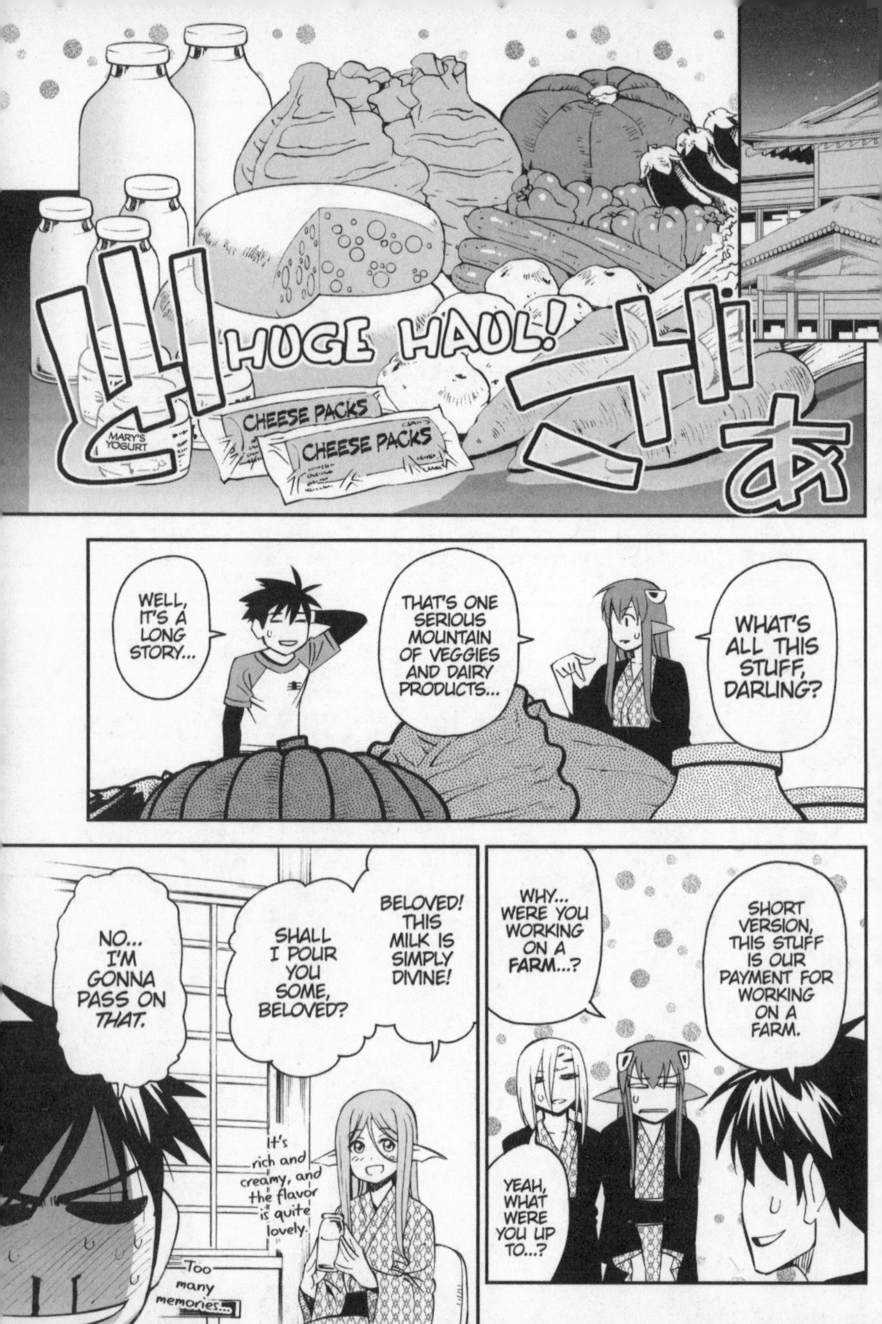
HUGE HAUL!
MARY'S YOGURT
CHEESE PACKS
CHEESE PACKS
WHAT'S ALL THIS STUFF, DARLING?
THAT'S ONE SERIOUS MOUNTAIN OF VEGGIES AND DAIRY PRODUCTS...
WELL, IT'S A LONG STORY...
SHORT VERSION, THIS STUFF IS OUR PAYMENT FOR WORKING ON A FARM.
WHY... WERE YOU WORKING ON A FARM...?
YEAH, WHAT WERE YOU UP TO...?
BELOVED! THIS MILK IS SIMPLY DIVINE!
SHALL I POUR YOU SOME, BELOVED?
It's rich and creamy, and the flavor is quite lovely.
NO... I'M GONNA PASS ON *THAT.*
Too many memories...

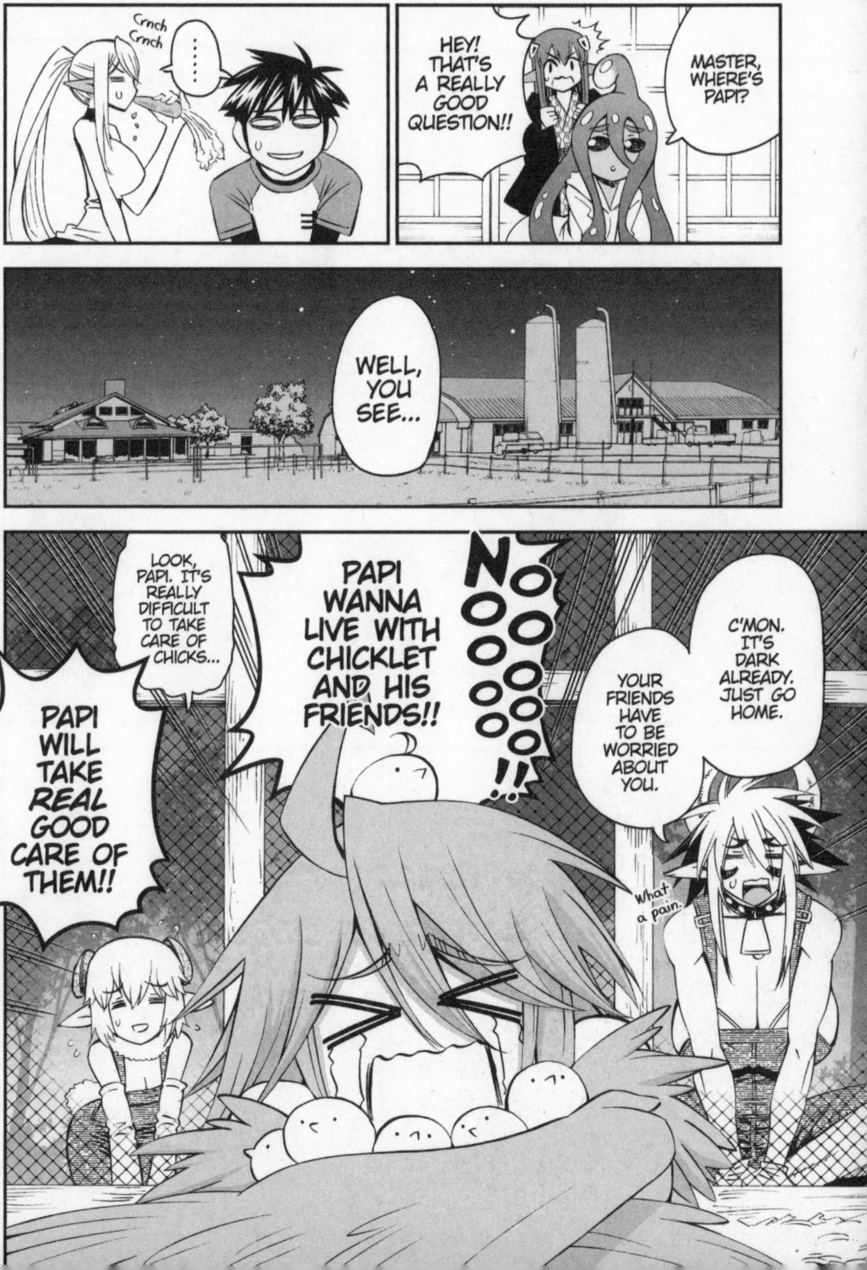
MASTER, WHERE'S PAPI?
HEY! THAT'S A REALLY GOOD QUESTION!!
Crnch Crnch
......
WELL, YOU SEE...
C'MON. IT'S DARK ALREADY. JUST GO HOME.
YOUR FRIENDS HAVE TO BE WORRIED ABOUT YOU.
NOOOOOOOOOO!!
PAPI WANNA LIVE WITH CHICKLET AND HIS FRIENDS!!
LOOK, PAPI. IT'S REALLY DIFFICULT TO TAKE CARE OF CHICKS...
What a pain.
PAPI WILL TAKE REAL GOOD CARE OF THEM!!

Monster Musume

Everyday Life with Monster Girls

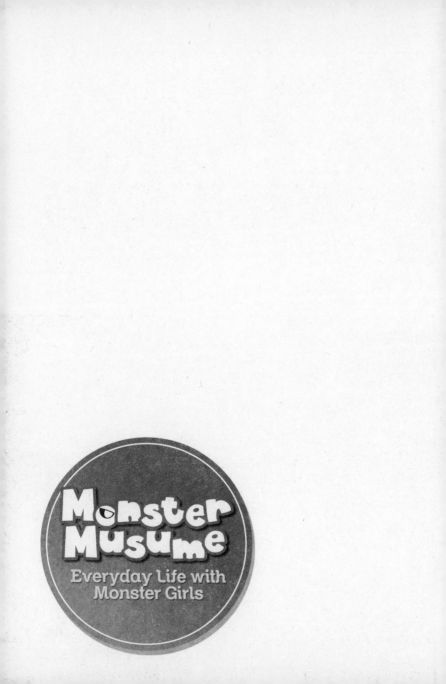

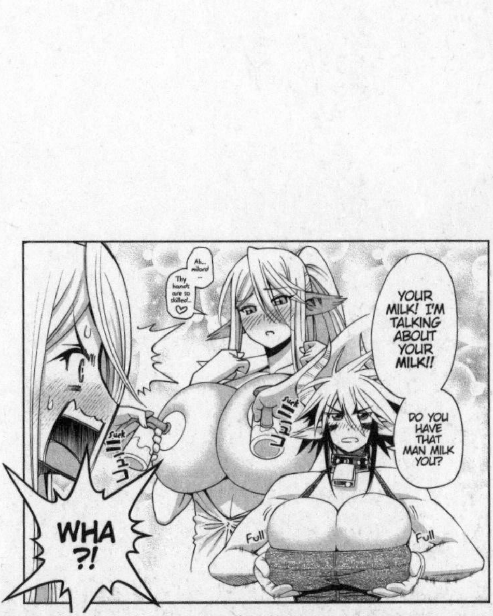
YOUR MILK! I'M TALKING ABOUT YOUR MILK!!
DO YOU HAVE THAT MAN MILK YOU?
Ah... milord! ... Thy hands are so skilled... ♡
Suck
Full
Full
Suck
WHA?!

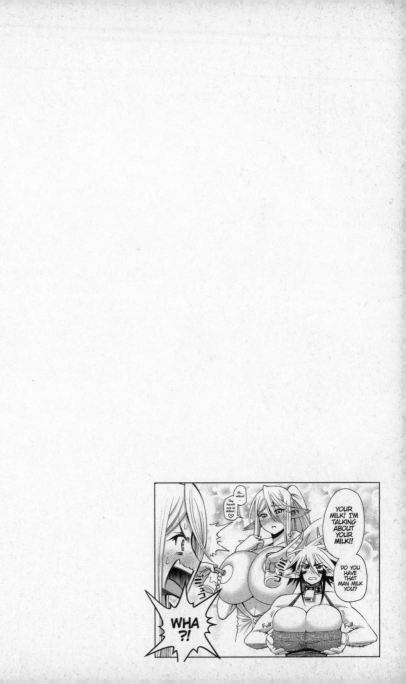

Chapter 34

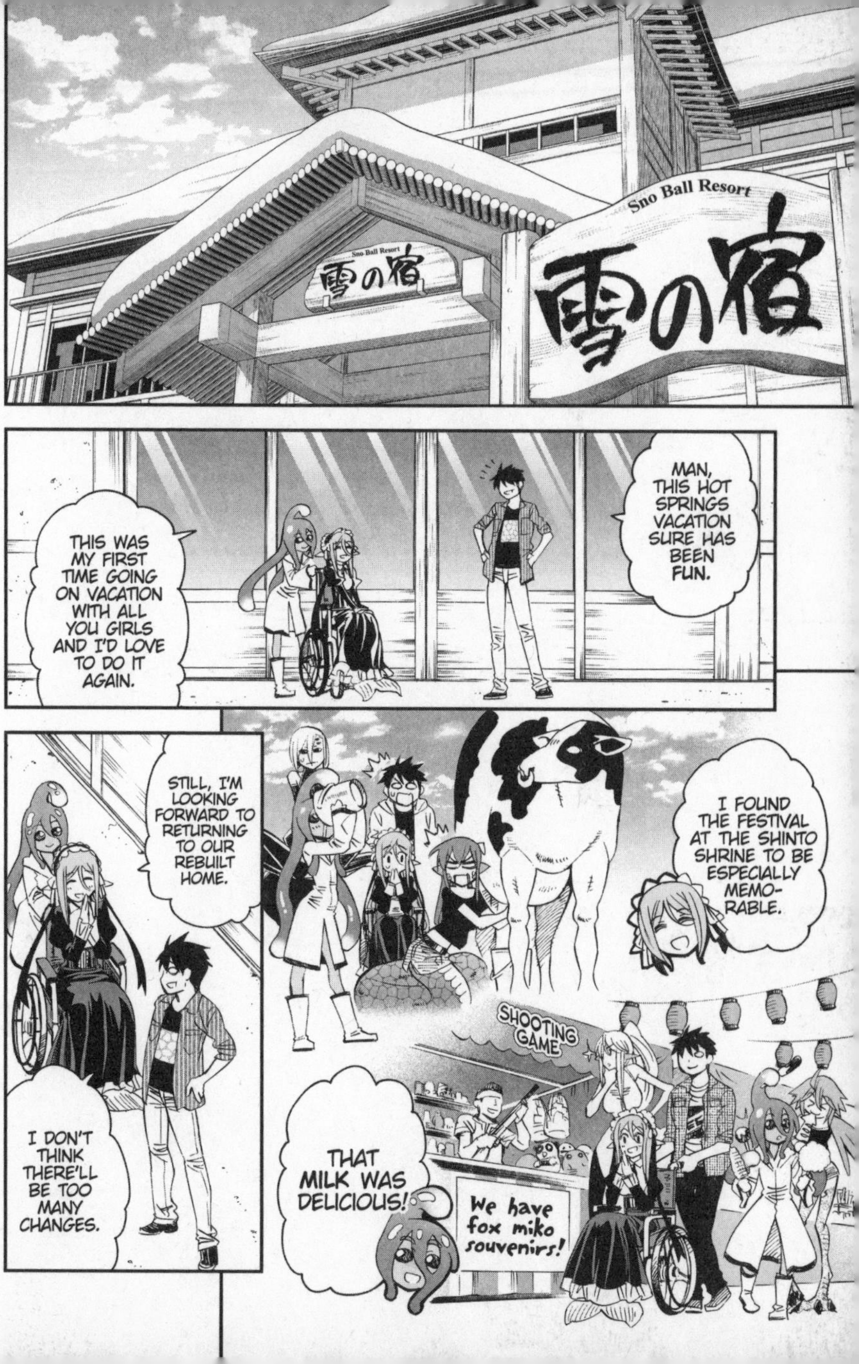
Sno Ball Resort
雪の宿
Sno Ball Resort
雪の宿
MAN, THIS HOT SPRINGS VACATION SURE HAS BEEN FUN.
THIS WAS MY FIRST TIME GOING ON VACATION WITH ALL YOU GIRLS AND I'D LOVE TO DO IT AGAIN.
I FOUND THE FESTIVAL AT THE SHINTO SHRINE TO BE ESPECIALLY MEMO-RABLE.
SHOOTING GAME
We have fox miko souvenirs!
THAT MILK WAS DELICIOUS!
STILL, I'M LOOKING FORWARD TO RETURNING TO OUR REBUILT HOME.
I DON'T THINK THERE'LL BE TOO MANY CHANGES.

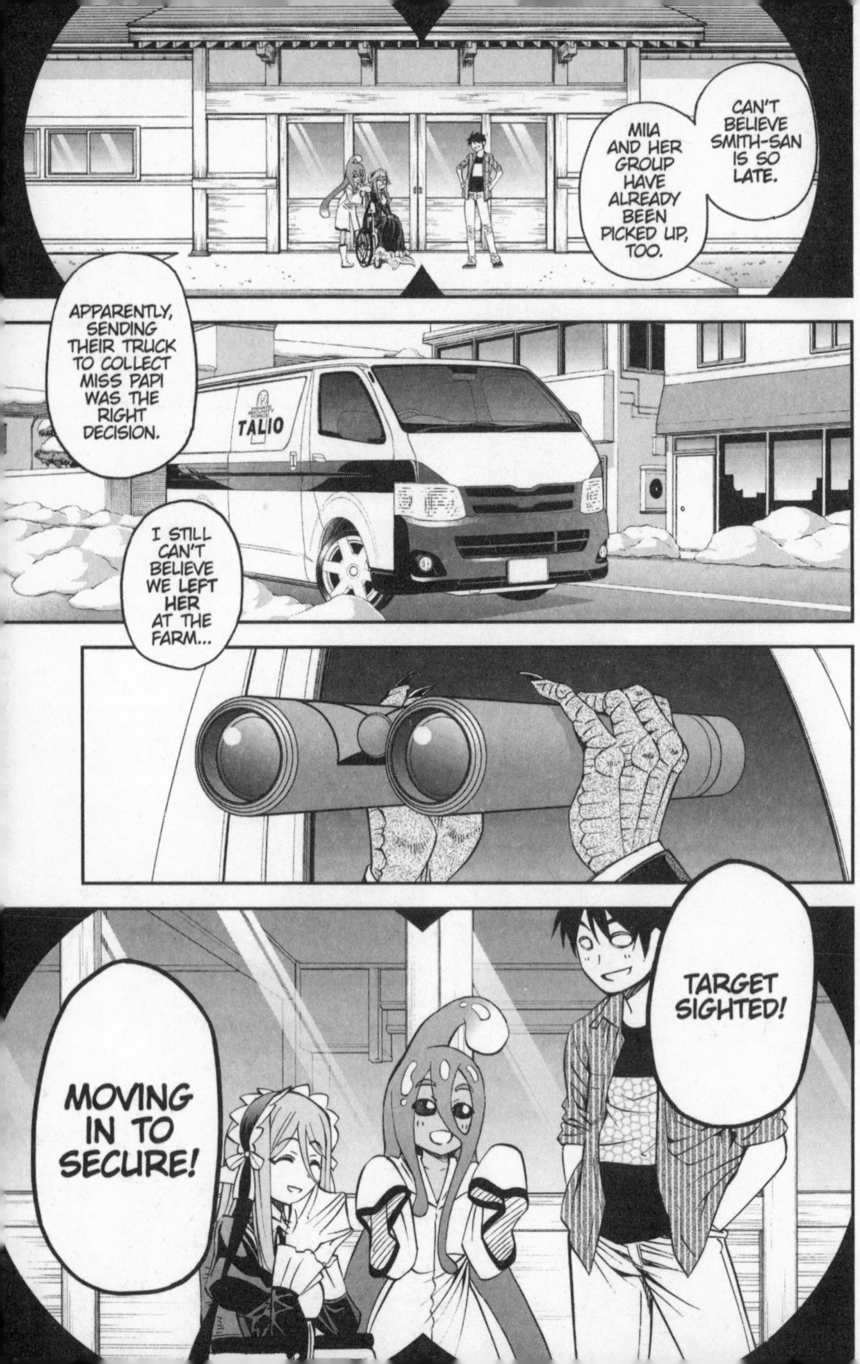
CAN'T BELIEVE SMITH-SAN IS SO LATE.
MIIA AND HER GROUP HAVE ALREADY BEEN PICKED UP, TOO.
APPARENTLY, SENDING THEIR TRUCK TO COLLECT MISS PAPI WAS THE RIGHT DECISION.
TALIO
I STILL CAN'T BELIEVE WE LEFT HER AT THE FARM...
TARGET SIGHTED!
MOVING IN TO SECURE!

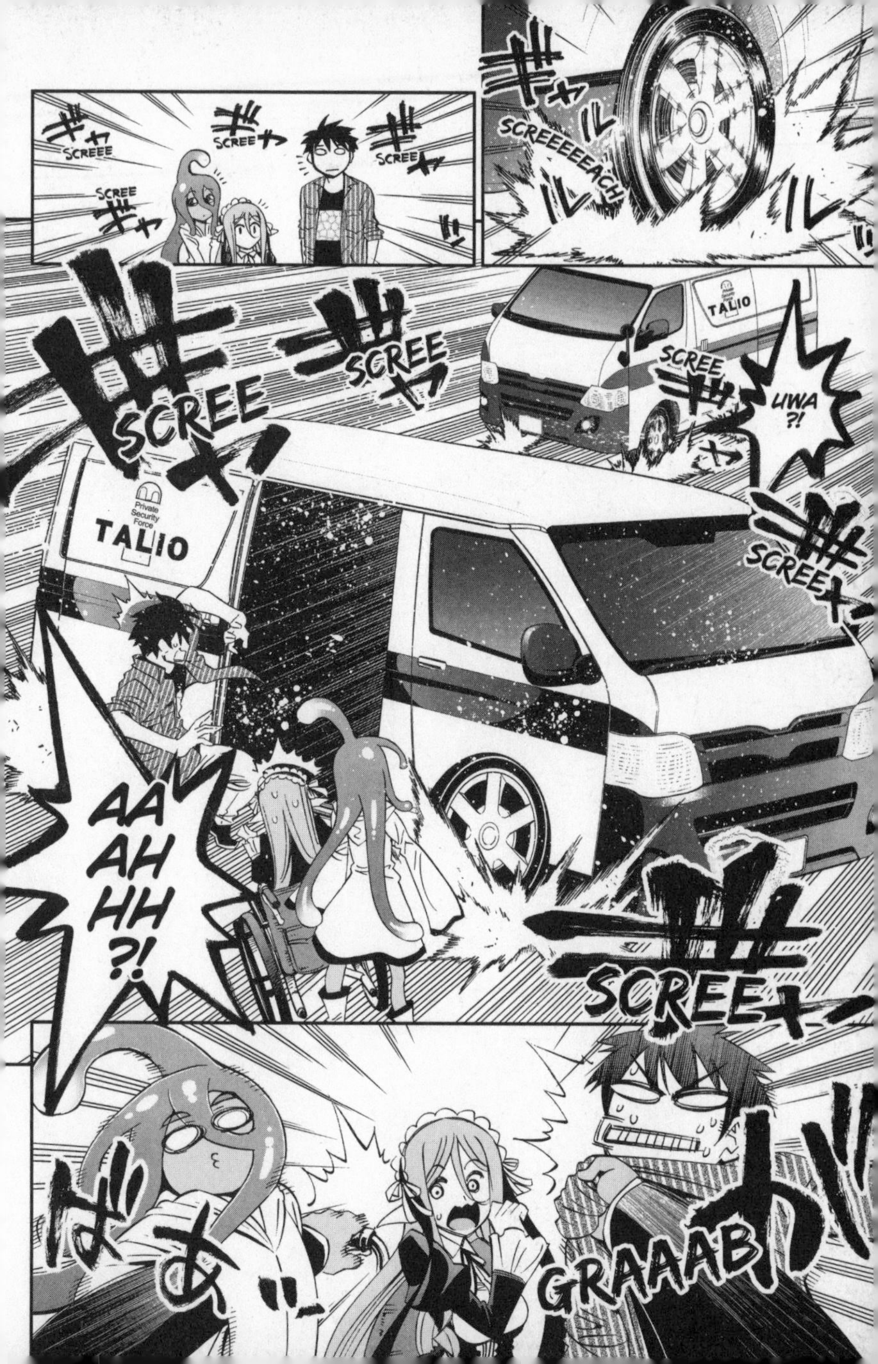
SCREEEEEEACH
SCREE
SCREE
SCREEE
SCREE
TALIO
SCREE
UWA ?!
SCREE
SCREE
SCREE
Private Security Force
TALIO
SCREE
AAAHHH?!
GRAAAB

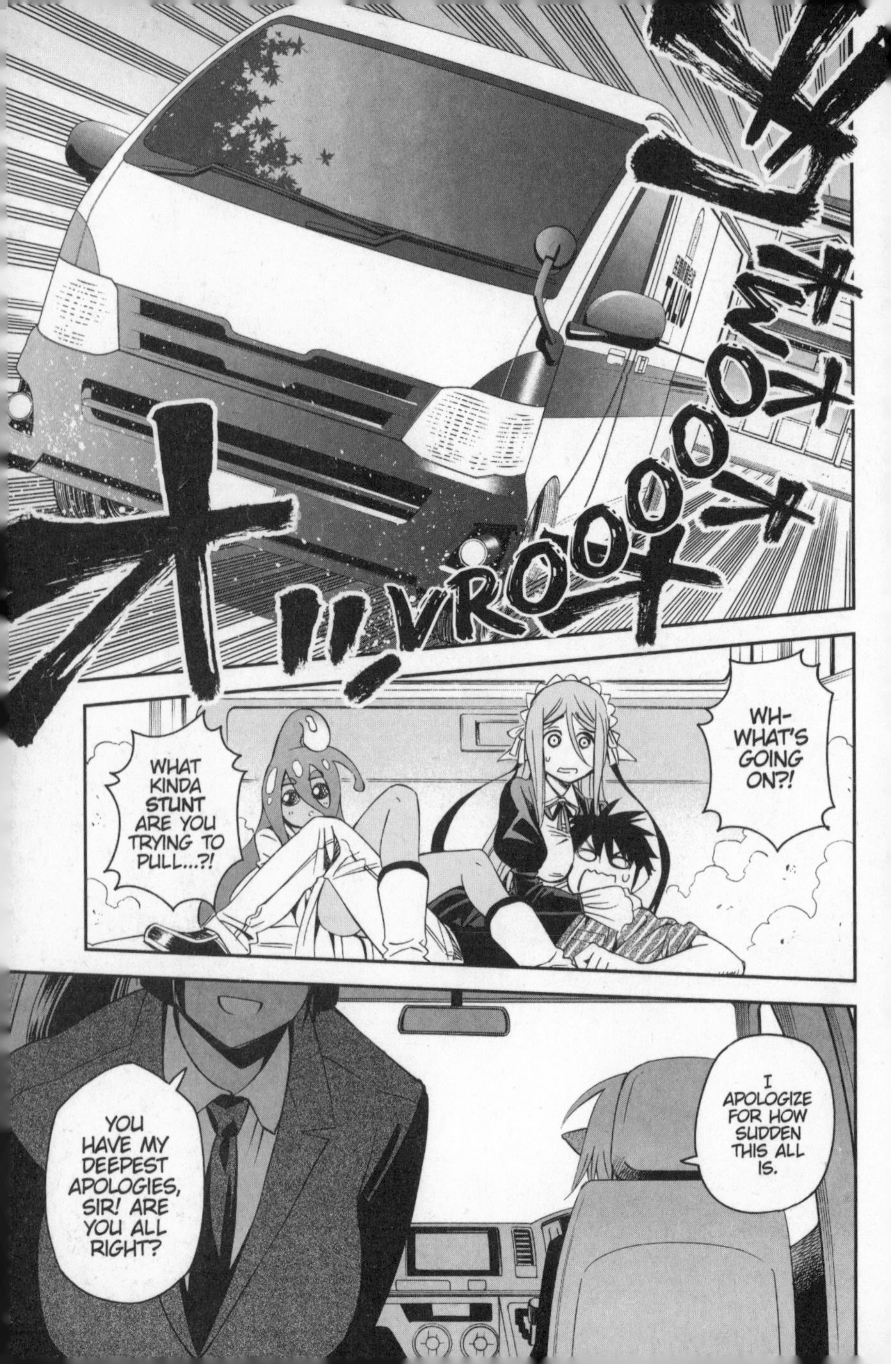
TALIO
VROOOOOOM!!
WH-WHAT'S GOING ON?!
WHAT KINDA STUNT ARE YOU TRYING TO PULL...?!
I APOLOGIZE FOR HOW SUDDEN THIS ALL IS.
YOU HAVE MY DEEPEST APOLOGIES, SIR! ARE YOU ALL RIGHT?

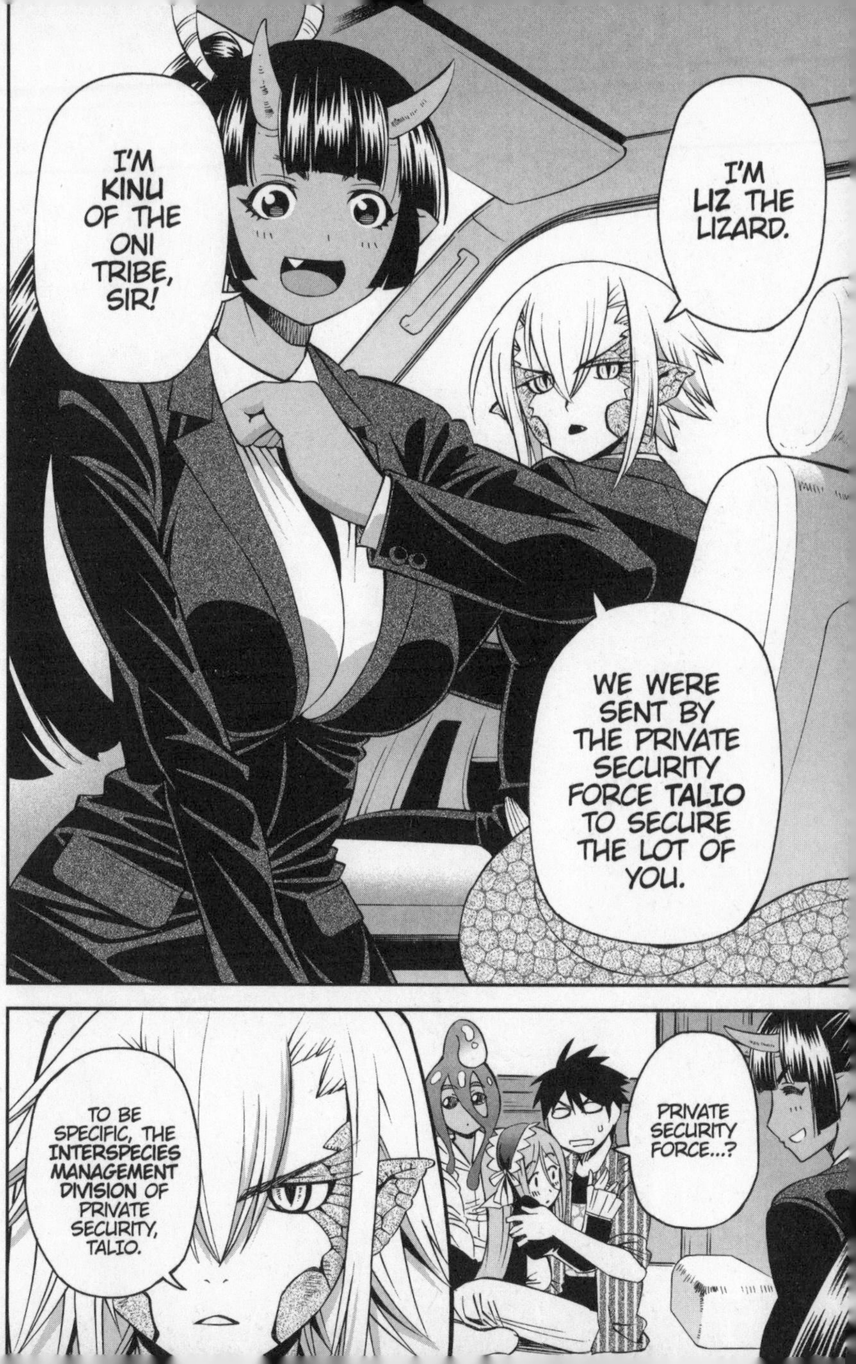
I'M LIZ THE LIZARD.
I'M KINU OF THE ONI TRIBE, SIR!
WE WERE SENT BY THE PRIVATE SECURITY FORCE TALIO TO SECURE THE LOT OF YOU.
PRIVATE SECURITY FORCE...?
TO BE SPECIFIC, THE INTERSPECIES MANAGEMENT DIVISION OF PRIVATE SECURITY, TALIO.

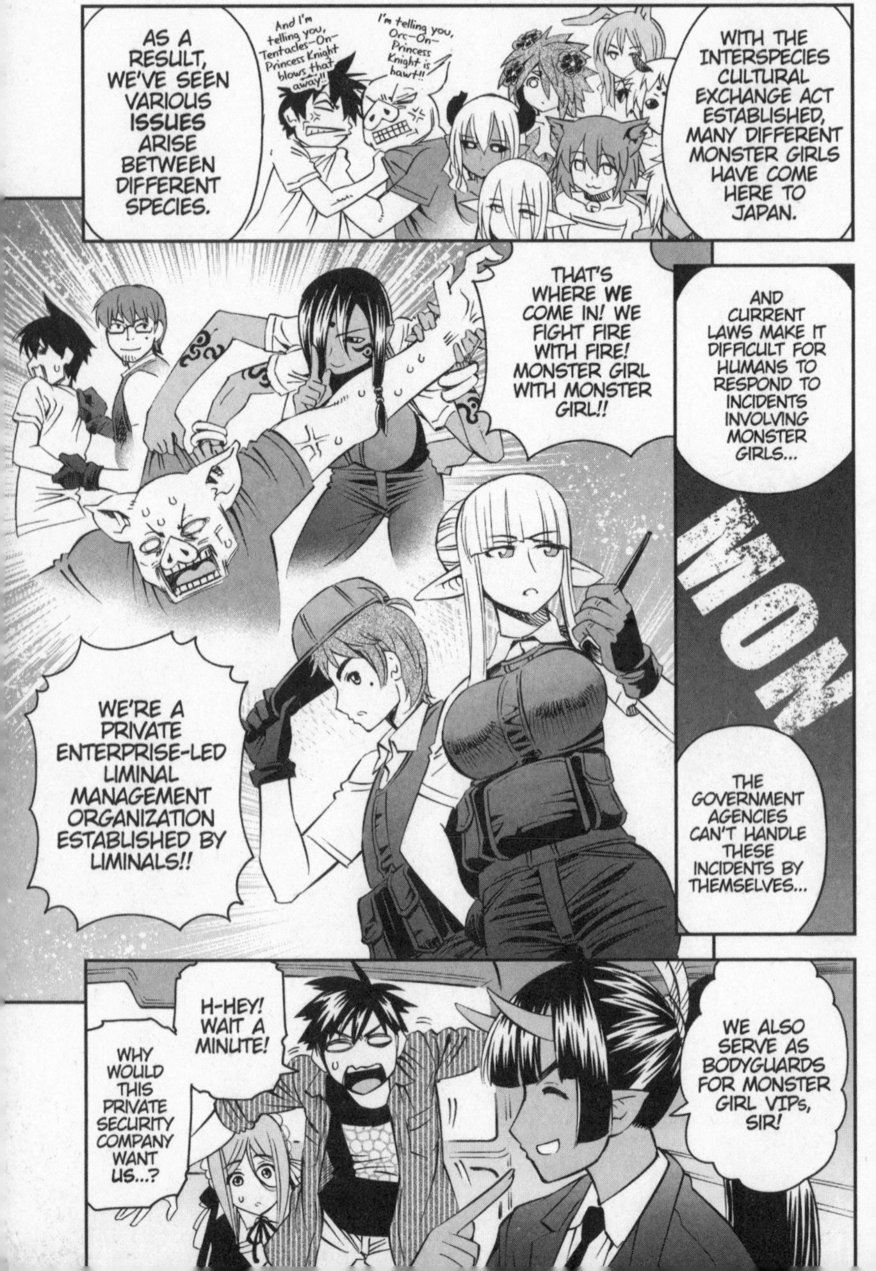
WITH THE INTERSPECIES CULTURAL EXCHANGE ACT ESTABLISHED, MANY DIFFERENT MONSTER GIRLS HAVE COME HERE TO JAPAN.
I'm telling you, Orc-On-Princess Knight is hawt!!
And I'm telling you, Tentacles-On-Princess Knight blows that away!!
AS A RESULT, WE'VE SEEN VARIOUS ISSUES ARISE BETWEEN DIFFERENT SPECIES.
AND CURRENT LAWS MAKE IT DIFFICULT FOR HUMANS TO RESPOND TO INCIDENTS INVOLVING MONSTER GIRLS...
MON
THE GOVERNMENT AGENCIES CAN'T HANDLE THESE INCIDENTS BY THEMSELVES...
THAT'S WHERE WE COME IN! WE FIGHT FIRE WITH FIRE! MONSTER GIRL WITH MONSTER GIRL!!
WE'RE A PRIVATE ENTERPRISE-LED LIMINAL MANAGEMENT ORGANIZATION ESTABLISHED BY LIMINALS!!
WE ALSO SERVE AS BODYGUARDS FOR MONSTER GIRL VIPs, SIR!
H-HEY! WAIT A MINUTE!
WHY WOULD THIS PRIVATE SECURITY COMPANY WANT US...?

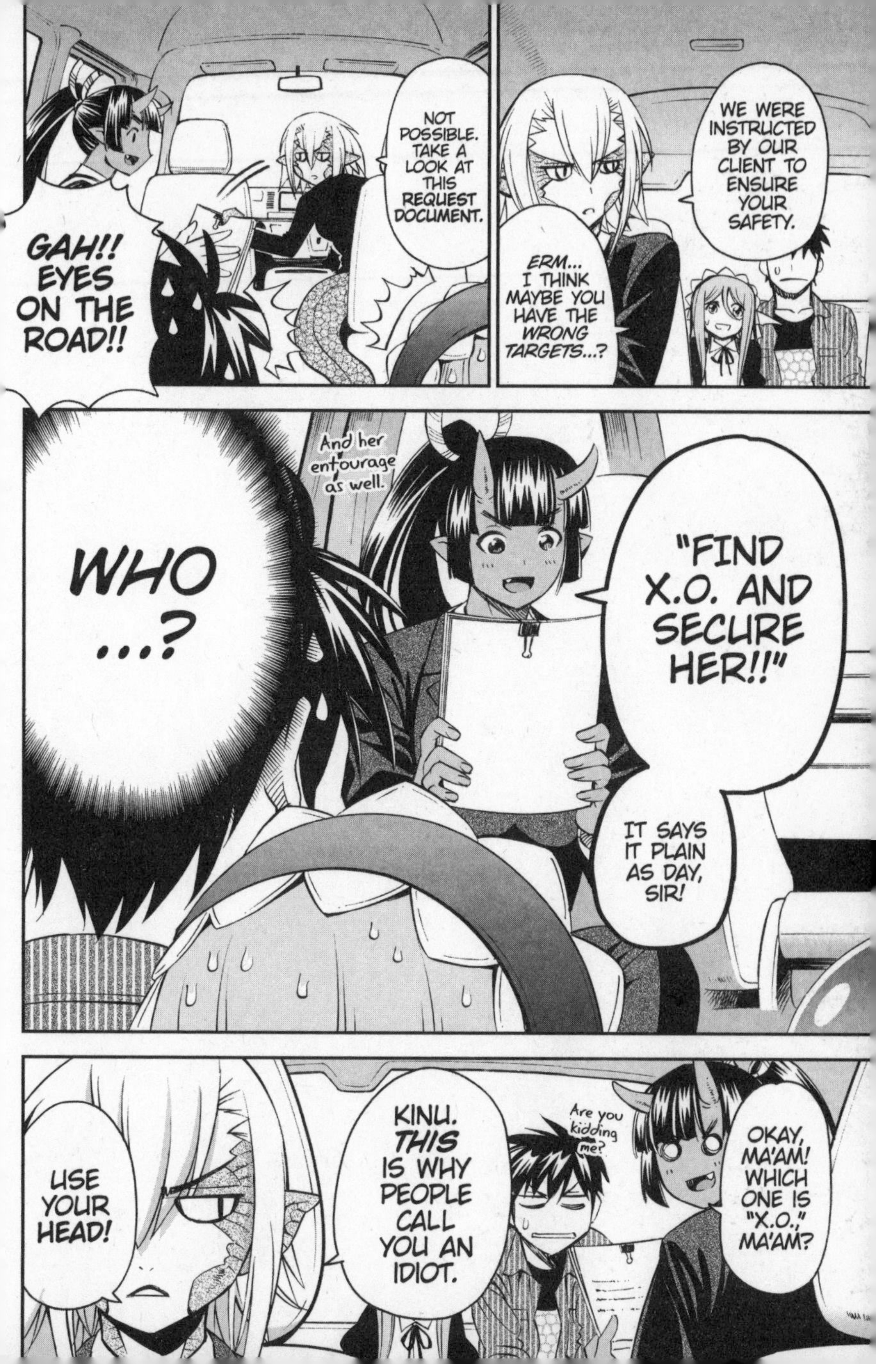
WE WERE INSTRUCTED BY OUR CLIENT TO ENSURE YOUR SAFETY.
ERM... I THINK MAYBE YOU HAVE THE *WRONG* TARGETS...?
NOT POSSIBLE. TAKE A LOOK AT THIS REQUEST DOCUMENT.
GAH!! EYES ON THE ROAD!!
"FIND X.O. AND SECURE HER!!"
IT SAYS IT PLAIN AS DAY, SIR!
And her entourage as well.
WHO ...?
OKAY, MA'AM! WHICH ONE IS "X.O.," MA'AM?
Are you kidding me?
KINU. *THIS* IS WHY PEOPLE CALL YOU AN IDIOT.
USE YOUR HEAD!

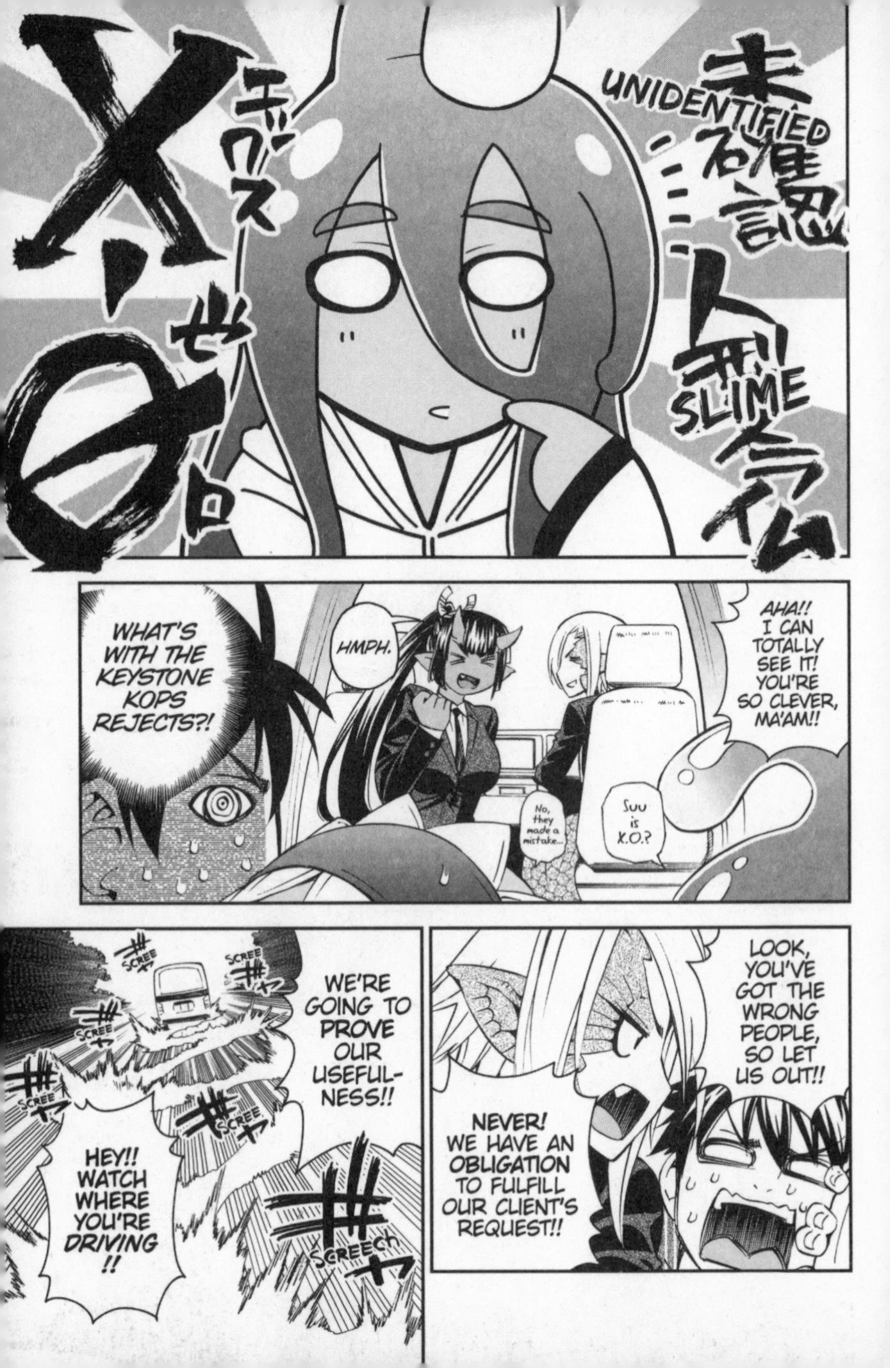
UNIDENTIFIED
未確認スライム
SLIME
エックスゼロ
X・0
AHA!! I CAN TOTALLY SEE IT! YOU'RE SO CLEVER, MA'AM!!
Suu is X.O.?
No, they made a mistake...
HMPH.
WHAT'S WITH THE KEYSTONE KOPS REJECTS?!
LOOK, YOU'VE GOT THE WRONG PEOPLE, SO LET US OUT!!
NEVER! WE HAVE AN OBLIGATION TO FULFILL OUR CLIENT'S REQUEST!!
WE'RE GOING TO PROVE OUR USEFUL-NESS!!
SCREE
SCREE
SCREE
SCREE
SCREE
HEY!! WATCH WHERE YOU'RE DRIVING!!
SCREECH

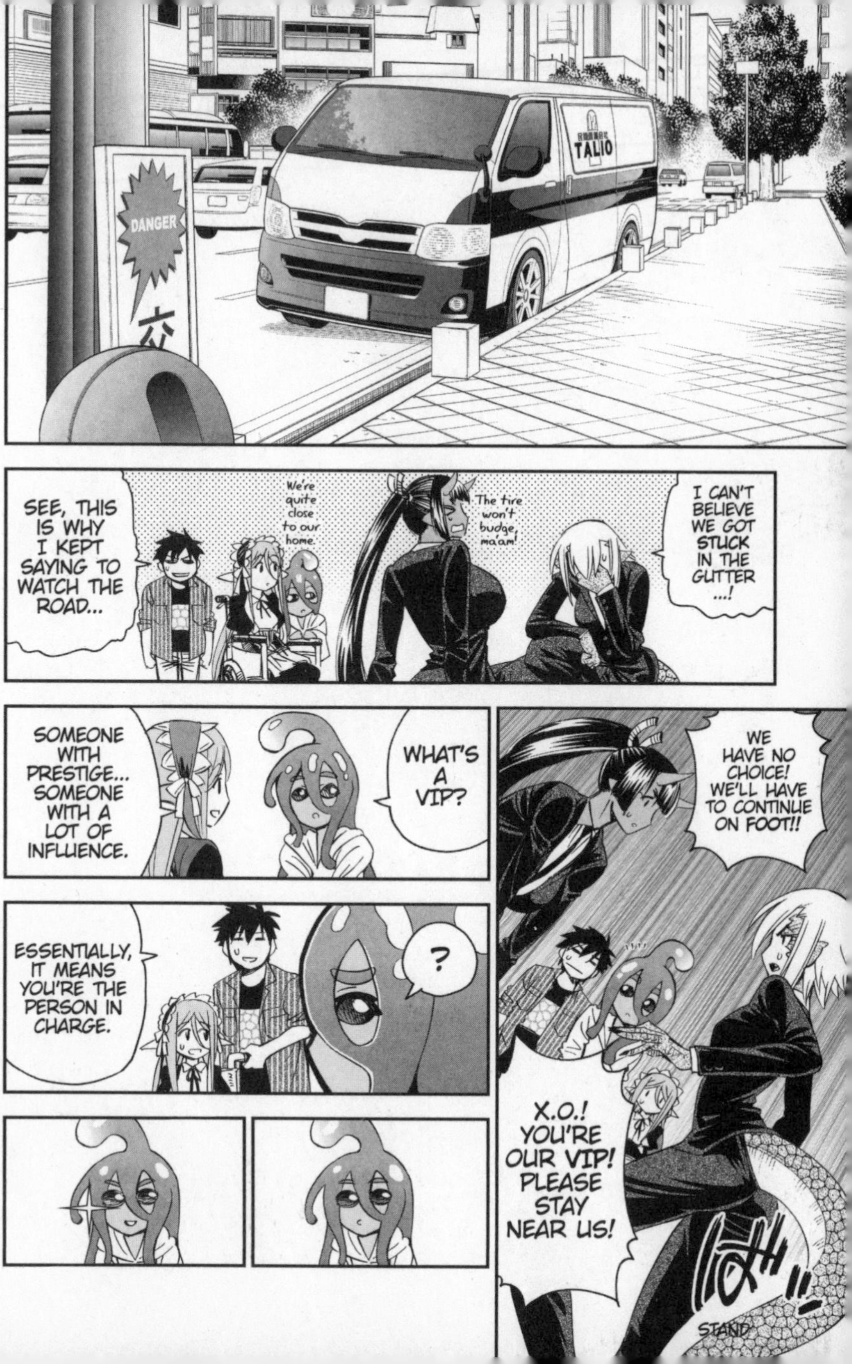
DANGER
TALIO
I CAN'T BELIEVE WE GOT STUCK IN THE GUTTER ...!
The tire won't budge, ma'am!
We're quite close to our home.
SEE, THIS IS WHY I KEPT SAYING TO WATCH THE ROAD...
WE HAVE NO CHOICE! WE'LL HAVE TO CONTINUE ON FOOT!!
X.O.! YOU'RE OUR VIP! PLEASE STAY NEAR US!
STAND
WHAT'S A VIP?
SOMEONE WITH PRESTIGE... SOMEONE WITH A LOT OF INFLUENCE.
?
ESSENTIALLY, IT MEANS YOU'RE THE PERSON IN CHARGE.

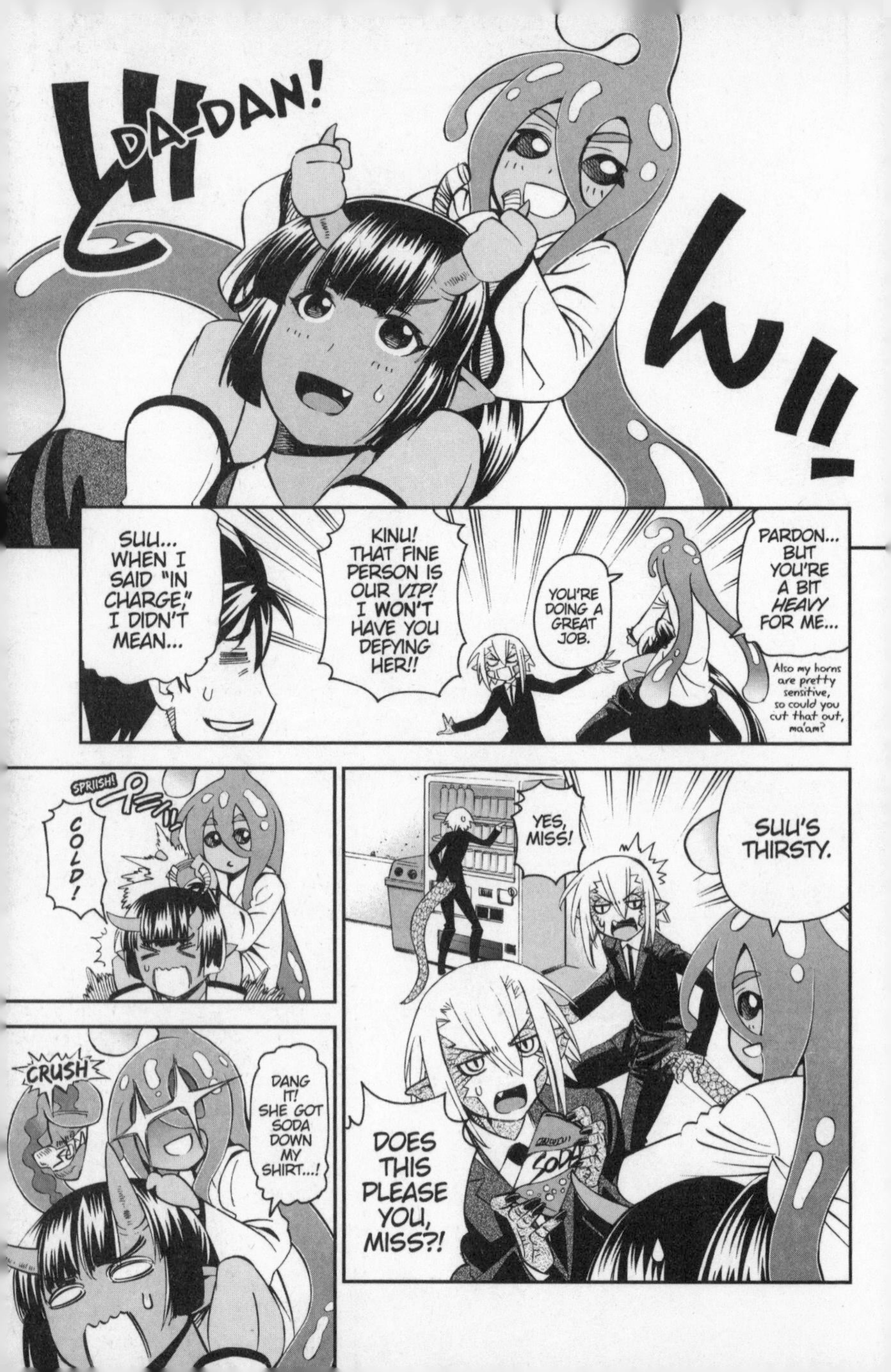
DA-DAN!
PARDON... BUT YOU'RE A BIT HEAVY FOR ME...
Also my horns are pretty sensitive, so could you cut that out, ma'am?
YOU'RE DOING A GREAT JOB.
KINU! THAT FINE PERSON IS OUR VIP! I WON'T HAVE YOU DEFYING HER!!
SUU... WHEN I SAID "IN CHARGE," I DIDN'T MEAN...
SUU'S THIRSTY.
YES, MISS!
DOES THIS PLEASE YOU, MISS?!
SPRIISH!
COLD!
CRUSH
DANG IT! SHE GOT SODA DOWN MY SHIRT...!

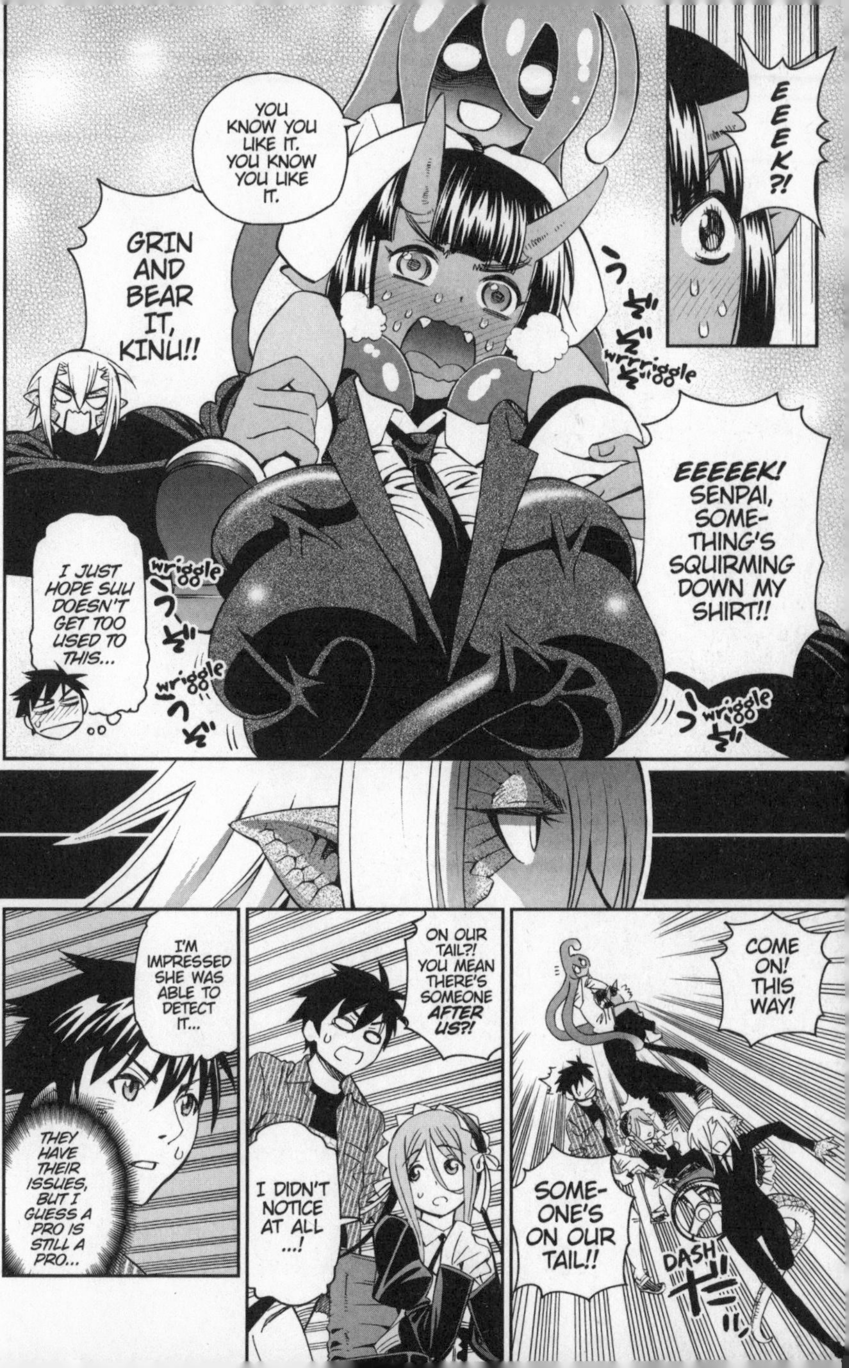
EEEK?!
YOU KNOW YOU LIKE IT. YOU KNOW YOU LIKE IT.
GRIN AND BEAR IT, KINU!!
wrrriggle
EEEEEK! SENPAI, SOME-THING'S SQUIRMING DOWN MY SHIRT!!
wriggle
wriggle
wriggle
I JUST HOPE SUU DOESN'T GET TOO USED TO THIS...
COME ON! THIS WAY!
SOME-ONE'S ON OUR TAIL!!
DASH
ON OUR TAIL?! YOU MEAN THERE'S SOMEONE *AFTER US?!*
I DIDN'T NOTICE AT ALL ....!
I'M IMPRESSED SHE WAS ABLE TO DETECT IT...
THEY HAVE THEIR ISSUES, BUT I GUESS A PRO IS STILL A PRO...

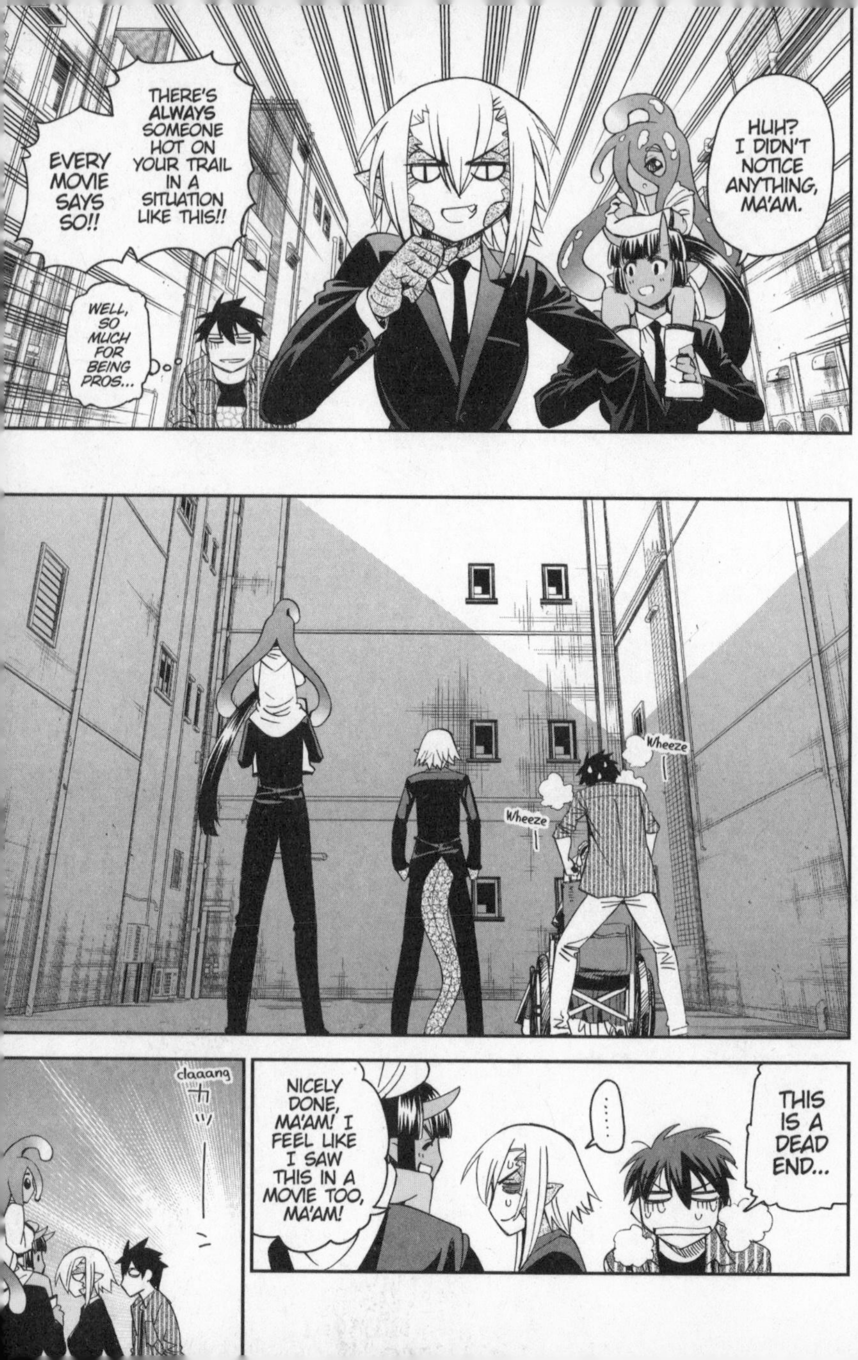
HUH? I DIDN'T NOTICE ANYTHING, MA'AM.
THERE'S ALWAYS SOMEONE HOT ON YOUR TRAIL IN A SITUATION LIKE THIS!!
EVERY MOVIE SAYS SO!!
WELL, SO MUCH FOR BEING PROS...
Wheeze
Wheeze
THIS IS A DEAD END...
......
NICELY DONE, MA'AM! I FEEL LIKE I SAW THIS IN A MOVIE TOO, MA'AM!
claaang
カッー

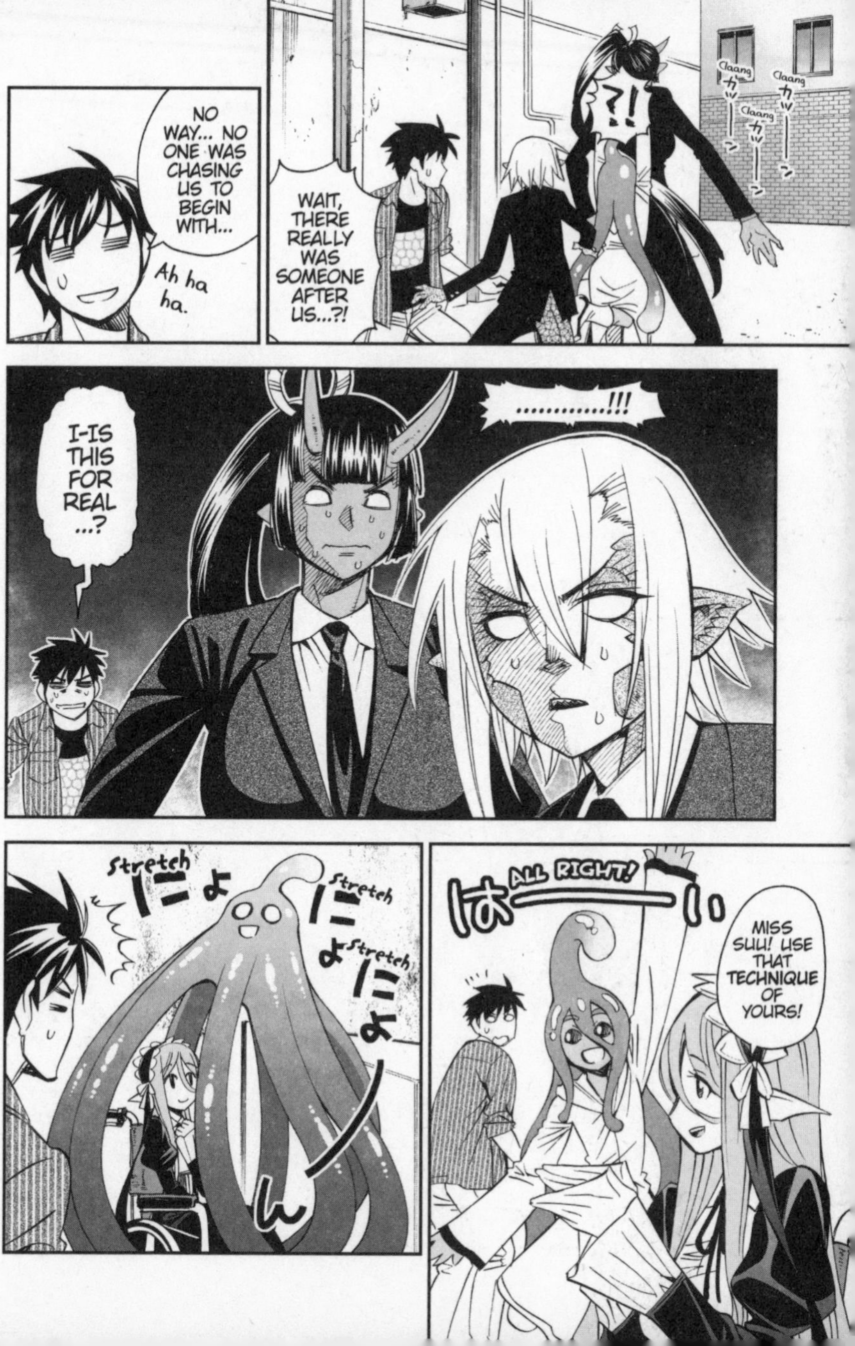

Claang
Claang
Claang
?!
WAIT, THERE REALLY WAS SOMEONE AFTER US...?!
NO WAY... NO ONE WAS CHASING US TO BEGIN WITH...
Ah ha ha.
............!!!
I-IS THIS FOR REAL...?
ALL RIGHT!
MISS SUU! USE THAT TECHNIQUE OF YOURS!
Stretch
Stretch
Stretch

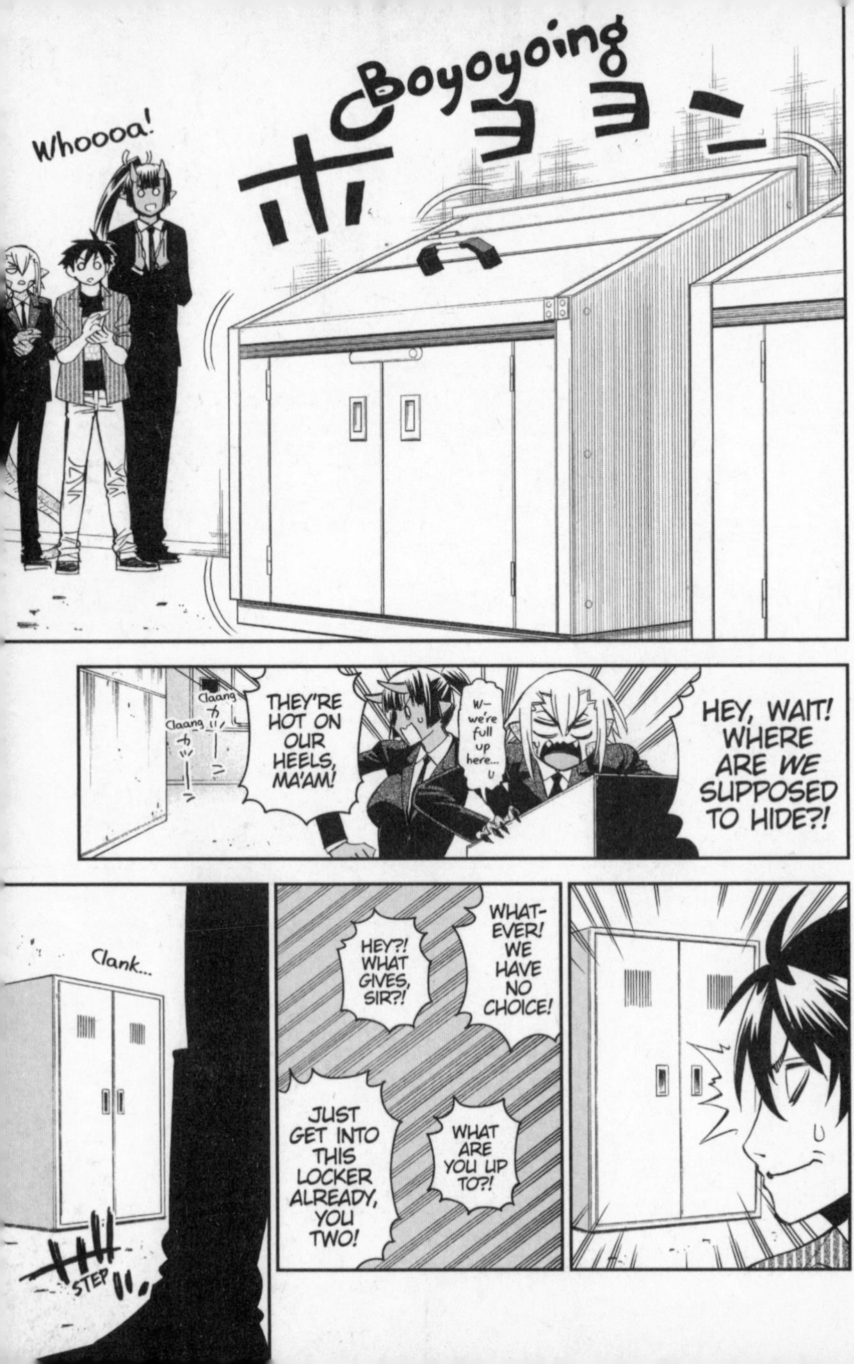
Boyoyoing
Whoooa!
HEY, WAIT! WHERE ARE WE SUPPOSED TO HIDE?!
W-we're full up here...
THEY'RE HOT ON OUR HEELS, MA'AM!
Claang
Claang
WHAT-EVER! WE HAVE NO CHOICE!
HEY?! WHAT GIVES, SIR?!
WHAT ARE YOU UP TO?!
JUST GET INTO THIS LOCKER ALREADY, YOU TWO!
Clank...
STEP

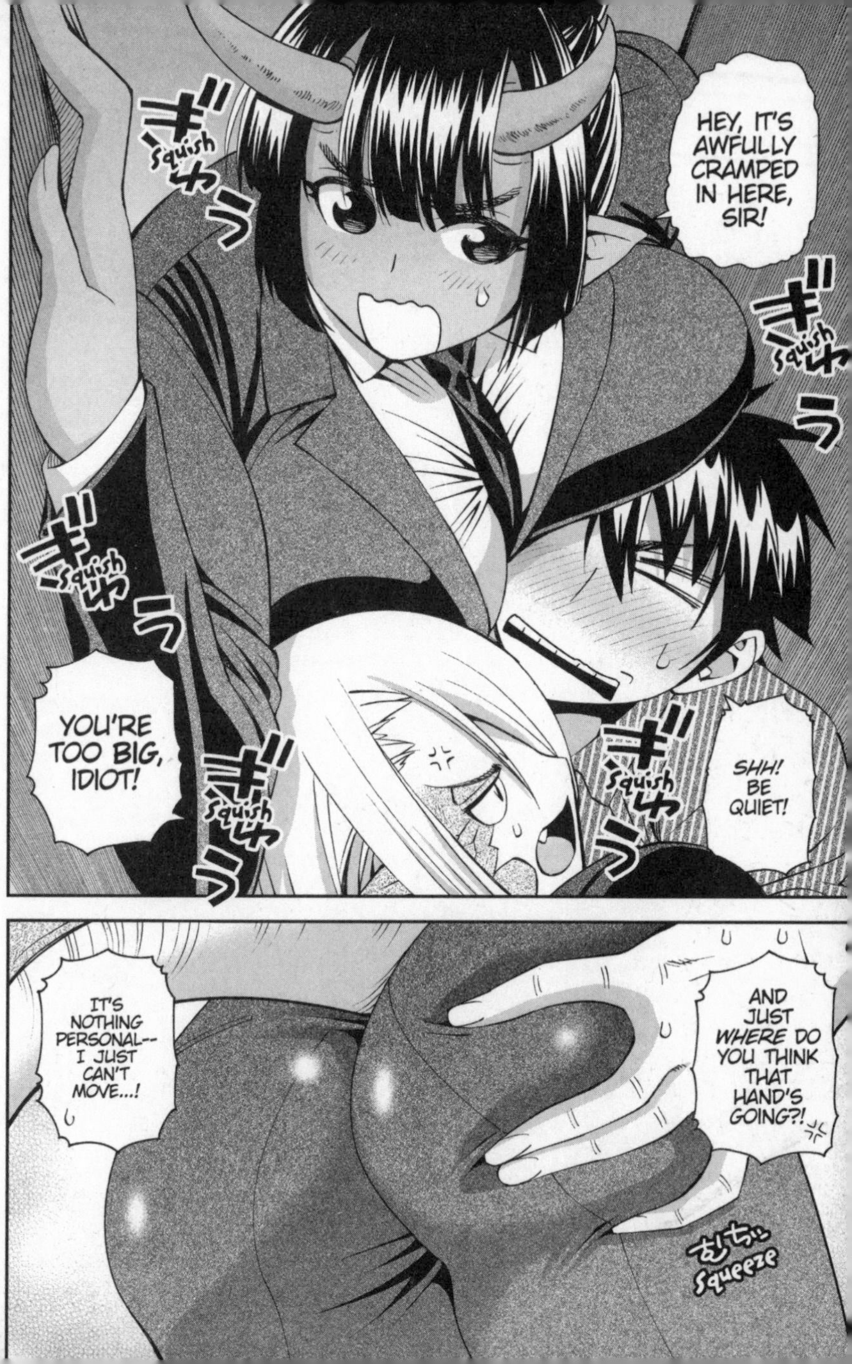
HEY, IT'S AWFULLY CRAMPED IN HERE, SIR!
ぎゅう squish
ぎゅう squish
SHH! BE QUIET!
ぎゅう squish
ぎゅう squish
ぎゅう squish
YOU'RE TOO BIG, IDIOT!
AND JUST *WHERE* DO YOU THINK THAT HAND'S GOING?!
IT'S NOTHING PERSONAL-- I JUST CAN'T MOVE...!
むにっ squeeze

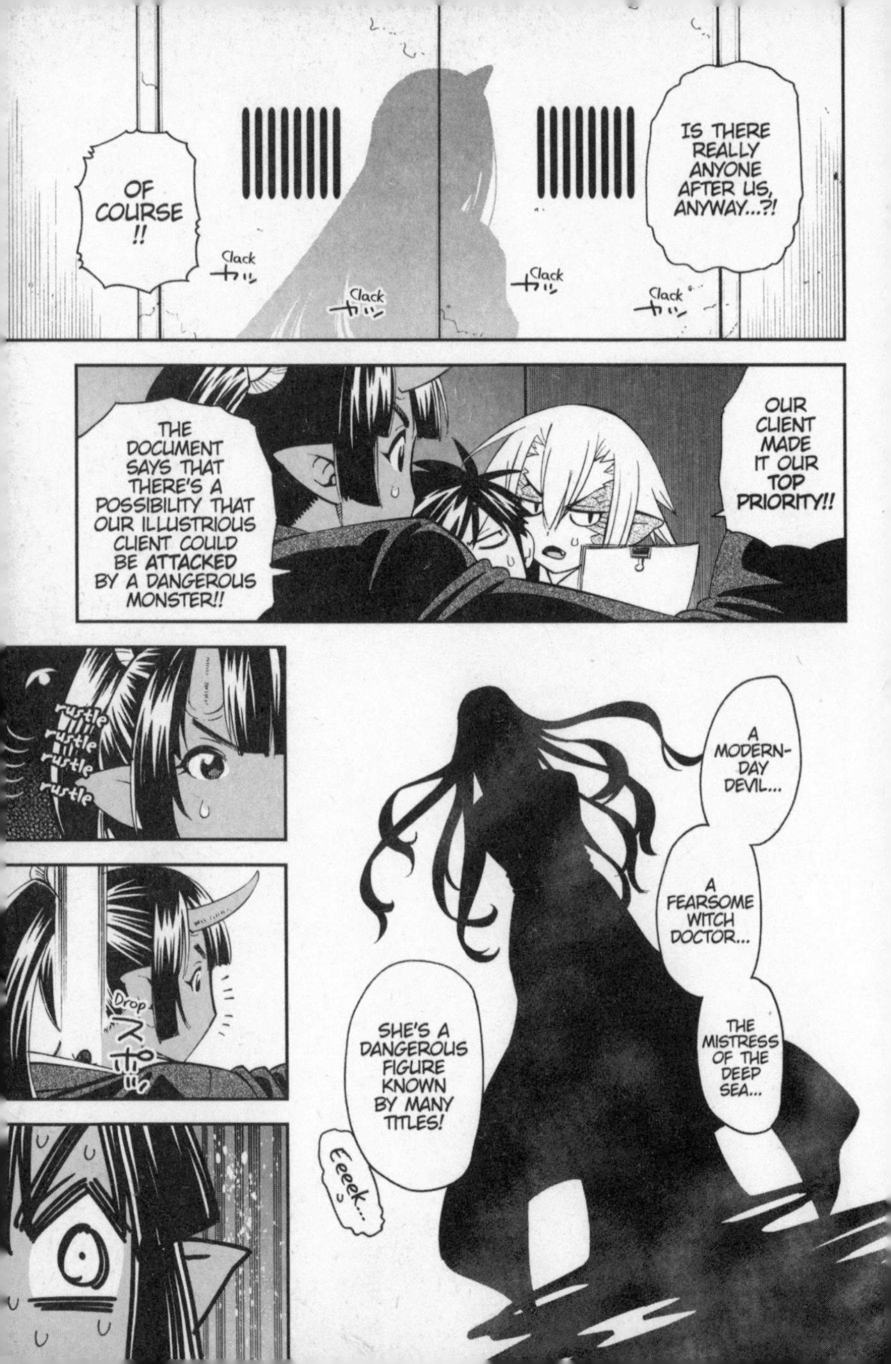

IS THERE REALLY ANYONE AFTER US, ANYWAY...?!
Clack カッ
Clack カッ
Clack カッ
Clack カッ
OF COURSE!!
OUR CLIENT MADE IT OUR TOP PRIORITY!!
THE DOCUMENT SAYS THAT THERE'S A POSSIBILITY THAT OUR ILLUSTRIOUS CLIENT COULD BE ATTACKED BY A DANGEROUS MONSTER!!
A MODERN-DAY DEVIL...
A FEARSOME WITCH DOCTOR...
THE MISTRESS OF THE DEEP SEA...
SHE'S A DANGEROUS FIGURE KNOWN BY MANY TITLES!
Eeeek...
rustle rustle rustle rustle
Drop

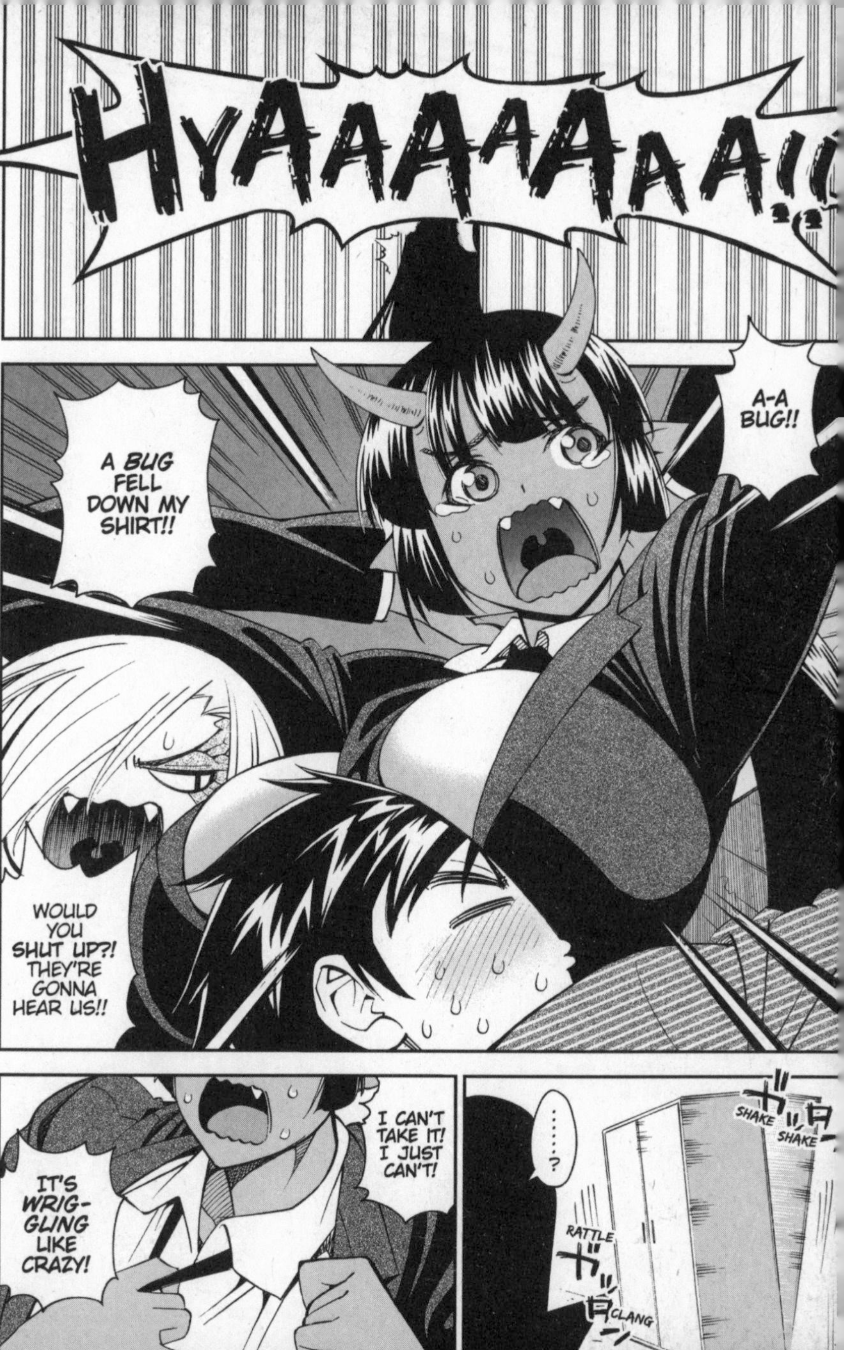
HYAAAAAAA!!
A-A BUG!!
A BUG FELL DOWN MY SHIRT!!
WOULD YOU SHUT UP?! THEY'RE GONNA HEAR US!!
SHAKE
SHAKE
......?
RATTLE
CLANG
I CAN'T TAKE IT! I JUST CAN'T!
IT'S WRIGGLING LIKE CRAZY!

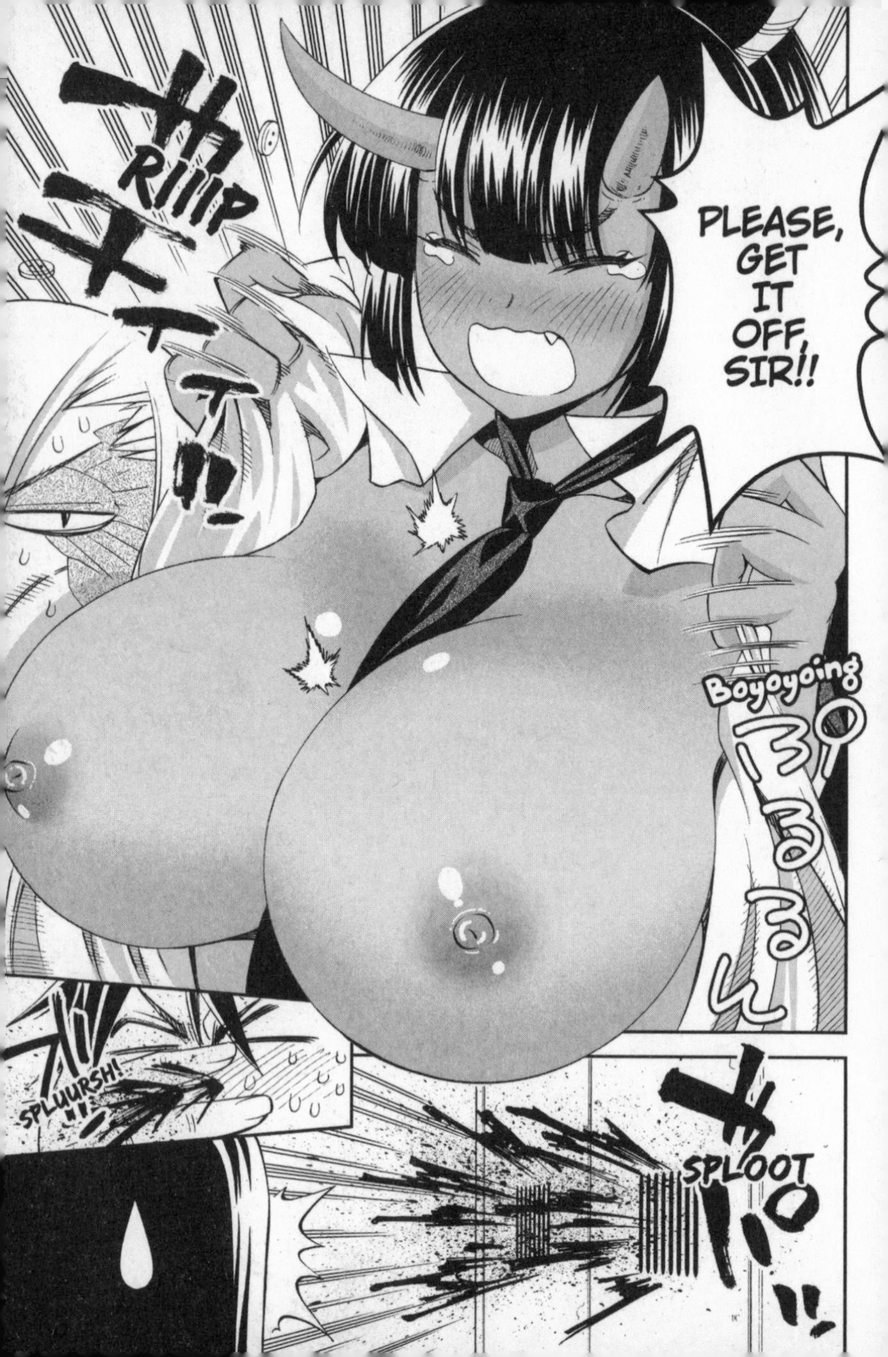
PLEASE, GET IT OFF, SIR!!
Boyoyoing
RIIIP
SPLOOT
SPLUURSH!

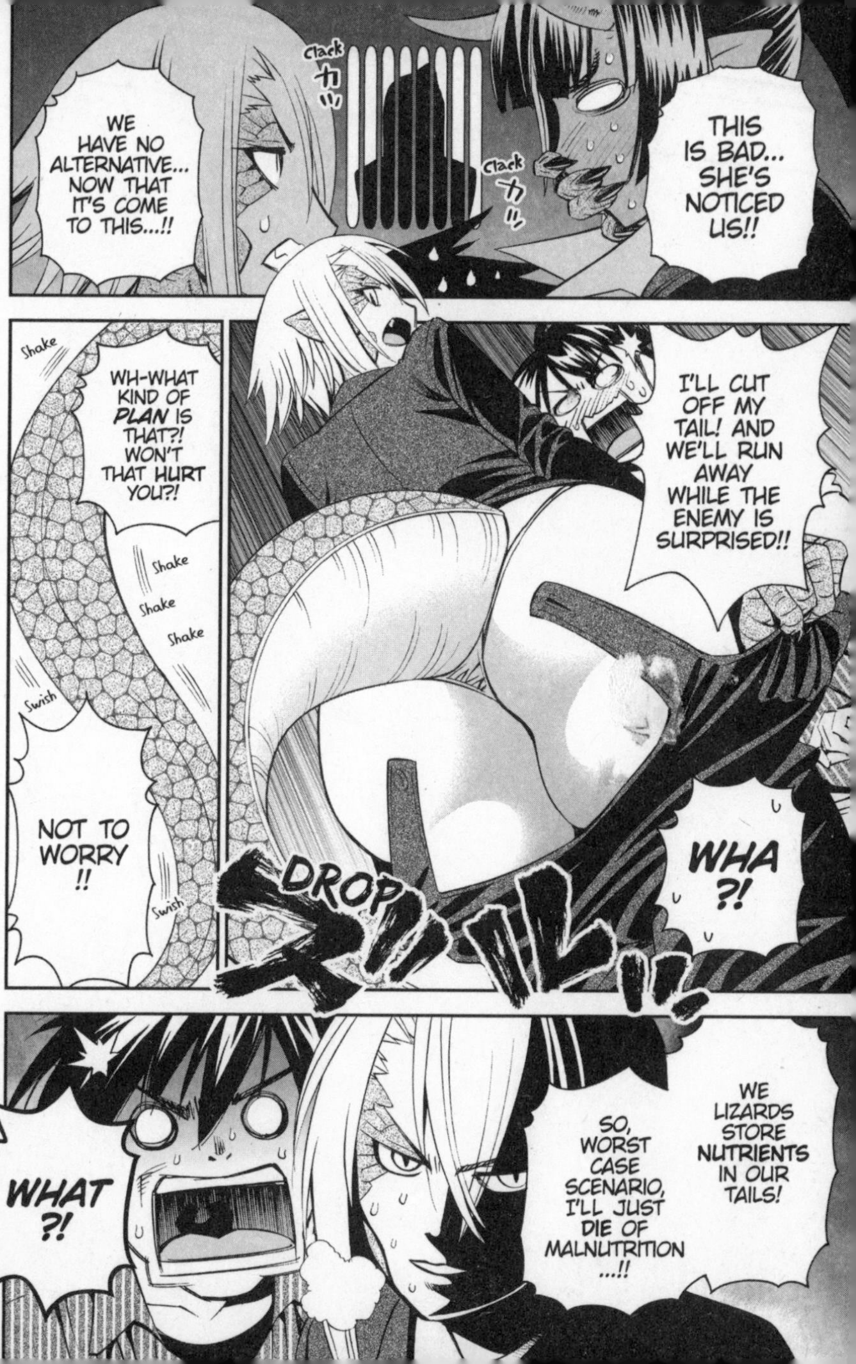
Clack
Clack
THIS IS BAD... SHE'S NOTICED US!!
WE HAVE NO ALTERNATIVE... NOW THAT IT'S COME TO THIS...!!
I'LL CUT OFF MY TAIL! AND WE'LL RUN AWAY WHILE THE ENEMY IS SURPRISED!!
WHA ?!
DROP
Shake
WH-WHAT KIND OF *PLAN* IS THAT?! WON'T THAT HURT YOU?!
Shake
Shake
Shake
Swish
NOT TO WORRY !!
Swish
WE LIZARDS STORE NUTRIENTS IN OUR TAILS!
SO, WORST CASE SCENARIO, I'LL JUST DIE OF MALNUTRITION ...!!
WHAT ?!

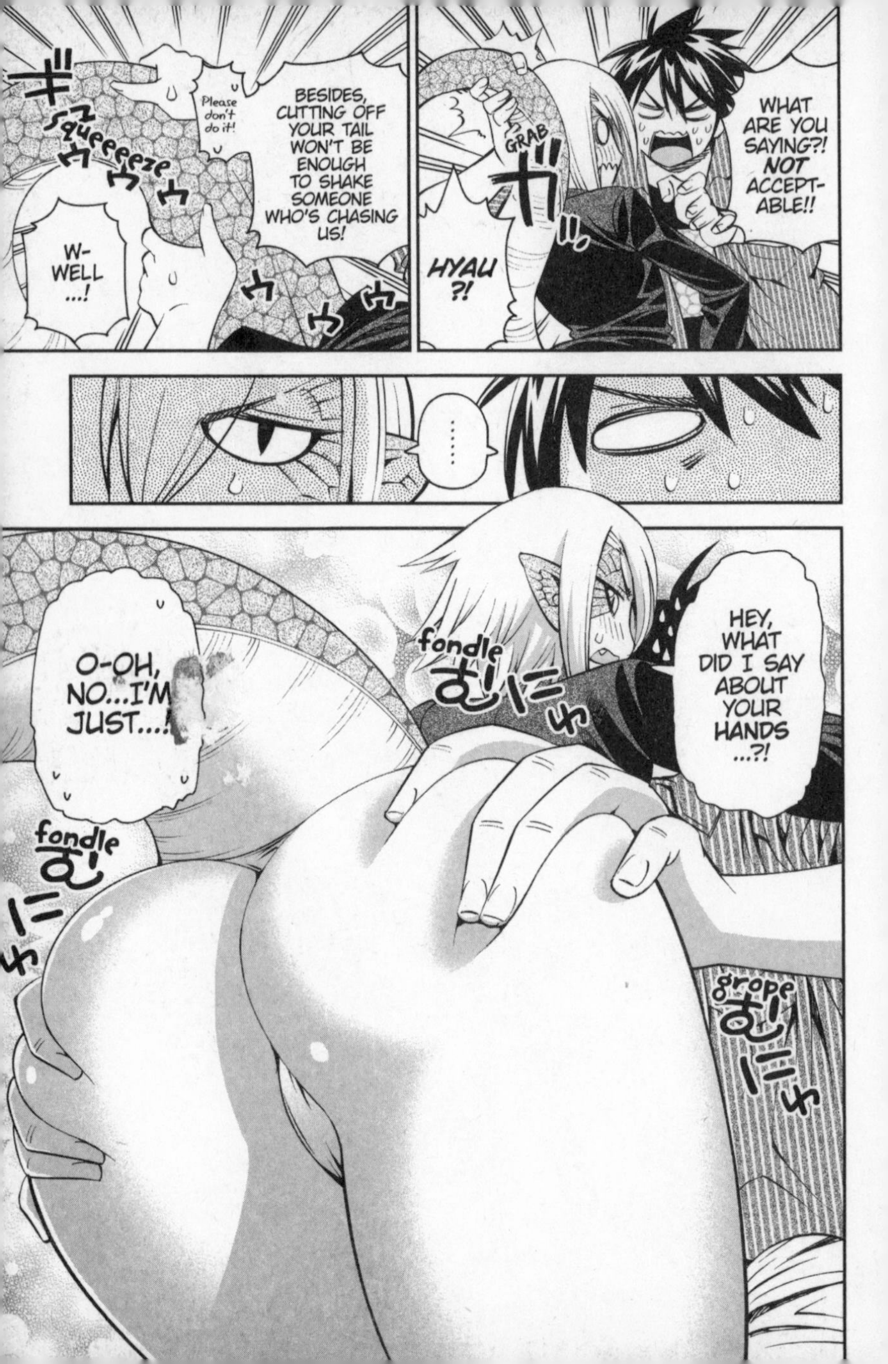
WHAT ARE YOU SAYING?! NOT ACCEPTABLE!!
GRAB
HYAU?!
BESIDES, CUTTING OFF YOUR TAIL WON'T BE ENOUGH TO SHAKE SOMEONE WHO'S CHASING US!
Please don't do it!
squeeeeeze
W-WELL...!
......
HEY, WHAT DID I SAY ABOUT YOUR HANDS...?!
fondle
O-OH, NO...I'M JUST...!
fondle
grope

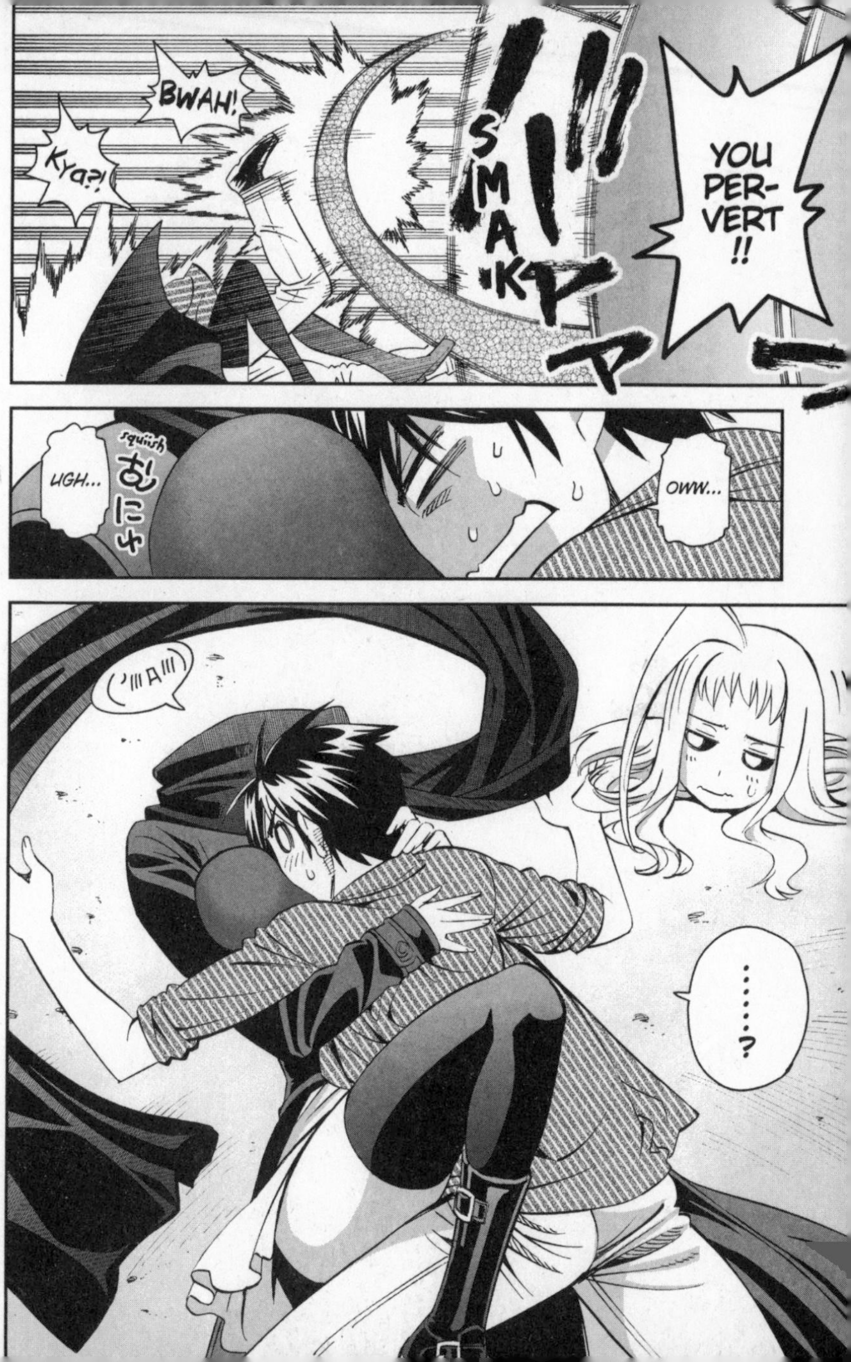
YOU PER-VERT!!
SMAK
BWAH!
Kya?!
OWW...
むにゅ
squish
UGH...
('|||A|||)
......?

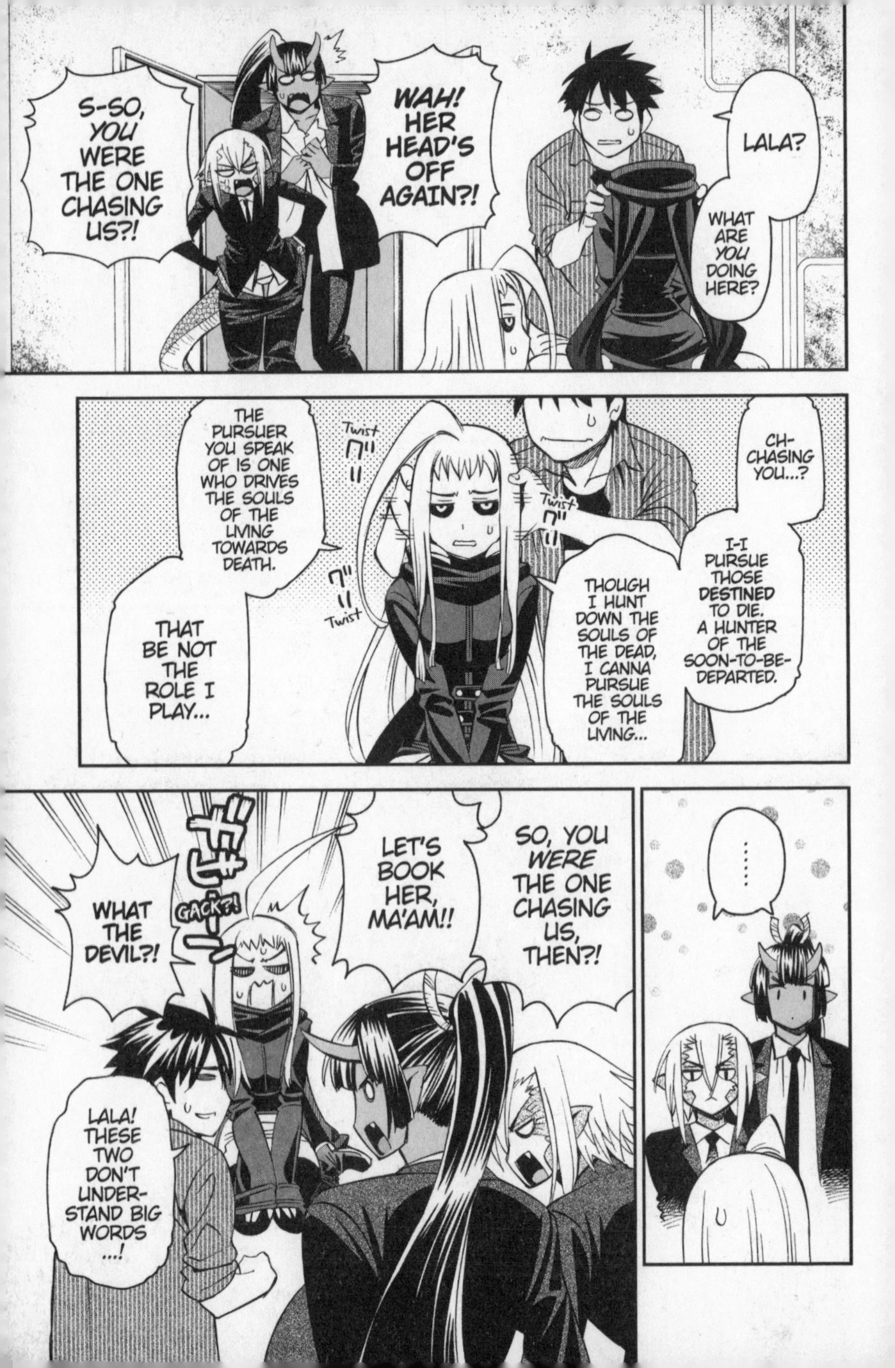
LALA?
WHAT ARE YOU DOING HERE?
WAH! HER HEAD'S OFF AGAIN?!
S-SO, YOU WERE THE ONE CHASING US?!
CH-CHASING YOU...?
I-I PURSUE THOSE DESTINED TO DIE. A HUNTER OF THE SOON-TO-BE-DEPARTED.
THOUGH I HUNT DOWN THE SOULS OF THE DEAD, I CANNA PURSUE THE SOULS OF THE LIVING...
Twist
Twist
THE PURSUER YOU SPEAK OF IS ONE WHO DRIVES THE SOULS OF THE LIVING TOWARDS DEATH.
Twist
THAT BE NOT THE ROLE I PLAY...
......
SO, YOU WERE THE ONE CHASING US, THEN?!
LET'S BOOK HER, MA'AM!!
GACK?!
WHAT THE DEVIL?!
LALA! THESE TWO DON'T UNDER-STAND BIG WORDS ...!

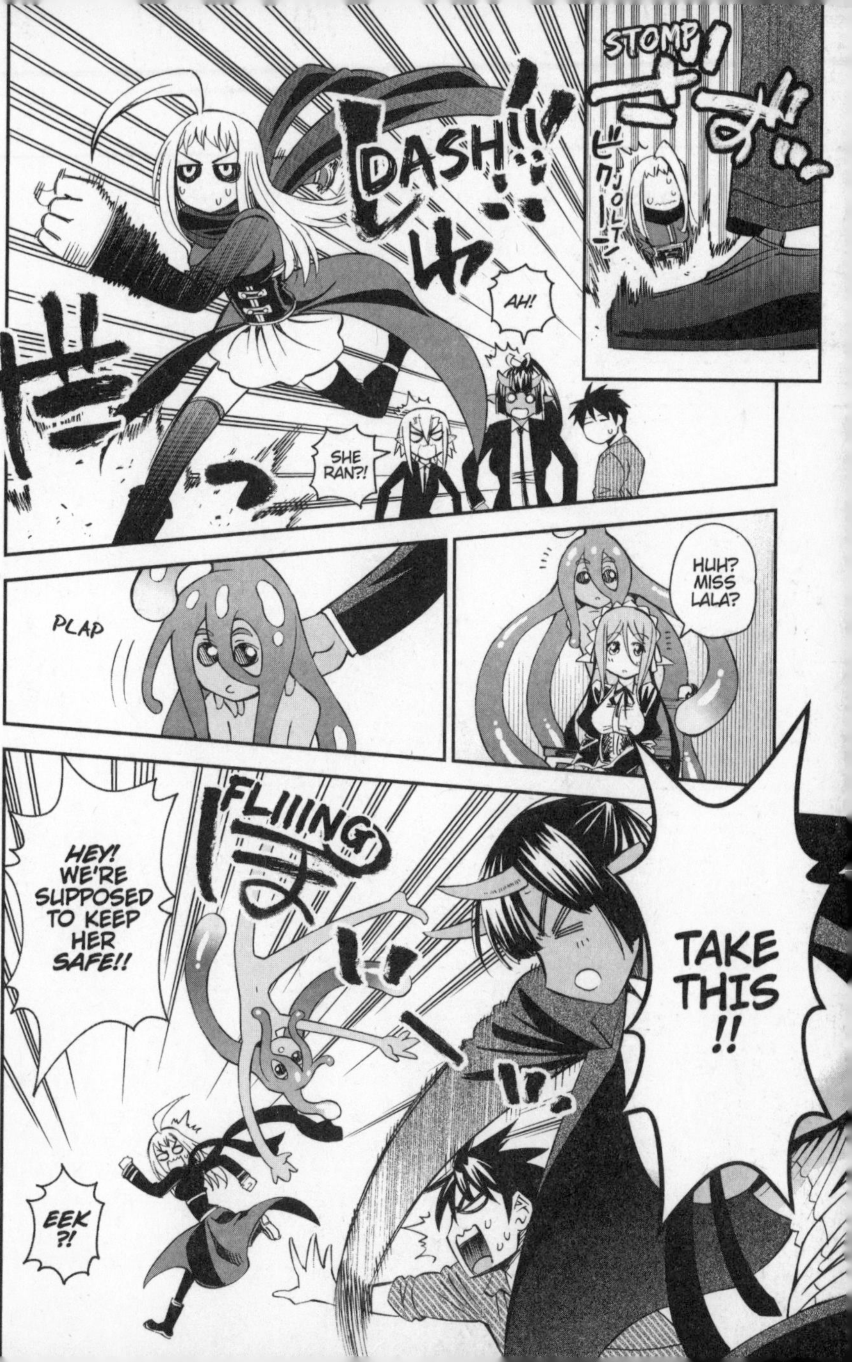
STOMP!
JOLT
DASH!!!
AH!
SHE RAN?!
HUH? MISS LALA?
PLAP
TAKE THIS!!
FLIIING
HEY! WE'RE SUPPOSED TO KEEP HER SAFE!!
EEK?!

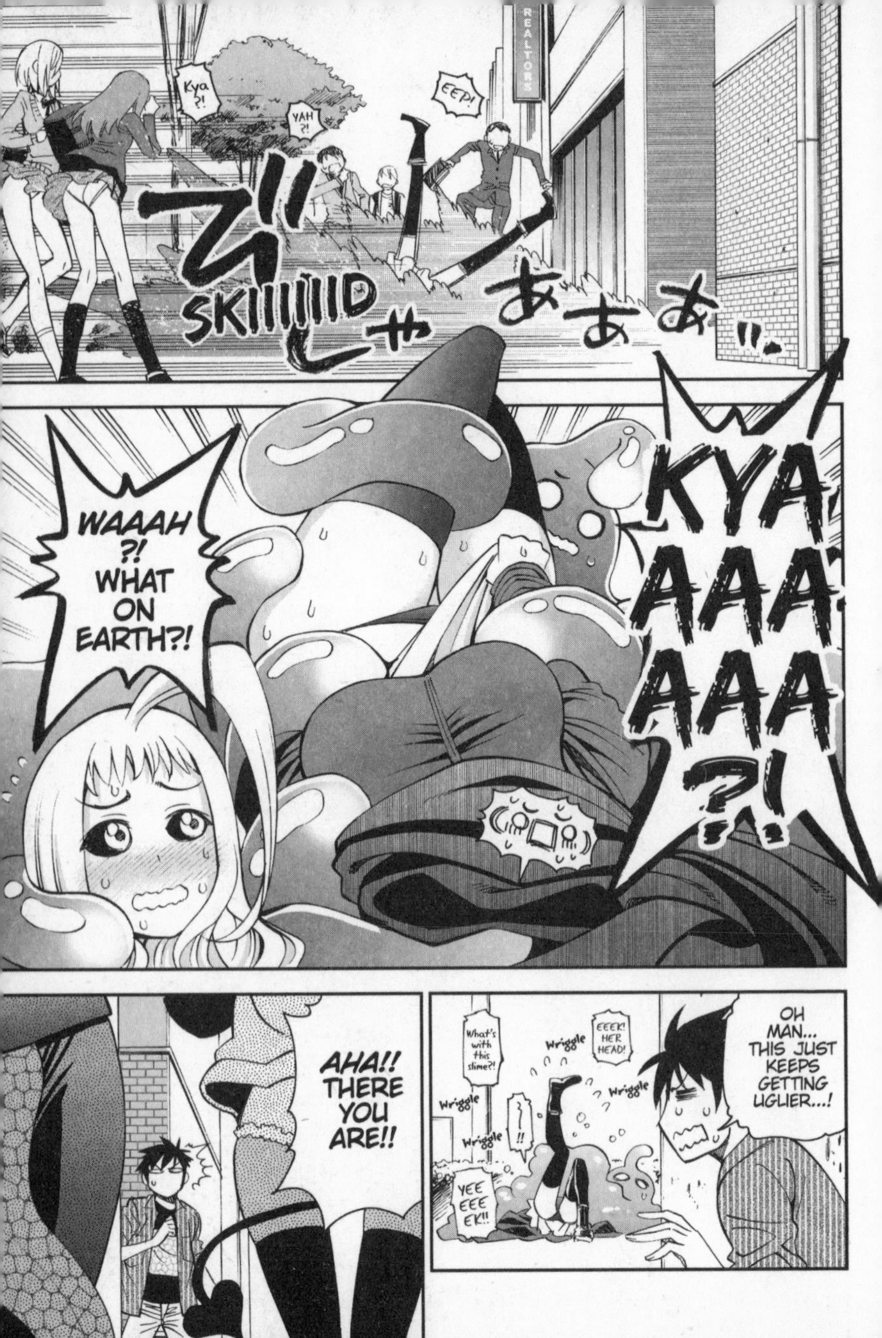
REALTORS
EEP!
YAH ?!
Kya ?!
SKIIIIIID
KYA AAA AAA ?!
WAAAH ?! WHAT ON EARTH?!
OH MAN... THIS JUST KEEPS GETTING UGLIER...!
EEEK! HER HEAD!
Wriggle
What's with this slime?!
Wriggle
Wriggle
Wriggle
YEE EEE EK!!
AHA!! THERE YOU ARE!!
Kya

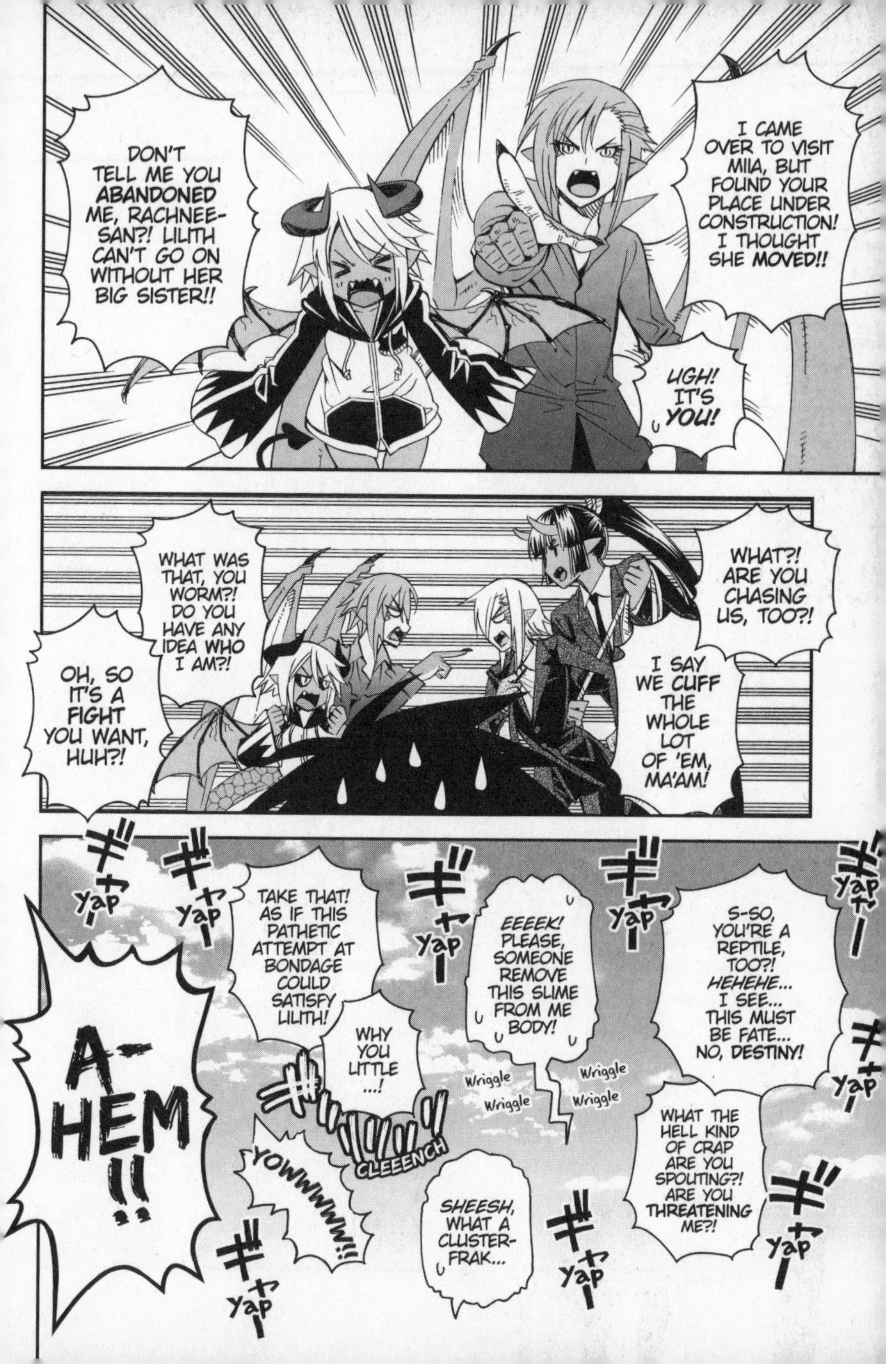

I CAME OVER TO VISIT MIIA, BUT FOUND YOUR PLACE UNDER CONSTRUCTION! I THOUGHT SHE MOVED!!
UGH! IT'S YOU!
DON'T TELL ME YOU ABANDONED ME, RACHNEE-SAN?! LILITH CAN'T GO ON WITHOUT HER BIG SISTER!!
WHAT?! ARE YOU CHASING US, TOO?!
I SAY WE CUFF THE WHOLE LOT OF 'EM, MA'AM!
WHAT WAS THAT, YOU WORM?! DO YOU HAVE ANY IDEA WHO I AM?!
OH, SO IT'S A FIGHT YOU WANT, HUH?!
yap
S-SO, YOU'RE A REPTILE, TOO?! HEHEHE... I SEE... THIS MUST BE FATE... NO, DESTINY!
yap
WHAT THE HELL KIND OF CRAP ARE YOU SPOUTING?! ARE YOU THREATENING ME?!
yap
yap
EEEEK! PLEASE, SOMEONE REMOVE THIS SLIME FROM ME BODY!
Wriggle
Wriggle
Wriggle
Wriggle
yap
SHEESH, WHAT A CLUSTER-FRAK...
TAKE THAT! AS IF THIS PATHETIC ATTEMPT AT BONDAGE COULD SATISFY LILITH!
WHY YOU LITTLE ...!
CLEEENCH
YOWWWWWW!!
yap
yap
yap
A-HEM!!

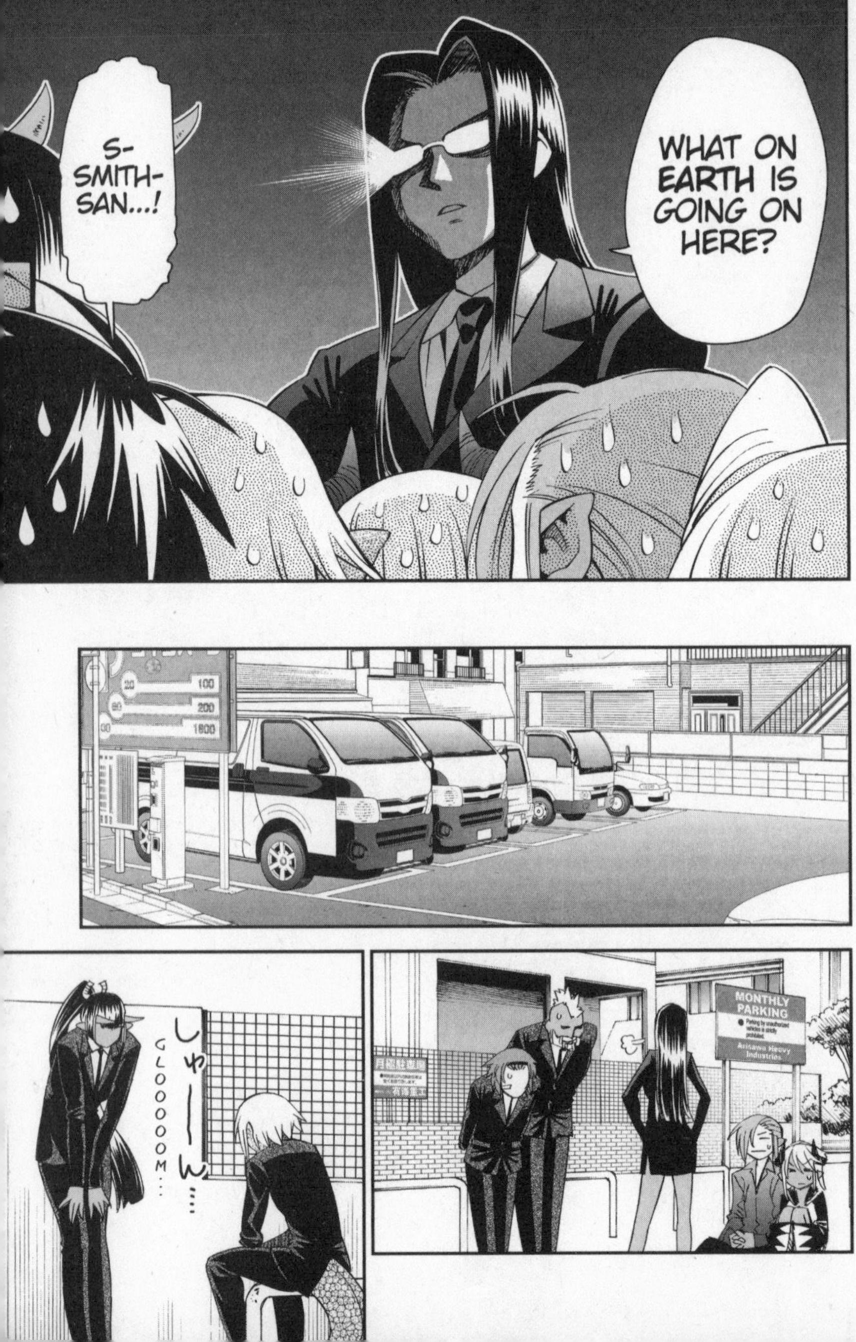
WHAT ON EARTH IS GOING ON HERE?
S-SMITH-SAN...!
MONTHLY PARKING
Arisawa Heavy Industries
しゅーーん…
GLOOOOOM...

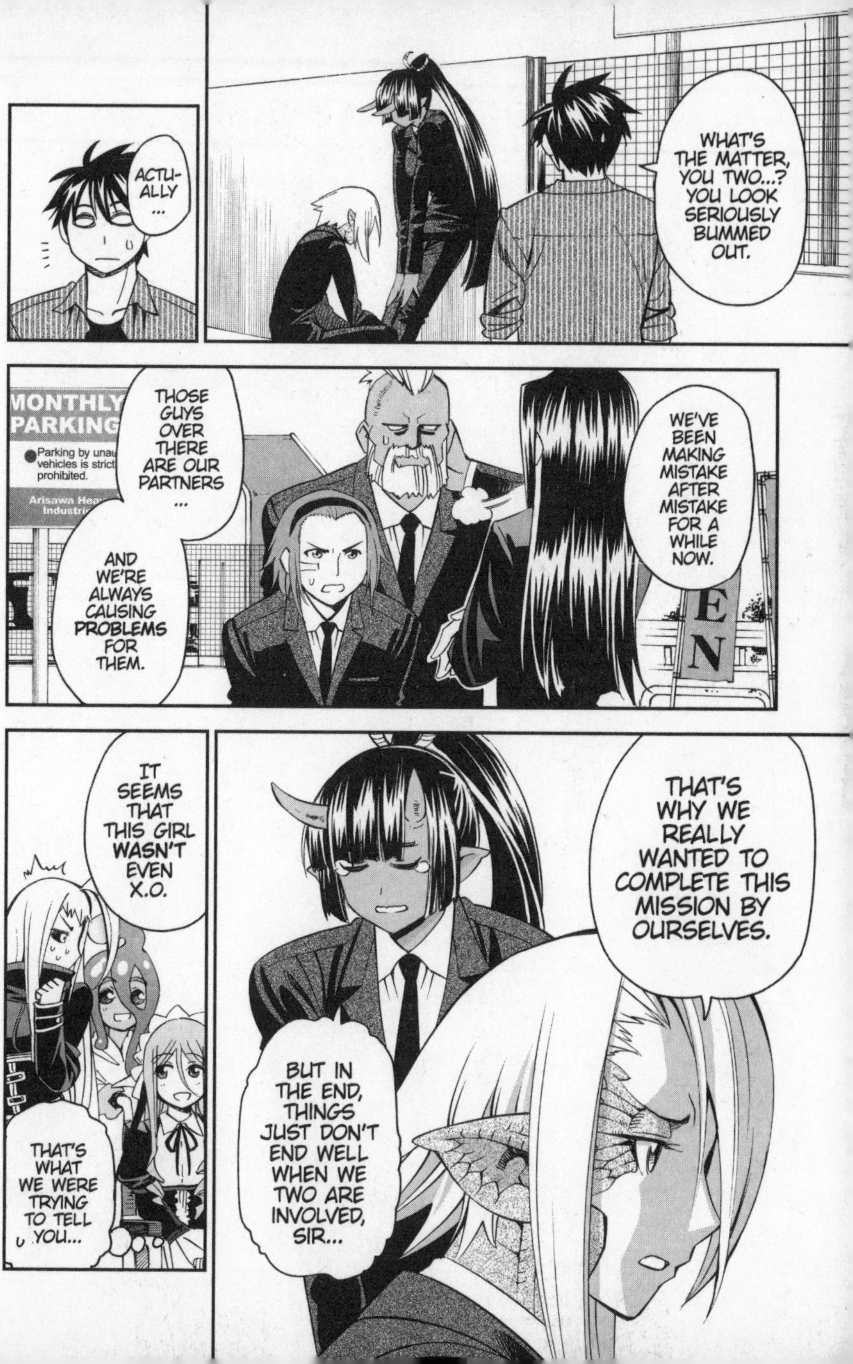
WHAT'S THE MATTER, YOU TWO...? YOU LOOK SERIOUSLY BUMMED OUT.
ACTU-ALLY ...
MONTHLY PARKING
WE'VE BEEN MAKING MISTAKE AFTER MISTAKE FOR A WHILE NOW.
THOSE GUYS OVER THERE ARE OUR PARTNERS ...
AND WE'RE ALWAYS CAUSING PROBLEMS FOR THEM.
THAT'S WHY WE REALLY WANTED TO COMPLETE THIS MISSION BY OURSELVES.
BUT IN THE END, THINGS JUST DON'T END WELL WHEN WE TWO ARE INVOLVED, SIR...
IT SEEMS THAT THIS GIRL WASN'T EVEN X.O.
THAT'S WHAT WE WERE TRYING TO TELL YOU...

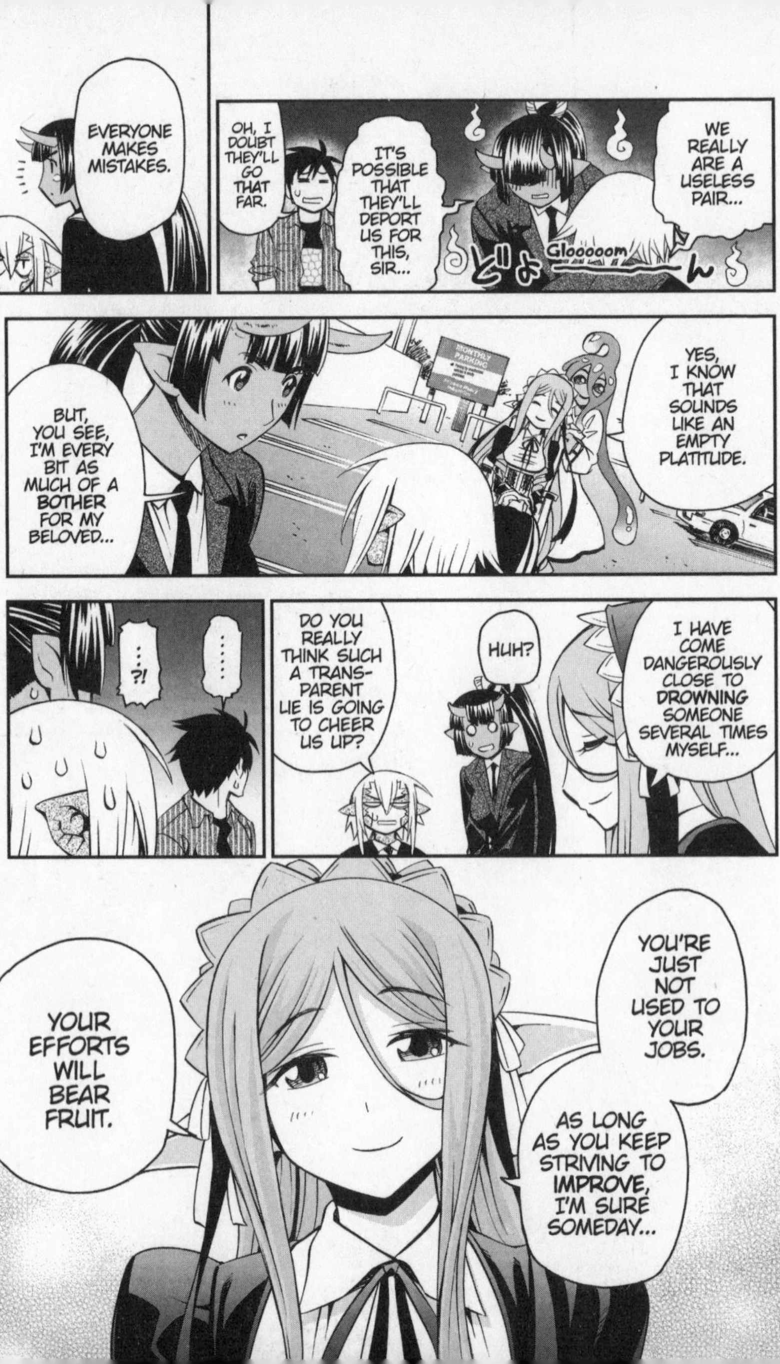
WE REALLY ARE A USELESS PAIR...
どよ Gloooom ん
IT'S POSSIBLE THAT THEY'LL DEPORT US FOR THIS, SIR...
OH, I DOUBT THEY'LL GO THAT FAR.
EVERYONE MAKES MISTAKES.
YES, I KNOW THAT SOUNDS LIKE AN EMPTY PLATITUDE.
MONTHLY PARKING
BUT, YOU SEE, I'M EVERY BIT AS MUCH OF A BOTHER FOR MY BELOVED...
I HAVE COME DANGEROUSLY CLOSE TO DROWNING SOMEONE SEVERAL TIMES MYSELF...
HUH?
DO YOU REALLY THINK SUCH A TRANSPARENT LIE IS GOING TO CHEER US UP?
......
...?!
YOU'RE JUST NOT USED TO YOUR JOBS.
AS LONG AS YOU KEEP STRIVING TO IMPROVE, I'M SURE SOMEDAY...
YOUR EFFORTS WILL BEAR FRUIT.

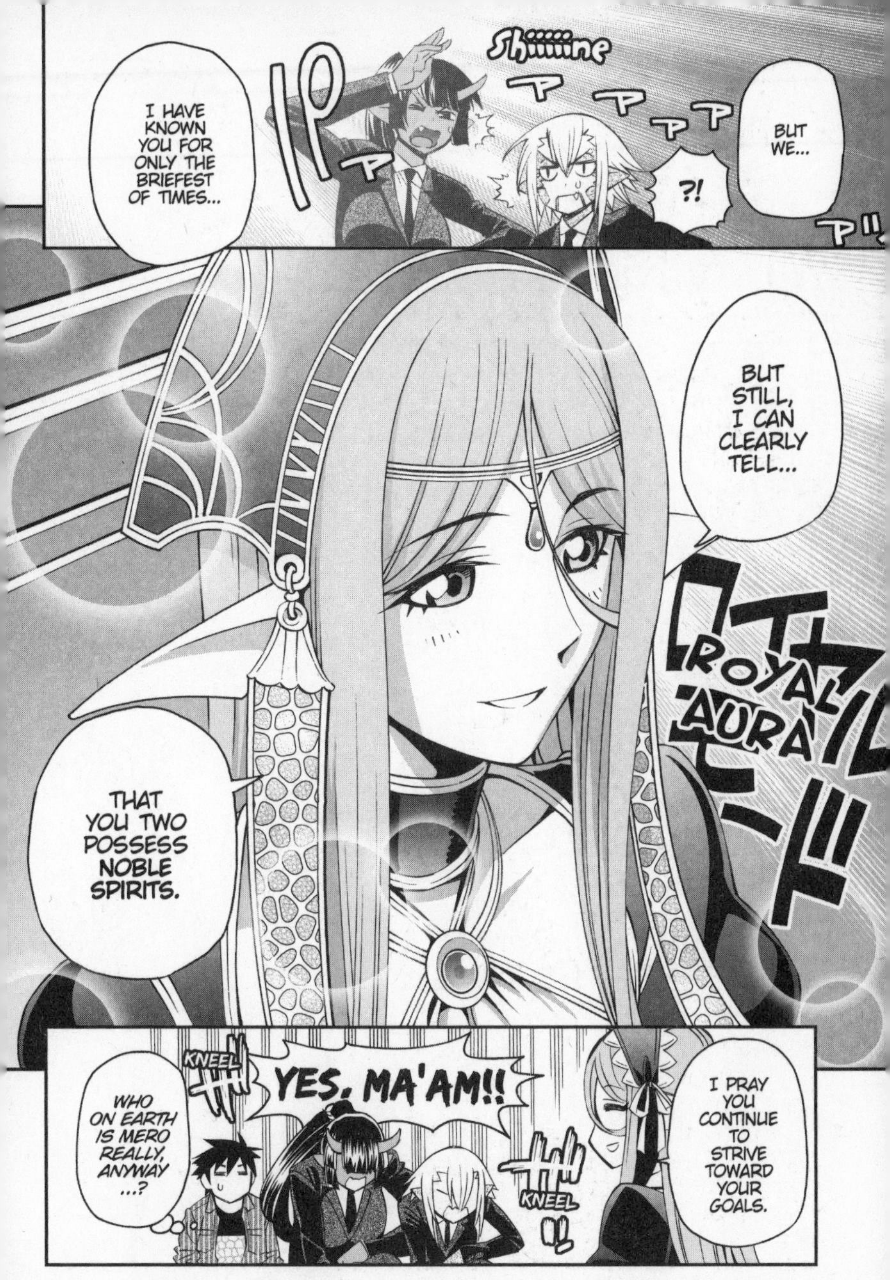
BUT WE...
?!
Shiiiiine
I HAVE KNOWN YOU FOR ONLY THE BRIEFEST OF TIMES...
BUT STILL, I CAN CLEARLY TELL...
ROYAL AURA
THAT YOU TWO POSSESS NOBLE SPIRITS.
I PRAY YOU CONTINUE TO STRIVE TOWARD YOUR GOALS.
KNEEL
YES, MA'AM!!
KNEEL
WHO ON EARTH IS MERO REALLY, ANYWAY...?

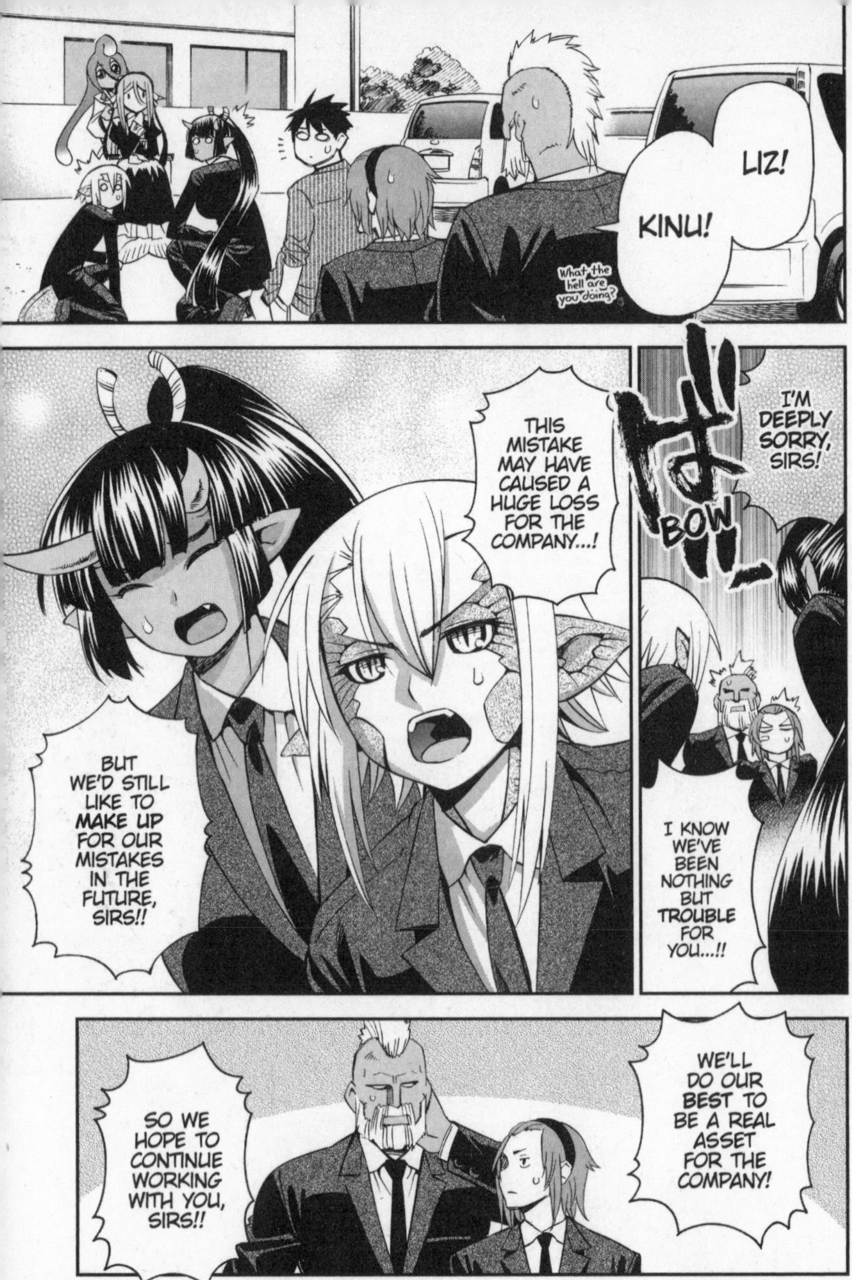
LIZ!
KINU!
What the hell are you doing?
I'M DEEPLY SORRY, SIRS!
BOW
I KNOW WE'VE BEEN NOTHING BUT TROUBLE FOR YOU...!!
THIS MISTAKE MAY HAVE CAUSED A HUGE LOSS FOR THE COMPANY...!
BUT WE'D STILL LIKE TO MAKE UP FOR OUR MISTAKES IN THE FUTURE, SIRS!!
WE'LL DO OUR BEST TO BE A REAL ASSET FOR THE COMPANY!
SO WE HOPE TO CONTINUE WORKING WITH YOU, SIRS!!

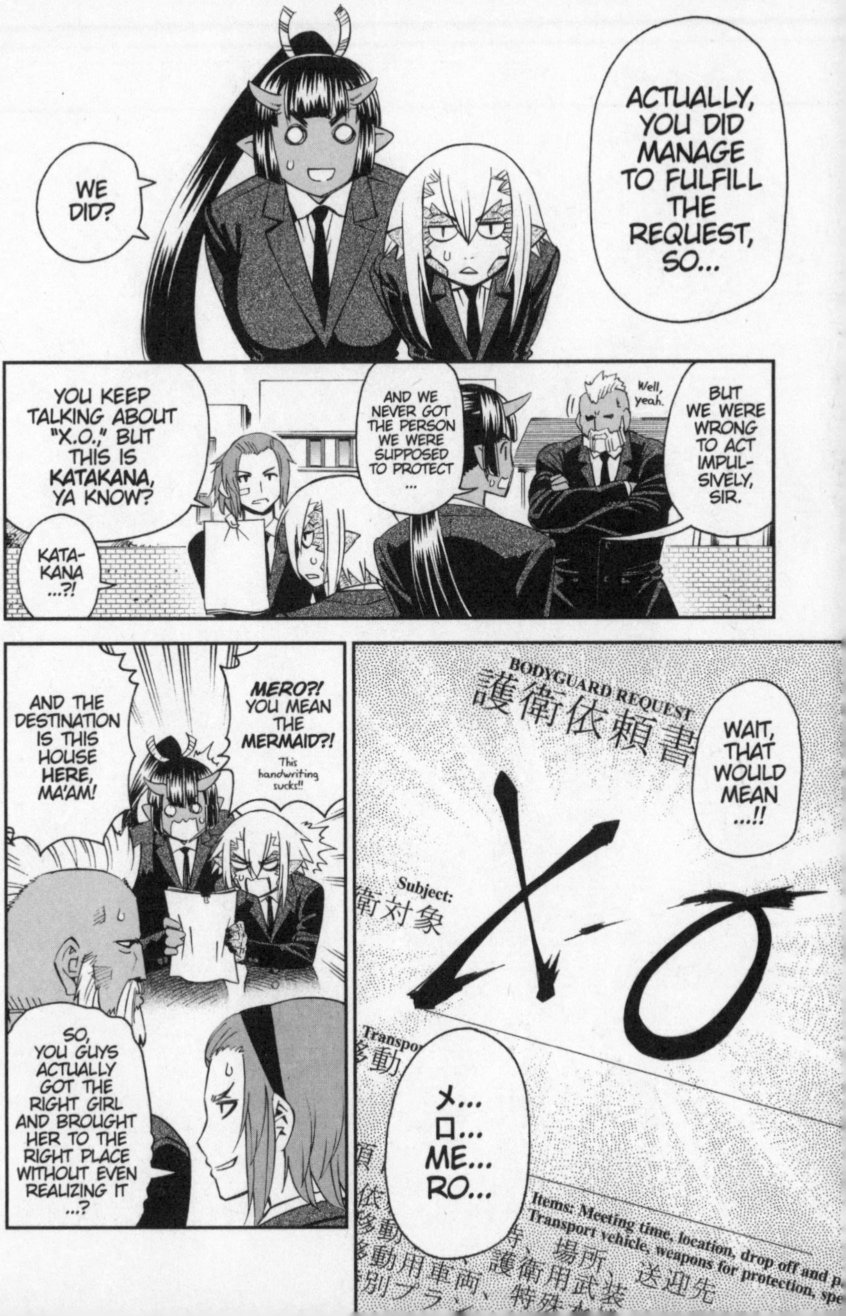
ACTUALLY, YOU DID MANAGE TO FULFILL THE REQUEST, SO...
WE DID?
Well, yeah.
BUT WE WERE WRONG TO ACT IMPULSIVELY, SIR.
AND WE NEVER GOT THE PERSON WE WERE SUPPOSED TO PROTECT ...
YOU KEEP TALKING ABOUT "X.O.," BUT THIS IS KATAKANA, YA KNOW?
KATAKANA ...?!
BODYGUARD REQUEST
護衛依頼書
WAIT, THAT WOULD MEAN ...!!
Subject:
メ... ロ... ME... RO...
Items: Meeting time, location, drop off and
Transport vehicle, weapons for protection,
場所、送迎先
移動用車両、護衛用武装
MERO?! YOU MEAN THE MERMAID?!
This handwriting sucks!!
AND THE DESTINATION IS THIS HOUSE HERE, MA'AM!
SO, YOU GUYS ACTUALLY GOT THE RIGHT GIRL AND BROUGHT HER TO THE RIGHT PLACE WITHOUT EVEN REALIZING IT ...?

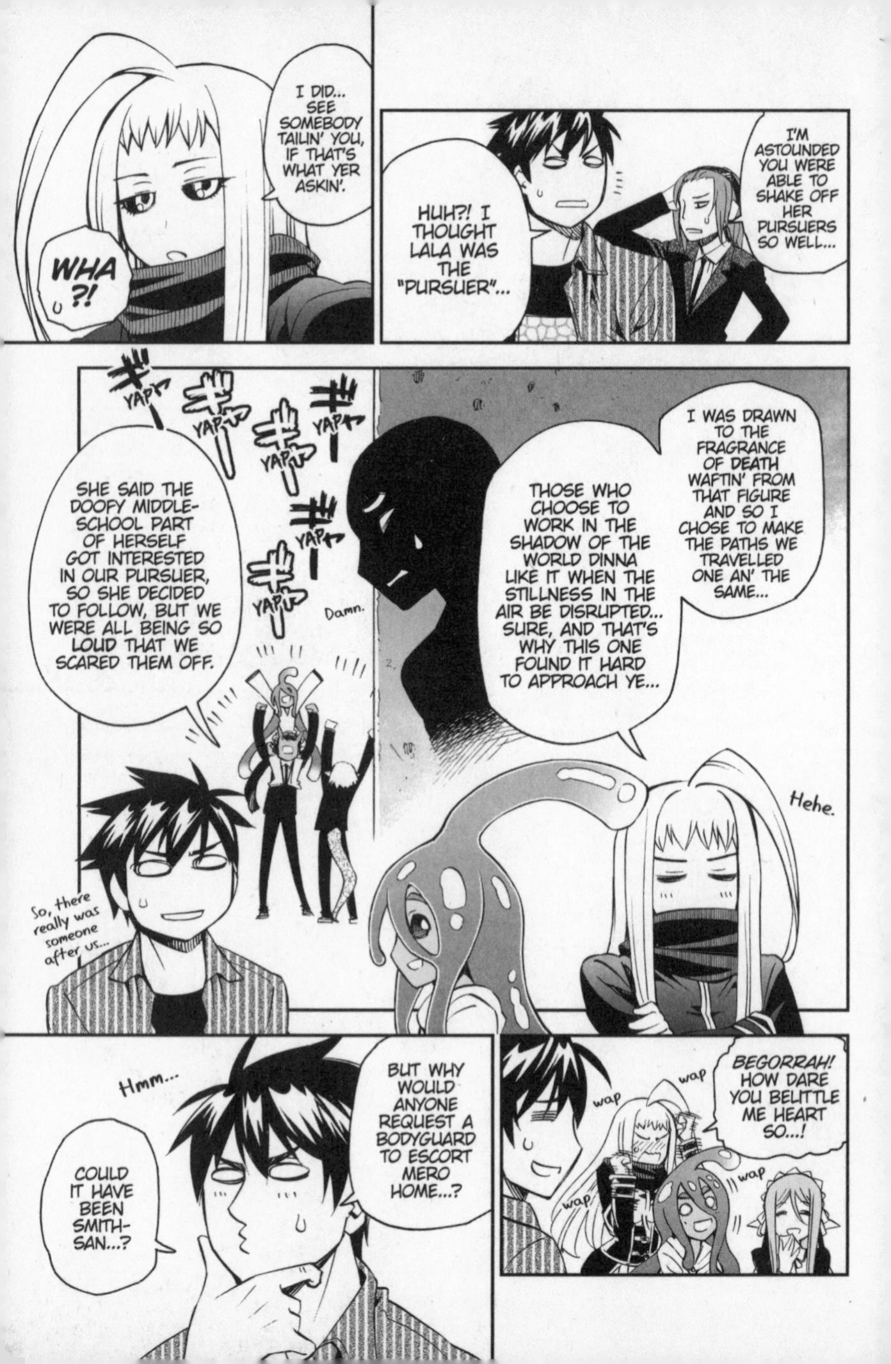
I'M ASTOUNDED YOU WERE ABLE TO SHAKE OFF HER PURSUERS SO WELL...
HUH?! I THOUGHT LALA WAS THE "PURSUER"...
I DID... SEE SOMEBODY TAILIN' YOU, IF THAT'S WHAT YER ASKIN'.
WHA ?!
I WAS DRAWN TO THE FRAGRANCE OF DEATH WAFTIN' FROM THAT FIGURE AND SO I CHOSE TO MAKE THE PATHS WE TRAVELLED ONE AN' THE SAME...
THOSE WHO CHOOSE TO WORK IN THE SHADOW OF THE WORLD DINNA LIKE IT WHEN THE STILLNESS IN THE AIR BE DISRUPTED... SURE, AND THAT'S WHY THIS ONE FOUND IT HARD TO APPROACH YE...
YAP
YAP
YAP
YAP
YAP
YAP
YAP
SHE SAID THE DOOFY MIDDLE-SCHOOL PART OF HERSELF GOT INTERESTED IN OUR PURSUER, SO SHE DECIDED TO FOLLOW, BUT WE WERE ALL BEING SO LOUD THAT WE SCARED THEM OFF.
Damn.
Hehe.
So, there really was someone after us...
BEGORRAH! HOW DARE YOU BELITTLE ME HEART SO...!
wap
wap
wap
wap
BUT WHY WOULD ANYONE REQUEST A BODYGUARD TO ESCORT MERO HOME...?
Hmm...
COULD IT HAVE BEEN SMITH-SAN...?

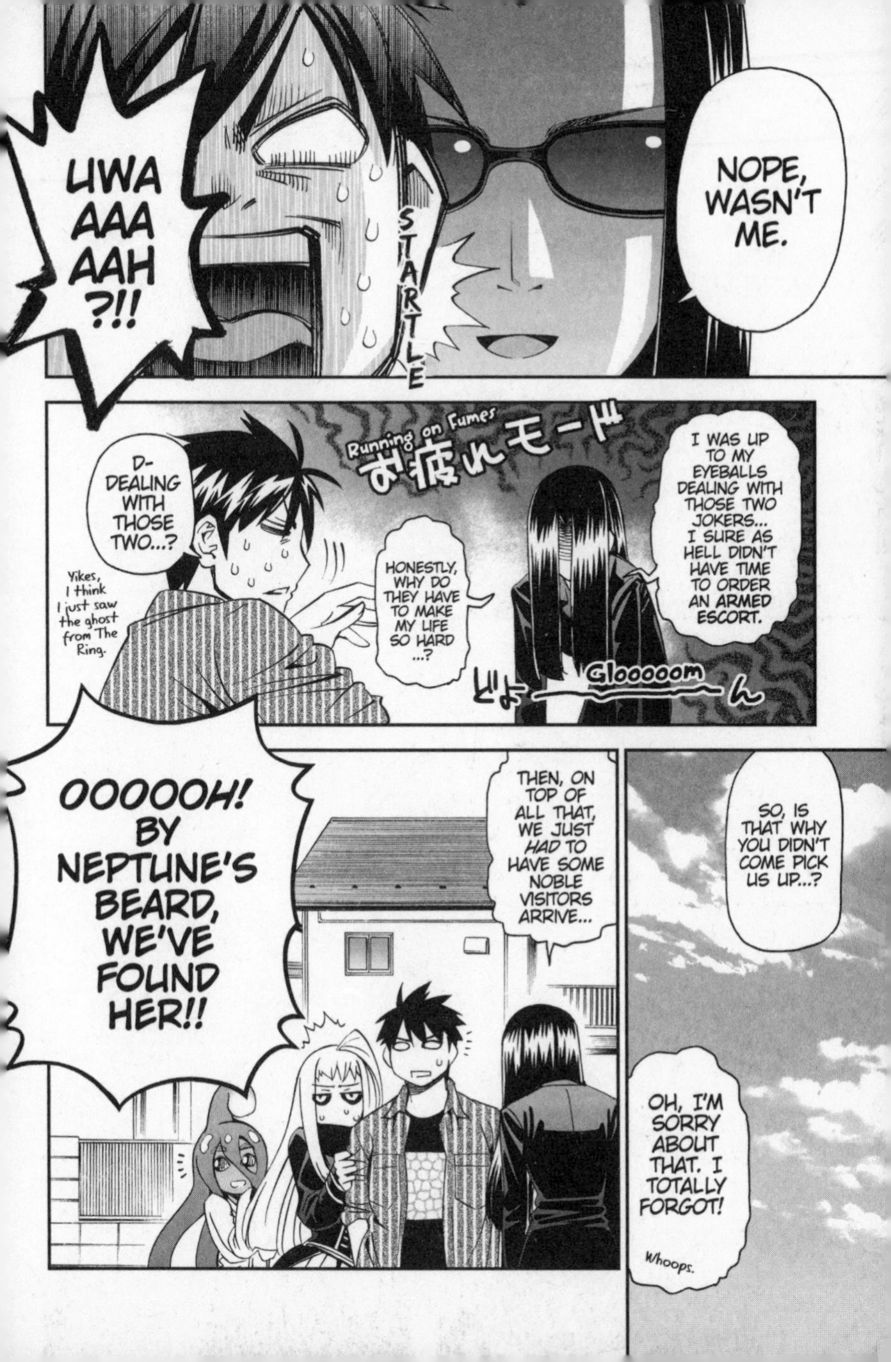
NOPE, WASN'T ME.
STARTLE
UWAAAAAAAH?!!
Running on Fumes
お疲れモード
I WAS UP TO MY EYEBALLS DEALING WITH THOSE TWO JOKERS... I SURE AS HELL DIDN'T HAVE TIME TO ORDER AN ARMED ESCORT.
HONESTLY, WHY DO THEY HAVE TO MAKE MY LIFE SO HARD ...?
D-DEALING WITH THOSE TWO...?
Yikes, I think I just saw the ghost from The Ring.
どよ——Glooooom——ん
SO, IS THAT WHY YOU DIDN'T COME PICK US UP...?
OH, I'M SORRY ABOUT THAT. I TOTALLY FORGOT!
Whoops.
THEN, ON TOP OF ALL THAT, WE JUST *HAD* TO HAVE SOME NOBLE VISITORS ARRIVE...
OOOOOH! BY NEPTUNE'S BEARD, WE'VE FOUND HER!!

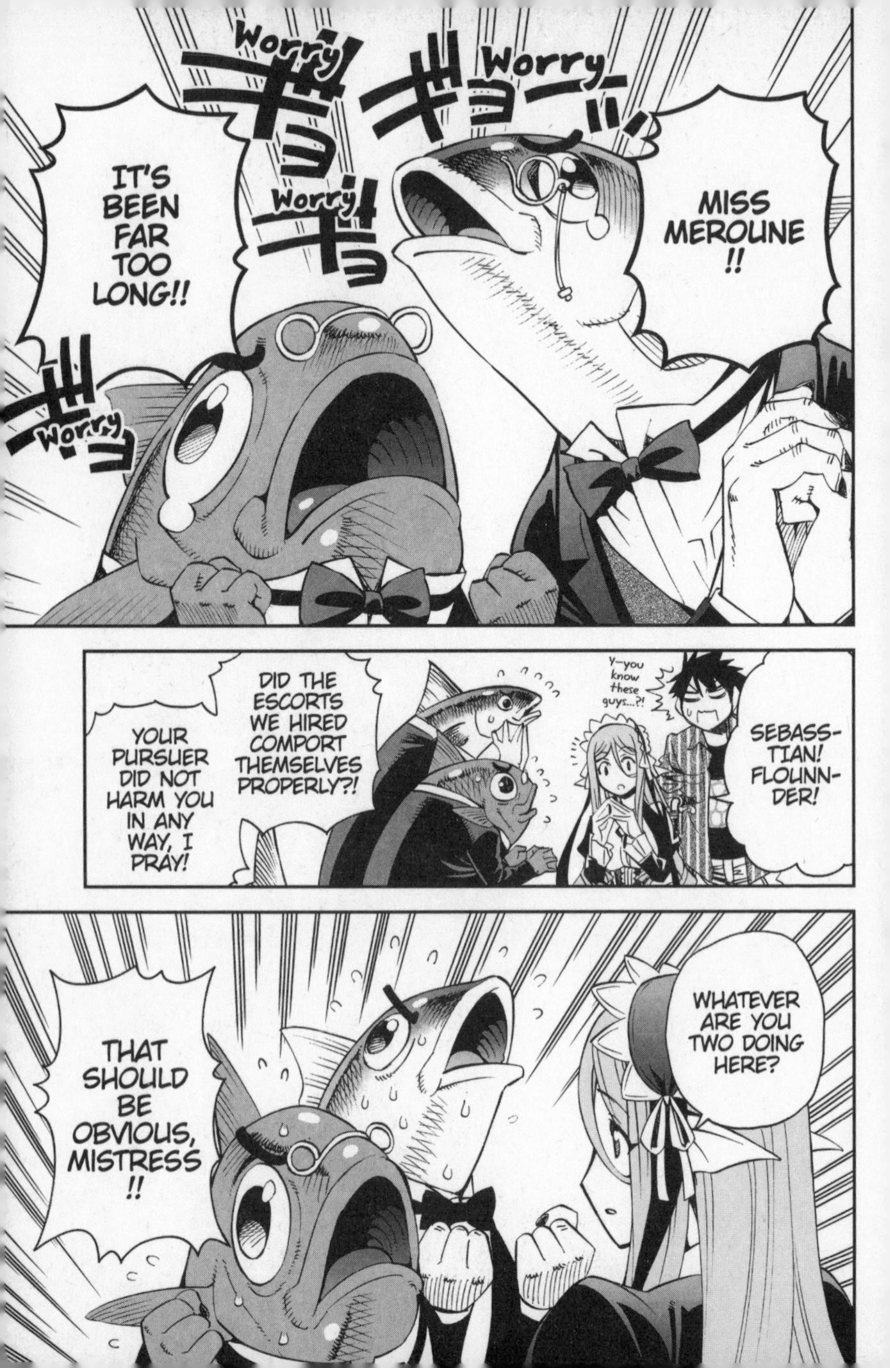
Worry
MISS MEROUNE !!
Worry
Worry
IT'S BEEN FAR TOO LONG!!
Worry
SEBASS-TIAN! FLOUNN-DER!
Y-you know these guys...?!
DID THE ESCORTS WE HIRED COMPORT THEMSELVES PROPERLY?!
YOUR PURSUER DID NOT HARM YOU IN ANY WAY, I PRAY!
WHATEVER ARE YOU TWO DOING HERE?
THAT SHOULD BE OBVIOUS, MISTRESS !!

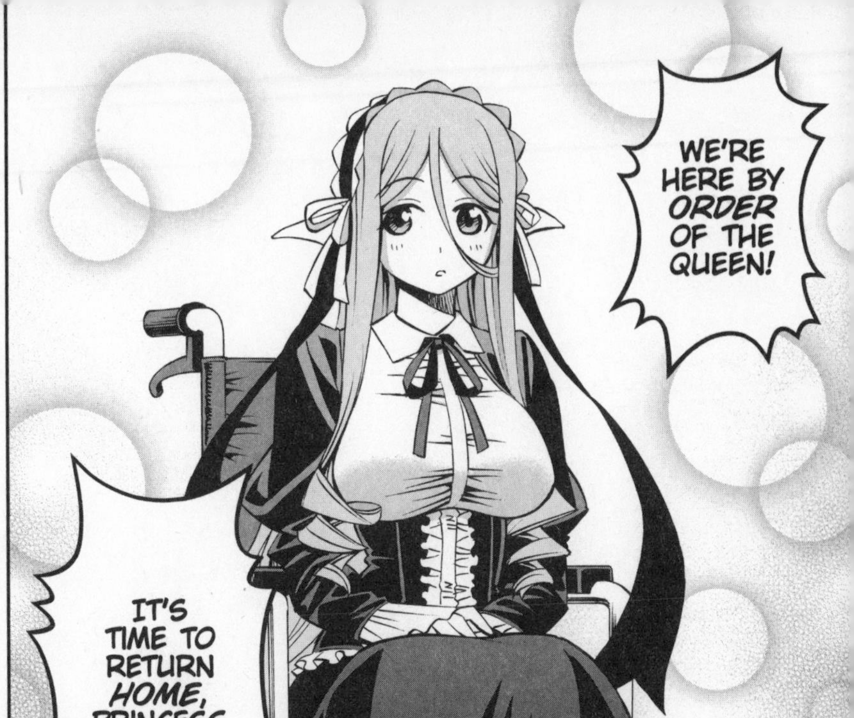
WE'RE HERE BY *ORDER* OF THE QUEEN!
IT'S TIME TO RETURN *HOME*, PRINCESS MEROUNE!!
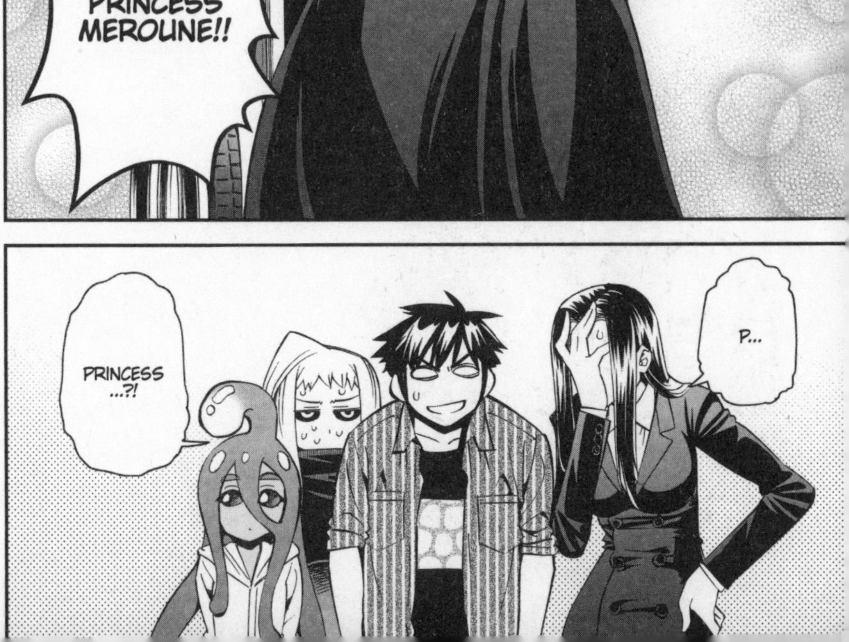
P...
PRINCESS ...?!

Monster Musume

Everyday Life with Monster Girls

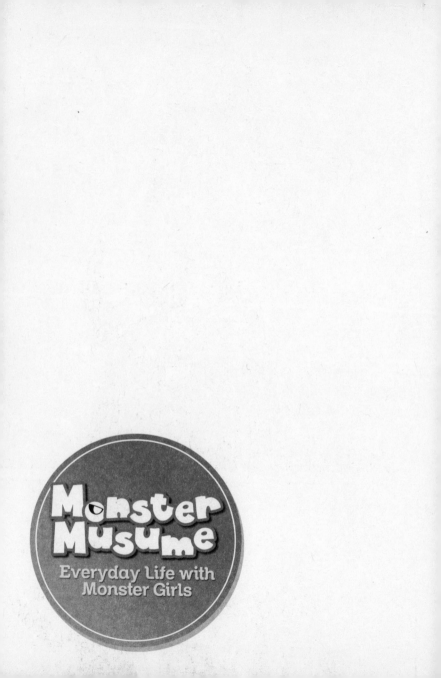

YUKI-ONNA
SAY YES TO YUKIO

HEIGHT: 170CM
WEIGHT: 58KG
MEASUREMENTS: 89-57-86

F CUP

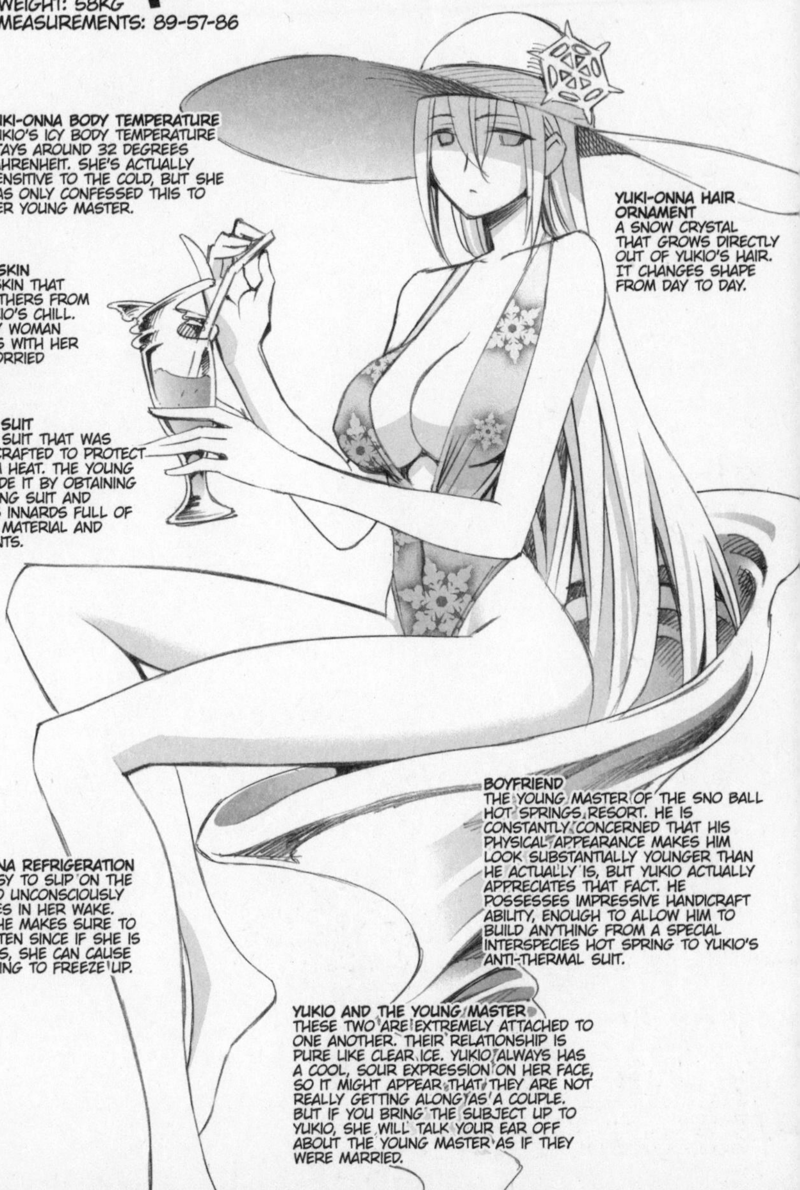

YUKI-ONNA BODY TEMPERATURE
YUKIO'S ICY BODY TEMPERATURE STAYS AROUND 32 DEGREES FAHRENHEIT. SHE'S ACTUALLY SENSITIVE TO THE COLD, BUT SHE HAS ONLY CONFESSED THIS TO HER YOUNG MASTER.

YUKI-ONNA HAIR ORNAMENT
A SNOW CRYSTAL THAT GROWS DIRECTLY OUT OF YUKIO'S HAIR. IT CHANGES SHAPE FROM DAY TO DAY.

IKI-ONNA SKIN
ILE BLUE SKIN THAT IELTERS OTHERS FROM ELING YUKIO'S CHILL. IE ELDERLY WOMAN IAT WORKS WITH HER OFTEN WORRIED BOUT HER.

IKI-ONNA SUIT
THERMAL SUIT THAT WAS PECIALLY CRAFTED TO PROTECT IKIO FROM HEAT. THE YOUNG ASTER MADE IT BY OBTAINING USED DIVING SUIT AND ACKING ITS INNARDS FULL OF ISULATING MATERIAL AND EFRIGERANTS.

BOYFRIEND
THE YOUNG MASTER OF THE SNO BALL HOT SPRINGS RESORT. HE IS CONSTANTLY CONCERNED THAT HIS PHYSICAL APPEARANCE MAKES HIM LOOK SUBSTANTIALLY YOUNGER THAN HE ACTUALLY IS, BUT YUKIO ACTUALLY APPRECIATES THAT FACT. HE POSSESSES IMPRESSIVE HANDICRAFT ABILITY, ENOUGH TO ALLOW HIM TO BUILD ANYTHING FROM A SPECIAL INTERSPECIES HOT SPRING TO YUKIO'S ANTI-THERMAL SUIT.

YUKI-ONNA REFRIGERATION
IT IS EASY TO SLIP ON THE ICE YUKIO UNCONSCIOUSLY PRODUCES IN HER WAKE. STILL, SHE MAKES SURE TO SAVE OFTEN SINCE IF SHE IS CARELESS, SHE CAN CAUSE EVERYTHING TO FREEZE UP.

YUKIO AND THE YOUNG MASTER
THESE TWO ARE EXTREMELY ATTACHED TO ONE ANOTHER. THEIR RELATIONSHIP IS PURE LIKE CLEAR ICE. YUKIO ALWAYS HAS A COOL, SOUR EXPRESSION ON HER FACE, SO IT MIGHT APPEAR THAT THEY ARE NOT REALLY GETTING ALONG AS A COUPLE. BUT IF YOU BRING THE SUBJECT UP TO YUKIO, SHE WILL TALK YOUR EAR OFF ABOUT THE YOUNG MASTER AS IF THEY WERE MARRIED.

KYŪBI

NOTES ON ILS NINETA

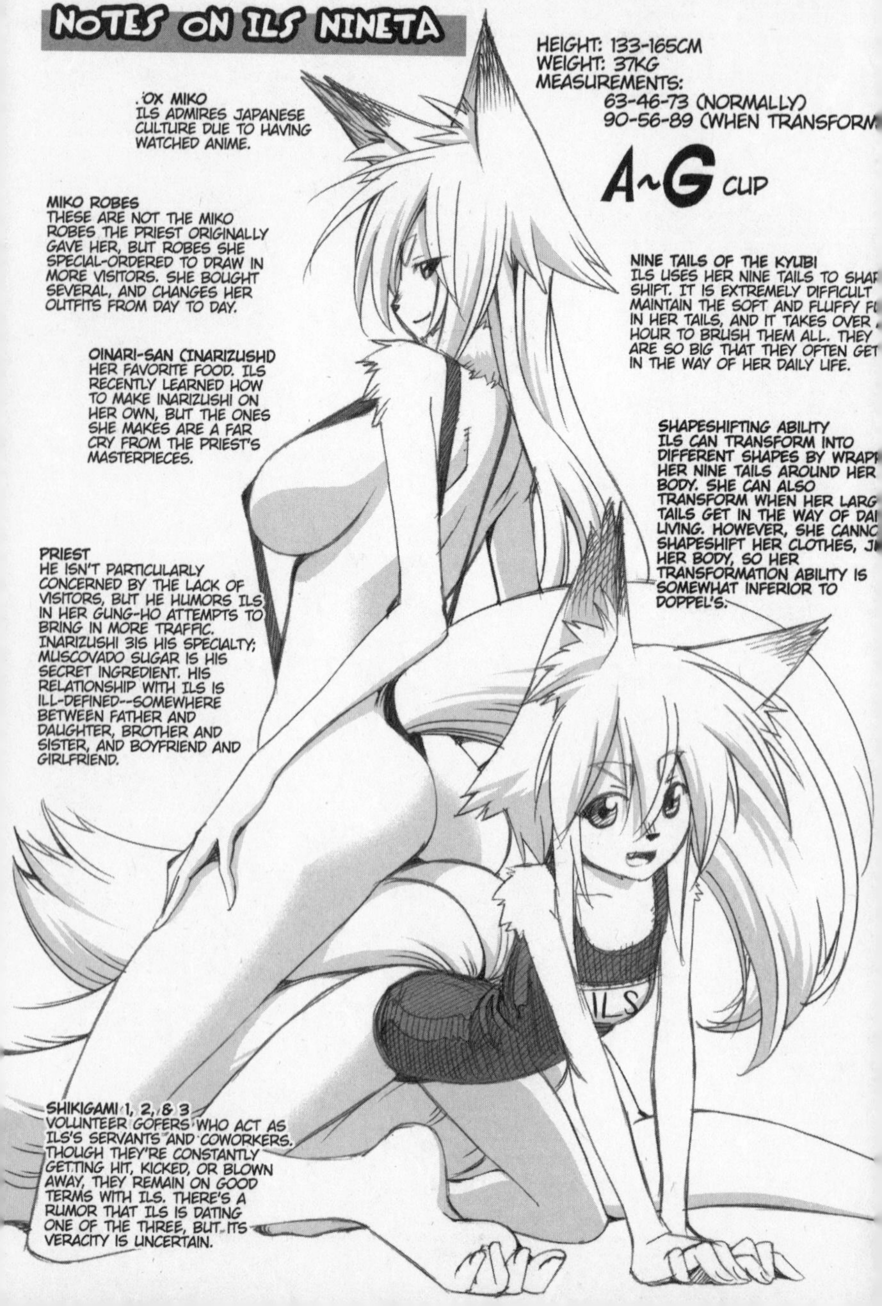

HEIGHT: 133-165CM
WEIGHT: 37KG
MEASUREMENTS:
63-46-73 (NORMALLY)
90-56-89 (WHEN TRANSFORM

A~G CUP

.'OX MIKO
ILS ADMIRES JAPANESE CULTURE DUE TO HAVING WATCHED ANIME.

MIKO ROBES
THESE ARE NOT THE MIKO ROBES THE PRIEST ORIGINALLY GAVE HER, BUT ROBES SHE SPECIAL-ORDERED TO DRAW IN MORE VISITORS. SHE BOUGHT SEVERAL, AND CHANGES HER OUTFITS FROM DAY TO DAY.

OINARI-SAN (INARIZUSHI)
HER FAVORITE FOOD. ILS RECENTLY LEARNED HOW TO MAKE INARIZUSHI ON HER OWN, BUT THE ONES SHE MAKES ARE A FAR CRY FROM THE PRIEST'S MASTERPIECES.

PRIEST
HE ISN'T PARTICULARLY CONCERNED BY THE LACK OF VISITORS, BUT HE HUMORS ILS IN HER GUNG-HO ATTEMPTS TO BRING IN MORE TRAFFIC. INARIZUSHI 3IS HIS SPECIALTY; MUSCOVADO SUGAR IS HIS SECRET INGREDIENT. HIS RELATIONSHIP WITH ILS IS ILL-DEFINED--SOMEWHERE BETWEEN FATHER AND DAUGHTER, BROTHER AND SISTER, AND BOYFRIEND AND GIRLFRIEND.

NINE TAILS OF THE KYUBI
ILS USES HER NINE TAILS TO SHAF SHIFT. IT IS EXTREMELY DIFFICULT MAINTAIN THE SOFT AND FLUFFY FU IN HER TAILS, AND IT TAKES OVER HOUR TO BRUSH THEM ALL. THEY ARE SO BIG THAT THEY OFTEN GET IN THE WAY OF HER DAILY LIFE.

SHAPESHIFTING ABILITY
ILS CAN TRANSFORM INTO DIFFERENT SHAPES BY WRAPP HER NINE TAILS AROUND HER BODY. SHE CAN ALSO TRANSFORM WHEN HER LARG TAILS GET IN THE WAY OF DAI LIVING. HOWEVER, SHE CANNC SHAPESHIFT HER CLOTHES, JU HER BODY, SO HER TRANSFORMATION ABILITY IS SOMEWHAT INFERIOR TO DOPPEL'S.

SHIKIGAMI 1, 2, & 3
VOLUNTEER GOFERS WHO ACT AS ILS'S SERVANTS AND COWORKERS. THOUGH THEY'RE CONSTANTLY GETTING HIT, KICKED, OR BLOWN AWAY, THEY REMAIN ON GOOD TERMS WITH ILS. THERE'S A RUMOR THAT ILS IS DATING ONE OF THE THREE, BUT ITS VERACITY IS UNCERTAIN.

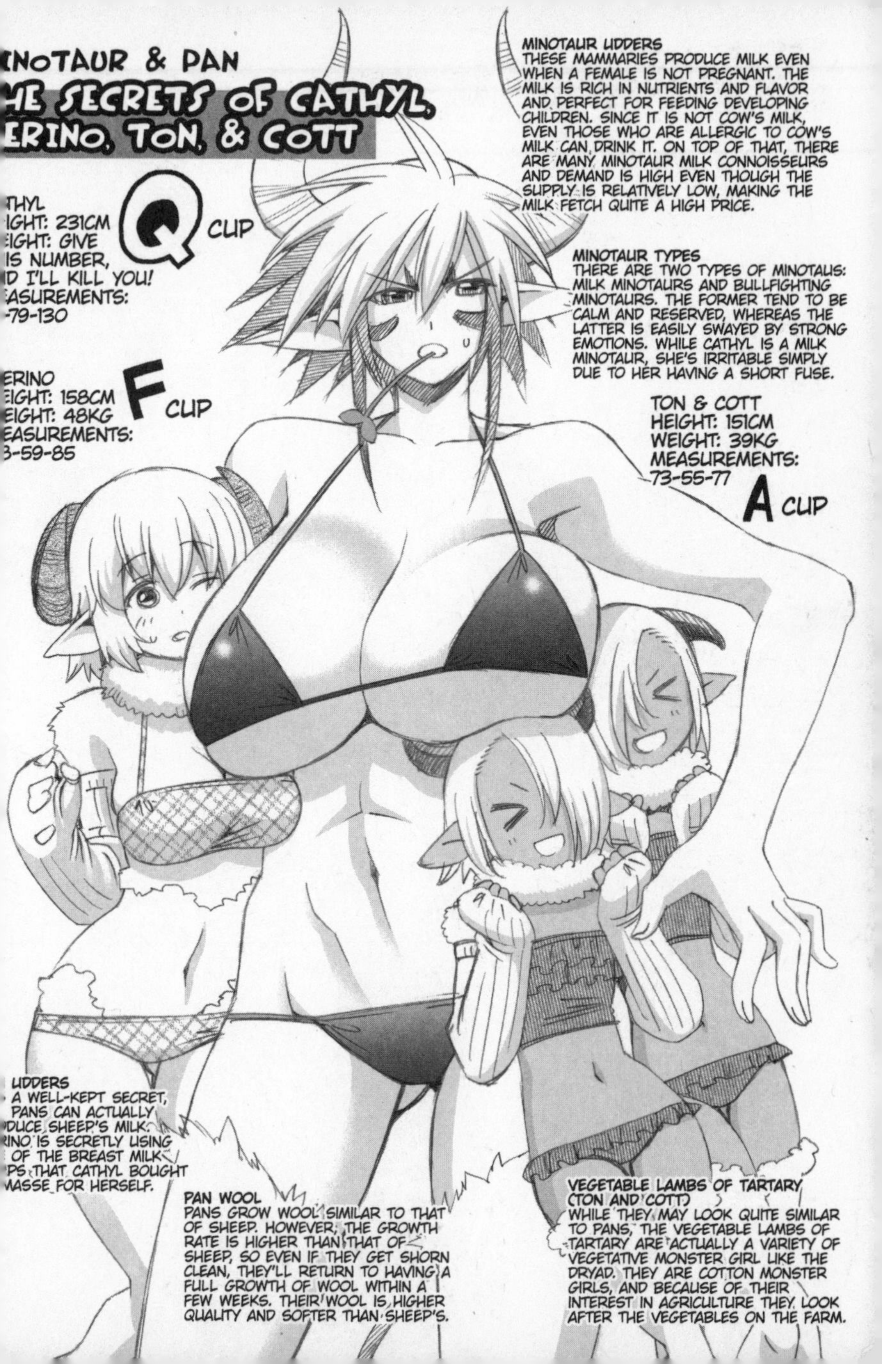

INOTAUR & PAN
HE SECRETS OF CATHYL, ERINO, TON, & COTT
THYL
IGHT: 231CM
EIGHT: GIVE
IS NUMBER,
D I'LL KILL YOU!
EASUREMENTS:
-79-130
Q CUP
ERINO
IGHT: 158CM
EIGHT: 48KG
EASUREMENTS:
3-59-85
F CUP
MINOTAUR UDDERS
THESE MAMMARIES PRODUCE MILK EVEN WHEN A FEMALE IS NOT PREGNANT. THE MILK IS RICH IN NUTRIENTS AND FLAVOR AND PERFECT FOR FEEDING DEVELOPING CHILDREN. SINCE IT IS NOT COW'S MILK, EVEN THOSE WHO ARE ALLERGIC TO COW'S MILK CAN DRINK IT. ON TOP OF THAT, THERE ARE MANY MINOTAUR MILK CONNOISSEURS AND DEMAND IS HIGH EVEN THOUGH THE SUPPLY IS RELATIVELY LOW, MAKING THE MILK FETCH QUITE A HIGH PRICE.
MINOTAUR TYPES
THERE ARE TWO TYPES OF MINOTAUS: MILK MINOTAURS AND BULLFIGHTING MINOTAURS. THE FORMER TEND TO BE CALM AND RESERVED, WHEREAS THE LATTER IS EASILY SWAYED BY STRONG EMOTIONS. WHILE CATHYL IS A MILK MINOTAUR, SHE'S IRRITABLE SIMPLY DUE TO HER HAVING A SHORT FUSE.
TON & COTT
HEIGHT: 151CM
WEIGHT: 39KG
MEASUREMENTS:
73-55-77
A CUP
UDDERS
A WELL-KEPT SECRET, PANS CAN ACTUALLY ODUCE SHEEP'S MILK. RINO IS SECRETLY USING OF THE BREAST MILK PS THAT CATHYL BOUGHT MASSE FOR HERSELF.
PAN WOOL
PANS GROW WOOL SIMILAR TO THAT OF SHEEP. HOWEVER, THE GROWTH RATE IS HIGHER THAN THAT OF SHEEP, SO EVEN IF THEY GET SHORN CLEAN, THEY'LL RETURN TO HAVING A FULL GROWTH OF WOOL WITHIN A FEW WEEKS. THEIR WOOL IS HIGHER QUALITY AND SOFTER THAN SHEEP'S.
VEGETABLE LAMBS OF TARTARY (TON AND COTT)
WHILE THEY MAY LOOK QUITE SIMILAR TO PANS, THE VEGETABLE LAMBS OF TARTARY ARE ACTUALLY A VARIETY OF VEGETATIVE MONSTER GIRL LIKE THE DRYAD. THEY ARE COTTON MONSTER GIRLS, AND BECAUSE OF THEIR INTEREST IN AGRICULTURE THEY LOOK AFTER THE VEGETABLES ON THE FARM.

LIZARD & ONI

LET'S LOOK AT LIZ & KINU

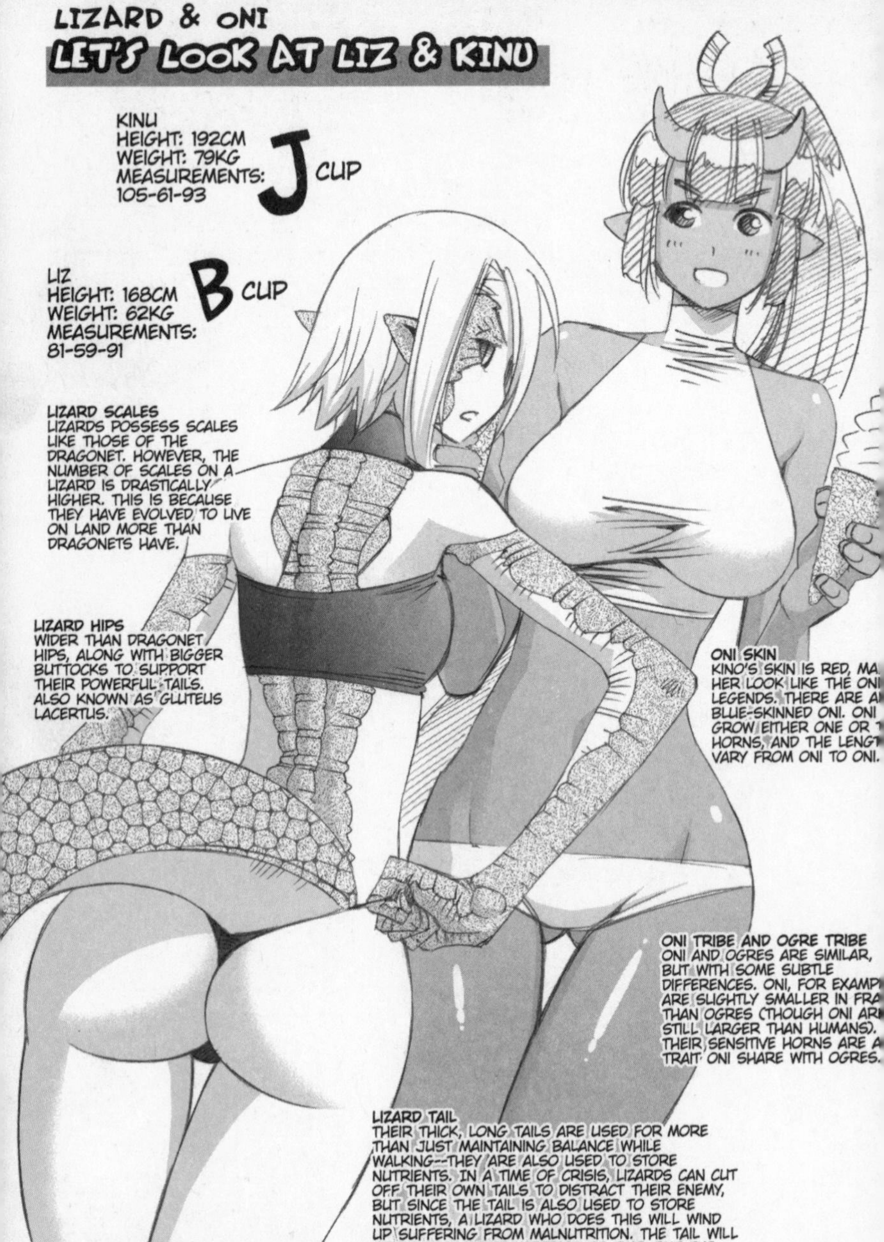

KINU
HEIGHT: 192CM
WEIGHT: 79KG
MEASUREMENTS:
105-61-93
J CUP

LIZ
HEIGHT: 168CM
WEIGHT: 62KG
MEASUREMENTS:
81-59-91
B CUP

LIZARD SCALES
LIZARDS POSSESS SCALES LIKE THOSE OF THE DRAGONET. HOWEVER, THE NUMBER OF SCALES ON A LIZARD IS DRASTICALLY HIGHER. THIS IS BECAUSE THEY HAVE EVOLVED TO LIVE ON LAND MORE THAN DRAGONETS HAVE.

LIZARD HIPS
WIDER THAN DRAGONET HIPS, ALONG WITH BIGGER BUTTOCKS TO SUPPORT THEIR POWERFUL TAILS. ALSO KNOWN AS GLUTEUS LACERTUS.

ONI SKIN
KINO'S SKIN IS RED, MA
HER LOOK LIKE THE ONI
LEGENDS. THERE ARE A
BLUE-SKINNED ONI. ONI
GROW EITHER ONE OR T
HORNS, AND THE LENGT
VARY FROM ONI TO ONI.

ONI TRIBE AND OGRE TRIBE
ONI AND OGRES ARE SIMILAR,
BUT WITH SOME SUBTLE
DIFFERENCES. ONI, FOR EXAMP
ARE SLIGHTLY SMALLER IN FRA
THAN OGRES (THOUGH ONI AR
STILL LARGER THAN HUMANS).
THEIR SENSITIVE HORNS ARE A
TRAIT ONI SHARE WITH OGRES.

LIZARD TAIL
THEIR THICK, LONG TAILS ARE USED FOR MORE THAN JUST MAINTAINING BALANCE WHILE WALKING--THEY ARE ALSO USED TO STORE NUTRIENTS. IN A TIME OF CRISIS, LIZARDS CAN CUT OFF THEIR OWN TAILS TO DISTRACT THEIR ENEMY, BUT SINCE THE TAIL IS ALSO USED TO STORE NUTRIENTS, A LIZARD WHO DOES THIS WILL WIND UP SUFFERING FROM MALNUTRITION. THE TAIL WILL GROW BACK AFTER A PERIOD OF TIME, BUT THE BONE WILL NOT REGENERATE, SO LIZARDS CAN ONLY CUT OFF THEIR TAILS ONCE.

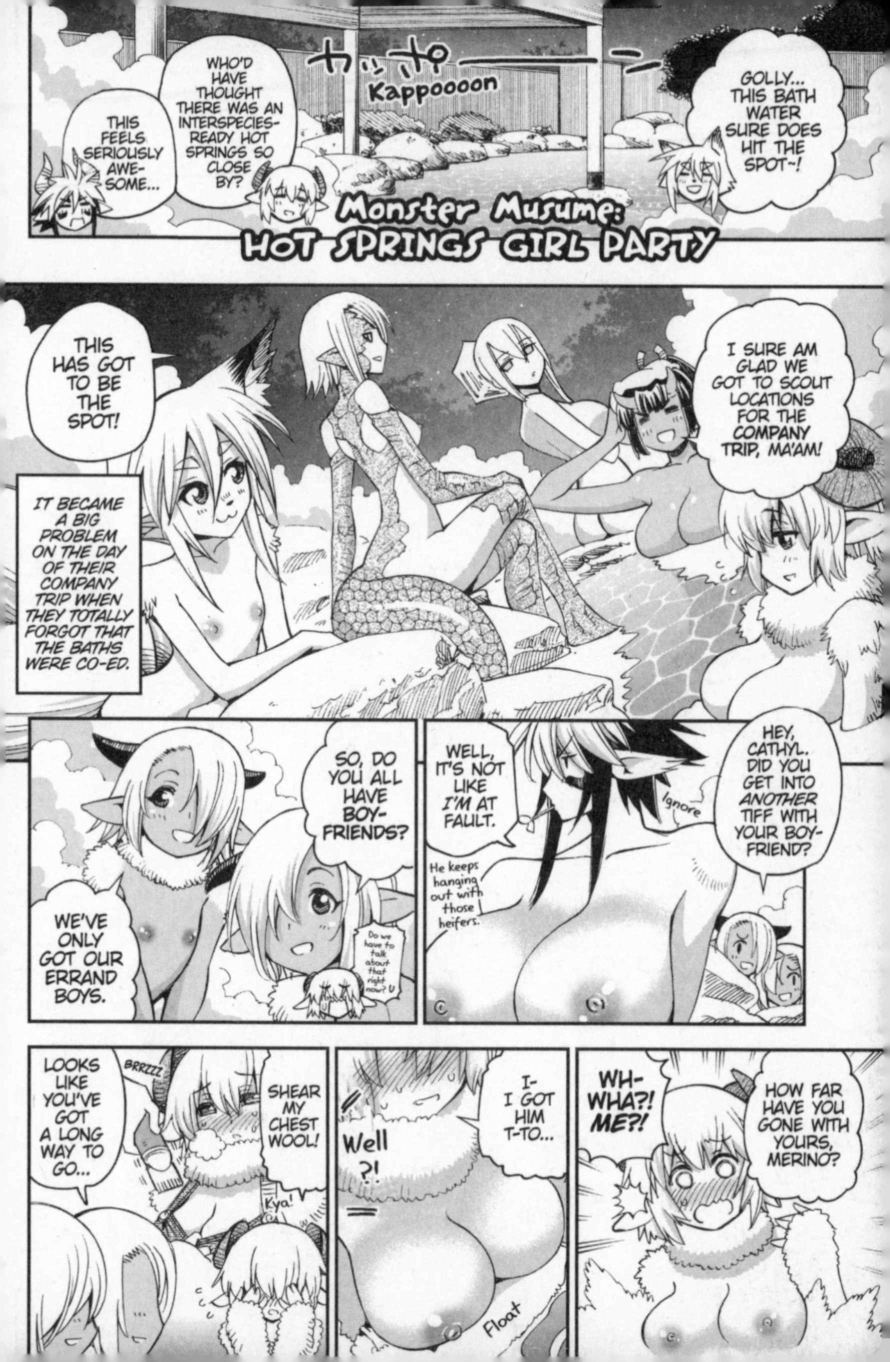
GOLLY... THIS BATH WATER SURE DOES HIT THE SPOT~!
Kappooooon
WHO'D HAVE THOUGHT THERE WAS AN INTERSPECIES-READY HOT SPRINGS SO CLOSE BY?
THIS FEELS SERIOUSLY AWE-SOME...
Monster Musume:
HOT SPRINGS GIRL PARTY
I SURE AM GLAD WE GOT TO SCOUT LOCATIONS FOR THE COMPANY TRIP, MA'AM!
THIS HAS GOT TO BE THE SPOT!
IT BECAME A BIG PROBLEM ON THE DAY OF THEIR COMPANY TRIP WHEN THEY TOTALLY FORGOT THAT THE BATHS WERE CO-ED.
HEY, CATHYL. DID YOU GET INTO ANOTHER TIFF WITH YOUR BOY-FRIEND?
Ignore
WELL, IT'S NOT LIKE I'M AT FAULT.
He keeps hanging out with those heifers.
SO, DO YOU ALL HAVE BOY-FRIENDS?
Do we have to talk about that right now?
WE'VE ONLY GOT OUR ERRAND BOYS.
HOW FAR HAVE YOU GONE WITH YOURS, MERINO?
WH-WHA?! ME?!
I- I GOT HIM T-TO...
Well ?!
Float
SHEAR MY CHEST WOOL!
BRRZZZ
Kya!
LOOKS LIKE YOU'VE GOT A LONG WAY TO GO...

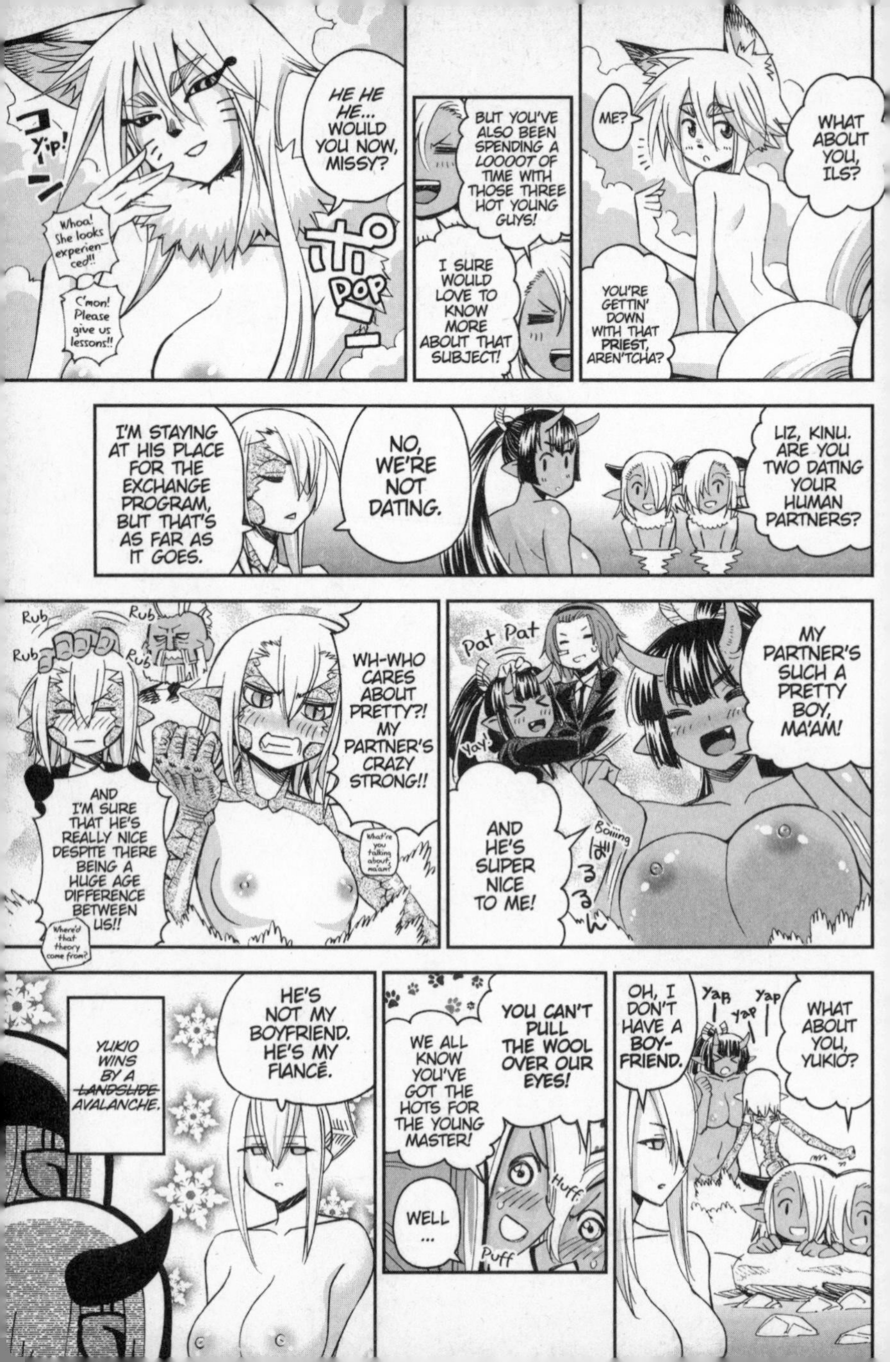
WHAT ABOUT YOU, ILS?
ME?
YOU'RE GETTIN' DOWN WITH THAT PRIEST, AREN'TCHA?
BUT YOU'VE ALSO BEEN SPENDING A LOOOOT OF TIME WITH THOSE THREE HOT YOUNG GUYS!
I SURE WOULD LOVE TO KNOW MORE ABOUT THAT SUBJECT!
HE HE HE... WOULD YOU NOW, MISSY?
Yip!
POP
Whoa! She looks experienced!!
C'mon! Please give us lessons!!
LIZ, KINU. ARE YOU TWO DATING YOUR HUMAN PARTNERS?
NO, WE'RE NOT DATING.
I'M STAYING AT HIS PLACE FOR THE EXCHANGE PROGRAM, BUT THAT'S AS FAR AS IT GOES.
MY PARTNER'S SUCH A PRETTY BOY, MA'AM!
Pat Pat
Yay!
AND HE'S SUPER NICE TO ME!
Boiiing
WH-WHO CARES ABOUT PRETTY?! MY PARTNER'S CRAZY STRONG!!
Rub
Rub
Rub
Rub
What're you talking about, ma'am?
AND I'M SURE THAT HE'S REALLY NICE DESPITE THERE BEING A HUGE AGE DIFFERENCE BETWEEN US!!
Where'd that theory come from?
WHAT ABOUT YOU, YUKIO?
Yap
Yap
Yap
OH, I DON'T HAVE A BOY-FRIEND.
YOU CAN'T PULL THE WOOL OVER OUR EYES!
WE ALL KNOW YOU'VE GOT THE HOTS FOR THE YOUNG MASTER!
Huff
WELL ...
Puff
HE'S NOT MY BOYFRIEND. HE'S MY FIANCÉ.
YUKIO WINS BY A ~~LANDSLIDE~~ AVALANCHE.

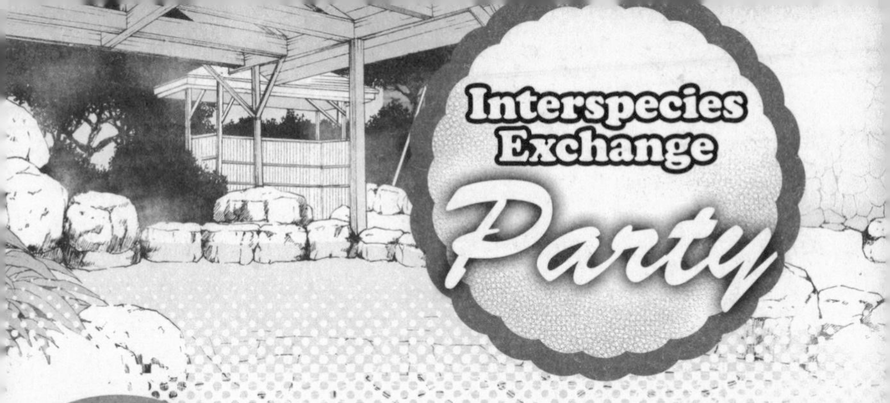

Interspecies Exchange Party

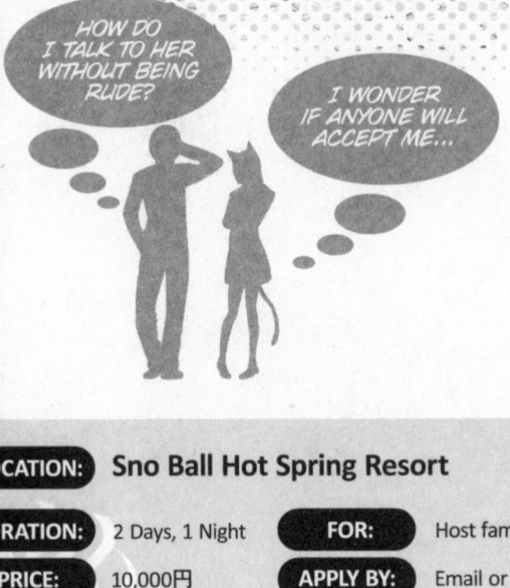

HOW DO I TALK TO HER WITHOUT BEING RUDE?
I WONDER IF ANYONE WILL ACCEPT ME...

"I want to take part in the Interspecies Cultural Exchange, but I don't even know where to begin when talking with liminals."

Is this you? If so, we have exciting news!

You can find a compatible partner at our Interspecies Exchange Party under the careful supervision of an Interspecies Exchange Coordinator, with the support of our administration, and at a reasonable price, all while contributing to the success of the Interspecies Exchange Program.

OCATION: Sno Ball Hot Spring Resort

URATION: 2 Days, 1 Night

FOR: Host families approved for interspecies exchanges

PRICE: 10,000円

APPLY BY: Email or Phone

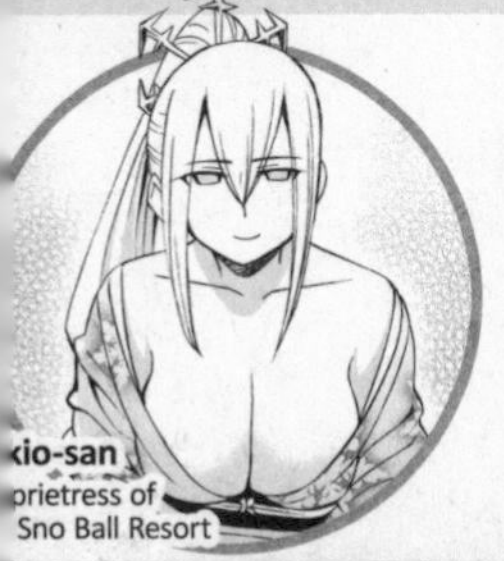

I was inspired to organize this party by one of my friends, but I never dreamed that so many of our clients would participate, or that it would result in so many successful pairings.

In fact, a stay at this resort is what brought me together with my current boyfriend. I'll never forget that day. That young man was very kind to me. He always considered my wants and needs before his own, and I've been with him ever since...(remainder omitted)

kio-san
prietress of
Sno Ball Resort

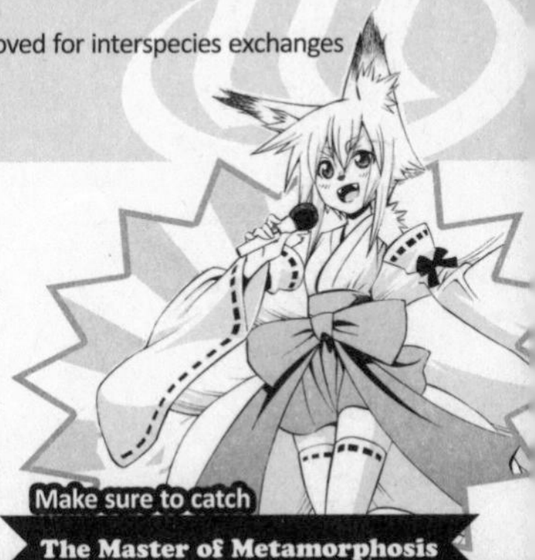

Make sure to catch

The Master of Metamorphosis
Fox Miko Show

after the party!!

CHEDULE

- **14:00** Post-reception Profile Check
- **15:00** Party
- **18:00** Mingling
- **20:00** Mixed-bathing party (Free time until the next morning)
- **08:00** Announcement of Host Family assignments

TOKUMA SHOTEN